# Princess & 18-22 Series Owners Workshop Manual

## by J H Haynes
Member of the Guild of Motoring Writers

## and P G Strasman

**Models covered**

Austin/Morris/Wolseley 18-22 Series : 1800, 1800 HL and 2200 HL; 1798 cc and 2227 cc
Princess: 1800, 1800 HL, 2200 HL and 2200 HLS, including Special Six; 1798 cc and 2227 cc
Princess 2: 2200 HL, 2200 HLS and 2.2 HLS; 2227 cc

*Does not cover Princess 2 models with four-cylinder O-series engine*

**ISBN 0 85696 976 1**

Printed in England   *(286-11J2)*

**HAYNES PUBLISHING GROUP**
**SPARKFORD YEOVIL SOMERSET BA22 7JJ ENGLAND**
*distributed in the USA by*
**HAYNES PUBLICATIONS INC**
**861 LAWRENCE DRIVE**
**NEWBURY PARK**
**CALIFORNIA 91320**
**USA**

# Acknowledgements

Thanks are due to the Austin Morris subsidiary of BL Cars Limited for the provision of technical information, to Castrol Limited who supplied the lubrication data, and to the Champion Sparking Plug Company who supplied the illustrations showing the various spark plug conditions.

The Section in Chapter 10, dealing with the suppression of electrical interference, was originated by Mr. I. P. Davey., and was first published in *Motor* magazine.

Our project car, a Morris 2200 HL, was supplied by Westover Motors Limited, Old Christchurch Road, Bournemouth.

Lastly, special thanks are due to all of those people at Sparkford who helped in the production of this manual.

# About this manual

## Its aims

The aim of this manual is to help you get the best value from your car. It can do so in several ways. It can help you decide what work must be done (even should you choose to get it done by a garage), provide information on routine maintenance and servicing, and give a logical course of action and diagnosis when random faults occur. However, it is hoped that you will use the manual by tackling the work yourself. On simpler jobs it may even be quicker than booking the car into a garage, and going there twice to leave and collect it. Perhaps most important, a lot of money can be saved by avoiding the costs the garage must charge to cover its labour and overheads.

The manual has drawings and descriptions to show the function of the various components so that their layout can be understood. Then the tasks are described and photographed in a step-by-step sequence so that even a novice can do the work.

## Its arrangement

The manual is divided into thirteen Chapters, each covering a logical sub-division of the car. The Chapters are each divided into Sections, numbered with single figures, eg 5; and the Sections into paragraphs (or sub-sections), with decimal numbers following on from the Section they are in, eg 5.1, 5.2, 5.3 etc.

It is freely illustrated, especially in those parts where there is a detailed sequence of operations to be carried out. There are two forms of illustration: figures and photographs. The figures are numbered in sequence with decimal numbers, according to their position in the Chapter: eg Fig.6.4 is the 4th drawing/illustration in Chapter 6. Photographs are numbered (either individually or in related groups) the same as the Section or sub-section of the text where the operation they show is described.

There is an alphabetical index at the back of the manual as well as a contents list at the front.

References to the 'left' or 'right' of the vehicle are in the sense of a person in the driver's seat facing forwards.

Unless otherwise stated, nuts and bolts are removed by turning anti-clockwise and tightened by turning clockwise.

Vehicle manufacturers continually make changes to specifications and recommendations, and these when notified are incorporated into our manuals at the earliest opportunity.

**Whilst every care is taken to ensure that the information in this manual is correct no liability can be accepted by the authors or publishers for loss, damage or injury caused by any errors in, or omissions from, the information given.**

# Contents

# Introduction to the
# Leyland Cars 18-22 and Princess models

Originally introduced in March 1975, by British Leyland the car was available with either a 4 or 6 cylinder engine as a Morris or Austin or with a 6 cylinder power unit under the Wolseley marque.

In October 1975, the range was redesignated Princess by the newly restructured Leyland organisation and was offered with a 4 or 6 cylinder engine. Austin, Morris and Wolseley variants ceased.

Automatic transmission is available on all models and HL or HLS versions may be encountered which offer a variation in trim, equipment and accessories.

The car is of four door design and features an exciting and up-to-date 'wedge' shape.

Mechanically the car follows accepted transverse engine, front wheel drive layout.

Morris 2200 HL (1975). This is the actual car used in our workshops

# Buying spare parts and vehicle identification numbers

## Buying spare parts

Spare parts are available from many sources, for example: BL/ Leyland garages, other garages and accessory shops, and motor factors. Our advice regarding spare parts is as follows:

*Officially appointed BL/Leyland garages* - This is the best source of parts which are peculiar to your car and otherwise not generally available (eg; complete cylinder heads, internal gearbox components, badges, interior trim etc). It is also the only place at which you should buy parts if your car is still under warranty; non-BL/Leyland components may invalidate the warranty. To be sure of obtaining the correct parts it will always be necessary to give the storeman your car's engine and chassis number, and if possible to take the old part along for positive identification. Remember that many parts are available on a factory exchange scheme - any parts returned should always be clean! It obviously makes good sense to go to the specialists on your car for this type of part for they are best equipped to supply you.

*Other garages and accessory shops* - These are often very good places to buy material and components needed for the maintenance of your car (eg; oil filters, spark plugs, bulbs, fan belts, oils and grease, touch-up paint, filler paste etc). They also sell general accessories, usually have convenient opening hours, charge lower prices and can often be found not far from home.

*Motor factors* - Good factors will stock all of the more important components which wear out relatively quickly (eg; clutch components, pistons, valves, exhaust systems, brake cylinders/pipes/hoses/seals/shoes and pads etc). Motor factors will often provide new or reconditioned components on a part exchange basis - this can save a considerable amount of money.

## Vehicle identification numbers

Modifications are a continuing and unpublicised process in vehicle manufacture quite apart from major model changes. Spare parts manuals and lists are compiled upon a numberical basis, the individual vehicle number being essential to correct identification of the component required.

*The vehicle number* may be obtained from the identification plate within the engine compartment and the *engine number* is stamped on the cylinder block. Both numbers are also shown in the vehicle registration document

Engine number

Vehicle identification plate

# Routine maintenance

Maintenance is essential for ensuring safety and desirable for the purpose of getting the best in terms of performance and economy from the car. Over the years the need for periodic lubrication - oiling, greasing and so on - has been drastically reduced if not totally eliminated. This has unfortunately tended to lead some owners to think that because no such action is required the items either no longer exist or will last for ever. This is a serious delusion. If follows therefore that the largest initial element of maintenance is visual examination. This may lead to repairs or renewals.

The threads used on nuts and bolts in these cars are either UNF or metric to ISO standards.

### Every 250 miles (400 km) or weekly

Check tyre pressures and inflate if necessary.
Check and top-up engine oil.
Check and top-up battery electrolyte level.
Check and top-up windscreen washer fluid level.
Check and top-up coolant level.
Check operation of all lights.

### Every 6000 miles (10,000 km)

Change engine oil and renew filter.
Top-up carburettor piston damper.
Check carburettor adjustment.
Check drive belt tension, renew if frayed.
Clean and adjust spark plugs.
Check, adjust or renew distributor contact breaker points.
Check ignition timing.
Check and top-up if necessary, clutch master cylinder fluid level.
Check and top-up automatic transmission fluid level.
Check for wear in all steering joints and condition of flexible dust excluders.
Check and top-up power steering pump fluid level.
Check and adjust if necessary the front wheel alignment.
Inspect brake fluid lines and hoses for leaks, damage or deterioration.
Inspect front disc pads for wear.
Check and top-up brake fluid reservoir.
Lubricate door hinges and controls.

### Every 12,000 miles (20,000 km)

Renew air cleaner element.
Renew engine breather filter.
Install new spark plugs.
Lubricate steering rack and pinion.
Inspect rear brake linings for wear.

### Every 24,000 miles (38,000 km)

Drain, flush and refill cooling system with antifreeze solution.

### Every 36,000 miles (60,000 km) - or at three yearly intervals

Renew brake servo filter element.
Renew fluid in brake hydraulic circuits and renew all system seals.

### Once a year or more often if the time can be spared

*Cleaning*
Examination of components requires that they are cleaned. The same applies to the body of the car, inside and out, in order that deterioration due to rust or unknown damage may be detected. Certain parts of the body frame, if rusted badly, can result in the vehicle being declared unsafe and it will not pass the annual test for roadworthiness.

*Exhaust system*
An exhaust system must be leakproof, and the noise level below a certain minimum. Excessive leaks may cause carbon monoxide fumes to enter the passenger compartment. Excessive noise constitutes a public nuisance. Both these faults may cause the vehicle to be kept off the road. Repair of replace defective sections when symptoms are apparent.

Topping up the engine oil

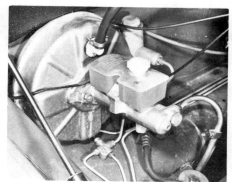
Brake master cylinder reservoir

Engine oil drain plug (4 cyl)

Engine oil drain plug (6 cyl)

Disposable cartridge oil filter (4 cyl)

Disposable oil filter (6 cyl)

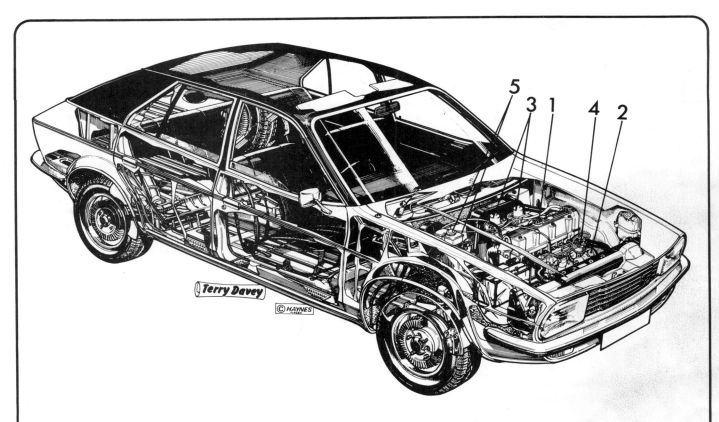

# Recommended lubricants and fluids

| | |
|---|---|
| Engine and manual gearbox (1) | Castrol GTX |
| Automatic gearbox | Castrol TQF |
| Power steering (2) | Castrol GTX |
| Steering rack | Castrol LM Grease |
| All grease points | Castrol LM Grease |
| Carburettor damper and distributor (3 & 4) | Castrol GTX |
| Hinges, locks, pivots etc | Castrol GTX |
| Brake and clutch master cylinders (5) | Castrol Girling Universal Brake & Clutch Fluid |

*Note: The above are general recommendations. Lubrication requirements vary from territory-to-territory and also depend on vehicle usage. Consult the operators handbook supplied with your car.*

# Jacking, towing and hoisting

The jack supplied with the car should only be used to raise the car for changing the roadwheels. If it is used in maintenance or repair operations, then it must be supplemented with axle stands. Two jacking points are provided on each side of the car, always chock the roadwheels not being raised. When using a workshop jack, it must only be located as described, otherwise distortion of the body may occur.

*To jack one front wheel,* locate the jack under the reinforcement member (2) (see illustration) to the rear of the suspension lower arm

rear bearing. Do not jack on the rear bearing itself.

*To jack both front wheels* at the same time, a steel section or baulk of timber should be placed across the reinforcement members as shown and a jack placed under the centre of the temporary support.

*To jack one rear wheel,* locate the jack under the rear suspension bracket (3).

*To jack both rear wheels,* locate the jack under the reinforcement plate (5) at the centre of the rear panel. Whenever repairs or adjustments are being carried out under the car, always supplement the jacks with

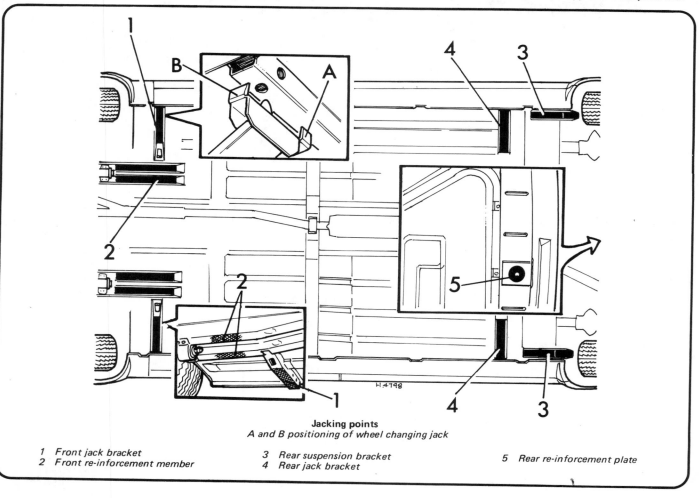

**Jacking points**
*A and B positioning of wheel changing jack*

1  Front jack bracket
2  Front re-inforcement member
3  Rear suspension bracket
4  Rear jack bracket
5  Rear re-inforcement plate

axle stands positioned under the wheel changing jacking brackets.

*To hoist the rear of the car,* hooks can be attached to the slots within the luggage boot and a spreader used.

*To hoist the front of the car,* hooks can be attached to the eyes within the engine compartment and a spreader used.

*The car may be towed* by another vehicle using the towing eyes located one each side of the front body member. A suspended tow must not be carried out using these eyes.

The lashing eyes located under the rear wheel arches must not be used for towing another vehicle but if eyes are found on the rear jacking plate then these may be used.

Where a caravan or trailer is to be towed, fit an approved towing kit and make sure that the total weight of the unit being towed does not exceed 2240 lbs (1016 kg).

If the car is equipped with automatic transmission, the car must not be towed by another vehicle unless an additional 3 Imp. pints (1.7 litres) of automatic transmission fluid are added and the towing speed is restricted to below 30 mph (50 km/h) and the distance towed to a maximum of 40 miles (65 km). When being towed, set the speed selector lever to 'N' and turn the ignition key to 'I'. If these conditions cannot be complied with, the front of the car must be raised and placed on a recovery trailer.

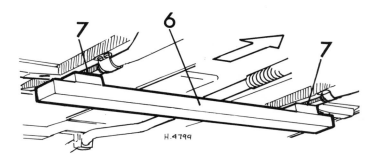

**Method of jacking both front wheels at the same time**

6  *Temporary support*            7  *Spacer blocks*

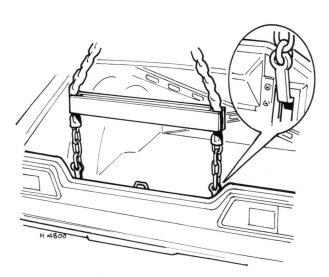

**Rear hoisting hook attachment**

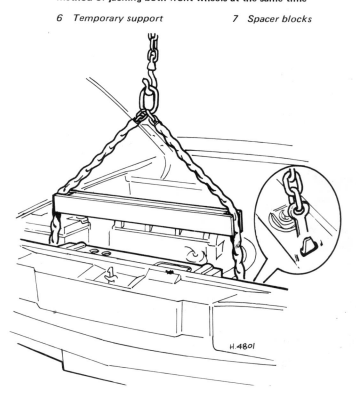

**Front hoisting hook attachment**

# General dimensions, weights and capacities

| Overall dimensions and weights | To 1975 | 1976 on |
|---|---|---|
| Length ... ... ... ... ... ... ... ... ... ... | 175.35 in (445.39 cm) | 175.41 in (445.55 cm) |
| Width ... ... ... ... ... ... ... ... ... ... | 67.84 in (172.33 cm) | 68.11 in (173.0 cm) |
| Height (unladen) ... ... ... ... ... ... ... ... | 55.50 in (141.10 cm) | 55.50 in (141.10 cm) |

**Weight (full fuel tank)**
Manual gearbox:
| | |
|---|---|
| 4 cylinder ... ... ... ... ... ... ... ... ... | 2560 lb (1160 kg) |
| 6 cylinder ... ... ... ... ... ... ... ... ... | 2610 lb (1183 kg) |

Automatic transmission:
| | |
|---|---|
| 4 cylinder ... ... ... ... ... ... ... ... ... | 2600 lb (1179 kg) |
| 6 cylinder ... ... ... ... ... ... ... ... ... | 2650 lb (1202 kg) |

*\* Wolseley add 40 lb (24 kg)*
*Capacities*

| | |
|---|---|
| **Fuel tank** ... ... ... ... ... ... ... ... ... | 16 Imp. gal. (73 litres) |

**Engine (plus filter)**
| | |
|---|---|
| 4 cylinder, plus manual gearbox ... ... ... ... ... ... | 10.25 Imp. pints (5.8 litres) |
| 4 cylinder, plus automatic transmission ... ... ... ... ... | 7.75 Imp. pints (4.4 litres) |
| 6 cylinder, plus manual gearbox ... ... ... ... ... ... | 13 Imp. pints (7.4 litres) |
| 6 cylinder, plus automatic transmission ... ... ... ... ... | 10 Imp. pints (5.7 litres) |

| | |
|---|---|
| **Automatic transmission** ... ... ... ... ... ... | 13 Imp. pints (7.4 litres) |
| (retained in torque converter) ... ... ... ... ... ... | 5 Imp. pints (3 litres) |

**Cooling system**
| | |
|---|---|
| 4 cylinder ... ... ... ... ... ... ... ... ... | 13 Imp. pints (7.3 litres) |
| 6 cylinder ... ... ... ... ... ... ... ... ... | 15 Imp. pints (8.5 litres) |

# Chapter 1 Engine

*For modifications, and information applicable to later models, see Supplement at end of manual*

## Contents

## Specifications

### Engine - general

| | 4 cylinder | 6 cylinder |
|---|---|---|
| Type | 18H | 23H |
| Bore | 3.160 in (80.26 mm) | 3.00 in (76.2 mm) |
| Stroke | 3.5 in (88.9 mm) | 3.20 in (81.28 mm) |
| Capacity | 1798 cc (109.7 cu in) | 2227 cc (135.8 cu in) |
| Firing order | 1 - 3 - 4 - 2 | 1 - 5 - 3 - 6 - 2 - 4 |
| Valve operation | Overhead pushrod | Overhead camshaft |
| Compression ratio | 9.0 : 1 | 9.0 : 1 |

| | 4 cylinder | 6 cylinder |
|---|---|---|
| Torque ... ... ... ... ... ... ... ... ... | 101 lb/ft @ 3000 rpm (14 kg/m) | 125 lb/ft @ 3500 rpm (17.3 kg/m) |

## Crankshaft

| | 4 cylinder | 6 cylinder |
|---|---|---|
| Main journal diameter ... ... ... ... ... ... ... ... | 2.1262 to 2.127 in (54.01 to 54.02 mm) | 2.2515 to 2.2520 in (57.20 to 57.21 mm) |
| Minimum regrind diameter ... ... ... ... ... ... | 2.0865 in (52.99 mm) | — |
| Crankpin journal diameter ... ... ... ... ... ... | 1.8759 to 1.8764 in (47.648 to 47.661 mm) | 1.8759 to 1.8764 in (47.62 to 47.64 mm) |
| Minimum regrind diameter ... ... ... ... ... ... | 1.836 in (46.632 mm) | |
| Crankshaft endfloat ... ... ... ... ... ... ... | 0.002 to 0.005 in (0.05 to 0.13 mm) | 0.004 to 0.007 in (0.10 to 0.18 mm) |
| Primary drive gear endfloat ... ... ... ... ... | — | 0.004 to 0.006 in (0.10 to 0.15 mm) |
| Undersizes ... ... ... ... ... ... ... ... ... | 0.010 in (0.25 mm) 0.020 in (0.51 mm) 0.030 in (0.76 mm) 0.040 in (1.02 mm) | 0.010 in (0.25 mm) 0.020 in (0.51 mm) 0.030 in (0.76 mm) 0.040 in (1.02 mm) |
| Main bearing number ... ... ... ... ... ... ... | 5 | 7 |
| Width: | | |
| Front centre and rear ... ... ... ... ... ... | 1.125 in (28.57 mm) | — |
| Intermediate ... ... ... ... ... ... ... ... | 0.875 in (22.23 mm) | — |
| All ... ... ... ... ... ... ... ... ... | — | 0.811 to 0.821 in (20.3 to 20.4 mm) |
| Running clearance ... ... ... ... ... ... ... | 0.001 to 0.0027 in (0.025 to 0.068 mm) | 0.001 to 0.0035 in (0.025 to 0.089 mm) |
| No. 4 bearing only ... ... ... ... ... ... ... | — | 0.002 to 0.004 in (0.05 to 0.10 mm) |

## Connecting rods

| | 4 cylinder | 6 cylinder |
|---|---|---|
| Length between centres ... ... ... ... ... ... | 6.5 in (165.1 mm) | 5.828 to 5.832 in (148.02 to 148.12 mm) |
| Endfloat at big-end ... ... ... ... ... ... ... | — | 0.006 to 0.010 in (0.15 to 0.25 mm) |
| Big-end bearing width ... ... ... ... ... ... | 0.775 to 0.785 in (19.68 to 19.94 mm) | 0.660 to 0.665 in (16.75 to 16.89 mm) |
| Running clearance ... ... ... ... ... ... ... | 0.0015 to 0.0032 in (0.038 to 0.081 mm) | 0.0015 to 0.0030 in (0.038 to 0.076 mm) |

## Gudgeon pins

| | 4 cylinder | 6 cylinder |
|---|---|---|
| Fit ... ... ... ... ... ... ... ... ... | Interference in connecting rod Hand pressure in piston at 60°F (16°C) | Interference fit in connecting rod Hand pressure in piston at 68°F (20°C) |
| Diameter ... ... ... ... ... ... ... ... | 0.8124 to 0.8127 in (20.63 to 20.64 mm) | 0.8123 to 0.8125 in (20.63 to 20.64 mm) |

## Pistons

| | 4 cylinder | 6 cylinder |
|---|---|---|
| Type ... .... ... ... ... ... ... ... ... | Aluminium | Aluminium |
| Skirt clearance in bore: | | |
| At top ... ... ... ... ... ... ... ... | 0.0021 to 0.0037 in (0.0533 to 0.0939 mm) | 0.0018 to 0.0024 in (0.045 to 0.061 mm) |
| At bottom ... ... ... ... ... ... ... | 0.0018 to 0.0024 in (0.045 to 0.060 mm) | 0.001 to 0.0016 in (0.025 to 0.039 mm) |
| No. of rings: | | |
| Compression ... ... ... ... ... ... ... | 2 | 3 |
| Oil control ... ... ... ... ... ... ... | 1 | 1 |
| Ring groove width: | | |
| Top ... ... ... ... ... ... ... ... | 0.064 to 0.065 in (1.625 to 1.651 mm) | 0.064 to 0.065 in (1.625 to 1.651 mm) |
| Second ... ... ... ... ... ... ... ... | 0.064 to 0.065 in (1.625 to 1.651 mm) | 0.064 to 0.065 in (1.625 to 1.651 mm) |
| Third ... ... ... ... ... ... ... ... | — | 0.064 to 0.065 in (1.625 to 1.651 mm) |
| Oil control ... ... ... ... ... ... ... | 0.1578 to 0.1588 in (4.001 to 4.003 mm) | 0.1565 to 0.1575 in (4.962 to 4.987 mm) |
| Gudgeon pin bore ... ... ... ... ... ... | 0.8126 to 0.8128 in (20.645 to 20.650 mm) | 0.8126 to 0.8128 in (20.645 to 20.650 mm) |
| Oversizes ... ... ... ... ... ... ... ... | 0.020 in (0.51 mm) 0.040 in (1.02 mm) | 0.020 in (0.51 mm) |

## Piston rings

| | 4 cylinder | 6 cylinder |
|---|---|---|
| Width: | | |
| Top ... ... ... ... ... ... ... ... ... | 0.0615 to 0.0625 in (1.562 to 1.587 mm) | 0.0615 to 0.0625 in (1.562 to 1.587 mm) |
| Second ... ... ... ... ... ... ... ... | 0.0615 to 0.0625 in (1.562 to 1.587 mm) | 0.0615 to 0.0625 in (1.562 to 1.587 mm) |

| | | | | | | | | | 4 cylinder | 6 cylinder |
|---|---|---|---|---|---|---|---|---|---|---|
| Third | ... | ... | ... | ... | ... | ... | ... | ... | — | 0.0615 to 0.0625 in (1.562 to 1.587 mm) |
| **End gap:** | | | | | | | | | — | |
| Top | ... | ... | ... | ... | ... | ... | ... | ... | 0.012 to 0.017 in (0.304 to 0.431 mm) | 0.011 to 0.022 in (0.28 to 0.55 mm) |
| Second | ... | ... | ... | ... | ... | ... | ... | ... | 0.012 to 0.017 in (0.304 to 0.431 mm) | 0.011 to 0.022 in (0.28 to 0.55 mm) |
| Third | ... | ... | ... | ... | ... | ... | ... | ... | — | 0.011 to 0.022 in (0.28 to 0.55 mm) |
| **Ring to groove clearance:** | | | | | | | | | — | |
| Top | ... | ... | ... | ... | ... | ... | ... | ... | 0.0015 to 0.0035 in (0.038 to 0.088 mm) | 0.0015 to 0.0035 in (0.038 to 0.088 mm) |
| Second | ... | ... | ... | ... | ... | ... | ... | ... | 0.0015 to 0.0035 in (0.038 to 0.088 mm) | 0.0015 to 0.0035 in (0.038 to 0.088 mm) |
| Third | ... | ... | ... | ... | ... | ... | ... | ... | — | 0.0015 to 0.0035 in (0.038 to 0.088 mm) |
| **Oil control ring width** | | | | | | | | | — | |
| Pre 1976 | ... | ... | ... | ... | ... | ... | ... | ... | 0.1552 to 0.1562 in (3.942 to 3.967 mm) | 0.100 to 0.105 in (2.54 to 2.66 mm) |
| 1976 on | ... | ... | ... | ... | ... | ... | ... | ... | 0.1552 to 0.1562 in (3.942 to 3.967 mm) | 0.151 to 0.156 in (3.83 to 3.96 mm) |
| End gap | ... | ... | ... | ... | ... | ... | ... | ... | 0.015 to 0.045 in (0.381 to 1.143 mm) | 0.015 to 0.045 in (0.381 to 1.143 mm) |
| Ring to groove clearance | | | ... | ... | ... | ... | ... | ... | 0.0016 to 0.0036 in (0.040 to 0.091 mm) | — |

## Camshaft

| | | | | | | | | | 4 cylinder | 6 cylinder |
|---|---|---|---|---|---|---|---|---|---|---|
| Endfloat | ... | ... | ... | ... | ... | ... | ... | ... | 0.003 to 0.007 in (0.076 to 0.178 mm) | 0.002 to 0.007 in (0.05 to 0.17 mm) |
| Timing chain | ... | ... | ... | ... | ... | ... | ... | ... | 3/8 in (9.52 mm) X 52 | 3/8 in (9.52 mm) X 108 |
| **Journal diameters:** | | | | | | | | | | |
| Front (1) | ... | ... | ... | ... | ... | ... | ... | ... | 1.78875 to 1.78925 in (45.424 to 45.437 mm) | 1.9355 to 1.9365 in (49.185 to 49.197 mm) |
| Centre (2) | ... | ... | ... | ... | ... | ... | ... | ... | 1.72875 to 1.72925 in (43.910 to 43.923 mm) | 1.9668 to 1.9678 in (49.975 to 49.987 mm) |
| Rear (3) | ... | ... | ... | ... | ... | ... | ... | ... | 1.62275 to 1.62325 in (41.218 to 41.230 mm) | 1.998 to 1.999 in (50.762 to 50.775 mm) |
| (4) | ... | ... | ... | ... | ... | ... | ... | ... | — | 2.0293 to 2.0303 in (51.534 to 51.569 mm) |
| **Bearing internal diameters after reaming:** | | | | | | | | | | |
| Front | ... | ... | ... | ... | ... | ... | ... | ... | 1.79025 to 1.79075 in (45.472 to 45.485 mm) | — |
| Centre | ... | ... | ... | ... | ... | ... | ... | ... | 1.73025 to 1.73075 in (43.948 to 43.961 mm) | — |
| Rear | ... | ... | ... | ... | ... | ... | ... | ... | 1.62425 to 1.62475 in (41.256 to 41.269 mm) | — |
| Running clearance | ... | ... | ... | ... | ... | ... | ... | ... | 0.001 to 0.002 in (0.025 to 0.051 mm) | 0.002 to 0.003 in (0.05 to 0.09 mm) |

## Tappets

| | | | | | | | | | 4 cylinder | 6 cylinder |
|---|---|---|---|---|---|---|---|---|---|---|
| Outside diameter | ... | ... | ... | ... | ... | ... | ... | ... | 0.812 in (20.624 mm) | 0.812 in (20.624 mm) |
| Length | ... | ... | ... | ... | ... | ... | ... | ... | 1.500 to 1.505 in (38.10 to 38.22 mm) | — |
| Pushrod length | ... | ... | ... | ... | ... | ... | ... | ... | 10.38 to 10.41 in (263.7 to 264.4 mm) | — |

## Rocker gear

| | | | | | | | | | 4 cylinder | 6 cylinder |
|---|---|---|---|---|---|---|---|---|---|---|
| **Shaft length:** | | | | | | | | | 14.032 in (356.4 mm) | — |
| Diameter | ... | ... | ... | ... | ... | ... | ... | ... | 0.624 to 0.625 in (15.85 to 15.87 mm) | — |
| Rocker arm bush inside diameter (after reaming) | | | | | | ... | ... | ... | 0.6255 to 0.626 in (15.887 to 15.900 mm) | — |

## Valves

| | | | | | | | | | 4 cylinder | 6 cylinder |
|---|---|---|---|---|---|---|---|---|---|---|
| Seat angle | ... | ... | ... | ... | ... | ... | ... | ... | 45° 30' | 45° 15' |
| **Head diameter:** | | | | | | | | | | |
| Inlet, pre 1976 | ... | ... | ... | ... | ... | ... | ... | ... | 1.500 to 1.505 in (38.1 to 38.3 mm) | 1.500 to 1.505 in (38.1 to 38.3 mm) |
| Inlet, 1976 on | ... | ... | ... | ... | ... | ... | ... | ... | 1.562 to 1.567 in (39.67 to 39.80 mm) | 1.500 to 1.505 in (38.1 to 38.3 mm) |
| Exhaust | ... | ... | ... | ... | ... | ... | ... | ... | 1.343 to 1.348 in (34.11 to 34.23 mm) | 1.216 to 1.220 in (30.88 to 31.04 mm) |
| **Stem diameter:** | | | | | | | | | | |
| Inlet | ... | ... | ... | ... | ... | ... | ... | ... | 0.3429 to 0.3434 in (8.709 to 8.722 mm) | 0.3115 to 0.3120 in (7.91 to 7.93 mm) |

| | 4 cylinder | 6 cylinder |
|---|---|---|
| Exhaust ... ... ... ... ... ... ... ... ... | 0.3423 to 0.3428 in (9.694 to 9.707 mm) | 0.3115 to 0.3120 in (7.91 to 7.93 mm) |
| Oversize ... ... ... ... ... ... ... ... ... | — | 0.3331 to 0.3336 in (8.46 to 8.47 mm) |
| Stem to guide clearance: | | |
|   Inlet ... ... ... ... ... ... ... ... ... | 0.0008 to 0.0018 in (0.020 to 0.046 mm) | 0.0015 in (0.038 mm) |
|   Exhaust ... ... ... ... ... ... ... ... ... | 0.0014 to 0.0024 in (0.035 to 0.061 mm) | 0.0015 in (0.038 mm) |
| Valve lift ... ... ... ... ... ... ... ... ... | 0.347 in (8.81 mm) | 0.360 in (9.14 mm) |

## Valve guides
| | | |
|---|---|---|
| Length: | | |
|   Inlet ... ... ... ... ... ... ... ... ... | 1.88 in (47.75 mm) | — |
|   Exhaust ... ... ... ... ... ... ... ... ... | 2.22 in (56.39 mm) | — |
| Outside diameter ... ... ... ... ... ... ... | 0.5635 to 0.5640 in (14.30 to 14.32 mm) | — |
| Inside diameter ... ... ... ... ... ... ... ... | 0.3441 to 0.3448 in (8.743 to 8.755 mm) | — |

## Valve springs
| | | |
|---|---|---|
| Free-length ... ... ... ... ... ... ... ... ... | 1.92 in (48.77 mm) | 1.797 in (45.70 mm) |
| Number of working coils ... ... ... ... ... ... | 4½ | 5½ |

## Valve timing
| | | |
|---|---|---|
| Inlet valve: | | |
|   Opens ... ... ... ... ... ... ... ... ... | 5° BTDC | 9° 4' BTDC |
|   Closes ... ... ... ... ... ... ... ... ... | 45° ABDC | 50° 56' ABDC |
| Exhaust valve: | | |
|   Opens ... ... ... ... ... ... ... ... ... | 40° BBDC | 48° 56' BBDC |
|   Closes ... ... ... ... ... ... ... ... ... | 10° ATDC | 11° 4' ATDC |
| Valve clearances (cold): | | |
|   Inlet ... ... ... ... ... ... ... ... ... | 0.013 in (0.33 mm) | 0.016 to 0.018 in (0.41 to 0.46 mm) |
|   Exhaust ... ... ... ... ... ... ... ... ... | 0.013 in (0.33 mm) | 0.020 to 0.022 in (0.51 to 0.56 mm) |

## Oil pump clearances
| | |
|---|---|
| Oil pump outer ring endfloat ... ... ... ... ... | 0.004 to 0.005 in (0.10 to 0.12 mm) |
| Oil pump inner rotor endfloat ... ... ... ... ... | 0.0045 to 0.0055 in (0.11 to 0.14 mm) |
| Outer ring-to-body clearance ... ... ... ... ... | 0.011 in (0.28 mm) |
| Rotor lobe clearance ... ... ... ... ... | 0.0035 in (0.089 mm) |

## Lubrication
| | 4 cylinder | 6 cylinder |
|---|---|---|
| Oil pressure: | | |
|   Idling ... ... ... ... ... ... ... ... ... | 15/50 lb/in² (1.0 to 3.5 kg/cm²) | 15/60 lb/in² (1.0 to 4.2 kg/cm²) |
|   Running ... ... ... ... ... ... ... ... ... | 50/70 lb/in² (3.5 to 4.9 kg/cm²) | 65 lb/in² (4.6 kg/cm²) |

## Oil capacities
| | | |
|---|---|---|
| With manual gearbox (renewing filter) ... ... ... ... ... | 10.25 Imp pints (5.8 litres) | 13 Imp pints (7.4 litres) |
| With automatic transmission (renewing filter) ... ... ... ... | 7.75 pts (4.4 litres) | 10 pts (5.7 litres) |

## Torque wrench settings
| | 4 cylinder lb/ft | Nm | 6 cylinder lb/ft | Nm |
|---|---|---|---|---|
| Main bearing nuts ... ... ... ... ... ... ... ... | 70 | 97 | 70 | 97 |
| Flywheel bolts ... ... ... ... ... ... ... ... | 40 | 55 | 60 | 83 |
| Big-end bolts ... ... ... ... ... ... ... ... | 35 | 48 | 35 | 48 |
| Cylinder head nuts or bolts ... ... ... ... ... ... ... | 50 | 69 | 70 | 97 |
| Rocker pedestal nuts ... ... ... ... ... ... ... | 25 | 35 | — | — |
| Oil pump to crankcase ... ... ... ... ... ... ... | 14 | 19 | 20 | 28 |
| Transmission case to crankcase ... ... ... ... ... | 25 | 35 | 25 | 35 |
| Side cover screws ... ... ... ... ... ... ... | 4 | 6 | — | — |
| Timing cover screws: | | | | |
|   Small ... ... ... ... ... ... ... ... ... | 6 | 8 | 6 (Studs) | 8 |
|   Larger ... ... ... ... ... ... ... ... ... | 14 | 19 | 18 (Nuts) | 25 |
| Crankshaft pulley bolt ... ... ... ... ... ... ... | 70 | 97 | 60 | 83 |
| Camshaft sprocket nut ... ... ... ... ... ... ... | 70 | 97 | 35 | 48 |
| Front engine plate bolts ... ... ... ... ... ... | 20 | 28 | — | — |
| Rear plate bolts: | | | | |
|   Small ... ... ... ... ... ... ... ... ... | 20 | 28 | — | — |
|   Larger ... ... ... ... ... ... ... ... ... | 30 | 41 | — | — |
| Water pump bolts ... ... ... ... ... ... ... | 17 | 23 | 20 | 28 |
| Fan pulley screws ... ... ... ... ... ... ... | 18 | 25 | 10 | 14 |
| Manifold nuts ... ... ... ... ... ... ... | 15 | 21 | 15 | 21 |

## Torque wrench settings

| | 4 cylinder | | 6 cylinder | |
|---|---|---|---|---|
| | lb/ft | Nm | lb/ft | Nm |
| Clutch cover to flywheel bolts | 18 | 25 | 18 | 25 |
| Carburettor nuts | 15 | 21 | 15 | 21 |
| Spark plugs | 18 | 25 | 18 | 25 |
| Oil pressure valve dome nut | 40 | 55 | — | — |
| Adaptor plate bolts: | | | | |
| Small | 20 | 28 | 25 | 35 |
| Larger | 30 | 41 | 30 | 41 |
| Driveplate bolts (automatic) | 30 | 41 | 30 | 41 |
| Automatic transmission casing to crankcase | 30 | 41 | 30 | 41 |
| Timing chain guide bolts | — | — | 20 | 28 |
| Flywheel housing: | | | | |
| Studs | — | — | 6 | 8 |
| Nuts | — | — | 18 | 25 |
| Lifting bracket setscrews | — | — | 30 | 41 |
| Cam carrier to head: | | | | |
| Small | — | — | 25 | 35 |
| Large | — | — | 30 | 41 |
| Oil filter housing to crankcase: | | | | |
| Paper gasket | 20 | 28 | 20 | 28 |
| Cork gasket | 30 | 41 | 30 | 41 |

## 1 General description

1   1800 models are fitted with a 'B' series, 4 cylinder, 5 bearing, ohv engine (type 18H).
2200 models are fitted with an 'E' series, 6 cylinder, 7 bearing, ohc engine (type 23H).
2   Both engines are transversely mounted and the construction of the crankcase, cylinder block and cylinder head is of cast-iron (photos).
3   Pistons are of aluminium solid skirt type, the smaller engine having two compression and one oil control ring and the larger unit having three compression and one oil control ring.
4   Lubrication is provided by a rotor type pump on the 1800 engine and a concentric type pump on the 2200 unit. Both engines have a full-flow oil filter and a positive crankcase ventilation system.

## 2 Major operations with engine in position in car

The following operations can be carried out while the engine is still in position in the car:

### 1800 (4 cylinder)
*Removal and refitting of the:*
*Rocker shaft*
*Cylinder head*
*Tappets*
*Timing chain, gears and tensioner*
*Distributor driveshaft*
*Crankshaft spigot bush (after removal of flywheel housing and*

*clutch, see Chapter 5). (manual gearbox only)*
*Clutch, flywheel, flywheel housing and adaptor plate (manual gearbox)*
*Oil pick-up strainer*
*Oil pressure relief valve*

1.2A Front view of 6 cylinder engine

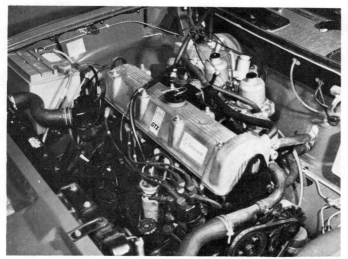
1.2B View of left-hand end of 6 cylinder engine

1.2C View of right-hand end of 6 cylinder engine

*Inlet and exhaust manifolds (see Chapter 3)*
*Engine mountings*

**2200 (6 cylinder)**
*Removal and refitting of the:*
*Camshaft cover*
*Camshaft and tappets (after removal of cylinder head)*
*Cylinder head*
*Crankshaft front oil seal and timing gear (manual gearbox only)*
*Oil pump*
*Distributor driveshaft (manual gearbox only)*
*Flywheel*
*Flywheel housing and clutch*
*Inlet and exhaust manifolds (see Chapter 3)*
*Engine mountings*

---

**3    Rocker shaft (4 cylinder) - removal and dismantling**

**If the engine is still in the car,** drain the cooling system and

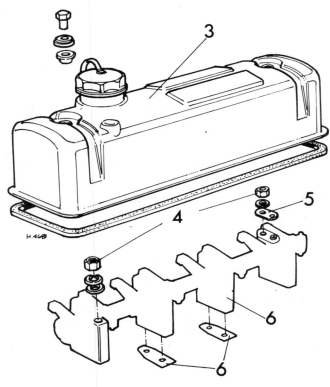

Fig. 1.1. 4 cylinder rocker cover (3), pedestal nut (4), locking plate
(5) and shims (6) (Sec. 3)

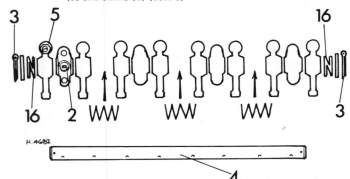

**Fig. 1.2. 4 cylinder rocker components (Sec. 3)**

| | |
|---|---|
| 2   Shaft locating screw | 5   Adjuster screw |
| 3   Split pin | 16  Double coil spring |
| 4   Shaft | washers |

disconnect the distributor vacuum pipe.

*Engine in or out of car*
1   Unbolt and remove the rocker cover.
2   Unscrew each of the rocker pedestal nuts half a turn at a time until any tension is released on the shaft and then lift the shaft away retaining the shims which are located beneath the two centre brackets. Four of the rocker pedestal securing nuts also act as cylinder head nuts.
3   To dismantle the rocker assembly, first extract the shaft locating screw and then withdraw the split pins from each end of the rocker shaft.
4   Slide the components from the shaft noting their sequence if they are to be refitted.

---

**4    Cylinder head (4 cylinder) - removal and dismantling**

**If the engine is still in the car,** drain the cooling system, disconnect the battery. Disconnect the radiator top hose, the exhaust pipe from the manifold and the brake servo hose from the manifold. Disconnect the lead from the water temperature switch.
If power steering is fitted, remove the pump drivebelt, withdraw the mounting bolts and place the pump to one side of the engine compartment.

*Engine in or out of car*
1   Remove the rocker shaft, as described in the preceding Section.
2   Withdraw the pushrods, keeping them in their original sequence. A piece of card with holes numbered 1 to 8 is useful for this purpose.
3   Remove the air cleaner.
4   Disconnect the carburettor vent pipe.
5   Disconnect the fuel pump pipes.
6   Remove the carburettor from the manifold.
7   Disconnect the HT leads from the spark plugs.
8   Unscrew and remove the remaining cylinder head nuts.
9   Withdraw the cylinder head upwards. If it is stuck, pour freeing fluid around the studs and tap the head all round with a hammer and a block of hardwood used as an insulator. With the spark plugs still in position, turning the crankshaft will generate compression to help break the seal.
10  Remove the cylinder head gasket from the block.
11  Commence dismantling by removing the spark plugs.
12  Unbolt the water outlet elbow and extract the thermostat.
13  Remove the water temperature switch and small cover plate and gasket (if essential).
14  Remove the flanged tube from the exhaust manifold shroud and then withdraw the shroud.
15  Unbolt the manifold assembly.
16  Using a suitable compressor, compress each of the valve springs in turn and extract the split cotters, cups, spring and collars. Remove

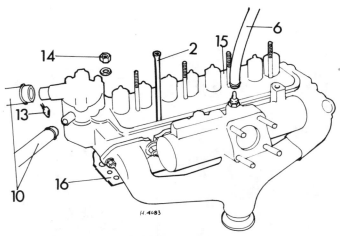

**Fig. 1.3. 4 cylinder cylinder head components (Sec. 4)**

| | |
|---|---|
| 2   Pushrod | 14  Cylinder head nuts |
| 6   Brake servo pipe | 15  Cylinder head |
| 10  Radiator top and heater hoses | 16  Cylinder head gasket |
| 13  Water temperature switch lead | |

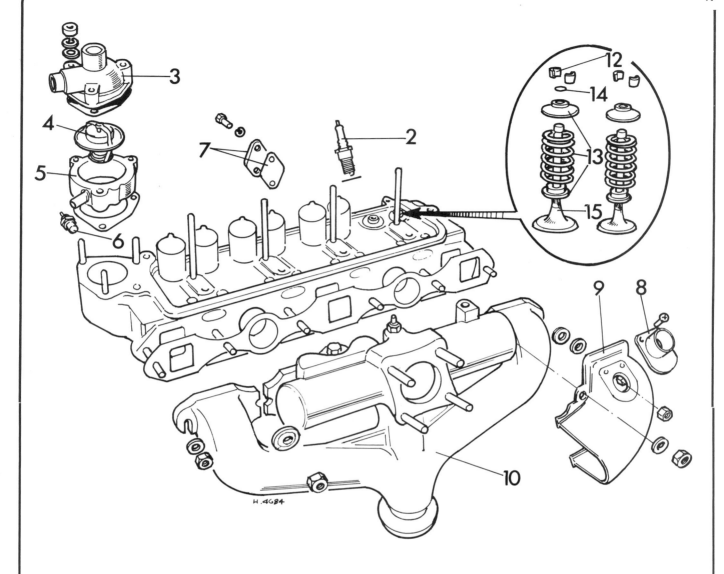

**Fig. 1.4. 4 cylinder cylinder head components (Sec. 4)**

| | | |
|---|---|---|
| 2 Spark plug | 6 Water temperature switch | 10 Exhaust manifold |
| 3 Water outlet | 7 Cover plate and gasket | 12 Split collets |
| 4 Thermostat | 8 Flanged tube | 13 Spring cup and collar |
| 5 Spacer plate | 9 Manifold shroud | 14 Inlet valve stem oil seal |
| | | 15 Valve |

4.16A Compressing a valve spring

4.16B Removing a valve spring and cup

4.17 Removing a valve from the cylinder head

the oil seals from the inlet valve stems (photos).

17 Withdraw the valves and retain them in their original sequence (photo).

## 5 Tappets (4 cylinder) - removal

**If the engine is still in the car,** disconnect the exhaust downpipe.

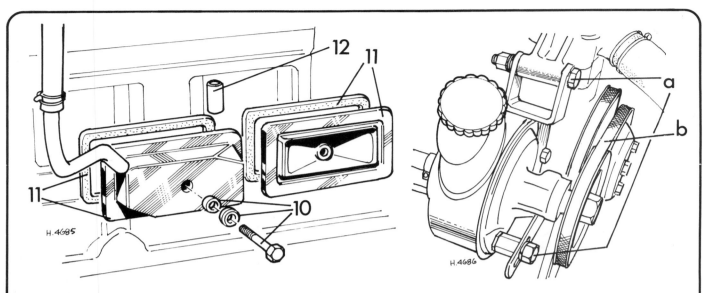

**Fig. 1.5. 4 cylinder tappet chamber side cover bolts (10), side cover and gasket (11) and tappet (12) (Sec. 5)**

**Fig. 1.6. 4 cylinder (optional) power steering pump mounting and adjustment bolts (a) and drivebelt (b) (Sec. 6)**

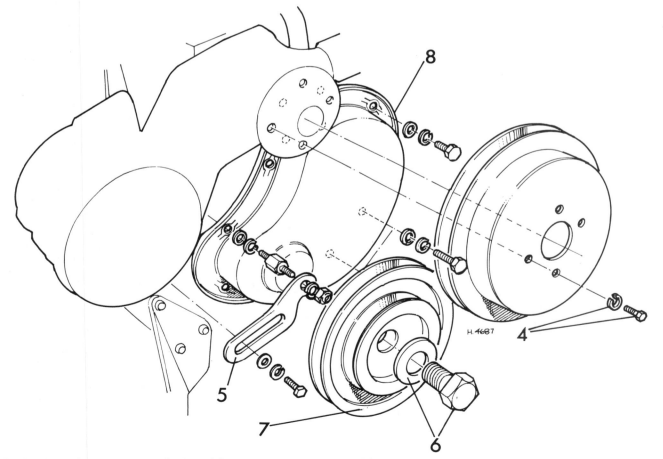

**Fig. 1.7. 4 cylinder water pump pulley bolts (4), alternator adjustment strap (5), crankshaft pulley bolt (6), crankshaft pulley (7), and timing cover (8) (Sec. 6)**

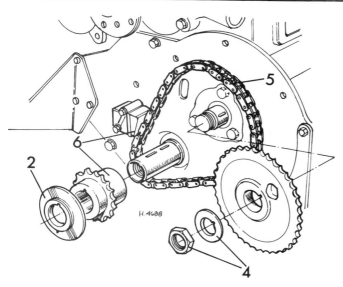

**Fig. 1.8. 4 cylinder timing components (Sec. 6)**

2  *Oil thrower*                           5  *Timing chain*
4  *Camshaft nut and locking plate*        6  *Tensioner slipper*

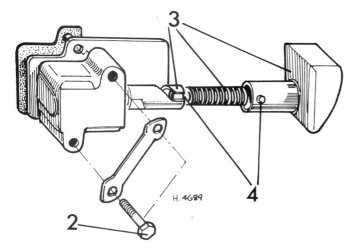

**Fig. 1.9. 4 cylinder timing chain tensioner components (Sec. 6)**

2  *Securing bolts*                        4  *Peg and slot*
3  *Tensioner*

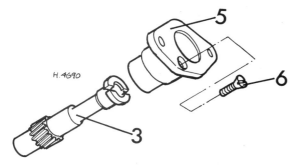

**Fig. 1.10. 4 cylinder distributor housing screw (3), housing (5) and driveshaft (6) (Sec. 7)**

*Engine in or out of car*
1  Disconnect the crankcase breather pipe from the carburettor.
2  Remove the air cleaner.
3  Remove the manifold shroud flanged tube and then withdraw the shroud.

4  Unbolt and remove the manifold assembly complete with carburettor.
5  Remove the rocker shaft (Section 3) and extract the pushrods, keeping them in their original sequence.
6  Remove the two adjacent side covers and gaskets.
7  Insert the fingers into the tappet chamber and extract the tappets, keeping them in strict order for refitting.

**6   Timing chain, gears and tensioner (4 cylinder) - removal**

If the engine is in the car, remove the water pump drivebelt and pulley and the alternator adjustment link. Where power steering is installed, slacken the pump mountings and push the pump towards the engine so that the drivebelt can be removed.

*Engine in or out of car*
1  Remove the crankshaft pulley bolt. To prevent the crankshaft rotating, engage a gear before applying a ring spanner to the bolt. On cars equipped with automatic transmission, remove the starter and jam the flywheel ring gear with a large screwdriver or cold chisel.
2  Remove the crankshaft pulley using a puller or two levers inserted at opposite points behind it.
3  Unbolt and remove the timing cover and peel off the gasket.
4  Extract the oil thrower.
5  Flatten the camshaft sprocket tab washer and unscrew the nut.
6  Withdraw the camshaft and crankshaft sprockets simultaneously until the camshaft sprocket can be removed from within the loop of the timing chain.
7  Do not let the timing chain tensioner inner cylinder and spring fly out but gradually release the tension and then remove these components from the tensioner body.
8  Pull off the crankshaft sprocket and unbolt and remove the chain tensioner body.

**7   Distributor driveshaft (4 cylinder) - removal**

1  Remove the cap from the distributor.
2  Disconnect the LT lead from the distributor and the vacuum pipe.
3  Release the clamp plate pinch bolt and withdraw the distributor.
4  Unbolt the clamp plate.
5  Remove the distributor housing (one screw) from the cylinder block.
6  Using a long 5/16 in. UNF bolt screw it into the hole in the end of the distributor driveshaft and extract the shaft.

**8   Crankshaft spigot bush (4 cylinder - manual gearbox) - removal**

If the engine is still in the car, refer to Section 28. Remove the air cleaner and disconnect all necessary controls and hoses and the exhaust downpipe so that the left-hand side of the engine can be lowered and supported on a block of wood in order to provide access to the spigot bush located in the centre of the crankshaft rear flange.

*Engine in or out of car*
1  The spigot bush may be extracted in one of two ways. Either tap a thread into it and then screw in a bolt, tightening it on a distance piece or fill the spigot bush with grease and tap in a close fitting rod. The hydraulic pressure created by the latter method, will eject the bush.
2  Installation is described in Section 42.

**9   Clutch, flywheel and adaptor plate (4 cylinder) - removal**

If the engine is in the car, drain the gearbox, disconnect the gearshift control rods and the right-hand driveshaft from the differential. Remove the battery and the starter motor and disconnect the brake servo hose, flywheel housing clips and the engine mountings after taking the weight of the power unit on a hoist. Also disconnect the exhaust pipe bracket from the gearbox casing.

*Engine in or out of car*
1  Remove the flywheel housing, as described in Section 28, paragraphs 1 to 6.
2  Slacken the clutch pressure plate cover bolts a turn at a time until the diaphragm spring pressure is relieved.

3   Disengage the pressure plate cover from the dowels on the flywheel and withdraw the pressure plate assembly and the driven plate.
4   Jam the flywheel starter ring gear and remove the flywheel securing bolts. Withdraw the flywheel.
5   Unscrew and remove the adaptor plate bolts and withdraw the adaptor plate, complete with integral oil seal and joint washer.

**10 Oil pick-up strainer and relief valve (4 cylinder) - removal**

*Manual gearbox*

1   Drain the transmission oil.
2   Disconnect the speedometer cable from its transmission front cover adaptor.
3   If power steering is fitted, detach the power steering pipe clips and remove the distance piece from the stud on the transmission casing. Remove the stud.
4   Unbolt and remove the front cover and gasket.
5   Unscrew and remove the locknut with flat and fibre washer which retain the oil strainer to the centre shaft. Withdraw the strainer and sealing ring.

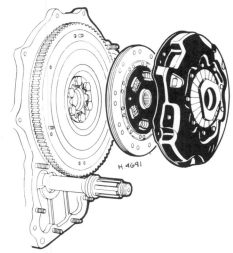

Fig. 1.11. 4 cylinder clutch and flywheel (Sec. 9)

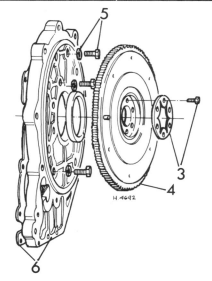

Fig. 1.12. 4 cylinder flywheel bolts and lockplate (3), flywheel (4), adaptor plate bolts (5) and gearbox adaptor plate and gasket (6) (Sec. 9)

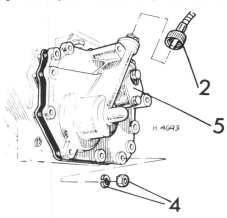

Fig. 1.13. 4 cylinder speedometer cable (2), transmission front cover nut (4), front cover plate (5) (Sec. 10)

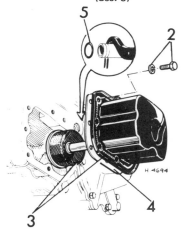

Fig. 1.14b. 4 cylinder (automatic transmission) oil pick-up strainer cover bolt (2), strainer and cover (3), cover gasket (4) and 'O' ring seal (5) (Sec. 10)

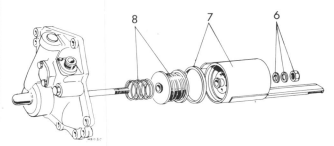

Fig. 1.14a. 4 cylinder engine (manual gearbox) oil pick-up strainer (Sec. 10)

6   *Locknut, flat and fibre washers*
7   *Oil pick-up strainer and sealing ring*
8   *Magnet and spring*

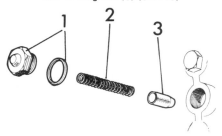

Fig. 1.15. 4 cylinder oil pressure relief valve (Sec. 10)

1   *Cap and washer*     2   *Spring*     3   *Valve*

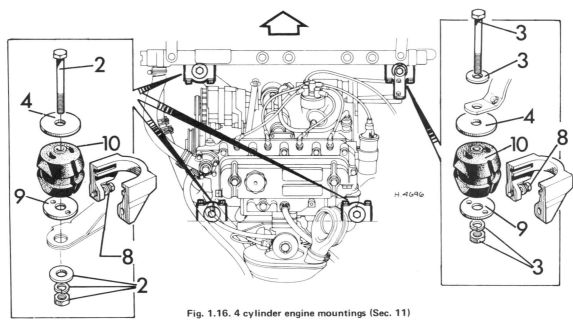

**Fig. 1.16. 4 cylinder engine mountings (Sec. 11)**

| 2 | Through bolt, plate and washers | 4 | Upper plate | 9 | Lower plate |
| 3 | Through bolt, nut and washers | 8 | Support bracket bolts | 10 | Flexible mounting |

6 Withdraw the magnet and spring from the front cover.

### Automatic transmission
7 Drain the engine oil.
8 Unbolt and remove the oil pick-up strainer cover.
9 Withdraw the strainer and cover and gasket.
10 Extract the 'O' ring from the strainer tube.

### All cars
11 Removal of the pressure relief valve is simply a matter of unscrewing its cap and extracting the internal components.

### 11 Engine mountings (4 cylinder) - removal (see also Section 86)

1 The engine mountings can be removed with the engine still in the car, provided the power unit is adequately supported with a hoist or jacks.
2 Withdraw the through bolt and upper plate from the front left-hand mounting bushes.
3 Withdraw the through bolt from the front right-hand mounting bush.
4 Raise the engine slightly and remove the upper plate from the right-hand front mounting bush.
5 Withdraw the through bolts from the rear left-hand and right-hand mounting bushes then extract the upper plates.
6 Lower the power unit slightly and extract the two bolts and two screws which retain each mounting bush support bracket to the body.
7 Withdraw the lower plates and the mounting bushes.

### 12 Camshaft cover (6 cylinder) - removal

**If the engine is still in the car,** disconnect the oil pressure pipe from the cylinder block adaptor from the cylinder block adaptor, (if fitted).

### Engine in or out of car
1 Remove the air cleaner assembly.
2 Disconnect the extractor hose from the top of the camshaft cover.
3 Disconnect the vacuum pipe from the distributor, and the fuel pipe from the carburettor.
4 Remove the camshaft cover screws, move the coil and the oil pressure pipe to one side and lift the cover and its gasket from the cylinder head.

### 13 Camshaft and tappets (6 cylinder) - removal

1 Remove the camshaft cover and gasket, as described in the preceding Section.

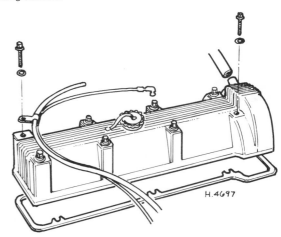

**Fig. 1.17. 6 cylinder camshaft cover showing extractor hose, distributor vacuum and oil pressure hoses (Sec. 12)**

2 Turn the crankshaft until the camshaft sprocket and camshaft carrier marks are in alignment (photo).
3 Remove the screw from the chain tensioner adaptor and insert a 1/8 in. Allen key into the screw aperture and turn the key clockwise to retract the tensioner (photos). (Fig. 1.18)
4 Remove the camshaft sprocket and retain the engagement of the chain with the crankshaft sprocket by supporting it on the chain guides (photo).
5 Remove the cylinder head (Section 14). Now slacken the camshaft carrier bolts in sequence until the tension of the valve springs has been relieved and then withdraw the bolts.
6 Lift the camshaft carrier about ½ in. (12.7 mm) from the cylinder head and support it in this position by inserting two small blocks or bars (photo).
7 Withdraw the camshaft from the carrier (in the direction of the clutch) taking care not to damage the bearings as the lobes of the

13.2 Camshaft sprocket and carrier alignment marks

13.3A Chain adjuster plug

13.3B Adjusting chain tensioner using an Allen key

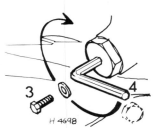

Fig. 1.18. 6 cylinder chain tensioner adaptor (Sec. 13)

3  Screw          4  Allen key

13.4 Timing chain supported on guides (cylinder head removed)

13.6 Camshaft and carrier supported on small blocks

13.8A Withdrawing a tappet

13.8B Interior of tappet showing shim

camshaft pass through.

8   Withdraw each tappet in strict sequence and extract the internal shim. If this is difficult to remove, wash out the oil in petrol to release the suction. Record carefully on paper the shim thickness of each tappet and keep them and their respective tappets in numbered sequence. It is imperative that they are returned to their original locations (photos).

## 14  Cylinder head (6 cylinder) - removal

**If the engine is in the car,** disconnect the battery and the lead from

the water temperature switch in the cylinder head. Disconnect the spark plug leads and remove the distributor cap. Drain the cooling system, remove the air cleaner and disconnect the camshaft cover breather hose. Disconnect the brake servo hose from the manifold. Disconnect the throttle cable. Disconnect the heater hoses and remove the exhaust manifold clamps. Disconnect the fuel pipe from the carburettor, also the vacuum pipe. Disconnect the radiator top hose and the water pump hose.

*Engine in or out of car*

1   Remove the camshaft cover (Section 12).
2   Turn the crankshaft so that No. 1 piston is at tdc on its compression

stroke. This can be determined by removing No. 1 spark plug and placing a finger over the plug hole. As the crankshaft pulley bolt is turned, compression will be felt being generated. Continue turning the crankshaft until the notch on the pulley is opposite the tdc mark on the index cast on the transmission casing front cover.

3   Align the camshaft sprocket and carrier marks.

4   Release the camshaft chain tensioner and remove the camshaft sprocket, keeping the chain in engagement with the crankshaft sprocket by tying it up with a piece of wire or by supporting it on the chain guides.

5   Slacken the cylinder head bolts, half a turn at a time and in diagonal sequence.

6   Lift the cylinder head from the block, allowing the chain to pass through the aperture using a piece of wire to retain the chain.

7   Lift the cylinder head gasket from the block.

8   Dismantling of the valves is as described in Section 4, paragraphs 16 and 17 for 4 cylinder engine cylinder heads.

### 15  Timing gear and crankshaft oil seal (6 cylinder) - removal

**If the engine is in the car**, these operations can only be carried out if a manual gearbox is fitted.

Remove the alternator drivebelt and the screw which secures it to the left-hand mounting bracket.

Remove the steering pump drivebelt. Refer also to Section 86.

*Engine in or out of car*

1   Knock back the crankshaft pulley bolt lock tab and unscrew and remove the pulley bolt and washer.

2   Using two levers or a puller, extract the crankshaft pulley.

3   If the engine is in the car, take its weight on a hoist or jacks and remove the through bolt which secures the left-hand mounting bracket to the front and rear mountings.

4   Remove the three screws which secure the left-hand engine mounting plate to the casing and remove the plate.

5   The crankshaft front oil seal can be levered from the cover or pulled using a suitable hooked tool (photo).

6   If the timing chain and sprockets are to be removed, retract the chain tensioner by removing the plug, unscrewing the locknut and inserting an Allen key. Turn the key fully clockwise. Remove the camshaft cover.

7   Align the camshaft sprocket and carrier marks, as described in Section 14, paragraphs 2 and 3 and then remove the camshaft sprocket.

8   Extract the oil thrower from the front face of the crankshaft sprocket.

9   Release any tension on the timing chain and when it is disengaged from the teeth of the crankshaft sprocket, withdraw the sprocket (rounded shoulder is against oil thrower) (photo).

10  If the chain must be removed for renewal, the rivets which secure the bright link will have to be extracted using a chain rivet extractor before the chain can be withdrawn.

11  If the timing chain guides are to be removed, unbolt the front cover and remove the gasket (Fig. 1.20).

12  Release the locknut and turn the chain guide adjuster a few turns inwards, using its end slot (photo).

13  Remove the two screws which secure the chain guides to the cylinder block. Extract the fixed guide.

15.5 Crankshaft front oil seal

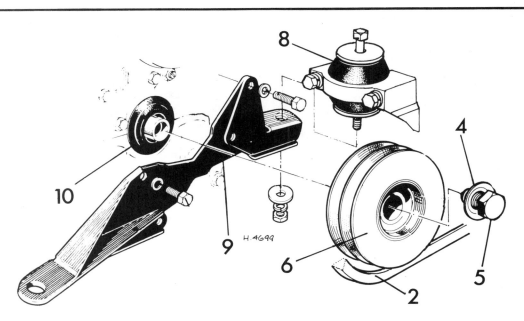

Fig. 1.19. 6 cylinder engine mounting components (Sec. 15)

| | | |
|---|---|---|
| 2  *Alternator drivebelt* | 5  *Crankshaft pulley retaining bolt* | 8  *LH mounting (manual gearbox)* |
| 4  *Crankshaft pulley bolt locking plate* | 6  *Pulley* | 9  *LH engine mounting plate (manual gearbox)* |
| | | 10  *Crankshaft front oil seal* |

15.9 Withdrawing crankshaft sprocket

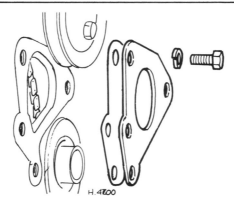

Fig. 1.20. Front cover and gasket (6 cylinder engine) (Sec. 15)

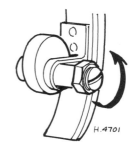

Fig. 1.21. Chain guide adjuster (6 cylinder engine) (Sec. 15)

15.12 Chain guide adjuster screw

16.1 Withdrawing distributor

16.4 Gearbox front cover

16.5 Withdrawing oil filter adaptor

16.6A Improvised method of unscrewing oil pump outlet connection

16.6B Extracting oil pump outlet connection

14 Disengage the lower end of the adjustable guide from the adjuster, turn the adjuster through 90° and remove the guide. The adjuster can be screwed into and removed from the engine interior.

## 16 Oil pump (6 cylinder - manual gearbox) - removal

**If the engine is still in the car,** drain the engine oil, raise the front of the car and support it on stands placed under the front side jacking points. Using a hoist, take the weight of the power unit and then release the clips which secure the power steering pipes to the gearbox. Remove the engine left-hand mounting plate.

*Engine in or out of car*
1   Mark the relationship of the distributor clamp plate to the cylinder block and then withdraw the distributor (photo).
2   Extract the oil pump driveshaft. A special tool (no. 18G1147) or a

pair of ground down long-nosed pliers will be needed to grip the squared end. Turning the crankshaft slightly may help to release the driveshaft.
3   Remove the crankshaft pulley (Section 15, paragraphs 1 and 2).
4   Remove the gearbox front cover and its gasket. These are secured by seven setscrews, one countersunk screw and a stud (photo).
5   Unscrew the securing bolt and withdraw the oil filter and adaptor assembly together with the gasket (photo).
6   Unscrew the pump outlet connection (photos).
7   If required, the sealed type oil pressure relief valve can be withdrawn and the filter cartridge unscrewed from the adaptor.
8   Remove the fuel pump and extract the operating rod from the guide tube (photo).
9   Remove the three screws which secure the oil pump pick-up pipe and withdraw the pipe and gasket.
10  Remove the oil pump securing bolts, retaining the sealing and spring washers.

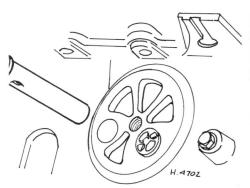

Fig. 1.22. Oil pressure relief valve (6 cylinder) (Sec. 16)

16.8 Removing fuel pump and operating rod

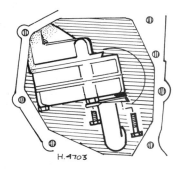

Fig. 1.23. Oil pump pick-up pipe screws (6 cylinder) (Sec. 16)

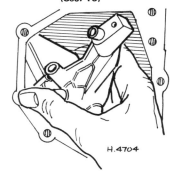

Fig. 1.24. Withdrawing the oil pump (6 cylinder) (Sec. 16)

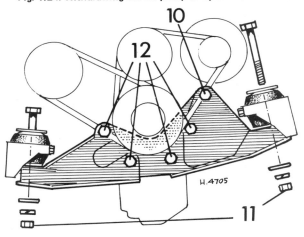

Fig. 1.25. Left-hand engine mounting plate (6 cylinder automatic transmission) (Sec. 17)

10 Alternator mounting bolt
11 Mounting nuts
12 Plate to end housing bolts

11 Withdraw the oil pump by pulling it downwards and at the same time, tilting it backwards.

### 17 Oil pump (6 cylinder - automatic transmission) - removal

If the engine is still in the car, jack-up the car and support it under the front left-hand jacking point. Drain the engine oil. Mark the relationship of the distributor clamp plate to the cylinder block and then withdraw the distributor. Withdraw the oil pump driveshaft after reference to Section 18, paragraphs 2 and 3. Disconnect the fuel inlet pipe from the fuel pump and plug the pipe. Use a hoist and take the weight of the power unit. Disconnect the clips which secure the power steering pipes to the front cover of the engine. Disconnect the power steering pump and tie it to the towing bracket below the car. Remove the screw which secures the alternator to the left-hand engine mounting plate. Remove the nut and spring which secures the left-

hand mounting plate to the two mountings. Remove the four screws which secure the left-hand mounting plate to the end housing and withdraw the plate.

#### Engine in or out of car
1 Remove the stud and six screws which secure the endhousing to the gearbox casing.
2 Remove the six end housing screws, noting the position of the clips. Remove the endhousing.
3 Extract the oil pick-up tube from the strainer within the gearbox casing.
4 Remove the oil pump after unscrewing the retaining screws. The ring dowels can be extracted by using a 5/16 in. (8.0 mm) tap.
5 Remove the securing screw and extract the pick-up strainer from the gearbox casing.
6 If required, the sealed type oil pressure relief valve can be withdrawn and the filter cartridge unscrewed from the adaptor (see Fig. 1.22).

### 18 Distributor driveshaft (6 cylinder - manual gearbox) - removal

If the engine is in the car, drain the engine oil and remove the alternator and power steering drivebelts.

#### Engine in or out of car
1 Remove the camshaft cover, (Section 12).
2 Withdraw the distributor, having first marked the relationship of the clamp plate to the cylinder block when the crankshaft is at tdc (No. 1) and the camshaft sprocket and carrier marks are in alignment.
3 Withdraw the oil pump driveshaft by gripping its squared-end with a special tool (18G1147) or long-nosed pliers, suitably ground. Turning the crankshaft slightly may ease its withdrawal.
4 Retract the chain tensioner (Section 13) and remove the camshaft sprocket, letting the chain hang over the guides.
5 Remove the fuel pump and extract the pushrod.
6 Remove the oil filter assembly and adaptor, also the oil pump assembly (Section 16).
7 Remove the crankshaft pulley (Section 15).
8 Extract the crankshaft front oil seal (Section 15).
9 Remove the crankshaft oil thrower and sprocket, followed by the distributor drivegear (photo).
10 The distributor driveshaft can now be withdrawn from its location. It will turn through 90° as it is removed. Retain the thrust washer.

### 19 Flywheel and clutch (6 cylinder) - removal

If the engine is in the car, disconnect and remove the battery and the battery tray. Support the weight of the engine either on a jack or by using a hoist. Release the right-hand front engine mounting, remove the nut and spring washer and extract the through-bolt. As the flywheel housing must be removed sideways due to lack of clearance, extract the long securing stud by locking two nuts together and unscrewing it.

#### Engine in or out of car
1 Slacken the eight screws which secure the clutch cover to the flywheel housing.
2 Remove the single nut from the clutch cover.

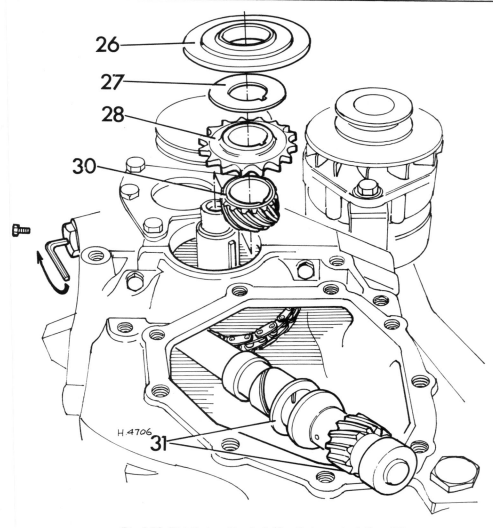

**Fig. 1.26. Distributor driveshaft (6 cylinder engine) (Sec. 18)**

26  Oil seal
27  Oil thrower

28  Crankshaft sprocket
30  Distributor drivegear

31  Distributor driveshaft and
     thrust washer

3   Remove the right-hand front engine mounting bracket.
4   Lower the engine as necessary and remove the six remaining screws noting the location of the earth cable and clip.
5   Free the clutch cover from the two dowel pins and the slave cylinder and withdraw the cover.
6   Remove the operating rod pivot pin and pull the operating rod from the throw-out plunger.
7   Remove the starter motor.
8   Remove the three setscrews and withdraw the clutch release plate.
9   Unbolt and remove the retaining plate.
10 Drive the clutch and flywheel assembly off the primary gear using a hide-faced mallet inserted through the starter motor aperture in the flywheel housing.
11 Place the assembly on the bench, clutch side uppermost.
12 Slacken the three diaphragm retaining bolts progressively and then remove the diaphragm cover.
13 Lift the flywheel from the pressure plate.
14 Extract the driven plate.
15 On cars equipped with automatic transmission the driveplate can only be removed from the crankshaft after removal of the power unit and separation of the units.

18.9 Removing distributor drivegear from crankshaft

**20 Flywheel housing (6 cylinder) - removal**

**If the engine is still in the car,** drain the coolant and the engine oil.

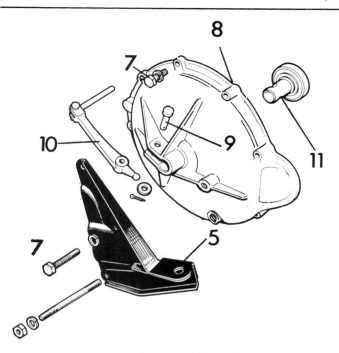

Fig. 1.27. Clutch cover (6 cylinder) (Sec. 19)

5  RH front engine mounting        9  Operating rod pivot
   bracket                            pin
7  Bolts                          10  Operating rod
8  Cover                          11  Release bearing

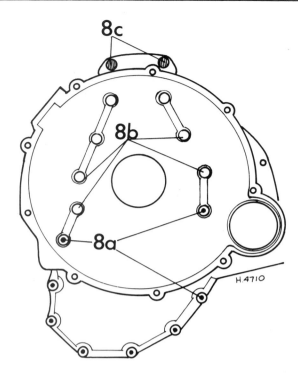

Fig. 1.29. Flywheel housing bolts (6 cylinder) (Sec. 19)

8a Nuts            8b Setscrews            8c Bolts

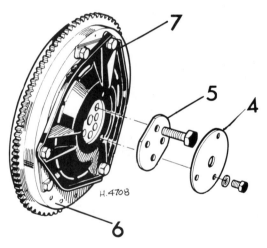

Fig. 1.28. Clutch release plate (4) and retaining plate (5), flywheel clutch assembly (6), diaphragm cover (7) on 6 cylinder power unit (Sec. 19)

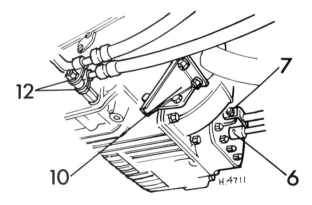

Fig. 1.30. 4 cylinder engine/gearbox attachments (Sec. 22)

6   Extension rod to selector shaft tension pin
7   Steady rod to mounting bracket bolt
10  Exhaust pipe bracket
12  Power steering steady pipe clips (if fitted)

*Engine in or out of car*
1  Remove the clutch and flywheel (see preceding Section).
2  Remove the clutch release lever and bearing from the clutch housing (see Chapter 5).
3  Release the clutch slave cylinder from the flywheel housing and tie it to one side.
4  Remove the right-hand and rear engine mounting bracket.
5  Knock back the locking tabs of the flywheel housing bolt, screws and nuts, unscrew the fastenings progressively and then withdraw the flywheel housing and its gasket. Tape the splines of the primary gear or fit a protective sleeve to prevent damage to the lips of the flywheel housing oil seal.
6  Remove the idler gear thrust washer, the crankcase breather filter and the flywheel housing inspection cover (if necessary). Extract the flywheel housing oil seal.

## 21 Engine mountings (6 cylinder) - removal

1  The removal of the engine mountings with the engine still in position in the car is similar to that described for 4 cylinder models in Section 11.

## 22 Engine/manual gearbox (4 cylinder) - removal

1  Raise the bonnet to its maximum vertical height.
2  Drain the engine oil.
3  Drain the transmission oil.
4  Remove the cylinder block drain plug and drain the cooling system.
5  Disconnect and remove the battery.

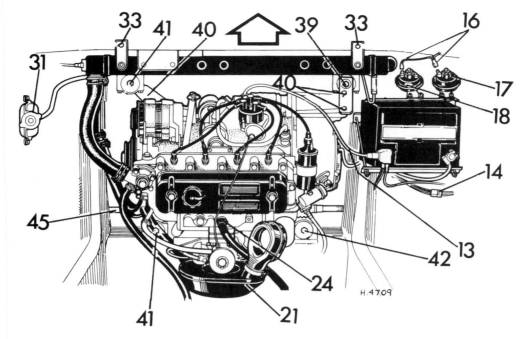

Fig. 1.31. 4 cylinder engine attachments (Sec. 22)

| | | | |
|---|---|---|---|
| 13 | Lead from battery positive terminal | 17 Horn | 31 Expansion tank | 41 LH front and rear mountings |

13  Lead from battery positive
    terminal
14  Engine harness connector
16  Horn leads

17  Horn
18  Horn
21  Air cleaner assembly
24  Servo pipe

31  Expansion tank
33  Radiator brackets
39  RH front mounting
40  Bracket

41  LH front and rear mountings
42  RH rear mounting
    bracket
45  LH driveshaft

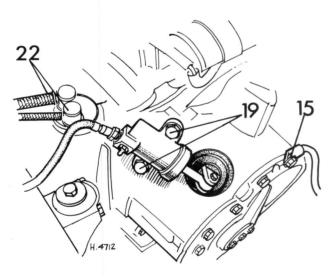

Fig. 1.32. 4 cylinder attachments (Sec. 22)

15  Earth strap                          22  Fuel pump
19  Clutch slave cylinder bolts              pipes

6   Raise the front of the car and support it under the front jacking
point.
7   Drive out the tension pin which secures the extension rod to the
gear selector shaft.
8   Remove the bolt which secures the steady rod to the mounting
bracket.
9   Disengage the extension rod from the gear selector shaft and tie
the rods to the exhaust pipe with a length of wire.
10 Disconnect the exhaust pipe bracket from the gearbox.
11 Lower the car to the ground.
12 On cars equipped with power steering, detach the pipe clips from

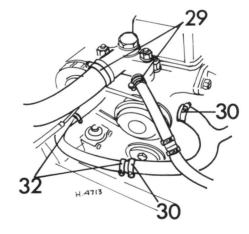

Fig. 1.33. 4 cylinder cooling hoses (Sec. 22)

29  Radiator top and heater          30  Radiator bottom hose
    hoses                            32  Bottom hose connector

the transmission casing.
13 Disconnect the leads from the battery positive terminal clamp.
14 Disconnect the engine wiring harness at the multi-connector plug.
15 Disconnect the earth lead from the transmission casing.
16 Disconnect the horn leads and remove the outer horn.
17 Remove the battery retaining bar complete with the inner horn.
18 Detach the clutch slave cylinder and withdraw it from the pushrod
and tie it to one side. There is no need to disconnect the hydraulic
lines.
19 Remove the air cleaner and temperature control device.
20 Disconnect the pipes from the fuel pump and plug them to prevent
loss of fuel.
22 Disconnect the breather and vacuum pipes from the carburettor.
23 Disconnect the brake servo pipe from the inlet manifold.
24 Remove the carburettor, gaskets, spacer and throttle bracket from

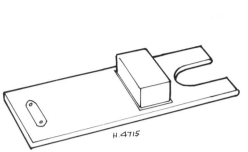

Fig. 1.34. Tool for disengaging driveshafts
(Sec. 22)

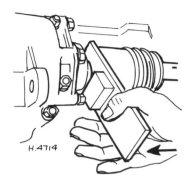

Fig. 1.35. Disengaging a driveshaft from
differential (4 cylinder) (Sec. 22)

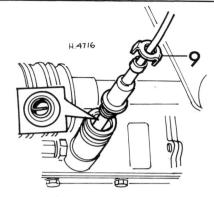

Fig. 1.36. Selector cable spring clip and
retainer (9), 4 cylinder automatic
transmission (Sec. 23)

the inlet manifold.
25 Disconnect the exhaust downpipe from the exhaust manifold.
26 Disconnect the speedometer drive cable from the transmission.
27 Disconnect the radiator top hose from the engine.
28 Disconnect the heater hose from the water outlet elbow.
29 Disconnect the radiator bottom hose from the water pump and its
connecting pipe.
30 Release the radiator expansion tank and pipe clips.
31 Disconnect the lead from the radiator cooling fan and then unbolt
and remove the radiator complete with expansion tank and connecting
pipe still attached.
32 On cars equipped with power steering, remove the pump mounting
bolts and tie the pump to the towing bracket.
33 Ideally, lifting hooks should now be fitted to the rocker cover studs.
Where these are not available, use chains or rope springs, so positioned
that the point of lift is in line with number 3 spark plug. Take the
weight of the power unit on the hoist or lifting tackle.
34 Slacken the right-hand front engine mounting through bolt and then
remove the two bracket bolts and pivot the bracket out of the way.
35 Remove the through-bolts from the three remaining engine
mountings and then remove the left-hand front mounting bracket from
the engine.
36 Release the right-hand driveshaft from its locator ring in the
differential. To do this, either borrow or purchase the official tool
(18G 1263) or make one up to suit. Strike the tool in the direction of
the differential to release the driveshaft. Do not attempt to pull the
driveshaft out of engagement as this will only serve to separate the
constant velocity joint.
37 Move the engine/gearbox as far as possible to the left-hand side of
the engine compartment and then raise it about 3 in. (76.0 mm) using
the hoist.
38 Disengage the right-hand driveshaft completely from the differential.
39 Disengage the left-hand driveshaft in a similar manner to the
right-hand one, again using the special tool to release it and moving the
power unit as far as possible to the right. To completely disengage the
driveshaft, the engine/gearbox should be raised about 6 in. (152.4 mm)
by means of the hoist.
40 Raise the hoist and lift the engine/gearbox carefully from the engine
compartment.

## 23 Engine/automatic transmission (4 cylinder) - removal

1 The procedure is similar to that described in the preceding Section
with the following differences.
2 The transmission fluid need only be drained if the unit is to be
subsequently dismantled.
3 Disconnect the leads from the starter inhibitor switch.
4 Set the selector lever in 'P', release the selector cable clip, prise out
the spring clip and disengage the cable.
5 Release the kick-down cable trunnion from the throttle bracket and
disconnect the kickdown cable from the carburettor linkage.

## 24 Engine/manual gearbox (6 cylinder) - removal

1 Disconnect the bonnet struts from the body brackets so that the

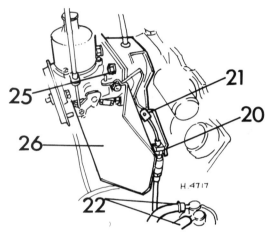

Fig. 1.37. 4 cylinder automatic transmission attachments (Sec. 23)

20 Kickdown cable trunnion
21 Kickdown cable connection
   to carburettor
22 Fuel pump hoses
25 Carburettor flange nuts
26 Carburettor heat shield

bonnet can be tied back in the fully open position. Mark the location of
any leads, hoses or pipes which are likely to cause confusion when
reconnecting (photo).
2 Drain the engine oil and cooling system.
3 Disconnect the leads from the battery and remove the battery and
its securing clamp.
4 Disconnect the starter motor, coil, distributor, water temperature
switch and radiator fan switch leads. Disconnect the reversing lamp
leads at the gearbox switch (photo).
5 Release the wiring harness clip from the flywheel housing and the
earth strap from the clutch housing.
6 Disconnect the radiator top and bottom hoses from the engine.
7 Disconnect the expansion tank hose from the radiator.
8 Remove the two radiator support brackets from the bonnet lock
platform, tilt the radiator so that the fan motor lead can be disconnected
and then lift the radiator from the engine compartment (photos).
9 Remove the air cleaner assembly.
10 Disconnect the throttle return spring from its bracket, lift the
linkage and release the throttle cable (one screw). Press the cable from
the bracket and remove the trunnion return spring. Disconnect the
mixture control cable and remove the trunnion.
11 Disconnect the brake vacuum servo hose from the manifold.
12 Disconnect the heater hoses from the engine.
13 Disconnect the speedometer cable from the transmission.
14 Disconnect the exhaust downpipe from the manifold.
15 Unbolt the clutch slave cylinder and tie it to one side out of the
way (photo).
16 Jack-up the front of the car and support it under the side jacking
points.

17 Remove the left-hand front roadwheel.
18 Remove the caliper from the left-hand swivel hub (see Chapter 9) and tie the caliper up to prevent strain on the flexible hose (photo).
19 Disconnect the trackrod-end balljoint from the steering arm using a suitable extractor (photo).
20 Disconnect the upper and lower swivel joints from the left-hand suspension arms (photo).
21 Drive out the tension pin which secures the extension rod to the gear selector shaft. Detach the steady rod from the differential housing and tie the gearchange rods to the exhaust pipe (photo).
22 Disconnect the exhaust pipe from the transmission casing.
23 Release the power steering pipes from the gearbox support stud.
24 Release both driveshafts from their differential locating rings using the tool described in Section 22, paragraph 36. Strike the tool towards the differential.
25 Disconnect the fuel inlet pipe from the fuel pump and plug the pipe.
26 Slacken the outlet pipe union on the power steering pump. Unbolt the pump and temporarily tie it to the left-hand suspended tow hook which is welded to the left-hand bodyframe sidemember within the engine compartment (photo).

27 Install suitable lifting gear and take the weight of the power unit.
28 Remove the four engine mounting through bolts.
29 Remove the right-hand front mounting bracket from the flywheel housing.
30 Remove the left-hand front engine mounting from both the body frame and the engine and then untie and lower the steering pump downwards to the left of the oil filter (photo).
31 Using the hoist, lift the power unit until the end of the left-hand engine mounting bracket is above the bodyframe member.
32 Pull the left-hand driveshaft (already released see paragraph 24), from the differential and support it on a block or axle stand. It will be easier and less likely to damage the oil seal if the top left-hand suspension swivel joint is first disconnected.
33 Push the engine/gearbox hard against the left-hand side of the engine compartment and disconnect the left-hand driveshaft (photo).
34 Raise the power unit until it is level with the upper surface of the front wings and then pull the wiring plug from the alternator and release the two clips on the gearbox flange.
35 Lift the power unit away from the car (photo).

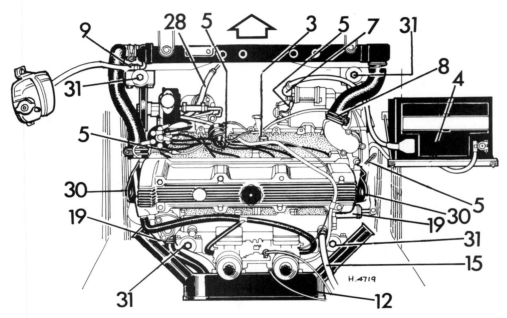

Fig. 1.38. 6 cylinder engine/manual gearbox attachments (Sec. 24)

| | | | | |
|---|---|---|---|---|
| 3 | Cylinder block drain plug | 8 | Radiator top and bottom hoses | 16  Heater hoses |
| 4 | Battery | | | 19  Clutch slave cylinder |
| 5 | Water temperature switch, coil, distributor and starter solenoid leads | 9 | Expansion tank hose | 28  Fuel pump inlet hose |
| | | 12 | Air cleaner | 30  Engine lifting brackets |
| 7 | Battery cable to solenoid | 15 | Brake servo hose | 31  Engine mountings |

24.1 Bonnet strut

24.4 Reversing lamp switch leads at gearbox selector housing

24.8A Radiator tilted forward to reveal fan lead connector

24.8B Lifting radiator from engine compartment

24.18 Caliper supported pending driveshaft removal

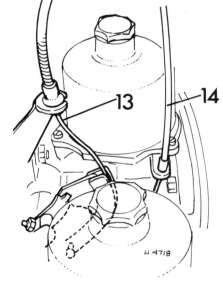
Fig. 1.39. Throttle cable (13) and choke cable (14) on 6 cylinder engine (Sec. 24)

24.15 Clutch slave cylinder

24.19 Disconnecting trackrod end from steering arm

24.20 Disconnecting suspension upper swivel joint

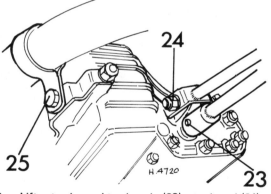
Fig. 1.40. Gearshift extension rod tension pin (23), steady rod (24) and exhaust pipe clip (25) on 6 cylinder manual gearbox (Sec. 24)

24.21 Extension rod and steady rod connections at gearbox

24.26 Power steering pump

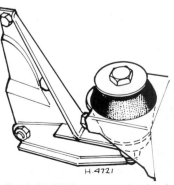
Fig. 1.41. RH front mounting bracket attached to 6 cylinder flywheel housing (Sec. 24)

24.30 Left-hand front engine mounting

24.33 Disconnecting left-hand driveshaft from differential

Fig. 1.42. Alternator wiring plug (6 cylinder) (Sec. 24)

24.35 Removing 6 cylinder engine/gearbox assembly

27.1 Removing 6 cylinder manifold/carburettor assembly

27.3A Engine oil dipstick guide tube

27.3B Removing coolant filler housing

27.3C Removing water pump

27.3D Location of ignition coil

## 25 Engine/automatic transmission (6 cylinder) - removal

1   The procedure is similar to that described in the preceding Section, but with the following differences.
2   Release the selector cable from the transmission, as described in Section 23, paragraph 4.
3   The steering pump is withdrawn downwards between the transmission housing and the engine compartment front panel.
4   Lifting brackets are incorporated in the engine to which the hoist or lifting bar should be attached and the weight of the power unit taken.
5   Disconnect the engine mountings in the following order; left-hand mounting bracket from the transmission casing (five setscrews), through-bolt from the right-hand rear mounting followed by the mounting bracket from the torque converter housing. Remove the through-bolt from the right-hand front mounting followed by the bracket.
6   Using the hoist, raise the power unit about 5 in. (13.0 cm) and

disengage the (already released) driveshafts. Unplug the alternator leads and lift the engine/transmission away from the car.

## 26 Engine dismantling - general

1   With the power unit removed, clean the external surfaces before commencing dismantling. If accumulations of dirt and oil are light, brushing with paraffin and wiping dry will suffice but heavier contamination is best removed using a water soluble solvent. Take care when hosing it off however that water does not enter the carburettor or electrical components.
2   Try and anticipate overhaul requirements by buying in advance, gasket sets, jointing compound, lockplates and washers, oil etc.
3   To strip the engine, work from the top down but where attention to a specific component or assembly only is required, follow the description given in the appropriate Section of this Chapter - do not

dismantle unnecessarily.

4 During dismantling, always make a sketch of fitting sequences or mark the parts with a piece of tape if there is any possibility of refitting them incorrectly. This applies particularly to bolts of different lengths securing the same unit.

## 27 Engine - removing ancillary components

1 With the power unit removed and a major overhaul anticipated, strip the ancillary components.

*Alternator — Chapter 10*
*Distributor — Chapter 4*
*Starter — Chapter 10*
*Manifolds and carburettor — Chapter 3 (photo)*

2 Detailed descriptions of the removal procedure are given in the Chapters indicated.

3 The oil and water sender units, the oil dipstick guide tube, the coolant filler housing, water pump and coil can be removed if damage is likely to be caused to them (photos).

## 28 Engine/manual gearbox (4 cylinder) - separation

1 Remove the ten screws and three nuts which secure the transmission primary drive cover and withdraw the cover and joint washer. Be prepared to catch some oil which will be released.

2 Flatten the locking tab and unscrew and remove the first motion shaft nut. Jam the starter ring gear to prevent the first motion shaft turning.

3 Remove the idler gear, marking it carefully to ensure that it is

refitted the correct way round.

4 Withdraw the gear from the first motion shaft.

5 Remove the right-hand rear engine mounting bracket.

6 Remove the flywheel housing from the adaptor plate. This necessitates removal of one dowel bolt and seven nuts, one of which is situated deep inside the flywheel housing.

**If the engine is in the car,** remove the flywheel housing by:
a) Lowering the power unit and pushing it against the left-hand valance.
b) Raising the right-hand end of the power unit about 2.5 in (65 mm).

After the flywheel housing has been released from the adaptor plate, manoeuvre the housing around the first motion shaft and withdraw it.

7 Withdraw the special washer from the first motion shaft.

8 Unbolt and remove the clutch assembly from the flywheel.

9 Flatten the locking tabs and unbolt and remove the flywheel from the crankshaft. Again jam the flywheel ring gear to prevent the flywheel turning when unscrewing the retaining bolts.

10 Remove the adaptor plate screws and withdraw the adaptor plate and joint washer.

11 Extract the four laygear thrust springs from their holes in the gearbox casing.

12 Withdraw the engine oil dipstick and then remove the bolts, screws and nuts which secure the gearbox casing to the engine cylinder block. These comprise: six nuts on the differential side, five bolts on the filter side, two setscrews on the casing front and on the rear of the casing, one screw to the main bearing cap and one screw to the cylinder block.

13 Lift the engine from the gearbox and remove the gasket and 'O' ring seal from the oil feed.

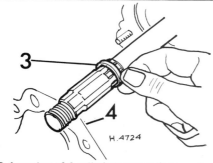

Fig. 1.43. Location of 4 cylinder gearbox first motion shaft special washer (3) and flywheel housing (4) (Sec. 28)

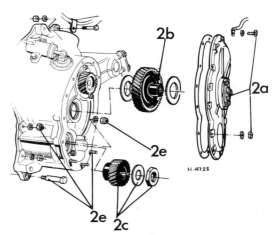

Fig. 1.44. 4 cylinder manual gearbox components (Sec. 28)

2a Primary drive cover bolts
2b Idler gear
2c First motion shaft, nut and lockplate
2e Flywheel housing adaptor plate bolts and nuts

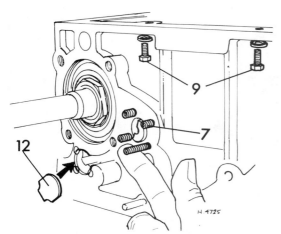

Fig. 1.45. Location of laygear thrust springs (7), gearbox to cylinder block bolts (9) and fork rod retaining plate (12), 4 cylinder manual gearbox (Sec. 28)

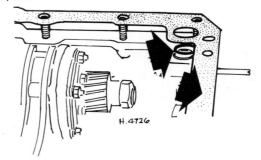

Fig. 1.46. Location of gasket and oil feed 'O' ring seal after removal of 4 cylinder engine from manual gearbox (Sec. 28)

## 29 Engine/automatic transmission (4 cylinder) - separation

1   Working through the starter motor aperture, unscrew each of the four screws which secure the driveplate to the torque converter. The crankshaft will have to be turned by means of its pulley bolt to bring each driveplate bolt in turn into view.
2   Remove the engine rear mounting bracket (two bolts).
3   Remove the harness clip from the top of the torque converter housing.
4   Extract the screw which secures the main transmission casing to the engine crankcase lower extension and is accessible from between the casing and the torque converter housing.
5   Remove the screws which secure the transmission casing to the crankcase extension. These comprise: ten screws on the distributor side and six screws on the differential side.
6   Working through the starter motor aperture, push the torque converter fully into its housing, support the engine and lift it from the transmission in a straight-line until the driveplate has cleared the converter housing.
7   Detach the transmission casing to crankcase lower extension gasket, unbolt the driveplate from the crankshaft also the adaptor plate with integral oil seal and remove the gasket.

## 30 Engine/manual gearbox (6 cylinder) - separation

1   Remove the clutch, flywheel and flywheel housing, as described in Sections 19 and 20, of this Chapter.
2   Remove the primary gear and thrust washer.
3   Flatten the locking plate and unscrew the crankshaft pulley bolt.
4   Remove the crankshaft pulley using two levers or a puller.
5   Remove the left-hand mounting plate (three screws) and the alternator mounting plate screw.
6   If not already removed, withdraw the distributor and remove the fuel pump and operating pushrod.
7   Withdraw the alternator bracket from the cylinder block (photo).
8   Remove the bolts and screws which secure the gearbox casing to the cylinder block. These comprise: two bolts at the front, six screws on the differential side (note clips) one of which screws downwards and has a UNC thread and seven screws on the oil filter side.
9   Lift the engine from the gearbox, watching to see that the oil pump driveshaft is not bent during the operation. Discard the crankshaft front oil seal (photo).

## 31 Engine/automatic transmission (6 cylinder) - separation

1   The procedure is similar to that described in Section 29 for 4 cylinder models, with the following differences:

30.7 Alternator mounting bracket

2   Remove the engine oil filter to prevent damage.
3   Remove the distributor and oil pump drive spindle (see Section 18).
4   Removal is required of the two through bolts which secure the transmission casing to the engine crankcase.

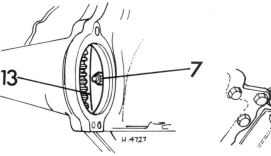

Fig. 1.47. Driveplate to torque converter bolts (7) and driveplate (13), 6 cylinder automatic transmission (Sec. 29)

Fig. 1.48. 6 cylinder automatic transmission casing to engine crankcase lower extension securing bolt (Sec. 29)

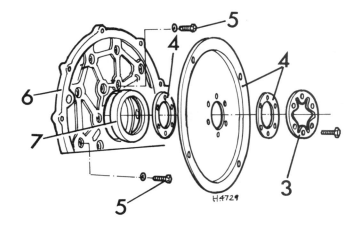

Fig. 1.49. Lockplate (3), driveplate, backing plate (4), bolts (5), adaptor plate (6) and oil seal (7) on 4 cylinder automatic transmission (Sec. 29)

30.9 Separating engine from transmission (6 cylinder)

## 32 Engine - dismantling after removal and separation from transmission

Dismantling of components which is possible when the engine is still in the car has already been covered in Sections 2 to 21 of this Chapter and, of course, equally applies when the engine is removed and separated from the transmission. **The operations described in the following Sections (33 to 40) can only be carried out with the engine/transmission removed.**

## 33 Camshaft and bearings (4 cylinder) - removal

1 Remove the timing chain and gears (Section 6).
2 Remove the tappets (Section 5).
3 Remove the distributor driveshaft (Section 7).
4 Remove the fuel pump and withdraw the actuating pushrod.
5 Unbolt and remove the camshaft locating plate and carefully withdraw the camshaft taking care not to damage the bearings as the cam lobes pass through.
6 Removal of the camshaft bearings is best left to your Leyland dealer due to the need for special tools (see Section 46).

## 34 Connecting rod/piston (4 cylinder) - removal

1 With the engine separated from the transmission, remove the cylinder head (Section 4).
2 Check the connecting rod and big-end cap markings both in respect of position in the block (1 to 4 numbering from the crankshaft pulley end of the engine), and to which side the numbers face. If no marks are evident, dot punch the rods and caps before dismantling.
3 Remove the big-end nuts, caps and extract the bearing shells.
4 Push the piston/connecting rod assembly out from the top of the

block taking care not to scratch the surfaces of the cylinder bore during the process. The operation will be found easier if the crankshaft is rotated to bring each big-end cap to its lowest point, in turn, before removing the cap nuts.

## 35 Crankshaft (4 cylinder) - removal

1 With the engine separated from the transmission, remove the clutch, flywheel and adaptor plate (Section 28).
2 Remove the timing chain, tensioner and gears (Section 6).
3 Remove the camshaft location plate and the front mounting plate from the cylinder block.
4 Remove the keys and shims from the crankshaft.
5 Check the main bearing cap markings in respect of position (1 to 5 numbering from the crankshaft sprocket end) and to which side the numbers face. If no marks are evident, dot punch the caps and adjacent crankcase surfaces before dismantling.
6 With the big-end caps disconnected (Section 34) remove the main bearing caps and the thrust washers which are located each side of the centre main bearing.
7 Lift out the crankshaft and extract the bearing shells from the crankcase.
8 Remove the upper halves of the thrust washers. If by any chance, the original bearing shells are to be refitted, they must be identified in respect of cap or crankcase recess and fitting sequence. Do not scratch the shells but mark them with a piece of masking tape.

## 36 Oil pump (4 cylinder) - removal

1 With the engine separated from the transmission, remove the three oil pump setscrews and withdraw the pump and its gasket.

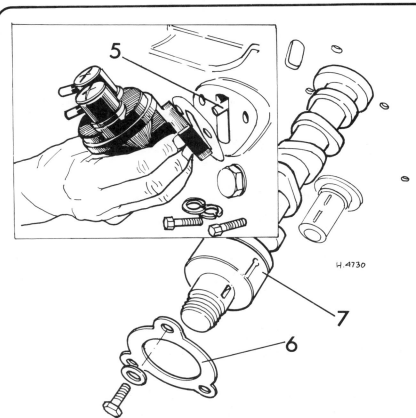

Fig. 1.50. Fuel pump operating rod (5), camshaft locating plate (6), and camshaft (7) on 4 cylinder engine (Sec. 33)

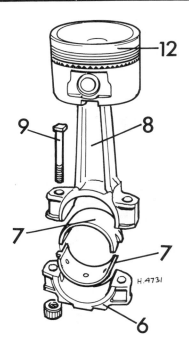

Fig. 1.51. 4 cylinder piston/con-rod assembly (Sec. 34)

6  Big-end cap
7  Shell bearings
8  Connecting rod
9  Bolt
12  Piston

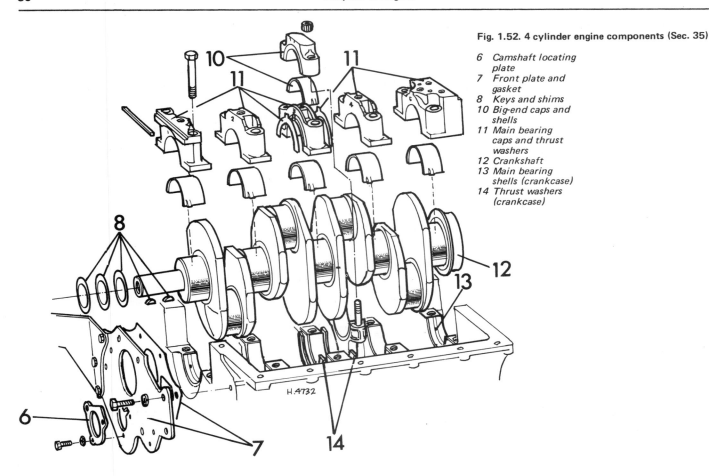

**Fig. 1.52. 4 cylinder engine components (Sec. 35)**

6   Camshaft locating
    plate
7   Front plate and
    gasket
8   Keys and shims
10  Big-end caps and
    shells
11  Main bearing
    caps and thrust
    washers
12  Crankshaft
13  Main bearing
    shells (crankcase)
14  Thrust washers
    (crankcase)

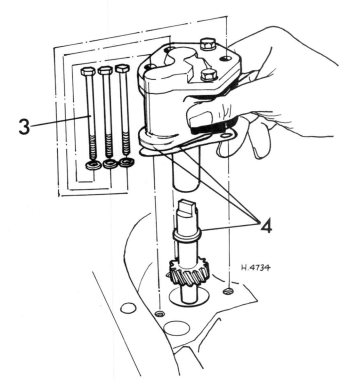

**Fig. 1.53. Retaining bolt (3) and oil pump assembly (4), 4 cylinder
engine (Sec. 36)**

### 37 Distributor driveshaft (6 cylinder - automatic transmission) - removal

1   The operations are similar to those described in Section 18 except
that the engine/transmission is removed and the end housing is then
withdrawn from the gearbox casing and crankcase lower extension
(12 screws, one stud).

### 38 Connecting rod/piston (6 cylinder) - removal

1   With the engine separated from the transmission, remove the
cylinder head (Section 14).
2   Repeat the operations described in Section 34, paragraphs 2 to 4
inclusive except, of course, that there are six assemblies instead of four.

### 39 Crankshaft rear oil seal (6 cylinder - automatic transmission) - removal

The crankshaft rear oil seal on manual gearbox cars can be renewed
after withdrawal of the flywheel housing (Section 20) while the engine
is still in the car.
1   On cars equipped with automatic transmission, remove and separate
the engine and automatic transmission unit, remove the driveplate from
the crankshaft rear flange.
2   Prise out the oil seal using a suitable pointed tool.

### 40 Crankshaft (6 cylinder) - removal

1   With the engine separated from the transmission, remove the
camshaft cover, camshaft sprocket, crankshaft front oil seal, oil thrower,
crankshaft sprocket, distributor drive gear and shaft, all as described in
Sections 12, 13, 15, 18 or 37.

2  **On cars equipped with automatic transmission,** remove the engine oil dipstick tube by releasing its cylinder block union and bracket.

Remove the ten inner and four outer screws which secure the crankcase extension to the crankcase. Remove the extension and gaskets.

*On all cars*
3  Check the main bearing cap markings in respect of position (1 to 7 numbering from the crankshaft sprocket end) and to which side the numbers face. If no marks are evident, dot-punch the caps and adjacent crankcase surfaces before dismantling.

4  With the big-end caps disconnected (Section 38) remove the main bearing caps and thrust washers which are located each side of No. 4 bearing.
5  Lift out the crankshaft and extract the bearing shells from the crankcase.
6  Remove the upper halves of the thrust washers. If for any reason, the original bearing shells are to be refitted, they must be identified in respect of cap or crankcase recess and fitting sequence. Do not scratch the shells but mark them with a piece of masking tape. Note that No. 4 bearing shells are oversize and are marked with a coloured edge.

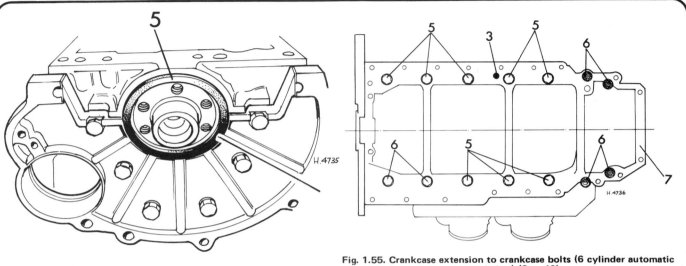

Fig. 1.54. Crankshaft rear oil seal (5) on 6 cylinder automatic transmission (Sec. 39)

Fig. 1.55. Crankcase extension to crankcase bolts (6 cylinder automatic transmission) (Sec. 40)

3  *Dipstick tube*
5  *Ten setscrews*

6  *Four setscrews (outside case)*
7  *Crankcase lower extension*

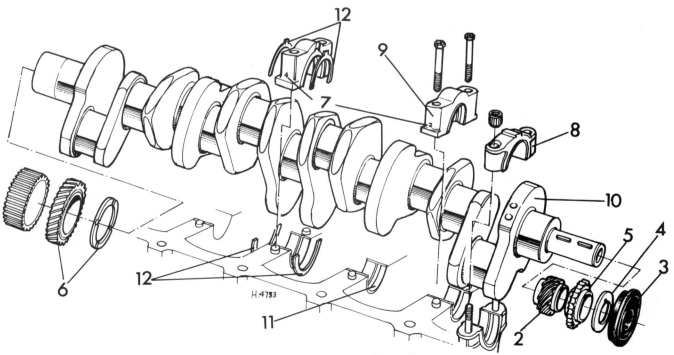

Fig. 1.56. 6 cylinder crankshaft components (Sec. 40)

2  *Distributor drivegear*
3  *Crankshaft front oil seal*
4  *Washer*

5  *Sprocket*
6  *Crankshaft primary gear and thrust washer*

7  *Main bearing identification numbers*
8  *Big-end cap*

9  *Main bearing cap*
10 *Crankshaft*
11 *Bearing shell*
12 *Crankshaft thrust washers*

## 41 Engine - examination and renovation (general)

1  With the engine stripped, all components should be thoroughly cleaned and examined for wear, as described in the following Sections. Where a high mileage has been covered, consideration should be given to renewing an assembly on an exchange basis rather than renewing an individual component in a well worn unit.

## 42 Crankshaft and main bearings - examination and renovation

1  Examine the crankpin and main journal surfaces for signs of scoring or scratches. Check the ovality of the crankpins at different positions with a micrometer. If more than specified out of round, the crankpin will have to be reground. It will also have to be reground if there are any scores or scratches present. Also check the journals in the same fashion.
2  If it is necessary to regrind the crankshaft and fit new bearings your local Leyland garage or engineering works will be able to decide how much metal to grind off and the size of new bearing shells.
3  Full details of crankshaft regrinding tolerances and bearing undersizes are given in Specifications.
4  The main bearing clearances may be established by using a strip of Plastigage between the crankshaft journals and the main bearing/shell caps. Tighten the bearing cap bolts to the specified torque. Remove the cap and compare the flattened Plastigage strip with the index provided. The clearance should be compared with the tolerances in Specifications.
5  To check the crankshaft endfloat, temporarily fit the upper halves of the main bearing shells to the crankcase and install the upper segments of the thrust washers. Lower the crankshaft into position and fit the main bearing caps complete with bearing shells, also the lower segments of the thrust washers. Tighten the main bearing bolts to specified torque and then push and pull the crankshaft and measure the endfloat using a dial gauge or a feeler blade inserted between No. 4 cap and the face of the thrust washer. If the endfloat is outside the specified tolerance, renew the thrust washers from the selective thicknesses available.
6  On 6 cylinder engines, the crankshaft primary gear endfloat must now be checked. To do this, fit the thrust washer (chamfer to crankshaft) and the primary gear to the crankshaft. Press hard on the end face of the primary gear and measure the gap 'C' which should be between 0.003 and 0.005 in. (0.08 and 0.13 mm). If it is outside this tolerance, renew the thrust washer with one of the six selective thicknesses available.
7  On 4 cylinder engines, check the condition of the spigot bush and renew it if worn. The bush can be renewed with the engine still in position on manual gearbox cars (Section 8) but only after engine removal on cars equipped with automatic transmission.
8  When refitting a spigot bush to cars with a manual gearbox, drive it into its recess until dimension 'A' (Fig. 1.58) is as shown.
9  When refitting a spigot bush to cars equipped with automatic transmission, measure the depth of the bush recess from the face of the crankshaft flange and then select a bush from those available and listed in the following table. The correct bush will provide a driveplate preload depth of between 0.030 and 0.051 in. (0.76 and 1.29 mm).

| Recess depth | Bush to install |
|---|---|
| 0.969 to 0.972 in. | 0.930 to 0.935 in. |
| (24.61 to 24.86 mm) | (23.62 to 23.74 mm) |
| 0.980 to 0.996 in. | 0.945 to 0.950 in. |
| (24.89 to 25.29 mm) | (24.00 to 24.13 mm) |
| 0.997 to 1.013 in. | 0.962 to 0.967 in. |
| (25.32 to 25.73 mm) | (24.43 to 24.56 mm) |
| 1.014 to 1.026 in. | 0.978 to 0.984 in. |
| (25.79 to 26.06 mm) | (24.68 to 24.99 mm) |

10  Drive the selected bush into the full depth of the crankshaft recess.

## 43 Connecting rods and bearings - examination and renovation

1  Big-end bearing failure is indicated by a knocking from within the crankcase and is accompanied by a slight drop in oil pressure.
2  Examine the big-end bearing surfaces for pitting and scoring. Renew the shells with ones of the same original size or if the crankshaft has been reground, the correct undersize big-end bearing shells will be supplied by the repairer.
3  The gudgeon pin is an interference fit in the connecting rod small end and a push fit in the piston. It is recommended that where the connecting rod must be renewed due to twist or to slackness in the small end, then this operation is left to your dealer due to the need for special tools.
4  Measurement of the big-end bearing clearances may be carried out in a similar manner to that described for the main bearings in the preceding Section. Connecting rod side-float should be as specified, otherwise the rod must be renewed.

## 44 Cylinder bores - examination and renovation

1  The cylinder bores must be examined for taper, ovality, scoring and scratches. Start by carefully examining the top of the cylinder bores. If they are at all worn a very slight ridge will be found on the thrust side. This marks the top of the piston ring travel. The owner will have a good indication of the bore wear prior to dismantling the engine, or removing the cylinder head. Excessive oil consumption accompanied by blue smoke from the exhaust is a sure sign of worn cylinder bores and piston rings.
2  Measure the bore diameter just under the ridge with a micrometer and compare it with the diameter at the bottom of the bore which is not subject to wear. If the difference between the two measurements is more than 0.008 in. (0.2032 mm) then it will be necessary to fit special pistons and rings or to have the cylinders rebored and fit oversize pistons. If no micrometer is available remove the rings from a piston and place the piston in each bore in turn about ¾ in. below the top of the bore. If an 0.0012 in. (0.0254 mm) feeler gauge slid between the piston and the cylinder wall requires more than a pull of between 1.1 and 3.3 lbs (0.5 and 1.5 kg) to withdraw it, using a spring balance then remedial action must be taken. Oversize pistons are available as listed in Specifications.
3  These are accurately machined to just below the indicated measurements so as to provide correct running clearances in bores bored out to the exact oversize dimensions.
4  If the bores are slightly worn but not so badly worn as to justify reboring, then special oil control rings and pistons can be fitted which will restore compression and stop the engine burning oil. Several different types are available and the manufacturer's instructions concerning their fitting must be followed closely.
5  If new pistons are being fitted and the bores have not been reground, it is essential to slightly roughen the hard glaze on the sides of the bores with fine glass paper so the new piston rings will have a chance to bed in properly.
6  On 4 cylinder engines, if the bores have been bored out to their oversize limit, it is possible for 'dry' type cylinder liners to be fitted.

## 45 Pistons and piston rings - examination and renovation

1  If the original pistons are to be refitted, carefully remove the piston rings. This is best achieved by using a twisting motion and sliding them over the piston lands having inserted two or three old feeler blades between the ring and piston.
2  Clean the grooves and rings free from carbon, taking care not to scratch the aluminium surfaces of the pistons.
3  If new rings are to be fitted, then order the top compression ring to be stepped to prevent it impinging on the 'wear ring' which will almost certainly have been formed at the top of the cylinder bore.
4  Before fitting the rings to the pistons, push each ring in turn down to its lower limit of normal travel in its respective cylinder bore (use an inverted piston to do this and to keep the ring square in the bore) and measure the ring end gap. The gaps should be as listed in Specifications Section.
5  Now test the side clearance of the compression rings which again should be as shown in Specifications Section.
6  Where necessary a piston ring which is slightly tight in its groove may be rubbed down holding it perfectly squarely on an oilstone or a sheet of fine emery cloth laid on a piece of plate glass. Excessive tightness can only be rectified by having the grooves machined out.
7  Check that the ends of the oil control ring expanders are butting but not overlapping.
8  On 4 cylinder engines, there are two compression rings and one oil

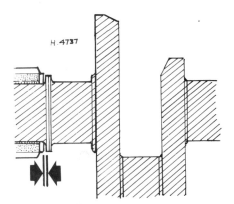

Fig. 1.57. Crankshaft primary gear endfloat (6 cylinder) (Sec. 42)

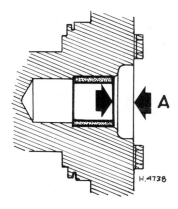

Fig. 1.58. Crankshaft spigot bush installation diagram (manual gearbox) A = 0.30 in (7.62 mm) (Sec. 42)

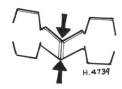

Fig. 1.59. Oil control ring expander butt joint (Sec. 45)

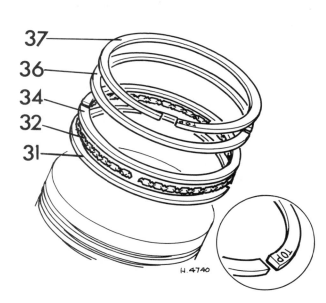

Fig. 1.60. 4 cylinder piston ring assembly (Sec. 45)

31 Oil control ring rail
32 Expander
34 Upper rail
36 Second (tapered or stepped) compression ring
37 Top compression ring

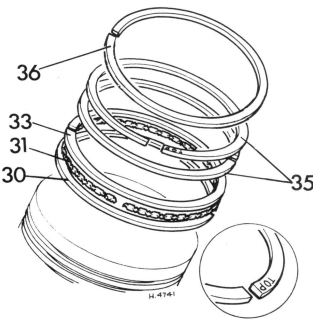

Fig. 1.61. 6 cylinder piston ring assembly (Sec. 45)

30 Oil control ring rail
31 Expander
33 Upper rail
35 Second and third (tapered) compression rings
36 Top compression ring

control ring. Assemble as follows:

Oil control ring, located in bottom groove, set the end gaps in rails and expander at 90° to each other.

Tapered or stepped compression ring, word 'TOP' or step uppermost located in second groove from top of piston.

Plain compression ring, word 'TOP' uppermost, located in top groove of piston.

9 On 6 cylinder engines, there are three compression rings and one oil control ring. Assemble as follows:

Oil control ring, located in bottom groove, set the end gaps in rails and expander at 90° to each other.

Tapered compression rings, word 'TOP' uppermost, located in second and third grooves. These are the two thinner compression rings.

Plain compression ring, word 'TOP' uppermost, located in top groove of piston.

10 The piston ring end gaps should be positioned at 90° to each other and away from the thrust side of the piston.

## 46 Camshaft and camshaft bearings - examination and renovation

1 Carefully examine the camshaft bearings for wear. If they are worn or pitted, then on 4 cylinder engines they can be renewed but special tools are needed and the bearings must be in-line reamed and it is best to leave this job to your dealer. On 6 cylinder engines, the bearings are integral with the camshaft carrier and the complete assembly must be renewed in the event of bearing wear.

2 The camshaft itself should show no signs of wear, but, if very slight scoring on the cams is noticed, the score marks can be removed by gentle rubbing down with a very fine emery cloth. The greatest care should be taken to keep the cam profiles smooth.

3 Examine the skew gear for wear, chipped teeth or other damage.

4 Carefully examine the camshaft locating plate. Excessive endfloat (more than 0.007 in. (0.17 mm) will be visually self-evident and will require the fitting of a new plate.

## 47 Valves and valve seats - examination and renovation

1   Examine the heads of the valves for pitting and burning, especially the heads of the exhaust valves. The valve seatings should be examined at the same time. If the pitting on valve and seat is very slight the marks can be removed by grinding the seats and valves together with coarse, and then fine, valve grinding paste.
2   Where bad pitting has occurred to the valve seats it will be necessary to recut them and fit new valves. If the valves seats are so worn that they cannot be recut, then it will be necessary to fit new valve seat inserts. These latter two jobs should be entrusted to the local dealer or engineering works. In practice it is very seldom that the seats are so badly worn that they require renewal. Normally, it is the valve that is too badly worn for replacement, and the owner can easily purchase a new set of valves and match them to the seats by valve grinding.
3   Valve grinding is carried out as follows:
     Smear a trace of coarse carborundum paste on the seat face and apply a suction grinder tool to the valve head. With a semi-rotory motion, grind the valve head to its seat, lifting the valve occasionally to redistribute the grinding paste. When a dull matt even surface finish is produced on both the valve seat and the valve, wipe off the paste and repeat the process with fine carborundum paste, lifting and turning the valve to redistribute the paste as before. A light spring placed under the valve head will greatly ease this operation. When a smooth unbroken ring of light grey matt finish is produced, on both valve and valve seat faces, the grinding operation is completed.
4   Scrape away all carbon from the valve head and the valve stem. Carefully clean away every trace of grinding compound, taking great care to leave none in the ports or in the valve guides. Clean the valves and valve seats with a paraffin soaked rag then with a clean rag, and finally if an air line is available, blow the valves, valve guides and valve ports clean.

## 48 Valve guides - examination and renovation

1   After a considerable mileage, the valve guide bore may wear oval in shape. Insert each valve into its respective guide and check for excessive clearance. Establish whether it is the guide or valve stem which is worn or both, by reference to Specifications or by testing a new valve in the guide.
2   On 4 cylinder engines, the old valve guide should be pressed out and the new one pressed in from the top face of the cylinder head. Inlet valve guides should project above the machined face of the valve spring seating by 0.75 in. (19.05 mm) and exhaust valve guides by 0.625 in. (15.87 mm). In view of the pressing facilities required, these operations are probably best left to your dealer.
3   On 6 cylinder engines, the valve guides are integral with the cylinder head and must be reamed to accept oversize valves. Where this is carried out, remember that oversize inlet valve stem oil seals will be required. The seals are identified by having two rings moulded on their flanges instead of the single ring on standard seals.

## 49 Timing sprockets, chain and tensioner - examination and renovation

1   Examine the camshaft and crankshaft sprocket teeth for a hooked appearance which indicates wear and renew if necessary.
2   Examine the chain tensioner slipper for grooving or deterioration and renew it if necessary.
3   On 4 cylinder engines, the endless type timing chain is best renewed if it shows that it has stretched when comparing it with a new one.
4   On 6 cylinder engines, the chain will have been 'broken' for removal by extracting rivets (Section 15) and it can be held by its end links in a horizontal attitude (sideplates facing downwards). If the chain takes on a deeply bowed appearance then it should be renewed.

## 50 Rockers and rocker shaft (4 cylinder) - examination and renovation

1   Thoroughly clean the rocker shaft and then check the shaft for straightness by rolling it on plate glass. It is most unlikely that it will deviate from normal, but if it does, purchase a new shaft. The surface of the shaft should be free from any worn ridges caused by the rocker arms. If any wear is present, renew the shaft.

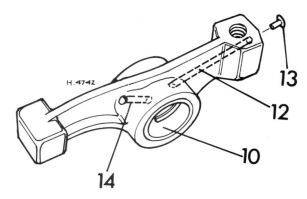

Fig. 1.62. Rocker arm detail (4 cylinder) (Sec. 50)

*10 Bush*          *12 & 14   Oilways*     *13   Plug*

2   Check the rocker arms for wear of the rocker bushes, for wear at the rocker arm face which bears on the valve stem, and for wear of the adjusting ball ended screws. Wear in the rocker arm bush can be checked by gripping the rocker arm tip and holding the rocker arm in place on the shaft, noting if there is any lateral rocker arm shake. If shake is present, and the arm is very loose on the shaft, a new bush or rocker arm must be fitted.
3   If a new rocker arm bush is fitted, it must be pressed in so that the butt joint is at the top and the oil groove at the bottom. Also remove the rocker arm adjusting screw after the bush has been installed and then drill out the plug in the rocker arm and drill the oil way in the bush using a twist drill of 0.093 in. (2.36 mm) diameter. This hole should be continued on the opposite side of the bush using a drill of 0.0785 in. (1.98 mm) diameter. The rocker bush should now be burnish reamed to the diameter given in Specifications, and a new plug welded into position.

## 51 Pushrods and tappets (4 cylinder) - examination and renovation

1   Check the pushrods for straightness by rolling them on a piece of plate glass. Renew any that are bent.
2   Examine the bearing surface of the tappets which lie on the camshaft. Any indentation in this surface or any cracks indicate serious wear and the tappets should be renewed. Thoroughly clean them out, removing all traces of sludge. It is most unlikely that the sides of the tappets will prove worn, but, if they are a very loose fit in their bores and can readily be rocked, they should be exchanged for new units. It is very unusual to find any wear in the tappets, and any wear is likely to occur only at very high mileages.

## 52 Tappets (6 cylinder) - examination and renovation

1   Examine the contact face of the tappet and the ground faces of the shim for grooves or pitting and renew any that show such signs. Remember that the shim thicknesses were recorded at dismantling and any replacement must be identical to the one discarded.

## 53 Flywheel or driveplate - examination and renovation

1   It is not recommended that the surface of the flywheel is machined or surface ground to remove scoring but rather a new component is fitted.
2   The starter ring gear on 6 cylinder engine flywheels can be renewed. To do this, split the old ring gear and heat the new one to between 572 and 752°F (300 to 400°C) indicated by a surface colour of light blue.
3   Locate the new ring gear so that the chamfer on the teeth are away from the flywheel mounting flange.
4   If the starter ring gear on 4 cylinder engine flywheels or any automatic transmission driveplate is worn, renew the complete assembly.
5   When installing a new flywheel to a 6 cylinder engine, the three small dowel holes in the flywheel and the crankshaft rear mounting

flange must be line - reamed to accept oversize dowels which will provide a good interference fit.

### 54 Oil pump - examination and renovation

#### 4 cylinder engines

1  Withdraw the pump driving spindle and unbolt the pump cover. Note that it is held in position by two locating dowels. Extract all components and clean them. Re-install the parts making sure that the

chamfered edge of the outer rotor is at the driving end of the body recess.
2  Using feeler blades, check:
   (A)   Inner and outer rotor to body endface endfloat.
   (B)   Outer ring to pump body clearance.
   (C)   Inner to outer rotor lobe clearances.

#### 6 cylinder engines

3  Remove the five suction housing bolts and separate the filter housing from the pump body. On manual gearbox cars, remove the oil strainer and gasket.

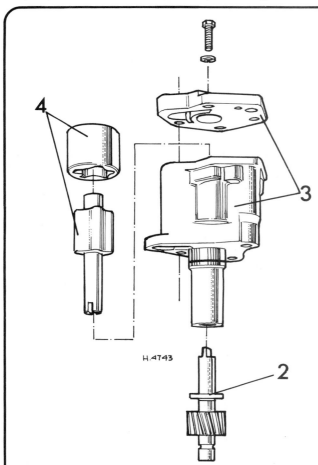

Fig. 1.63. 4 cylinder oil pump (Sec. 54)

2   Driving spindle     3   Pump cover and body   4   Rotors

Fig. 1.64. 6 cylinder oil pump (Sec. 54)

2   Suction housing bolts     4   Oil strainer and gasket
3   Filter housing                  (manual gearbox only)

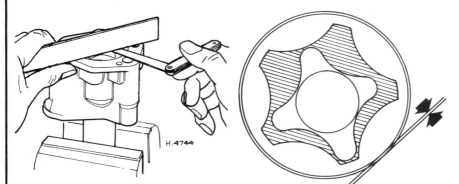

Fig. 1.65. Checking oil pump endfloat (Sec. 54)

Fig. 1.66. Checking oil pump outer ring to body clearance (Sec. 54)

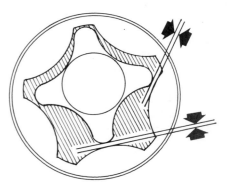

Fig. 1.67. Checking oil pump rotor lobe clearances (Sec. 54)

4   Clean all components and re-install them to the pump body and then check the clearances, as described in paragraph 2.

*All engines*

5   Where the clearances are outside those given in the Specification Section, renew the oil pump as a complete assembly.

## 55 Cylinder head - decarbonising and examination

1   With the cylinder head removed, use a blunt scraper to remove all trace of carbon and deposits from the combustion spaces and ports. A wire brush in an electric drill will speed up the carbon removal operation. Scrape the cylinder head free from scale or old pieces of gasket or jointing compound. Clean the cylinder head by washing it in paraffin and take particular care to pull a piece of rag through the ports and cylinder head bolt holes. Any dirt remaining in these recesses may well drop onto the gasket or cylinder block mating surface as the cylinder head is lowered into position and could lead to a gasket leak after reassembly is complete.

2   With the cylinder head clean, test for distortion if a history of coolant leakage has been apparent. Carry out this test using a straight edge and feeler gauges or a piece of plate glass. If the surface shows any warping in excess of 0.039 in. (0.1015 mm) then the cylinder head will have to be resurfaced which is a job for a specialist engineering company.

3   Clean the pistons and top of the cylinder bores. If the pistons are still in the block then it is essential that great care is taken to ensure that no carbon gets into the cylinder bores as this could scratch the cylinder walls or cause damage to the piston and rings. To ensure this does not happen, first turn the crankshaft so that two of the pistons are at the top of their bores. Stuff rag into the other bores or seal them off with paper and masking tape to prevent particles of carbon entering the cooling system and damaging the water pump.

4   Rotate the crankshaft and repeat the carbon removal operations on the remaining pistons and cylinder bores.

5   Thoroughly clean all particles of carbon from the bores and then inject a little light oil round the edges of the pistons to lubricate the piston rings.

## 56 Engine - preparation for reassembly

1   To ensure maximum life with reliability from a rebuilt engine, not only must everything be correctly assembled but all components must be spotlessly clean and the correct spring or plain washers used where originally located. Always lubricate bearing and working surfaces with clean engine oil during reassembly of engine parts.

2   Before reassembly commences, renew any bolts ot studs the threads of which are damaged or corroded.

3   As well as your normal tool kit, gather together clean rags, oil can, a torque wrench and a complete (overhaul) set of gaskets and oil seals.

4   The installation sequence recommended is as follows:

| 4 cylinder | 6 cylinder |
|---|---|
| *Crankshaft* | *Crankshaft* |
| *Connecting rods/pistons* | *Connecting rods/pistons* |
| *Camshaft* | *Chain guides and tensioner* |
| *Oil pump* | *Distributor driveshaft and gear* |
| *Clutch/flywheel/adaptor* | *Crankshaft sprocket* |
| *Distributor driveshaft* | *Cylinder head/camshaft* |
| *Timing chain and gears* | *Clutch/flywheel* |
| *Tappets and pushrods* | *Front cover and crankshaft* |
| *Cylinder head* | *Pulley* |
| *Rocker shaft* | |

## 57 Oil pump (4 cylinder) - refitting

1   This is a reversal of the operations given in Section 36, but use a new pump flange gasket and tighten the bolts to the specified torque.

## 58 Crankshaft (4 cylinder) - installation

1   This is a reversal of removal (Section 35) but observe the following

points.

2   Oil the crankcase bearing shells liberally and install the thrust washers at the centre bearing so that their tabs engage in the slots and the oil grooves are towards the crankshaft webs.

3   Make sure that the caps are fitted in their correct sequence and the right way round.

4   Smear the horizontal joint of the rear main bearing cap with jointing compound.

5   Renew the cork seal in No. 1 main bearing cap having first saturated it with engine oil.

6   Tighten the main bearing cap bolts to the specified torque and then re-check the endfloat (Section 42).

7   Install the engine front mounting plate using a new gasket.

## 59 Connecting rod/piston (4 cylinder) - installation

1   Check that the piston/connecting rod has been correctly assembled with the word 'FRONT' or notch on the piston crown facing the front of the engine when the numbers stamped on the connecting rod and big-end cap are towards the camshaft. Check the piston ring installation (Section 45) (photo).

2   Oil the cylinder bores and piston rings and insert the bearing shells into the caps and rods (photo).

3   Fit a piston ring compressor and install No. 1 piston/connecting rod. To do this, rest the compressor squarely on the top face of the cylinder block and then drive the assembly out of the compressor into the bore by applying the wooden handle of a hammer to the crown of the piston (photo).

4   Arrange No. 1 crankpin at the lowest point of its 'throw' and connect the rod to it. Oil the big-end bearing cap bearing shell and fit the cap so that the numbers are adjacent and towards the camshaft (photo).

5   Tighten the big-end nuts to the specified torque.

6   Repeat the operations on the remaining three connecting rod/piston assemblies.

## 60 Camshaft (4 cylinder) - installation

1   This is a reversal of removal (Section 33) but oil the bearings before installation and check the endfloat (Section 46) when the locating plate is finally tightened.

## 61 Oil pick-up strainer and relief valve (4 cylinder) - refitting

1   This is a reversal of removal (Section 10) but on cars fitted with a manual gearbox, renew the sealing rings and fibre washers, tightening the nut just enough to compress the sealing ring.

2   Make sure that the leg on the strainer engages in the cut-out in the front cover and use a new front cover gasket.

3   Locate the front cover on the dowels making sure that the torque of the speedometer drive wheel engages with the slot in the end of the third motion shaft.

4   Tighten the front cover nuts to the specified torque.

5   *On cars equipped with automatic transmission,* fit a new 'O' ring seal to the strainer tube and install a new cover gasket.

## 62 Clutch, flywheel and adaptor plate (4 cylinder) - installation

1   This is a reversal of removal (Section 9) but fit a new oil seal to the adaptor plate so that seal lip is towards the front of the engine.

2   Install a new adaptor plate joint washer and tighten the adaptor plate bolts to specified torque. Note that the bottom two bolts have UNC threads and have a lower torque setting (see Specifications).

3   Install the flywheel, using a new bolt locking plate and tighten the bolts to the specified torque.

4   Install the clutch making sure to centralise the driven plate, as described in Section 13, Chapter 5.

5   *On cars equipped with automatic transmission,* the installation of the adaptor plate and driveplate is similar to the operations just described. Tighten the bolts strictly in accordance with the torque wrench settings specified at the beginning of this Chapter.

59.1 Typical piston markings

59.2 Connecting rod bearing shell

59.3 Installing a piston/connecting rod assembly

59.4 Installing a big-end cap

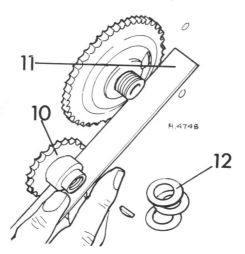

Fig. 1.68. Checking timing sprocket alignment (4 cylinder) (Sec. 63)

10 Crankshaft sprocket
11 Straight edge
12 Shims

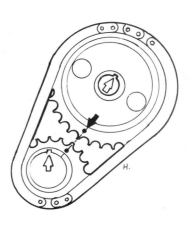

Fig. 1.69. Timing marks (4 cylinder) (Sec. 63)

## 63 Timing chain, gears and tensioner (4 cylinder) - installation

1   With the engine in its normal 'in car' attitude, turn the crankshaft until the keyway is vertical and uppermost.
2   Turn the camshaft so that the keyway is at the two o'clock position.
3   Install the crankshaft and camshaft sprockets and then using a straight-edge, check their alignment. If necessary, add or remove shims which will first require removal of the keys.
4   Assemble the chain tensioner by installing the inner cylinder and spring into the slipper head so that the slot in the inner cylinder engages with the peg in the slipper cylinder. Now by turning the inner cylinder clockwise against spring pressure, the lower serration in the slot engages with the peg and so retains the two cylinders together in the retracted state.
5   Fit the slipper head assembly into the chain tensioner body taking care not to release the spring tension.
6   Install the timing chain complete with crankshaft and camshaft sprockets, simultaneously, so that the timing marks on the sprockets are adjacent and in alignment with an imaginary line drawn through the centres of the camshaft and crankshaft.
7   Fit a new camshaft sprocket locking plate and tighten the nut to the specified torque then bend up the locking plate to secure it.
8   Fit the oil thrower to the front of the crankshaft sprocket so that the 'F' mark is away from the sprocket.
9   Renew the oil seal in the timing cover, making sure that the seal lips face inwards.

10  Install a new gasket and the timing cover but only tighten the securing bolts finger-tight at this stage.
11  Oil the seal contact surface of the crankshaft pulley and push it into position. As the cover bolts are not tight, the pulley will centralise the cover.
12  Screw in the pulley bolt, tighten to specified torque (jam the flywheel ring gear to prevent the crankshaft turning) and bend up the locking plate.
13  Refit the alternator adjustment strap and then fully tighten the timing cover bolts.
 4  If the engine is in the car, refit the ancillary units by reversing the procedure given in Section 6.

## 64 Tappets (4 cylinder) - refitting

This is a reversal of removal (Section 5) but make sure that the tappets are returned to their original locations.

## 65 Cylinder head (4 cylinder) - reassembly and installation

This is a reversal of the procedure given in Section 4 but observe the following points.
1   Make sure that the valves are returned to their original positions or, if new valves are being installed, to the seats into which they have been ground.

2   Install new valve springs if the original ones have covered 25,000 miles (40,000 km) or more or their free length is less than that specified for new ones.
3   Remember to install the inlet valve oil seals.
4   Ensure that the surfaces of the cylinder head and block are absolutely clean and then install a new cylinder head gasket so that the word 'TOP' is uppermost.
5   Lower the cylinder head into position, install the pushrods in their original sequence.
6   If the rocker shaft has been dismantled (Section 3), reassemble it by installing the parts in their original sequence noting that the double coil spring washers are located at the ends of the shaft. Use new split pins.
7   Locate the rocker shaft assembly on the eight cylinder head studs, making sure to insert the shims under the centre pedestal brackets and then screw on all nuts finger-tight. Make sure that the pushrods engage with the rocker arms.
8   Tighten the cylinder head nuts (including the four rocker shaft pedestal nuts which also act as cylinder head nuts) to the specified torque and in the sequence shown in Fig. 1.70.
9   Tighten the remaining rocker shaft pedestal nuts to the specified torque.
10 Set the valve clearances as described in the following Section.

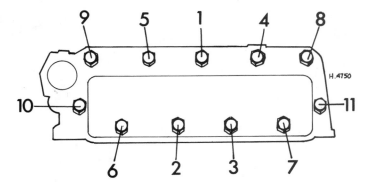

Fig. 1.70. Cylinder head bolt tightening sequence (4 cylinder) (Sec. 65)

## 66 Valve clearances (4 cylinder) - adjusting

1   The valve clearances should always be checked and adjusted with the engine cold.
2   With the rocker cover removed, turn the engine by applying a ring spanner to the crankshaft pulley bolt or by engaging top gear and pushing the car forward, and set the position of the valves in accordance with the following table. Rotation of the crankshaft will be easier if the spark plugs are not installed.
3   Using an 0.013 in. (0.33 mm) feeler blade inserted between the end of the valve stem and the rocker arm the blade should be a sliding fit. If it is not, release the rocker arm adjuster screw locknut and turn the screw as necessary. Retighten the locknut, holding the adjuster screw from moving with a screwdriver.

| Valve to adjust | Valve fully open |
|---|---|
| 1 | 8 |
| 3 | 6 |
| 5 | 4 |
| 2 | 7 |
| 8 | 1 |
| 6 | 3 |
| 4 | 5 |
| 7 | 2 |

4   The clearances for inlet and exhaust valves are the same.

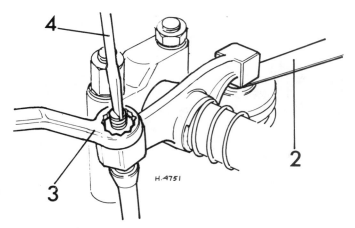

Fig. 1.71. Checking a valve clearance (4 cylinder) (Sec. 66)

2   Feeler blade          3   Ring spanner          4   Screwdriver

## 67 Distributor driveshaft (4 cylinder) - refitting

1   In order that the distributor can be pushed into its recess in the cylinder block and the ignition timing automatically reset, the installation of the distributor driveshaft is critical.
2   Apply a ring spanner to the crankshaft pulley bolt and turn the crankshaft until No. 1 piston is at TDC on its compression stroke. This is indicated when the valves of No. 4 cylinder are rocking (inlet valve just opening and exhaust valve just closing).
3   Insert the distributor driveshaft with its slot offset by approximately 7° from the centre-line of the engine and the larger segment uppermost. Use a 5/16 in. UNF bolt to hold the driveshaft as it is being installed. As the driveshaft engages with the camshaft, the slot will turn anticlockwise and take up a two o'clock position (30°) to the centre line of the engine.
4   Install the distributor housing using the original countersunk head securing screw which must not protrude above the housing face. Unscrew and remove the temporary 5/16 in. UNF bolt.

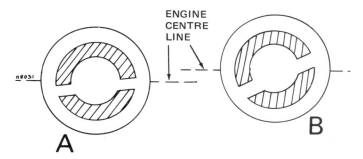

Fig. 1.72. Distributor driveshaft slot (Sec. 67)
A   Ready for installation          B   Installed

that the oil grooves are visible when the washers are in their seats (photo).
2   Make sure that the oversize main bearing shells (coloured edge) are installed on No. 4 bearing. IF THE CHAIN HAS NOT BEEN REMOVED, REMEMBER TO PASS THE FRONT OF THE CRANKSHAFT THROUGH IT BEFORE LOWERING THE CRANKSHAFT INTO POSITION IN THE CRANKCASE (PHOTOS).
3   Install the main bearing caps in correct sequence and the right way round. Note the thrust washer on No. 4 cap, with oil grooves visible (photo).
4   Tighten the main bearing cap bolts to the specified torque and then recheck the endfloat (Section 42 (photo).

## 68 Crankshaft (6 cylinder) - installation

1   This is a reversal of removal (Section 40) but oil the crankcase bearing shells liberally and install the thrust washers either side of No. 4 main bearing. Use thick grease to hold them in position and make sure

## 69 Connecting rod/piston (6 cylinder) - installation

1   The procedure is similar to that described in Section 59, for 4 cylinder engines.

68.1 Lubricating crankcase main bearing shells

68.2A Installing crankshaft to crankcase

68.2B Crankshaft installed through loop of timing chain

68.3 Installing a main bearing cap (no. 4 shown complete with thrust washers)

68.4 Tightening a main bearing cap bolt

72.2 Flywheel housing (6 cylinder)

## 70 Crankshaft rear oil seal (6 cylinder - automatic transmission) - refitting

1   When installing the rear oil seal, it may be necessary to cut the oil seal plugs off flush.
2   Install the seal using a piece of tubing as a drift and then the driveplate can be bolted to the crankshaft rear flange.

## 71 Distributor driveshaft (6 cylinder - automatic transmission) - installation

1   Installation is similar to that described in Section 74, for cars with a manual gearbox, except that it can only be carried out while the engine/transmission is removed from the car.
2   Refit the end housing to the gearbox casing and crankcase lower extension using new sections of gasket as necessary and applying jointing compound.

## 72 Flywheel housing (6 cylinder) - refitting

1   This is a reversal of removal (Section 20), tighten all bolts and nuts to the specified torque.
2   If a new oil seal is to be installed, drive it into the housing with its lip towards the housing flange (photo).

## 73 Flywheel, clutch assembly (6 cylinder) - installation

1   This is a reversal of removal (Section 19) but use a new bolt locking plate and tighten the bolts to the specified torque. Locate the clutch components, as described in Section 14, Chapter 5.

2   If a new flywheel is being fitted, the three small dowel holes in both the flywheel and crankshaft flange must be line-reamed.

## 74 Distributor driveshaft (6 cylinder - manual gearbox) - refitting

1   Install the original (or if worn a new) thrust washer to the distributor driveshaft.
2   Set No. 1 piston at tdc on its compression stroke.
3   Install the driveshaft so that its slot is at 10 o'clock (30°) to the centre-line of the engine and the larger segment is towards the cylinder block.
4   Install the distributor drive gear to the crankshaft. As the gear is pushed home, the distributor driveshaft will turn through approximately 60° in an anticlockwise direction, and its slot will take up a two o'clock position still with the large segment towards the cylinder block (as shown for 4 cylinder in Fig. 1.72, position B).
5   Insert the distributor and check that the contact end of the rotor arm points to No. 1 contact in the distributor cap when the contact breaker points are just about to open. Check the ignition timing precisely later (See Chapter 4).
6   Refer to Section 18 and reverse the procedure described in paragraphs 1 to 9. Make sure that No. 1 piston is not moved from its tdc position before installing the camshaft sprocket and chain with the camshaft sprocket and carrier marks in alignment.

## 75 Oil pump (6 cylinder - automatic transmission) - installation

1   This is a reversal of removal (Section 17) but install a new gasket section on the end housing using jointing compound.
2   Fit new sealing plugs and a new 'O' ring seal to the oil pump outlet.
3   Tighten the end housing bolts evenly and progressively to avoid distortion.

## 76 Oil pump (6 cylinder - manual gearbox) - installation

1  This is a reversal of removal (Section 16) but only locate the pump loosely on its bolts until the suction pipe and gasket have been fitted (photo).

## 77 Timing gear and crankshaft oil seal (6 cylinder) - refitting

1  This is a reversal of removal (Section 15).
2  If a new chain is to be fitted, it will have to be riveted securely after it has been passed round the crankshaft sprocket and both upper ends withdrawn from the crankcase aperture. Check that after riveting, no tight spots exist in the chain links.
3  Hang the upper loop of the chain over the side of the crankcase until the cylinder head and camshaft sprocket have been installed (Sections 78 and 79).
4  If the chain guides have been removed, fit the fixed guide so that the lower end pin engages in the hole in the cylinder block lug. Fit the adjustable guide, engaging the lower end with the adjuster cam. This adjuster cam must be set so that the chain guide is in vertical alignment with the chain sprockets and an even gap will exist between the chain and its guide after the cylinder head and camshaft have been installed (Sections 78 and 79).
5  Install the front cover.
6  Tighten the front cover and guide screws.
7  The chain should be hung over the side of its crankcase aperture pending fitting of the camshaft sprocket and adjustment of the chain tensioner (Section 79).
8  Before installing a new crankshaft front oil seal, check the projection (and cut flush if necessary) the transmission casing sealing plugs.
9  Oil the lips of the oil seal and fit it to the casing.

## 78 Cylinder head (6 cylinder) - reassembly and installation

1  This is a reversal of removal and dismantling (Section 14), **but if the engine is in the car, the camshaft and tappets must be fitted BEFORE installation** as there is insufficient space to install the camshaft if the head is fitted first.
2  Remember to fit oversize inlet valve stem oil seals if the valve guides have been reamed and oversize valves installed (Section 48) (photo).
3  Pass the timing chain through the aperture in the cylinder head as the head is lowered onto a new cylinder head gasket and retain the chain with the guides (photos).
4  Insert the cylinder head bolts and tighten them to the specified torque in the sequence shown in Fig. 1.74.

76.1 Installing oil pump (6 cylinder manual gearbox)

## 79 Camshaft and tappets (6 cylinder) - refitting

1  Place the camshaft carrier on the cylinder head and insert the tappets and shims into their respective holes.
2  Raise the carrier ½ in. (12.7 mm) and support it, then oil the camshaft bearings and install the camshaft to the carrier.
3  Lower the camshaft onto the cylinder head. Insert and tighten the camshaft carrier bolts to the specified torque, noting that the two thicker bolts are installed at the chain end of the carrier.
4  *If the valves have not been ground in* or renewed, proceed as described in paragraphs 13 to 17 of this Section.
5  *If the valves have been ground in* or renewed, the valve clearances must be checked. Turn the camshaft as required by temporarily fitting the camshaft sprocket.
6  Using a feeler blade, check the clearance between the back of the cam and the tappet. Work to the following table. Record carefully each of the valve clearances (twelve in number) on a piece of paper.

| Tappet to check | Valve fully open |
|---|---|
| 1 | 12 |
| 7 | 6 |
| 9 | 4 |
| 2 | 11 |
| 5 | 8 |
| 10 | 3 |
| 12 | 1 |
| 6 | 7 |
| 4 | 9 |
| 11 | 2 |
| 8 | 5 |
| 3 | 10 |

7  Remove the camshaft again keeping the tappets and shims in strict original order. Extract each shim in turn, note its marking and compare it with the feeler gauge clearance recorded previously. Work to the following formula and obtain new shims from the sixteen thicknesses available from your dealer. In practice it will probably be found that some of the existing shims will meet the requirement of other valves and so the actual number of new shims required may be few.
8  If the valve clearance 'A' is found to be too small, the shim thickness must be reduced by substituting one that is thinner by the amount left after subtracting 'A' from the specified valve clearance.
  *Inlet 0.016 to 0.018 in. (0.41 to 0.46 mm)*
  *Exhaust 0.020 to 0.022 in. (0.51 to 0.56 mm)*
9  If the valve clearance 'A' is found to be too large, the shim thickness must be increased by substitution of one that is thicker by the amount left after substracting the specified valve clearance from 'A'. Numbering from the timing chain end of the engine, inlet valves are: 2 - 3 - 6 - 7 - 10 - 11 and exhaust valves 1 - 4 - 5 - 8 - 9 - 12.
10  The numbers stamped on the shims correspond to the following thicknesses. If necessary, due to wear or poor marking, a micrometer can be used to measure the shim thickness (photo):

| 97 | 0.097 in. (2.47 mm) |
|---|---|
| 99 | 0.099 in. (2.52 mm) |
| 01 | 0.101 in. (2.56 mm) |
| 03 | 0.103 in. (2.62 mm) |
| 05 | 0.105 in. (2.67 mm) |
| 07 | 0.107 in. (2.72 mm) |
| 09 | 0.109 in. (2.77 mm) |
| 11 | 0.111 in. (2.83 mm) |
| 13 | 0.113 in. (2.87 mm) |
| 15 | 0.115 in. (2.93 mm) |
| 17 | 0.117 in. (2.98 mm) |
| 19 | 0.119 in. (3.03 mm) |
| 21 | 0.121 in. (3.08 mm) |
| 23 | 0.123 in. (3.13 mm) |
| 25 | 0.125 in. (3.18 mm) |
| 27 | 0.127 in. (3.23mm) |

11  Stick each shim into its respective tappet using a dab of grease. Install the tappets into the camshaft assembly onto the valves.
12  Tighten the camshaft carrier bolts to the specified torque and then install the cylinder head, as described in Section 78.
13  With No. 1 piston at tdc on the compression stroke (indicated by the notch on the crankshaft pulley being in alignment with the mark

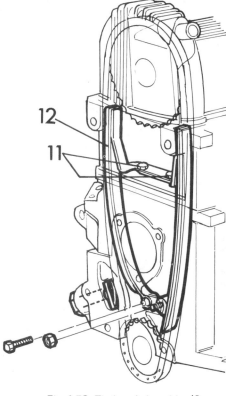

Fig. 1.73. Timing chain guides (6 cylinder) (Sec. 78)

11 Securing bolts
12 Fixed guide

78.2 Inlet valve (left) showing stem oil seal

78.3A Locating a new cylinder head gasket

78.3B Cylinder head correctly installed

79.10 Measuring the thickness of a tappet shim

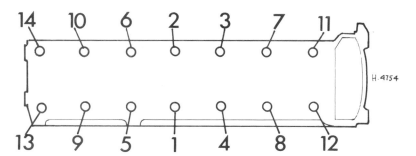

Fig. 1.74. Cylinder head bolt tightening sequence (6 cylinder) (Sec. 78)

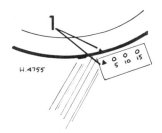

Fig. 1.75. Timing marks (6 cylinder) (Sec. 79)

on the scale) engage the camshaft sprocket within the loop of the timing chain and install the sprocket so that the mark on the sprocket is in alignment with the mark on the camshaft carrier.

14 Tighten the camshaft sprocket bolt to specified torque.

15 Turn the chain guide cam type adjuster screw until the timing chain is tight but not taut or under tension. Tighten the adjuster screw locknut.

16 Release the chain tensioner by inserting the Allen key and turning it fully anticlockwise. Remove the key, tighten the locknut and fit the sealing plug.

17 Install the camshaft cover using a new flange gasket if necessary.

## 80 Engine/manual gearbox (4 cylinder) - reconnection

1  This is a reversal of separation (Section 28) but make sure that the following operations are carried out.

2  Fit a new 'O' ring seal to the oil feed, connect the engine and gearbox and insert the bolts.

3  Position the layshaft cut-away to mate with the recess in the adaptor plate.

4  Insert the four laygear thrust springs into their holes in the gearbox casing.

5  Check that the fork rod retaining plate is in position.

6  Locate the special washer on the first motion shaft.

7  Centralise the clutch driven plate, as described in Chapter 5.

8  Tighten all bolts to the specified torque.

9  Fill the primary drive reservoir with oil. To do this, remove the primary drive cover filler plug and inject 1½ pints (0.8 litre) of engine oil.

## 81 Engine/automatic transmission (4 cylinder) - reconnection

1  This is a reversal of separation (Section 29) but make sure that the following operations are carried out.

2  Fit a new engine oil feed 'O' ring seal. (Fig. 1.76)

3  Smear both sides of the joint gasket with transmission fluid, position the gasket and then lower the engine until it is just clear of the transmission casing. Engage the torque converter spigot with the

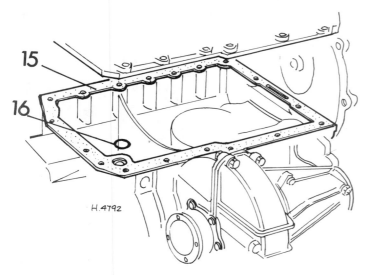

Fig. 1.76. Engine/automatic transmission gasket (15) and oil feed
'O' ring seal (16), 4 cylinder (Sec. 81)

crankshaft and then fully lower the engine onto the transmission casing.
4   Tighten the converter housing screws before those of the main casing
making sure all are tightened to the specified torque.

## 82 Engine/manual gearbox (6 cylinder) - reconnection

1   This is a reversal of separation (Section 30) but make sure that the
following operations are carried out.
2   Fit a new oil feed 'O' ring seal (photo).
3   Fit two sealing plugs to the oil seal face (photo).
4   Use new gaskets and tighten all bolts to the specified torque.

## 83 Engine/automatic transmission (6 cylinder) - reconnection

1   This is a reversal of separation (Section 31) but note specially the
operations listed in Section 81 which apply.

## 84 Engine ancillaries - refitting

1   These can either be refitted now or after the engine/transmission

has been installed in the car.
2   Refer to Section 27, and then to the appropriate Chapters, for full
refitting procedures.
3   Screw on the oil filter cartridge using hand-pressure only.

## 85 Engine/transmission - installation

1   This is a reversal of removal according to engine and transmission
type. Remember that the engine is slung from beneath the mountings,
not above when lowering the unit into position.
   *Section 22 – 4 cylinder with manual gearbox*
   *Section 23 – 4 cylinder with automatic transmission*
   *Section 24 – 6 cylinder with manual gearbox*
   *Section 25 – 6 cylinder with automatic transmission*
2   The following points should be noted however.
3   Take care not to damage the oil seals when entering the driveshafts into
the differential unit.
4   If any problem is found in locking the driveshafts into the
differential unit, install a worn drive clip around the driveshaft inner
joint and then drive the joint into the differential, using a drift applied
to the edge of the temporary clip.
5   Double check all lead and hose connections and adjust the alternator
drivebelt to give a deflection of ½ in. (12.7 mm) at the mid point of
the longest run of the belt.
6   Where power steering is fitted, release the bolts and the pipe union
nut (7) (Fig. 1.78) and adjust the drivebelt by moving the pump on its
pivots to give a deflection of ¼ in. (6.35 mm) at the mid-point of the
longest run of the belt. Note that the alternator drivebelt is shorter
than the one for the power steering pump.
7   Fill the cooling system with antifreeze mixture.
8   Fill the engine, gearbox or automatic transmission with the correct
grade and quantity of oil.

## 86 Engine mountings - installation

1   If the engine mountings are renewed at the time of engine
installation or at any other time when the engine is still in the car but
supported by a hoist, the following procedure should be followed. See
also Sections 11 and 15.

### 4 cylinder
2   Locate the mounting rubber in the support bracket with the flat
face of the rubber towards the bodyframe.
3   Install the lower plate over the pips on the mounting rubber.
Stretch the pips as the plate is pushed up against the mounting rubber
and then cut off the protruding portion of the pips flush with the plate.
4   The mounting rubbers are marked 'TOP' and they must be fitted
as colour matched pairs.
5   Refitting operations are a reversal of removal (Section 11).

82.2 Oil feed 'O' ring seal (6 cylinder engine to gearbox flange)

82.3 Oil seal face plugs

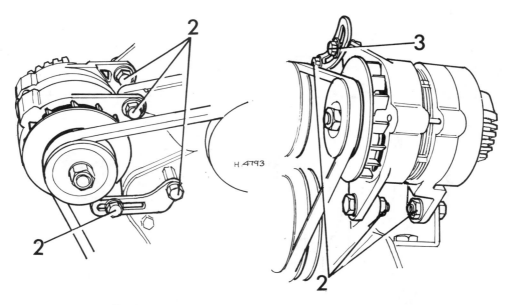

**Fig. 1.77 Alternator drivebelt tension adjustment (Sec. 85)**

2  *Mounting bolts*                                                3  *Adjuster bolts*

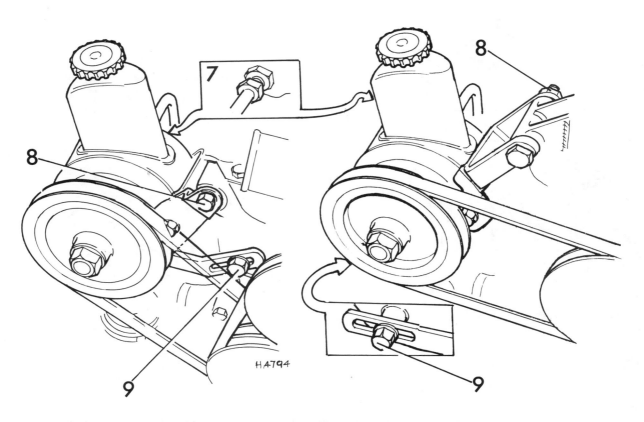

**Fig. 1.78 Power steering pump belt tension adjustment (Sec. 85)**

7  *Pipe union nut*              8  *Mounting bolts*              9  *Adjuster bolts*

*6 cylinder*

6   This is similar to the procedure just described for 4 cylinder mountings but note that the special plain washer locates under the head of the right-hand front through-bolt on cars equipped with automatic transmission.

**87 Initial start-up after major overhaul**

1   Adjust the throttle speed screw to provide a faster than normal

idling speed.

2   Start the engine and check for oil and water leaks.

3   Run the engine until normal operating temperature is reached and then adjust the slow-running (Chapter 3).

4   Dependent upon the number of new internal components which have been fitted so the engine speed should be restricted for the first few hundred miles. It is recommended that the engine oil and filter are changed and the valve clearances checked (4 cylinder), after the initial 1,000 miles (1600 km) running.

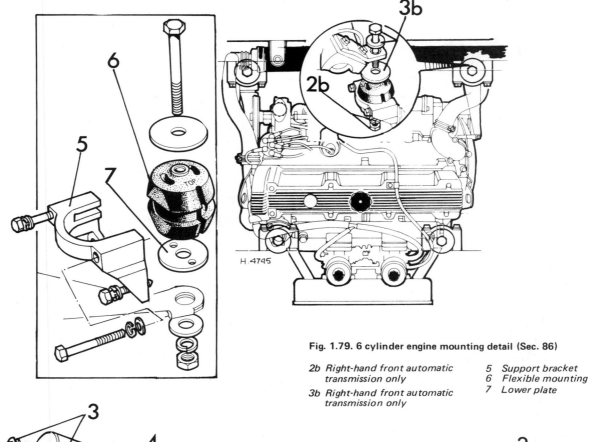

Fig. 1.79. 6 cylinder engine mounting detail (Sec. 86)

2b   Right-hand front automatic transmission only
3b   Right-hand front automatic transmission only
5   Support bracket
6   Flexible mounting
7   Lower plate

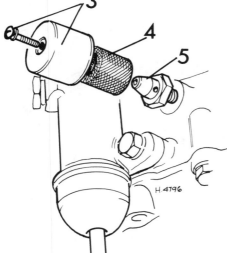

Fig. 1.80. Engine ventilator (renewable filter type), 6 cylinder (Sec. 88)

3   Screw and cap      4   Filter element      5   One-way valve

Fig. 1.81. Engine ventilator (sealed type), 6 cylinder (Sec. 88)

2   Locknut

### 88 Crankcase ventilation system filter - maintenance

1  Crankcase fumes are drawn through an extractor hose into the carburettor. Air to replace them is drawn in through a filter in the engine oil filler cap in the case of 4 cylinder engines.

2  With 6 cylinder engines, the filter is located on the flywheel housing (manual gearbox) or the engine adaptor plate (automatic transmission).
3  Some filters have a centre screw on the cap which when removed provides access to the renewable element.
4  On types without a centre screw, a complete filter assembly must be fitted at the specified service intervals.

### 89 Fault diagnosis - engine

| Symptom | Reason/s |
| --- | --- |
| Engine will not turn over when starter switch is operated | Flat battery.<br>Bad battery connections.<br>Bad connections at solenoid switch and/or starter motor.<br>Defective starter motor. |
| Engine turns over normally but fails to start | No spark at plugs.<br>No fuel reaching engine.<br>Too much fuel reaching the engine (flooding). |
| Engine starts but runs unevenly and misfires | Ignition and/or fuel system faults.<br>Incorrect valve clearances.<br>Burnt out valves.<br>Worn out piston rings. |
| Lack of power | Ignition and/or fuel system faults.<br>Incorrect valve clearances.<br>Burnt out valves.<br>Worn out piston rings. |
| Excessive oil consumption | Oil leaks from crankshaft, rear oil seal, timing cover gasket and oil seal, rocker cover gasket, oil filter gasket, sump gasket, sump plug washer.<br>Worn piston rings or cylinder bores resulting in oil being burnt by engine.<br>Worn valve guides and/or defective inlet valve stem seals. |
| Excessive mechanical noise from engine | Wrong valve clearances.<br>Worn crankshaft bearings.<br>Worn cylinders (piston slap).<br>Slack or worn timing chain and sprockets. |

*Note: When investigating starting and uneven running faults do not be tempted into snap diagnosis. Start from the beginning of the check procedure and follow it through. It will take less time in the long run. Poor performance from an engine in terms of power and economy is not normally diagnosed quickly. In any event the ignition and fuel systems must be checked first before assuming any further investigation needs to be made.*

# Chapter 2 Cooling system

*For modifications, and information applicable to later models, see Supplement at end of manual*

## Contents

## Specifications

**System type** ... ... ... ... ... ... ... ... ... Thermo syphon with water pump assistance. Pressurised with expansion tank and electric cooling fan

**Pressure cap rating** ... ... ... ... ... ... ... 15 lb sq in (1.05 kg/cm$^2$)

**Thermostat opening temperature**
Standard ... ... ... ... ... ... ... ... ... ... 165ºF (74ºC)
Cold climate ... ... ... ... ... ... ... ... ... 190ºF (88ºC)

**Thermostatic switch (fan) closing temperature** ... ... ... 194ºF (90ºC)

**Capacity (4 cylinder)** ... ... ... ... ... ... ... 13 Imp pints (7.3 litres)

**Capacity (6 cylinder)** ... ... ... ... ... ... ... 15 Imp pints (8.5 litres)

| Torque wrench settings | lb/ft | Nm |
|---|---|---|
| *4 cylinder* | | |
| Water pump to crankcase screws ... ... ... ... ... ... | 17 | 23 |
| Water pump pulley screws ... ... ... ... ... ... ... | 18 | 25 |
| Thermostat housing cover nuts ... ... ... ... ... ... | 8 | 11 |
| | | |
| *6 cylinder* | | |
| Water pump to crankcase screws ... ... ... ... ... ... | 20 | 28 |
| Water pump to body plug ... ... ... ... ... ... ... | 35 | 48 |
| Water pump pulley screws ... ... ... ... ... ... ... | 10 | 14 |
| Filler housing cover nuts ... ... ... ... ... ... ... | 10 | 14 |
| Thermostat housing cover nuts ... ... ... ... ... ... | 10 | 14 |

## 1 General description

1 The cooling system comprises a front mounted radiator, a water pump, belt driven from the crankshaft pulley and the necessary interconnecting hoses.
2 The system is pressurized and incorporates an expansion tank which removes the necessity of regular topping-up.
3 The expansion tank which is connected to the top of the radiator accepts the overflow of coolant as the cooling system warms up. When the system cools, the pressure in the radiator drops and the displaced coolant returns from the expansion tank.
4 When the car is in normal forward motion, the ram effect of the air cools the coolant in the radiator tubes but when the car is stationary or moving slowly in hot weather, a supplementary electrically-operated fan cuts in by means of a thermostatically controlled switch located on the side of the radiator. A thermostat is located in a housing in the cylinder head to prevent circulation of coolant until the engine has warmed up after starting from cold (photo).

## 2 Cooling system - draining

1 Unscrew and remove the pressure cap from the expansion tank. Unscrew it very slowly if the system is hot in order that the internal pressure may be released.
2 Unscrew and remove the filler plug which on four cylinder engines is located in the top of the thermostat housing and in six cylinder engines on the top of a special filler housing.
3 Unscrew the cylinder block drain plug and catch the coolant in a container if it is to be retained for further use.
4 *On four cylinder cars,* disconnect the water pump hose from its connecting pipe and catch the coolant which will drain from the system.
5 *On six cylinder cars,* disconnect the radiator bottom hose from the radiator.

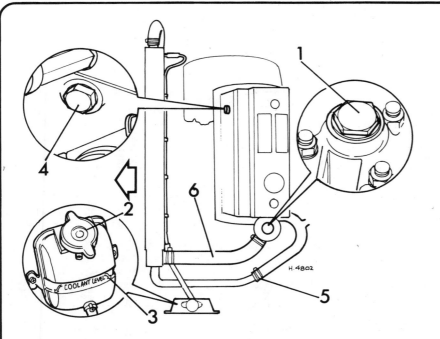

Fig. 2.1. Cooling system (4 cylinder)

1 Filler plug
2 Expansion tank cap
3 Level mark
4 Cylinder block drain plug
5 Bottom hose
6 Top hose

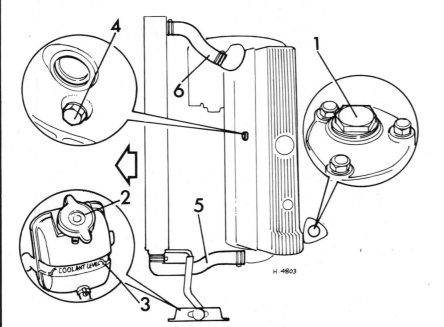

Fig. 2.2 Cooling system (6 cylinder)

1 Filler plug
2 Expansion tank cap
3 Level mark
4 Cylinder block drain plug
5 Bottom hose
6 Top hose

1.4 Location of fan thermostatically controlled switch

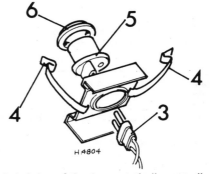

Fig. 2.3 Exploded view of the thermostatically controlled fan switch

3 Connector plug
4 Securing clips
5 Switch
6 Seal

## 3  Cooling system - flushing

1   Place the heater control to 'HOT' and leave the radiator bottom hose disconnected and the cylinder block drain plug out.
2   Remove the filler plug and insert a cold water hose. All ow the water to run until it emerges from both outlets quite clean.
3   In severe cases of contamination, remove the radiator (Section 6) and invert it. Place the cold water hose in the bottom outlet (which is now at the top) and reverse flush it.
4   If the cooling system is blocked or badly corroded due to neglect in routine changing of the antifreeze mixture or failure to maintain its strength, then a chemical cleaner or descaler can be used strictly in accordance with the manufacturer's instructions.

## 4  Cooling system - filling

1   Reconnect the radiator bottom hose and refit the cylinder block drain plug.
2   Disconnect the hose from the expansion tank.
3   Fill the system by pouring coolant through the engine coolant filler plug hole until coolant is seen to flow from the disconnected end of the expansion tank hose. Reconnect the expansion tank hose.
4   Pour coolant into the expansion tank until it is ¾ full and refit the expansion tank cap.
5   Pour more coolant into the filler plug hole until it reaches the bottom of the filler plug threads and then install the filler plug and 'O' ring seal.
6   Run the engine for 30 seconds at a fast idle and then switch off.
7   Release any pressure in the system by unscrewing the expansion tank cap to its stop and then removing it. Compress the top hose several times with the fingers.
8   Fill the expansion tank to half full and refit the cap.

## 5  Antifreeze mixture

1   The cooling system should always be filled with antifreeze mixture of suitable strength as apart from protecting the engine from frost damage, it will also prevent corrosion in the system.
2   It is recommended that the system is drained and refilled with fresh mixture every autumn.
3   Before adding the antifreeze mixture, check the tightness of all hose clips as the mixture is more searching than plain water and will find the smallest leak in the system.
4   The quantity of antifreeze which should be used for various levels of protection according to climate, is given in the following table:

| Solution | 4 cylinder | 6 cylinder | Protects to |
|---|---|---|---|
| | | Quantity | |
| 25% | 3.2 pints (1.9 litres) | 3.7 pints (2.1 litres) | 9°F (−13°C) |
| 33 1/3% | 4.3 pints (2.5 litres) | 5.0 pints (2.8 litres) | −2°F (−19°C) |
| 50% | 6.5 pints (3.5 litres) | 7.5 pints (4.3 litres) | −33°F (−36°C) |

5   Any topping-up of the antifreeze mixture should be carried out using a solution made up in similar proportions to the original, in order to avoid dilution.

## 6  Radiator - removal, inspection, refitting

1   Drain the cooling system, as described in Section 2.
2   Disconnect the plug connector from the thermostatic switch on the radiator.
3   Disconnect the radiator top and bottom hoses and the pipe which connects to the expansion tank.
4   Remove the screws which secure the radiator brackets and then tilt the radiator towards the engine and unplug the fan motor cable.
5   Lift the radiator out of the mounting bushes and withdraw it from the engine compartment.
6   Detach the electric fan and cowl from the radiator (four screws).
7   Release the clips and withdraw the thermostatic switch and sealing

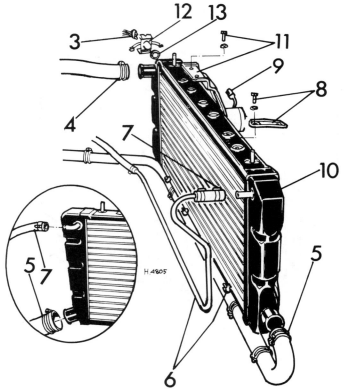

Fig. 2.4 Radiator assembly (4 cylinder): inset 6 cylinder variation (Sec. 6)

| | | | |
|---|---|---|---|
| 3 | Thermostatic switch connector plug | 8 | Brackets |
| 4 and 5 | hose clips | 9 | Fan connector plug |
| 6 | Expansion tank hose and clips | 10 | Radiator |
| 7 | Hose clip | 11 | Fan/cowl assembly |
| | | 12 | Thermostatic switch clip |
| | | 13 | Switch seal |

bush.
8   If the radiator has been removed because of a leak, it should be professionally repaired due to the need to localise the heat, otherwise further damage will be caused. Better still, exchange it for a reconditioned one.
9   Whenever the radiator is removed, take the opportunity of brushing away all accumulations of flies or dirt from the radiator fins or by applying air from a compressed air line in the reverse direction to normal airflow.
10  It is a good plan to have the expansion tank pressure cap tested at a service station periodically and if faulty, renewed with one of similar pressure rating.
11  Installation is a reversal of removal. Fill the system, as described in Section 4 of this Chapter.

## 7  Radiator fan - removal and installation

1   Removal of the electrically-operated cooling fan after withdrawing the radiator is described in the preceding Section. The fan can be removed and installed, however, without disconnecting the coolant hoses.
2   On four cylinder cars, disconnect the lead from the radiator thermostatic switch and release the clips which secure the expansion pipe to the radiator.
3   Disconnect the radiator brackets from the support platform and the fan cowl from the radiator.
4   Tilt the radiator towards the engine and unplug the fan connecting lead.
5   Lift the radiator from its bottom mounting bushes and free the cowl from the radiator.
6   Tilt the top of the radiator towards the engine and withdraw the fan/cowl assembly from between the side of the radiator and the front

panel.

7  *On six cylinder cars,* lift the radiator and move it towards the engine so that the fan and cowl assembly can be extracted from between the base of the radiator and the front panel.

8  Installation is a reversal of removal.

## 8  Fan motor - overhaul

1  Slacken the grub screw which secures the fan hub to the motor spindle and withdraw the fan blades.

2  Remove the three screws which secure the fan motor to the cowl and separate the two components.

3  Remove the two motor tie-bolts and then withdraw the end cover complete with armature from the motor yoke, noting the assembly marks on the end cover and on the yoke.

4  Remove the circlip from the armature spindle and withdraw the two shim washers and spring washer.

5  Withdraw the armature assembly from the end cover.

6  Withdraw the thrust washer from the armature spindle and then extract the circlip from the armature spindle.

7  Remove the three screws to release the brush carrier assembly from

Fig. 2.5 Fan/cowl removal (4 cylinder) (Sec. 7)

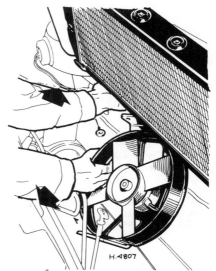

Fig. 2.6 Fan/cowl removal (6 cylinder) (Sec. 7)

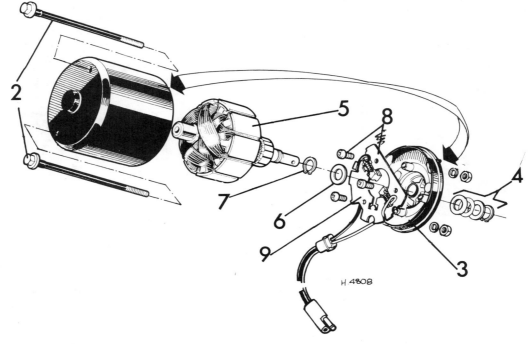

Fig. 2.7 Exploded view of the fan motor (Sec. 8)

| 2  Tie bolts | 4  Circlip, washers | 6  Thrust washer | 8  Brush carrier screws |
|---|---|---|---|
| 3  End cover | 5  Armature | 7  Circlip | 9  Brush carrier |

Alignment marks arrowed

the end cover.
8   Renew any worn components particularly the brushes after comparison with new ones.
9   Clean the commutator with a fuel moistened cloth and if essential, polish it with fine glass paper, not emery cloth. Do not undercut the segment insulators.
10   Reassembly is a reversal of dismantling but observe the following points: Lubricate sparingly, the bearings and bushes. Make sure that the yoke and end cover mating marks are in alignment. Position the spring washer **between** the two shims.
11   When fitting the fan to the shaft, ensure that the boss of the fan is away from the motor and engage the grub screw with the first indent in the shaft.

## 9   Thermostat (4 cylinder) - removal, testing and refitting

1   Remove the coolant filler plug and 'O' ring seal.
2   Partly drain the cooling system by removing the cylinder block drain plug. The withdrawal of 6 Imp. pints (3.4 litres) should be sufficient.
3   Release the thermostat housing cover (three nuts) and lift it off the housing and extract the joint gasket. Do not disturb the sandwich plate.
4   Lift the thermostat from the housing. If it is stuck tight, do not prise it by inserting a lever under the bridge piece but cut round its edge using a sharp pointed knife.
5   To test the thermostat, suspend it in a container of water and heat the water until the thermostat opens. By inserting a thermometer into the water, check the opening temperature of the thermostat and if this varies considerably from the figure stamped on it, fit a new one. Always renew the thermostat if it is stuck open or if one of incorrect rating (see Specifications) has been fitted by a previous owner. The fitting of a thermostat of incorrect rating will cause either overheating or cool running of the engine, slow warm up and an inefficient car interior heater.
6   Refitting is a reversal of removal, but use new gaskets.

## 10   Thermostat (6 cylinder) - removal, testing and refitting

1   Unscrew and remove the coolant filler plug from the filler housing.
2   Remove the drain plug from the front of the cylinder block and drain about 6 Imp. pints (3.4 litres) from the cooling system.
3   Release the thermostat housing cover and remove the cover, joint gasket and thermostat. If the thermostat is stuck tight, do not prise it by inserting a lever under the bridge piece but cut round its edge using a sharp pointed knife.
4   Test the thermostat, as described in the preceding Section.
5   Refitting is a reversal of removal but use new gaskets.

## 11   Water pump (4 cylinder) - removal, overhaul and refitting

1   Unscrew and remove the coolant filler plug and then drain the coolant from the cylinder block.
2   Slacken the alternator mounting and adjustment strap bolts and push the alternator towards the engine so that the drivebelt can be removed from the water pump pulley. Remove the power steering pump drivebelt (if fitted).
3   Remove the pulley from the water pump hub (four screws).
4   Remove the two bolts which secure the top of the alternator to the water pump and to the engine bracket and pull the alternator aside.
5   Disconnect the coolant hose from the water pump.
6   Unscrew the water pump securing screws, noting the location of the longer one. Peel off the joint gasket.
7   If the water pump has been in service for a considerable mileage, it is recommended that it is exchanged for a new or reconditioned one. Where preferred, it can be overhauled by first pressing the spindle out of the pulley hub.
8   Support the rear face of the pump and press out the bearing assembly complete with impeller and seal.
9   Press the spindle from the impeller and then extract the seal.
10   Renew any worn components (the bearing/spindle is supplied as an assembly).

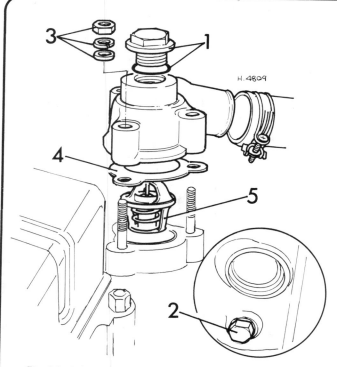

Fig. 2.8. Combined filler and thermostat housing (4 cylinder)
(Sec. 9)

1   Coolant filler plug
and seal
2   Cylinder block
drain plug
3   Cover nut and washers
4   Joint gasket
5   Thermostat

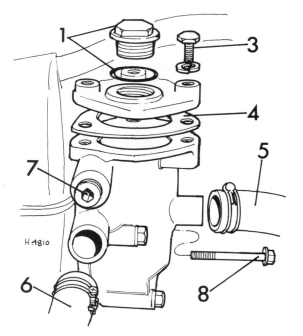

Fig. 2.9 Coolant filler housing (6 cylinder) (Sec. 10)

1   Filler plug and seal
3   Cover bolt
4   Joint gasket
5 and 6   hoses
7   Blanking plug
8   Housing bolt

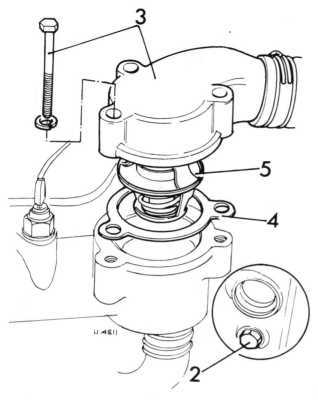

Fig. 2.10 Thermostat housing (6 cylinder) (Sec. 10)

2  Cylinder block drain plug    4  Joint gasket
3  Cover and bolt               5  Thermostat

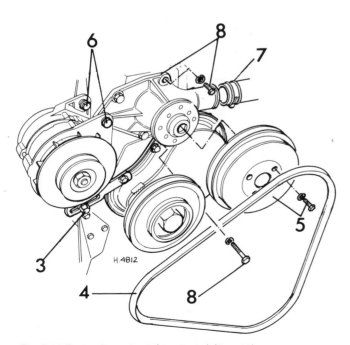

Fig. 2.11 Engine front detail (4 cylinder) (Sec. 11)

3  Alternator adjuster bolt     6  Alternator mounting bolts
4  Drive belt                   7  Hose
5  Pulley                       8  Water pump bolts

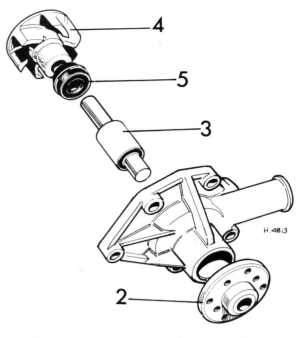

Fig. 2.12 Components of 4 cylinder water pump (Sec. 11)

2  Pulley hub                   4  Impeller
3  Bearing/spindle assembly     5  Seal

11 Press the bearing assembly into the water pump body, making sure to apply force only to the outer sleeve of the bearing.
12 Support the rear end of the spindle and press on the pulley hub.
13 Fit the seal and then support the spindle at its front end and press the impeller onto the rear, making sure that there is a final impeller vane to water pump body clearance of between 0.20 and 0.30 in. (0.508 and 0.762 mm).
14 Refitting is a reversal of removal, but use a new gasket and tighten all bolts to the specified torque.
15 Adjust the drivebelt tension, as described in Chapter 1, Section 85.

## 12 Water pump (6 cylinder) - removal and refitting

1  Unscrew and remove the coolant filler plug.
2  Drain the coolant from the cylinder block.
3  Slacken the alternator mounting and adjustment strap bolts and push the alternator in towards the engine so that the drivebelt can be removed from the pulleys (Fig. 1.13).
4  Remove the pulley from the water pump hub (three screws).
5  Disconnect both coolant hoses from the water pump.
6  Remove the alternator adjusting link and then extract the three water pump securing screws and remove the pump and joint gasket.
7  The pump cannot be overhauled and if faulty it should be renewed.
8  Refitting is a reversal of removal but make sure that the concave side of the pulley is against the water pump hub. Tighten all bolts to specified torque.
9  Adjust the drivebelt tension, as described in Chapter 1, Section 85.

## 13 Water temperature gauge and transmitter

1  The water temperature transmitter switch is screwed into the base of the filler/thermostat housing (four cylinder) or into the thermostat housing extension (six cylinder).
2  In the event of a faulty reading on the gauge, first check the security of the connecting leads.
3  If the temperature and fuel gauges are both giving incorrect readings, the instrument voltage stabiliser may be at fault (see Chapter 10).

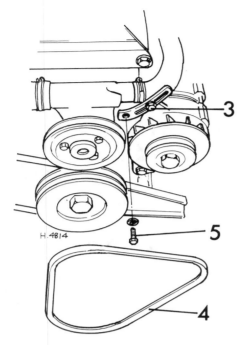

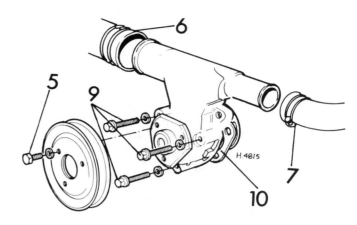

Fig. 2.14. 6 cylinder water pump (Sec. 12)

5   Pulley bolt
6 and 7 hose clips
9   Pump mounting bolts
10 Joint gasket

Fig. 2.13 Engine front detail (6 cylinder) (Sec. 12)

3   Alternator adjuster bolt        5   Adjuster strap to
4   Drivebelt                              water pump bolt

4   Checking the transmitter switch and the gauge can only be
satisfactorily carried out using special test equipment or by substitution
of new units. If the water temperature gauge must be removed, refer to
Chapter 10.

## 14 Fault diagnosis - cooling system

| Symptom | Reason/s |
| --- | --- |
| Heat generated in engine not being successfully disposed of by radiator | Insufficient water in cooling system. |
| | Drive belt slipping (accompanied by a shrieking noise on rapid engine acceleration). |
| | Radiator core blocked or radiator grille restricted. |
| | Bottom water hose collapsed, impeding flow. |
| | Thermostat not opening properly. |
| | Ignition advance and retard incorrectly set (accompanied by loss of power and perhaps misfiring). |
| | Carburettor incorrectly adjusted (mixture too weak). |
| | Exhaust system partially blocked. |
| | Oil level in sump too low. |
| | Blown cylinder head gasket (water/steam being forced down the expansion tank pipe under pressure). |
| | Engine not yet run-in. |
| | Brakes binding. |
| Too much heat being dispersed by radiator | Thermostat jammed open. |
| | Incorrect grade of thermostat fitted allowing premature opening of valve. |
| | Thermostat missing. |
| Leaks in system | Loose clips on water hoses. |
| | Top or bottom water hoses perished and leaking. |
| | Radiator core leaking. |
| | Expansion tank pressure cap spring worn or seal ineffective. |
| | Pressure cap spring worn or seal ineffective. |
| | Blown cylinder head gasket (pressure in system forcing water/steam down expansion tank pipe). |
| | Cylinder wall or head cracked. |

# Chapter 3 Fuel system and carburation

*For modifications, and information applicable to later models, see Supplement at end of manual*

## Contents

## Specifications

### Air cleaner type

| | |
|---|---|
| 4 cylinder ... ... ... ... ... ... ... ... ... | Disposable paper element with air temperature control device |
| 6 cylinder ... ... ... ... ... ... ... ... ... | Dual disposable paper elements without control device |

### Fuel pump type

Fuel pump type ... ... ... ... ... ... ... ...     SU mechanical

### Carburettors

| | 4 cylinder | | 6 cylinder (twin) | |
|---|---|---|---|---|
| | To 1975 | 1976 on | To 1975 | 1976 on |
| Type ... ... ... ... ... ... ... ... ... | SU HS6 | SU HS6 | SU HIF6 | SU HIF6 |
| Part No: | | | | |
|   Manual ... ... ... ... ... | AUD 68 | FZX 1079/1215/1216 | AUD 697 | AUD 697, FZX 1095/1219/1220 |
|   Automatic ... ... ... ... ... | AUD 635 | FZX 1080/1217/1218 | AUD 698 | AUD 698, FZX 1096/1221/1222 |
| Piston spring ... ... ... ... ... ... ... | Yellow | | Red | |
| Jet size ... ... ... ... ... ... ... ... | 0.100 in (2.54 mm) | | 0.100 in (2.54 mm) | |
| Needle ... ... ... ... ... ... ... ... | BBF | | BCP | |
| Idle speed... ... ... ... ... ... ... ... | 750 rev/min | | 750 rev/min | |
| Fast idle speed ... ... ... ... ... ... ... | 1200 rev/min | | 1400 rev/min | |

### Exhaust emission level

Exhaust emission level ... ... ... ... ... ... ...     3.0 to 4.5% CO                2.0% CO

### Fuel tank capacity

Fuel tank capacity ... ... ... ... ... ... ... ...     16 Imp gals (73.0 litres)

### Torque wrench settings

| | lb/ft | Nm |
|---|---|---|
| Carburettor to manifold nuts ... ... ... ... ... ... ... | 15 | 21 |
| Float chamber bolt (4 cylinder) ... ... ... ... ... ... | 8 | 11 |
| Manifold nuts and bolts ... ... ... ... ... ... ... | 15 | 21 |

## 1 General description

The fuel system comprises a rear mounted fuel tank, a mechanically operated fuel pump and a single SU carburettor on four cylinder models and twin SU carburettors on six cylinder models.

## 2 Air cleaner element (4 cylinder) - renewal

1 Every 12000 miles (19000 km) renew the disposable type air cleaner element.
2 Slacken the clamp (1) (Fig. 3.1) and disconnect the air temperature control valve.
3 Release the fuel pipe from its clip on the air cleaner.
4 Unscrew the square-headed nut (2) from the air cleaner cover (3) and then pull off the cover.
5 Discard the element and wipe clean the interior of the air cleaner components.
6 Install the new element and reassemble the components making sure that the sealing washer (6) is in good condition.

## 3 Air temperature control (4 cylinder) - description and testing

1 As an aid to maintaining a constant temperature level of the air entering the carburettor, an air temperature control device is attached to the intake nozzle of the air cleaner (Fig. 3.2a).
2 When the engine is cold, all air is drawn from the shrouded area of the exhaust manifold. As the temperature rises, the control valve in the device will open and admit cooler air to maintain a constant temperature level of air entering the carburettor air intake.
3 To test the operation of the valve, make sure that the engine is quite cold and then depress the valve and immediately release it. It should return at once to its original position. The valve must be renewed if it fails to operate in the correct manner.

## 4 Air cleaner elements (6 cylinder) - renewal

1 Every 12000 miles (19000 km) renew the air cleaner elements.
2 To do this, unscrew the two square headed nuts and withdraw the complete air cleaner assembly from the carburettor flanges.

3  Remove the wing nut, separate the lid from the casing and extract and discard the elements .

4  Clean the interior of the casing and install new elements.

5  Reassemble, making sure that the sealing rings and washers are in good condition.

## 5  Fuel pump - testing, removal and refitting

1  Operation of the fuel pump can be checked without removing it from the engine. Disconnect the fuel outlet pipe (connecting  to carburettor) and hold a small container under the open end of the pipe.

2  Disconnect the lead from the coil negative (−) terminal to prevent the engine firing and then have an assistant operate the ignition key to actuate the starter motor. Well defined spurts of fuel should be ejected from the pump if it is in good order.

3  *On four cylinder engines,* to remove the pump, disconnect the hoses and remove the securing bolts. Withdraw the pump and insulating spacer. Extract the pump pushrod.

4  *On six cylinder engines,* the procedure is similar except that on cars equipped with automatic transmission, a pump adaptor block is fitted as well as the flange insulating block.

5  The fuel pump is a sealed unit and no maintenance or repair is possible. In the event of a fault developing, renew the pump complete.

## 6  Fuel tank - removal, repair and installation

1  Disconnect the lead from the battery negative terminal.

2  Remove the fuel filler cap and fuel filler pipe cover.

3  Raise the rear of the car and support it under the rear jacking points.

4  Detach the lead from the tank transmitter unit and remove the lead also from the securing clips on the side of the fuel tank.

5  Disconnect the fuel outlet pipe from the tank transmitter unit and catch any fuel which drains in a suitable container.

6  Detach the fuel pipe from the two clips on the side of the tank.

7  Support the weight of the fuel tank on a jack and insulating wooden block and then remove the five screws and plates which secure the tank to the bodyframe.

8  Lower the fuel tank, carefully extracting the filler pipe from the body.

9  The tank transmitter unit can be released by turning it anticlockwise with a suitable lever or 'C' spanner.

10 Never attempt to repair a leaking fuel tank by soldering or welding. Even when empty, explosive gases will remain unless the tank is

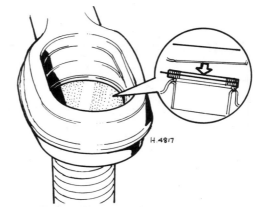

Fig. 3.2a. Air temperature control device (single carburettor air filter) (Sec. 3)

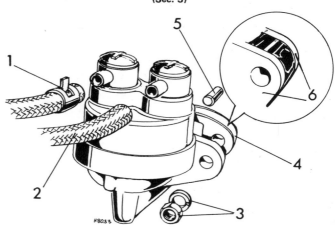

Fig. 3.2b. Typical fuel pump (Sec. 5)

| 1 | Fuel inlet | 4 | Insulator |
|---|---|---|---|
| 2 | Fuel outlet | 5 | Pushrod |
| 3 | Nut and washer | 6 | Gaskets |

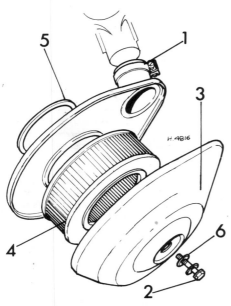

Fig. 3.1 Air cleaner (single carburettor) (Sec. 2)

| 1 | Clip | 3 | Cover | 5, 6 seals |
|---|---|---|---|---|
| 2 | Cover bolt | 4 | Filter element | |

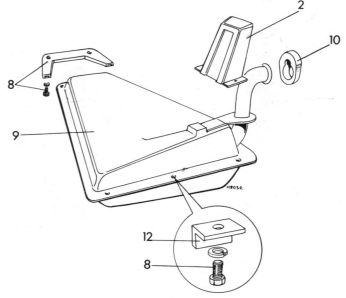

Fig.3.3a. Fuel tank and attachments (Sec. 6)

| 2 | Fuel filler pipe cover | 9 | Fuel tank |
|---|---|---|---|
| 8 | Mounting plates and bolts | 10 | Grommet |

steamed out or flushed through with boiling water for at least an hour. Have the tank professionally repaired or install a new one.
11 If the tank contains a quantity of sludge or sediment, use several changes of paraffin, shaking the tank vigorously to dislodge it but remove the transmitter unit first to prevent damaging it.
12 When installing the transmitter unit, use a new sealing gasket.
13 Installation is a reversal of removal.

## 7 Fuel contents gauge and transmitter unit

1 In the event of the fuel contents gauge reading incorrectly, first check the security and insulation of the wiring between the gauge and transmitter.
2 If the water temperature and fuel gauges are both giving incorrect readings, the instrument voltage stabiliser may be at fault (see Chapter 10).
3 Checking the transmitter and the gauge can only be satisfactorily carried out using special test equipment or by substitution of new units.
4 Removal of the tank transmitter unit is described in the preceding Section, while removal of the gauge is covered in Chapter 10.

## 8 Carburettors - general description

The carburettors are of SU type, a single unit being fitted to four cylinder engines and a twin installation to six cylinder power units.
The type of carburettor fitted differs between the two engines, also whether manual or automatic transmission is installed: for precise details, reference should be made to the specifications at the beginning of this Chapter.

## 9 Carburettor (single) - maintenance and adjustment

1 Every 6000 miles (9600 km) or at six monthly intervals, unscrew the cap from the top of the carburettor suction chamber and withdraw the damper. Pour in engine oil until the level is ½ in. (12.5 mm) above the top of the hollow piston rod. Push the damper assembly firmly back into position and tighten the cap with the fingers.
2 Before carrying out any adjustment to the carburettor, ensure that the tappet clearances and ignition settings are correct.
3 Check that the choke control is fully off when the control is pushed home and has in fact a slight free-movement before the cable actuates the lever on the carburettor.
4 Check that there is a clearance between the fast idle screw and the cam.
5 Remove the air cleaner and lift the piston with the finger. Allow it to drop unaided when it should fall as described in Section 11, paragraph 24.
6 In order to maintain the emission control characteristics of the carburettor, precise tuning is essential and this should only be carried out where a device such as a 'Colortune' is available or when a tachometer and exhaust gas analyser can be used. On later models, the carburettor adjustment screws are sealed with black or blue caps. The carburettor has been pre-set during manufacture to meet EEC regulations and in this case the screws should not be tampered with. However, if the carburettor has been overhauled and re-setting of mixture and idling is required, the caps must be broken off and new red coloured ones fitted on completion.
7 Have the engine running at normal operating temperature (with the air cleaner fitted) in neutral or 'P' on automatic transmission.
8 Adjust the throttle screw to give an engine idling speed of 750 rev/min. indicated on the tachometer.
9 Using either the combustion flame device in accordance with the manufacturer's instructions or the exhaust gas analyser, turn the jet adjusting nut one flat at a time (up weak, down rich) until the correct mixture setting is attained (3.0 to 4.5% CO). Readjust the throttle speed screw if necessary to give the specified idling speed.
10 To set the fast idle speed, have the engine running at the specified idling speed and then pull out the choke control knob until the linkage is just about to move the jet. Lock the knob in this position. Turn the fast idle screw until the correct fast idle speed (1200 rev/min.) is indicated on the tachometer.
11 Push the choke control knob fully home, switch off the engine and disconnect any tuning instruments.

12 If during the adjustment operations, the engine is kept idling for periods of longer than three minutes, momentarily raise the engine speed to clear the intake before continuing the adjustment.
13 It should be noted that the carburettor is set at the factory and any adjustment should be restricted to turning the throttle speed screw.

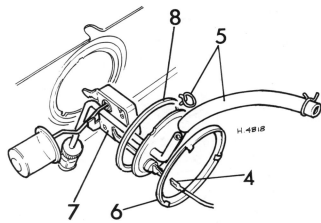

Fig. 3.3b Fuel tank transmitter unit (Sec. 6)

4 Lucar terminal
5 Fuel hose and clip
6 Locking ring
7 Transmitter unit
8 Sealing ring

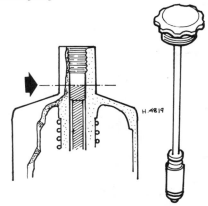

Fig. 3.4 Single carburettor damper and oil level (Sec. 9)

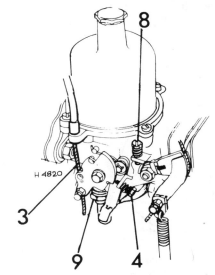

Fig. 3.5 Single carburettor adjustment screws (Sec. 9)

3 Choke cable
4 Fast idle screw
8 Throttle speed screw
9 Jet adjusting nut

## 10 Carburettors (twin) - maintenance and adjustment

The following procedure must not be regarded as routine and should only be carried out in the event of poor performance or after carburettor dismantling and reassembly. The units are set at the factory and should not be disturbed unnecessarily.

1 Every 6000 miles (9600 km) or at six monthly intervals, unscrew the cap on the top of each carburettor suction chamber and lift the piston and damper straight up to the limit of their travel. Fill the central recess with engine oil and push the damper down until the cap contacts the suction chamber. Repeat this procedure until the oil level is maintained at the bottom of the recess. Screw the caps down with the fingers.

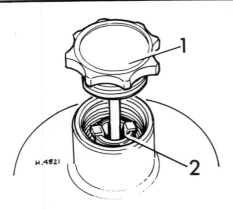

**Fig. 3.6 Twin carburettor type damper (Sec. 10)**

1   Cap                2   Recess for oil

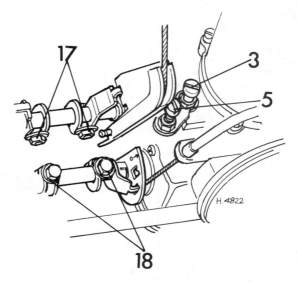

**Fig. 3.7 Twin carburettor adjustment points (Sec. 10)**

3   Throttle speed screw
5   Fast idle screw
17  Throttle spindle clamp bolt
18  Cold start interconnection clamp bolt

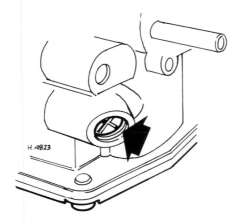

**Fig. 3.8 Location of jet adjusting screw (twin carburettor) (Sec. 10)**

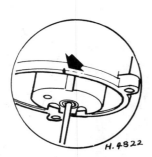

**Fig. 3.9a. Mark the position of the suction chamber relevant to the carburettor body ( Sec. 10)**

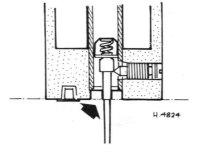

**Fig. 3.9b. Correct needle setting (flush with underside of piston) on twin carburettors (Sec. 10)**

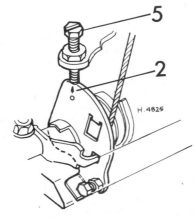

**Fig. 3.10 Cam to fast idle screw relationship during twin carburettor adjustment (Sec. 10)**

2   Alignment mark                5   Fast idle screw

2 Before carrying out any adjustments to the carburettors, ensure that the tappet clearance and ignition settings are correct.

3 Check that the choke control is fully off when the control is pushed home and has in fact a slight free-movement before the cable actuates the lever on the carburettor.

4 In order to maintain the emission control characteristics of the carburettors, precise tuning is essential and this should only be carried out where suitable tuning equipment is available or a tachometer, balance meter and exhaust gas analyser can be used.

5 Remove the air cleaner and unscrew each throttle speed adjusting screw until they clear the throttle stop (throttle closed). Screw each screw in one complete turn clockwise.

6 Unscrew each fast idle adjusting screw until it is well clear of the cam.

7 Mark the relative position of each suction chamber to the carburettor body and then remove them and turn each jet adjusting screw until the jets are flush with the bridge or as high as possible without exceeding the height of the bridge.

8 Turn each jet adjusting screw two turns (clockwise). If plugs have been fitted in the screw apertures, prise them out and discard them to obtain access to the jet adjusting screw.

9 Check that each needle shoulder is flush with the underside of the piston.

10 Refit the suction chamber assemblies after first having tested the movement of the pistons within the suction chambers as described in Section 12, paragraph 16.

11 Top-up the damper oil, as described earlier in this Section.

12 With the engine at a fast idle and at normal operating temperature in neutral or 'P' (automatic transmission), connect a tachometer in accordance with the manufacturer's instructions.

13 Slacken a clamp bolt on the throttle spindle interconnection.

14 Slacken a clamp bolt on the cold start interconnection.

15 Using the balance meter, balance the carburettors by altering one of the throttle speed adjusting screws until the air intake at each carburettor is of equal volume and gives the same reading on the meter. Now turn each throttle speed screw an equal amount until the engine idling speed is 750 rev/min. and recheck with the balance meter.

16 Turn the jet adjusting screws until the fastest engine speed is indicated on the tachometer. Turn each screw by the same amount, clockwise rich, anticlockwise weak.

17 Now turn each of the jet adjusting screws anticlockwise until the speed indicated on the tachometer just begins to fall and then give each screw a further quarter of a turn in an anticlockwise direction.

18 Re-adjust the idling speed, if necessary, to specification by turning each throttle speed screw by the same amount.

19 If the adjustment operations extend over a period of more than three minutes, momentarily raise the engine speed to clear the intake before continuing the adjustment.

20 If the adjustment has been carried out correctly, the exhaust gas analyser should give a reading of 2% at idling speed. If necessary, slight re-adjustment can be carried out by turning each of the jet adjusting screws by the same amount but not exceeding one half turn in either direction.

21 Set the throttle interconnecting levers so that both throttles will open simultaneously and a clearance will exist between the lever and the cam. Tighten the clamp bolt making sure that an endfloat of about 1/32 in. (0.8 mm) is evident on the interconnecting rod.

22 With the fast idle cams of both carburettors against their stops, set the cold start interconnections so that both cams will move together and that the cable has slight free-movement (see paragraph 3).

23 With the engine idling, pull out the choke control until the arrows marked on the cams are directly under the fast idle adjusting screws. Again using the balance meter, turn the fast idle adjusting screws very slowly until with the carburettors synchronised, the fast idle speed indicated on the tachometer is 1400 rev/min.

24 Switch off the engine, disconnect the tuning instruments and refit the air cleaner.

Note: Under normal circumstances, alteration of the factory set jet adjustment screws should be limited to one quarter turn in either direction and this only needed in the event of a change of operating altitude or fuel quality.

## 11 Carburettor (single type HS6) - removal, overhaul and refitting

1 Disconnect the lead from the battery negative terminal.

2 Remove the air cleaner and disconnect the engine breather pipe from the carburettor.

3 Disconnect the fuel inlet pipe from the carburettor, also the distributor vacuum pipe.

4 Disconnect the throttle and choke cables. On cars equipped with automatic transmission, disconnect the downshift cable from the carburettor.

5 Remove the carburettor from the intake manifold (four nuts) and detach the distance piece and heat shield.

6 Remove the air intake adaptor (two nuts) (photo).

7 Before dismantling, clean the outside of the carburettor and unscrew the damper and pour out any oil. Decide whether in view of the mileage covered it would be better to obtain a new unit, particularly if wear has

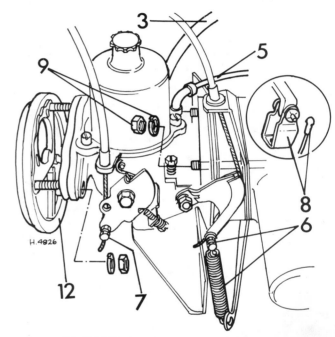

Fig. 3.11 Single carburettor controls (Sec. 11)

3 Engine breather pipe
5 Distributor vacuum pipe
6 Throttle return spring
7 Choke cable
8 Downshift cable (automatic transmission)
9 Carburettor securing nut
12 Air intake adaptor

11.6 Removing air intake adaptor (6 cylinder twin carburettor)

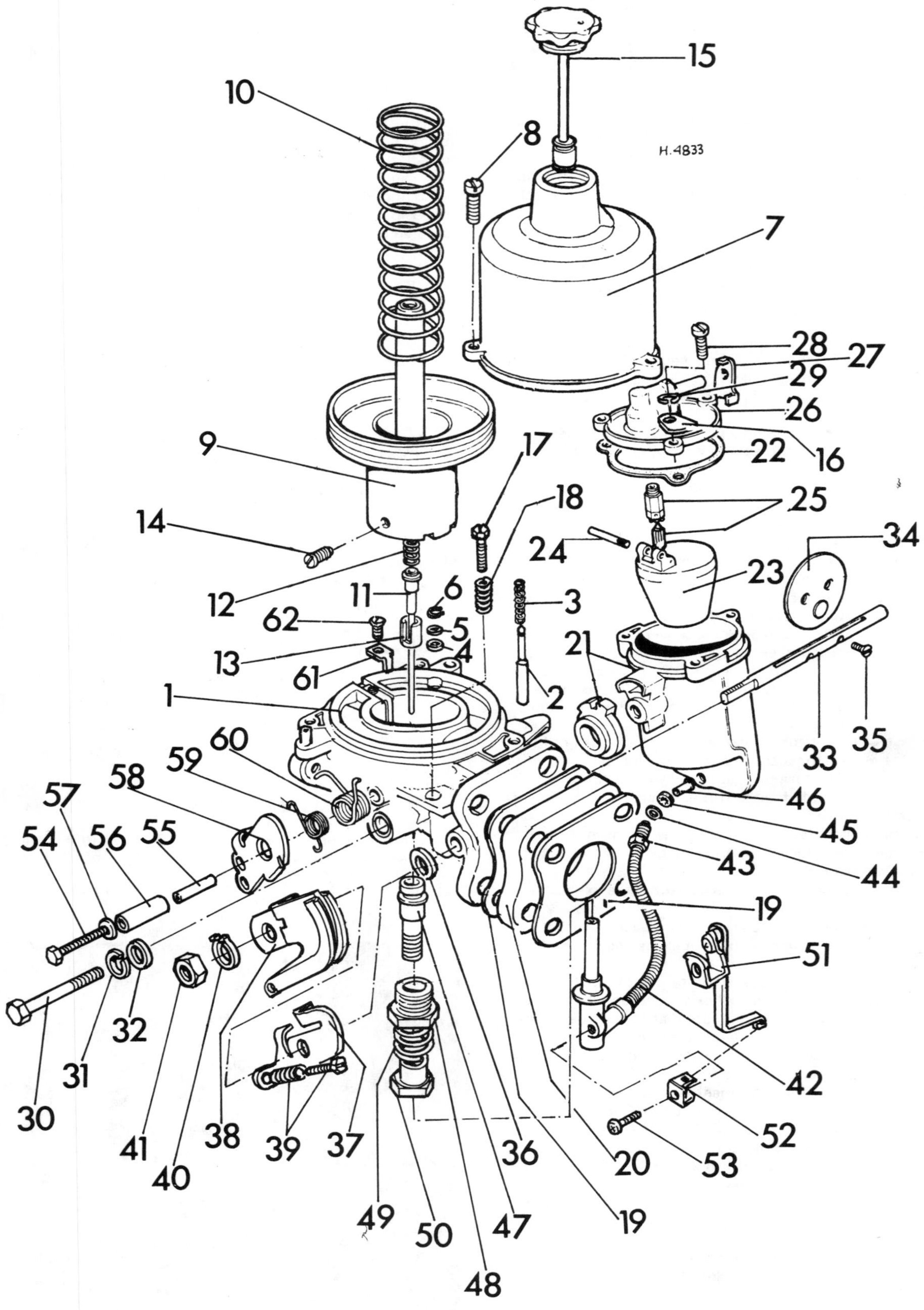

H.4833

Fig. 3.12 Exploded view of the single (type HS6) carburettor (Sec. 11)

**Fig. 3.12 Exploded view of the single (type HS6) carburettor (Sec. 11)**

1 Body
2 Piston lifting pin
3 Spring for pin
4 Sealing washer
5 Plain washer
6 Circlip
7 Piston chamber
8 Screw - piston chamber
9 Piston
10 Spring
11 Needle
12 Spring - needle
13 Support guide - needle
14 Needle locking grub screw
15 Piston damper
16 Identification tag
17 Throttle adjusting screw
18 Spring for screw
19 Joint washers
20 Insualtor block
21 Float - chamber and spacer
22 Joint washer - chamber
23 Float
24 Hinge pin - float
25 Fuel inlet needle valve/seat
26 Lid - float-chamber
27 Baffle plate
28 Screw - float-chamber lid
29 Spring washer
30 Bolt - securing float-chamber
31 Spring washer
32 Plain washer
33 Throttle spindle
34 Throttle butterfly valve plate
35 Screw - securing disc assembly
36 Washer - throttle spindle
37 Throttle return lever
38 Progressive throttle (snail cam)
39 Fast idle screw and spring
40 Lock washer - throttle spindle nut
41 Nut - throttle spindle
42 Jet assembly
43 Sleeve nut - jet flexible pipe
44 Washer
45 Gland
46 Ferrule
47 Sealing washer
48 Jet locating nut
49 Spring
50 Jet adjusting nut
51 Pick-up lever
52 Link - pick-up lever
53 Screw - securing lever to jet
54 Pivot bolt
55 Pivot bolt tube - inner
56 Pivot bolt tube - outer
57 Distance washer
58 Cam lever
59 Spring - cam lever
60 Spring - pick-up lever
61 Guide - suction chamber piston
62 Screw - securing guide

occurred in the throttle spindle or associated parts.

8   Remove the suction chamber after having first marked its position in relation to the carburettor body.

9   Remove the piston spring and lift out the piston assembly.

10  Extract the grub screw and withdraw the needle assembly.

11  Remove the needle from its guide and extract the spring from the needle.

12  Extract the circlip and dismantle the lifting pin.

13  Remove the screw which retains the jet pick-up link and link bracket (Fig. 3.16).

14  Unscrew the flexible jet tube union nut from the float-chamber and withdraw the jet assembly.

15  Remove the jet adjusting nut and spring followed by the jet locking nut and jet bearing.

16  Dismantle the lever assembly.

17  Remove the float-chamber and spacer (one bolt) and then mark the position of the lid and remove it (three screws).

18  Withdraw the float pivot pin by holding its knurled end with a pair of pliers. Extract the fuel inlet needle and float and then unscrew the needle seat from the lid.

19  Dismantle the throttle valve only if essential. First mark the relative position of the butterfly valve plate to the carburettor flange and then

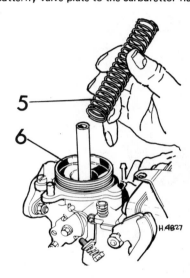

**Fig. 3.13 Single carburettor piston spring (5) and piston assembly (6) (Sec. 11)**

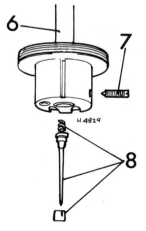

**Fig. 3.14 Needle assembly (single carburettor) (Sec. 11)**

6   Piston
7   Grub screw
8   Needle and spring

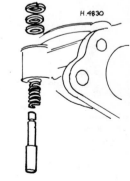

**Fig. 3.15 Lifting pin component (single carburettor) (Sec. 11)**

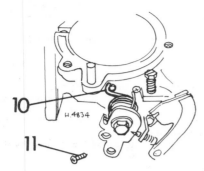

**Fig. 3.16 Attachment of jet pick-up lever return spring (single carburettor) (Sec. 11)**

10 Spring                              11 Link retaining screw

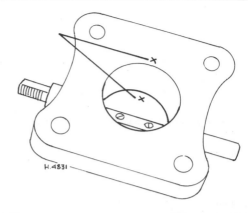

**Fig. 3.18 Throttle valve to flange alignment marks (single carburettor) (Sec. 11)**

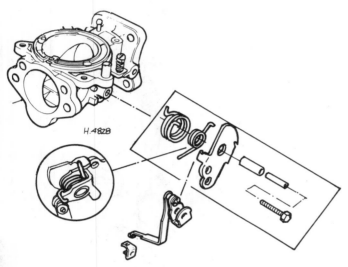

**Fig. 3.17 Attachment of cam lever spring (single carburettor) (Sec. 11)**

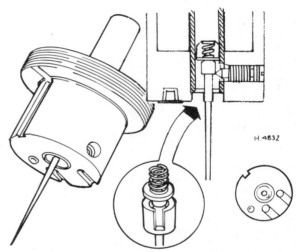

**Fig. 3.19 Needle setting (Secs. 11 and 12)**

dismantle the lever/cam components.

20 Pinch the split ends of the valve plate screws together and then remove them. Withdraw the valve plate from its slot and extract the throttle spindle.

21 With the carburettor completely dismantled, clean all components with fuel and renew any that are worn.

22 Reassembly is a reversal of dismantling but observe the following points:

   a) The countersunk sides of the holes in the throttle spindle must face outwards and the valve plate to flange marks must be in alignment before securing with new screws. Spread the ends of the screws to lock them.

   b) Fit the fuel inlet needle cone end first.

   c) The needle assembly must be fitted to the piston so that the guide is flush with the face of the piston and the etch mark aligned centrally between the piston transfer holes.

   d) Screw the jet adjustment nut up as far as possible and then down two complete turns to provide the initial setting.

23 Install the carburettor using all new joint washers.

24 Fill the piston damper with oil and then lift the piston with the finger. It should drop smoothly to the full extent of its travel in five to seven seconds. Provided the piston and chamber are clean (use fuel or methylated spirit only), any deviation from the time specified will necessitate renewal of the piston/chamber assembly as wear or distortion will be the cause.

25 Carry out the adjustments described in Section 9.

## 12 Carburettors (twin type HIF6) - removal, overhaul and refitting

1   Removal is very similar to the procedure described in Section 11,

paragraphs 1 to 7 for single carburettor installations.

2   Mark each suction chamber so that it can be refitted to its own body. Dismantle one carburettor at a time.

3   Unscrew the piston damper and pull the damper retainer directly from the piston rod.

4   Remove the suction chamber screws and lift the chamber vertically from the carburettor without tilting it. Extract the piston spring and piston assembly.

5   Remove the needle guide grub screw and withdraw the needle, guide and spring.

6   Mark the bottom cover plate in relation to the carburettor body and then remove the cover (four screws) and sealing ring.

7   Remove the jet adjusting screw and 'O' ring, the jet adjusting lever retaining screw and spring. The jet and lever assembly can now be withdrawn.

8   Remove the float pivot and fibre washer and extract the float.

9   Remove the fuel inlet needle valve and unscrew the valve seat.

10 Note how the ends of the fast idle cam lever return spring engage and then dismantle the cam lever and spring.

11 Remove the starter unit screws and cover plate, withdraw the starter unit and its gasket.

12 Remove the valve spindle and extract the 'O' ring seals and dust cap.

13 Note how the ends of the throttle lever return spring are engaged and remove the spring.

14 Dismantle the throttle levers and then close the throttle butterfly valve plate and mark the valve plate in relation to the carburettor flange. Remove the throttle plate screws, extract the valve plate, spindle and seals, taking care not to damage the over-run valve during the process.

15 Clean all components and examine for wear. Renew all rubber seals as a matter of routine.

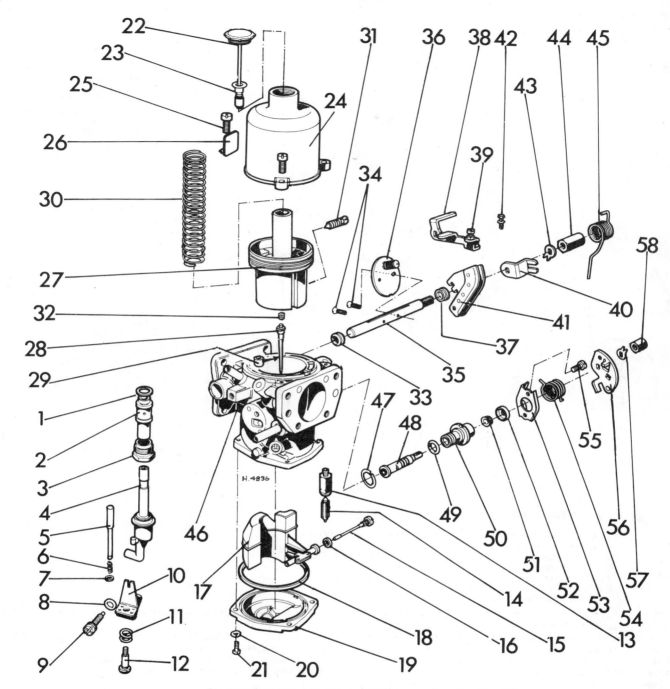

**Fig. 3.20 Exploded view of twin (HIF6) type carburettor (Sec. 12)**

1 Jet bearing washer
2 Jet bearing
3 Jet bearing nut
4 Jet assembly
5 Lifting pin
6 Lifting pin spring
7 Circlip
8 Adjusting screw seal
9 Jet adjusting screw
10 Bi-metal jet lever
11 Jet spring
12 Jet retaining screw
13 Fuel inlet needle seat
14 Fuel inlet needle valve
15 Float pivot

16 Pivot seat
17 Float
18 Float chamber cover seal
19 Float chamber cover
20 Spring washer
21 Cover screw
22 Piston damper
23 Damper retainer
24 Suction chamber - ball bearing
25 Chamber screw
26 Identity tag
27 Piston
28 Jet needle
29 Needle guide
30 Piston spring

31 Needle retaining grub screw
32 Needle spring
33 Throttle spindle seal
34 Throttle plate screws
35 Throttle spindle
36 Throttle butterfly valve plate
37 Throttle spindle seal
38 Throttle actuating lever
39 Fast idle screw and nut
40 Throttle lever
41 Cam lever - progressive throttle
42 Throttle adjusting screw and nut
43 Tab washer
44 Retaining nut

45 Throttle spring
46 Body
47 Cold start seal
48 Cold start spindle
49 'O' ring
50 Cold start body
51 Spindle seal
52 End cover
53 Retaining plate
54 Cold start spring
55 Retaining screw
56 Fast idle cam
57 Tab washer
58 Retaining nut

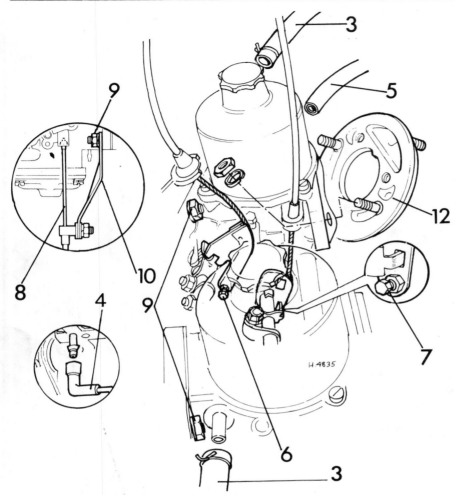

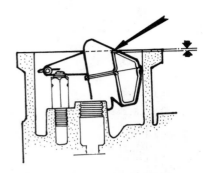

Fig. 3.22a Float setting diagrams (twin carburettor) (Sec. 12)

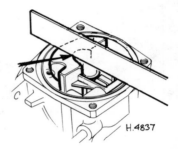

Fig. 3.22b Setting jet flush with bridge of carburettor body (twin carburettor) (Sec. 12)

Fig. 3.21 Twin carburettor controls (Sec. 12)

3   Engine extractor hoses
4   Distributor vacuum pipe
5   Fuel inlet hose
6   Throttle cable trunnion
7   Choke cable trunnion
8   Downshift cable
    (automatic transmission)
9   Carburettor securing nuts
10  Downshift cable support
    bracket (automatic
    transmission)
12  Air intake adaptor

16 Check that all the balls are in position in the piston ball race (2 rows of 6). Fit the piston to the suction chamber (without the damper or spring), and holding the assembly horizontally, spin the piston. There should be no tendency to stick. It it does, and the components have been cleaned, then it is probably due to distortion and the piston/chamber assembly must be renewed.

17 Reassembly is a reversal of dismantling but observe the following points:

a) Align the throttle valve plate marks before installing and check that the over-run valve is at the top of the bore with its spring towards the inside of the carburettor when the valve plate is closed. Always use new throttle plate screws and spread their ends to lock them.

b) Fit the starter unit valve with its cut-out towards the top retaining screw hole and its retaining plate having its slotted flange towards the throttle spindle.

c) Check the float level by inverting the carburettor and checking that the point indicated on the float is 0.04 in. (+0.02 in.) - 1.0 mm (+0.5 mm) below the face of the float chamber. Bend the brass tab if necessary to adjust the setting.

d) Engage the smaller diameter of the jet adjusting screw with the slot in the adjusting lever and then set the jet flush with the bridge of the carburettor body.

e) Use a new needle retaining grub screw, make sure that the etch mark on the needle is between the piston transfer holes and that

the shoulder of the needle is flush with the piston face (not the recess). (Fig. 3.19)

18 Install the carburettors by reversing the removal operations but using all new joint washers.

19 Carry out the adjustments described in Section 10 after having filled both piston dampers with engine oil.

## 13 Accelerator cable and pedal - removal and refitting

1   The accelerator (throttle) controls are correctly set when there is about 1/16 in. (2.0 mm) free-movement at the pedal before the cam on the carburettor begins to move.

2   To achieve this, adjust the position of the inner cable in the cam plate trunnion by slackening the pinch bolt.

3   To install a new cable, disconnect it from the carburettor cam plate trunnion and then pull off the spring clip and release the cable from the pedal arm cut-out.

4   Pull the complete cable assembly through the engine bulkhead grommet.

5   Refitting the new cable is a reversal of removal.

6   If the accelerator pedal is to be removed, this can be done after disconnecting the cable and unscrewing the pedal bracket securing nuts and setscrews.

Fig. 3.23 Method of securing accelerator cable to pedal arm (Sec. 13)

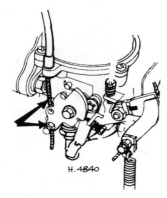

Fig. 3.25 Choke cable connection to single carburettor (Sec. 14)

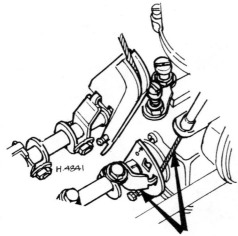

Fig. 3.26 Choke cable connection to twin carburettor (Sec. 14)

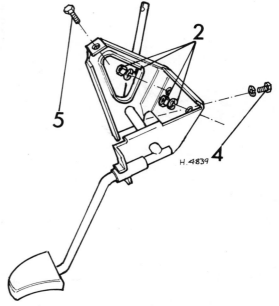

Fig. 3.24 Accelerator pedal attachment (Sec. 13)

2  Brake servo stud nuts                4 and 5 Setscrews

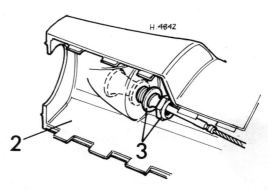

Fig. 3.27 Choke control (Sec. 14)

2  Steering column shroud              3  Locknut and lockwasher

## 14 Choke control cable - removal and refitting

1  To remove the choke cable, detach the cable from the carburettor lever.
2  Remove the left-hand steering column shroud (two screws) and release the choke knob locknut.
3  Pull the complete cable assembly into the car interior, extracting the locknut and lockwasher.
4  Refitting is a reversal of removal but make sure that the control knob has a little free-movement when the operating lever on the carburettor is in the fully off position.

## 15 Manifolds and exhaust system - removal and refitting

1  Remove the air cleaner and carburettor(s), as described in earlier Sections of this Chapter. Disconnect the brake servo hose.
2  *On four cylinder cars,* remove the heat shield from the intake manifold, also the insulation block, gaskets and throttle cable abutment bracket. Disconnect the exhaust pipe 'U' bolt from the stay on the

transmission casing. Release the downpipe from the exhaust manifold by unscrewing the clamp bolts.
3  Remove the hot air shroud flange (two screws) from the exhaust manifold hot air shroud.
4  Unbolt the manifold (six bolts) from the cylinder head and remove the hot air shroud, two distance washers, the manifold assembly and gasket.
5  *On six cylinder cars,* remove the alternator heat shield and disconnect the two exhaust downpipes by removing the clamps. Slacken the bolt which secures the front stay to the bracket on the transmission casing so that the downpipes can clear the manifold flanges (photo).
6  Unbolt the manifold and heater pipe from the cylinder head (ten bolts, two nuts) and remove it together with gasket.
7  Refitting is a reversal of removal but use new gaskets and tighten nuts and bolts to the specified torque wrench settings (photo).
8  Removal of the exhaust system is simply a matter of disconnecting the downpipes from the manifold and the transmission casing and then releasing the system mountings. Withdraw the complete system from beneath the car, jacking-up, if necessary, to obtain better access.
9  It is not recommended that corroded or damaged sections of the exhaust system are removed while the system is still in position as

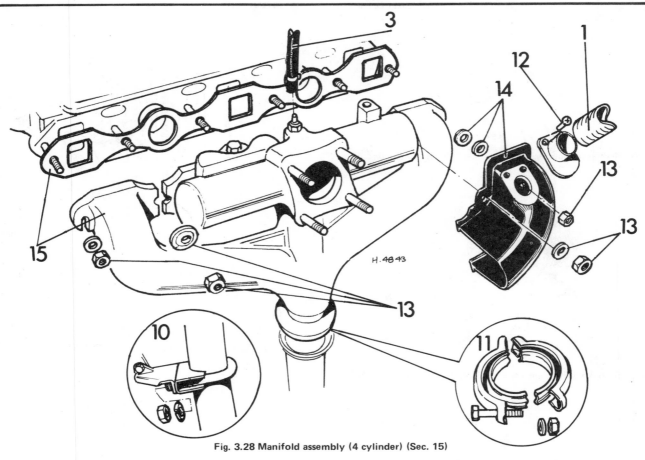

Fig. 3.28 Manifold assembly (4 cylinder) (Sec. 15)

1   Hot air duct
3   Brake servo hose
10  Exhaust 'U' bolt
    to transmission

11  Downpipe to
    manifold clamp
12  Hot air shroud
    securing screws

13  Manifold securing nuts
14  Hot air shroud and
    distance washers
15  Manifold and gasket

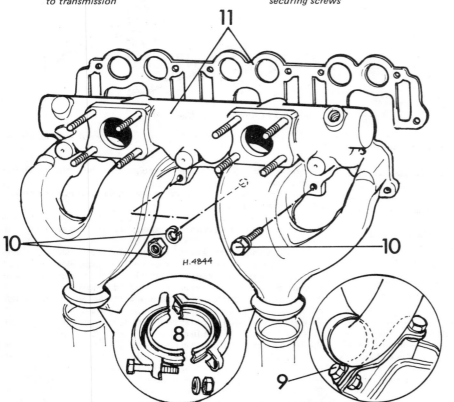

Fig. 3.29 Manifold assembly (6 cylinder)
(Sec. 15)

8   Twin downpipe clamps
9   Exhaust bracket to transmission
10  Securing bolts and nuts
11  Manifold and gasket

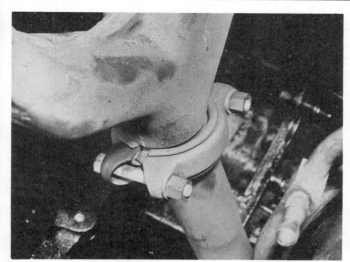

15.5 Correct installation of an exhaust downpipe clamp and bolts
(6 cylinder twin carburettor)

15.7 New manifold gasket installed (6 cylinder)

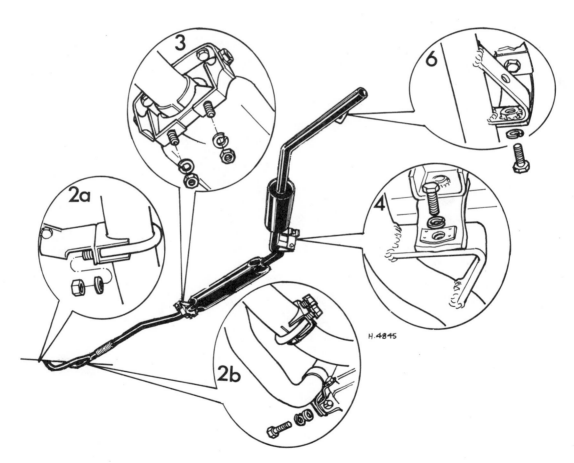

Fig. 3.30 Exhaust system components (Sec. 15)

2a  4 cylinder downpipe
2b  6 cylinder downpipe

3   Silencer front mounting
4   Intermediate mounting

6   Tailpipe mounting

further damage can be caused to good sections and the mountings distorted. It is better to remove the complete system where more purchase can be applied to disengage the sections.

10 Reassemble the new components but do not tighten any pipe clamps until the system has been installed on its mountings and the silencer and expansion box checked for correct alignment.

## 16 Fault diagnosis - fuel system and carburation

| Symptom | Reason/s |
| --- | --- |
| Fuel consumption excessive | Air cleaner choked giving rich mixture.<br>Leak from tank, pump or fuel lines.<br>Float chamber flooding due to incorrect level or worn needle valve.<br>Carburettor(s) incorrectly adjusted.<br>Idling speed too high.<br>Incorrect valve clearances. |
| Lack of power, stalling or difficult starting | Faulty fuel pump.<br>Leak on suction side of pump or in fuel line.<br>Intake manifold or carburettor flange gaskets leaking.<br>Carburettor(s) incorrectly adjusted. |
| Poor or erratic idling | Weak mixture.<br>Leak in intake manifold.<br>Leak in distributor vacuum pipe.<br>Leak in crankcase extractor hose.<br>Leak in brake servo hose. |

# Chapter 4 Ignition system

**Contents**

**Specifications**

**System type** ... ... ... ... ... ... ... ... ... Battery, coil and distributor

**Firing order**
4 cylinder ... ... ... ... ... ... ... ... ... 1 - 3 - 4 - 2
6 cylinder ... ... ... ... ... ... ... ... ... 1 - 5 - 3 - 6 - 2 - 4

**Ignition timing** (initial advance at 1000 rev/min, vacuum line disconnected)
4 cylinder ... ... ... ... ... ... ... ... ... $10^o$ BTDC
6 cylinder ... ... ... ... ... ... ... ... ... $12^o$ BTDC

**Note:** *These figures correspond to an approximate static setting of $8^o$ BTDC and $11^o$ BTDC respectively*

**Dwell angle**
4 cylinder ... ... ... ... ... ... ... ... ... $51^o \pm 5^o$
6 cylinder ... ... ... ... ... ... ... ... ... $33^o \pm 5^o$

**Spark plugs**
Type ... ... ... ... ... ... ... ... ... ... Champion N9Y
Gap ... ... ... ... ... ... ... ... ... ... 0.025 in (0.65 mm)

**Coil**
Type:
    Up to 1975 ... ... ... ... ... ... ... ... Lucas HA12
    1975 on 4 cylinder ... ... ... ... ... ... ... Lucas BA7 with ballast resistor
    1975 on 6 cylinder ... ... ... ... ... ... ... Lucas 16C-6 with ballast resistor
Condenser capacity ... ... ... ... ... ... ... ... 0.18 to 0.24 microfarad

**Distributor**
Type:
    4 cylinder ... ... ... ... ... ... ... ... Lucas 45D4 (no. 41415)
    6 cylinder ... ... ... ... ... ... ... ... Lucas 45D6 (no. 41440)
Rotation ... ... ... ... ... ... ... ... ... ... Anticlockwise
Contact breaker gap ... ... ... ... ... ... ... ... 0.014 to 0.016 in (0.35 to 0.40 mm)

| | 4 cylinder | 6 cylinder |
|---|---|---|
| Centrifugal advance: | | |
| Starts ... ... ... ... ... ... ... ... ... | 500 rev/min | 800 rev/min |
| | $2^o$ to $6^o$ @ 1200 | $1^o$ to $5^o$ @ 1300 |
| | $10^o$ to $14^o$ @ 2200 | $4^o$ to $8^o$ @ 1600 |
| | $18^o$ to $22^o$ @ 3200 | $9^o$ to $13^o$ @ 2000 |
| | 24 to $28^o$ @ 4400 | $14^o$ to $18^o$ @ 2400 |

Vacuum advance:
    4 cylinder, pre 1976
        Starts ... ... ... ... ... ... ... ... ... 1 in (25 mm) Hg
        Maximum... ... ... ... ... ... ... ... ... $12^o$ @ 7 in (188 mm) Hg
    4 cylinder, 1976 on
        Starts ... ... ... ... ... ... ... ... ... 4 in (102 mm) Hg
        Maximum... ... ... ... ... ... ... ... ... $16^o$ @ 12 in (305 mm) Hg
    6 cylinder:
        Starts ... ... ... ... ... ... ... ... ... 3 in (76 mm) Hg
        Maximum ... ... ... ... ... ... ... ... ... $16^o$ @ 9 in (230 mm) Hg

| **Torque wrench settings** | lb/ft | Nm |
|---|---|---|
| Spark plugs ... ... ... ... ... ... ... ... ... | 18 | 24 |

## 1  General description

In order that the engine can run correctly it is necessary for an electrical spark to ignite the fuel/air mixture in the combustion chamber at exactly the right moment in relation to engine speed and load. The ignition system is based on feeding low tension (LT) voltage from the battery to the coil where it is converted to high tension (HT) voltage. The high tension voltage is powerful enough to jump the spark plug gap in the cylinders many times a second under high compression pressures, providing that the system is in good condition and that all adjustments are correct.

The ignition system is divided into two circuits: the low tension circuit and the high tension circuit.

The low tension (sometimes known as the primary) circuit consists of the battery lead to the starter solenoid, lead to the ignition switch, lead from the ignition switch to the low tension or primary coil windings (terminal +), and the lead from the low tension coil windings (coil terminal —) to the contact breaker points and condenser in the distributor.

The high tension circuit consists of the high tension or secondary coil windings, the heavy ignition lead from the centre of the coil to the centre of the distributor cap, the rotor arm, and the spark plug leads and spark plugs.

The system functions in the following manner. Low tension voltage is changed in the coil into high tension voltage by the opening and closing of the contact breaker points in the low tension circuit. High tension voltage is then fed via the carbon brush in the centre of the distributor cap to the rotor arm of the distributor cap, and each time it comes in line with one of the metal segments in the cap, which are connected to the spark plug leads, the opening and closing of the contact breaker points causes the high tension voltage to build up, jump the gap from the rotor arm to the appropriate metal segment and so via the spark plug lead to the spark plug, where it finally jumps the spark plug gap before going to earth.

The ignition is advanced and retarded automatically, to ensure the spark occurs at just the right instant for the particular load at the prevailing engine speed.

The ignition advance is controlled both mechanically and by a vacuum operated system. The mechanical governor mechanism comprises two weights, which move out from the distributor shaft, and so advance the spark. The weights are held in position by two light springs and it is the tension of the springs which is largely responsible for correct spark advancement.

The vacuum control consists of a diaphragm, one side of which is connected via a small bore tube to the carburettor, and the other side to the contact breaker plate. Depression in the inlet manifold and carburettor, which varies with engine speed and throttle opening, causes the diaphragm to move, so moving the contact breaker plate, and advancing or retarding the spark. A fine degree of control is achieved by a spring in the vacuum assembly.

## 2  Contact breaker gap - adjustment

1  Prise off the distributor cap spring clips and remove the cap and lay it to one side. Do not disconnect the HT leads from it. Withdraw the rotor arm.
2  Turn the crankshaft until the heel of the breaker arm is on the high point of a cam lobe. The crankshaft can either be turned by applying a ring spanner to the crankshaft pulley bolt or by engaging top gear and pushing the car forward. Either method will be facilitated if the spark plugs are first removed.
3  Using feeler blades, check the gap is according to specification. If the points have been in use for a considerable mileage, do not make a false assessment of the gap as there will probably be a 'pip' on one face which will make precise checking impossible. In this case, the points should be dressed or renewed as described in the following Section (photo).
4  If adjustment is required, slacken the contact set securing screw and insert a screwdriver in the slot provided and gently move the breaker arm until the clearance is correct. Retighten the securing screw.
5  Before fitting the rotor arm, apply a few drops of oil to the felt pad in the centre of the cam and also squirt a few drops into the two holes in the baseplate to lubricate the mechanical advance mechanism. Smear the cam lobes with petroleum jelly.

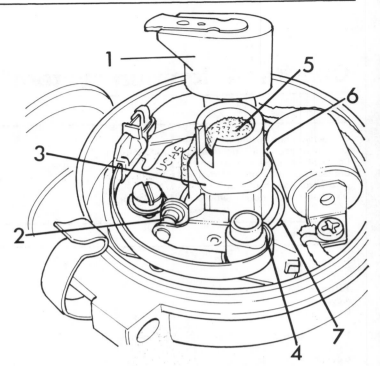

Fig. 4.1 View of distributor (6 cylinder) with cap removed (Sec. 2)

1  Rotor arm
2  Contact points
3  Cam
4  Pivot post
5  Felt lubrication pad
6 and 7  Oiling holes in baseplate

2.3 Checking points gap

6  Fit the rotor arm, wipe out the interior of the distributor cap and examine the central carbon brush before installing the cap.
7  It should be noted that where a dwell meter is available, a more precise gap setting will be obtained (refer to dwell angle - Specifications Section), using this instrument.

## 3  Contact breaker points - removal and refitting

1  Remove the distributor cap and rotor arm.
2  Remove the contact set securing screw together with the spring and flat washers.
3  Press the spring arm of the movable breaker arm towards the cam

**Measuring plug gap.** A feeler gauge of the correct size (see ignition system specifications) should have a slight 'drag' when slid between the electrodes. Adjust gap if necessary

**Adjusting plug gap.** The plug gap is adjusted by bending the earth electrode inwards, or outwards, as necessary until the correct clearance is obtained. Note the use of the correct tool

**Normal.** Grey-brown deposits, lightly coated core nose. Gap increasing by around 0.001 in (0.025 mm) per 1000 miles (1600 km). Plugs ideally suited to engine, and engine in good condition

**Carbon fouling.** Dry, black, sooty deposits. Will cause weak spark and eventually misfire. Fault: over-rich fuel mixture. Check: carburettor mixture settings, float level and jet sizes; choke operation and cleanliness of air filter. Plugs can be re-used after cleaning

**Oil fouling.** Wet, oily deposits. Will cause weak spark and eventually misfire. Fault: worn bores/piston rings or valve guides; sometimes occurs (temporarily) during running-in period. Plugs can be re-used after thorough cleaning

**Overheating.** Electrodes have glazed appearance, core nose very white — few deposits. Fault: plug overheating. Check: plug value, ignition timing, fuel octane rating (too low) and fuel mixture (too weak). Discard plugs and cure fault immediately

**Electrode damage.** Electrodes burned away; core nose has burned, glazed appearance. Fault: pre-ignition. Check: as for 'Overheating' but may be more severe. Discard plugs and remedy fault before piston or valve damage occurs

**Split core nose (may appear initially as a crack).** Damage is self-evident, but cracks will only show after cleaning. Fault: pre-ignition or wrong gap-setting technique. Check: ignition timing, cooling system, fuel octane rating (too low) and fuel mixture (too weak). Discard plugs, rectify fault immediately

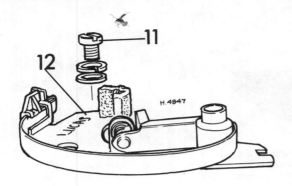

Fig. 4.2 Contact set (Sec. 3)

*11 Securing screw*            *12 Fixed contact*

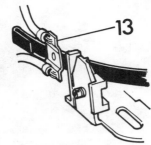

Fig. 4.3 Movable contact arm and terminal plate (13) (Sec. 3)

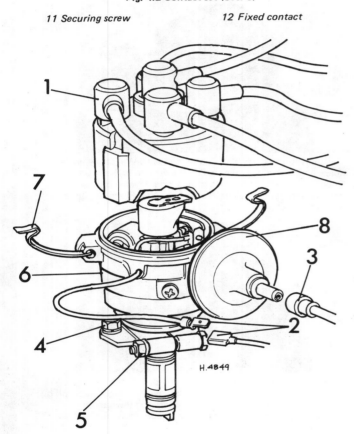

Fig. 4.4  4 cylinder type distributor
(Sec. 5)

1  HT lead              5  Pinch bolt
2  LT lead              6  Distributor body
3  Vacuum pipe          7  Cap clip
4  Clamp plate screw

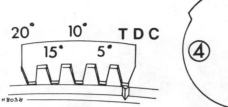

Fig. 4.5  Ignition timing marks
(4 cylinder)        (Sec. 5)

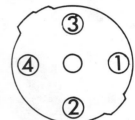

Fig. 4.6 Fitting sequence diagram
(4 cylinder distributor cap to
spark plugs) (Sec. 5)

## 4  Condenser (capacitor) - removal, testing and refitting

1   The condenser ensures that with the contact breaker points open, the sparking between them is not excessive to cause severe pitting. The condenser is fitted in parallel and its failure will automatically cause failure of the ignition system as the points will be prevented from interrupting the low tension circuit.
2   Testing for an unserviceable condenser may be effected by switching on the ignition and separating the contact points by hand. If this action is accompanied by a blue flash then condenser failure is indicated. Difficult starting, missing of the engine after several miles running or badly pitted points are other indications of a faulty condenser.
3   The surest test is by substitution of a new unit.
4   Removal of the condenser is by means of withdrawing the screw which retains it to the distributor baseplate. Replacement is a reversal of this procedure.

## 5  Distributor (4 cylinder) - removal and installation

1   To withdraw the distributor, disconnect the HT leads from the spark plugs.
2   Disconnect the LT lead at the terminal connector.
3   Disconnect the vacuum pipe.
4   Slacken one of the screws which secure the distributor clamp plate to the cylinder block and then slacken the clamp plate pinch bolt and withdraw the distributor complete.
5   *If the distributor driveshaft is not disturbed,* installation of the distributor is simply a matter of aligning the small and large segments of the driveshafts and pushing it into its recess.
6   Turn the crankshaft until the timing mark on the crankshaft pulley indicates 8° BTDC on the transmission case scale. The scale markings are in increments of 5°, so the setting will depend on the keenness of the eye; this setting allows for approximately 2° of additional advance at an engine speed of 1000 rev/min. Turn the distributor body until the contact points are just opening, and tighten the clamp plate bolts.
7   If the distributor driveshaft is removed, it must be installed, as described in Chapter 1, Section 67, before refitting the distributor.
8   Reconnect the spark plug leads in accordance with the diagram and remake all other connections (Fig. 4.6).
9   Check and adjust the ignition timing more precisely, as described in Section 7, using a stroboscope.

and release it from the terminal plate.
4   If the points are not badly pitted or corroded, draw a piece of fine 'wet and dry' paper between them to clean them and then refit them. If they are badly worn or pitted, renew them. Severely pitted points may be due to a poor earth (battery or engine earth strap), a faulty condenser or poor earth connection inside the distributor (condenser securing screw or baseplate earth wire).
5   Before fitting new points, wipe their faces clean with methylated spirit and lightly grease the pivot post.
6   After fitting the contact set, adjust the gap, as described in the preceding Section.
7   Apply a smear of petroleum jelly to the lobes of the cam.

## 6 Distributor (6 cylinder) - removal and installation

1   The procedure is similar to that described in the preceding Section, except that if the driveshaft is removed, then it must be installed after reference to Chapter 1, Sections 71 or 74, according to transmission type. The setting for 6 cylinder models should be 11° BTDC, which allows for approximately 1° of additional advance at an engine speed of 1000 rev/min.

## 7 Ignition timing - checking and adjustment

1   In order to obtain more precise ignition timing than is possible with

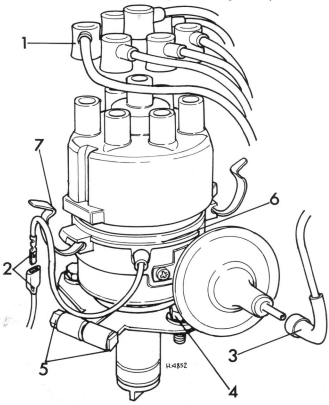

Fig. 4.7. 6 cylinder type distributor
(Sec. 6)

| | | | |
|---|---|---|---|
| 1 | HT lead | 5 | Pinch bolt |
| 2 | LT lead | 6 | Distributor body |
| 3 | Vacuum pipe | 7 | Cap clip |
| 4 | Clamp plate | | |

the method described in Section 5 or 6, carry out the following operations.

2   Mark the notch on the crankshaft pulley and the appropriate mark on the transmission cover scale (see Specifications according to engine type) with white paint or chalk.

3   Disconnect the vacuum pipe from the distributor and plug the pipe.

4   Connect a timing light (stroboscope) in accordance with the manufacturer's instructions. This is usually between the end of No. 1 spark plug lead and the spark plug terminal.

5   Start the engine and let it idle at 1000 rev/min.

6   Point the stroboscope at the white marks when they will appear stationary and if the timing is correct, in alignment. If the marks do not appear to be in alignment, release the distributor clamp plate pinch bolt and turn the distributor body fractionally in either direction until the timing marks coincide.

7   Retighten the pinch bolt, switch off the engine and remake the original connections.

## 8 Distributor - overhaul

1   Before overhauling a well worn distributor, consideration should be given to obtaining a factory reconditioned unit. If it is decided to dismantle the original unit, first check the availability of spare parts.

2   With the distributor removed as previously described in this Chapter, withdraw the cap and rotor arm and extract the felt lubrication pad from the centre of the cam.

3   Remove the two vacuum unit retaining screws, tilt the unit to disengage the operating arm and then withdraw the vacuum unit.

4   Push the low tension lead and grommet into the interior of the distributor body.

5   Remove the baseplate securing screw, prise the baseplate from its groove and lift it from the distributor body.

6   Drive out the pin which secures the drive dog to the distributor shaft and remove the dog and thrust washer.

7   Withdraw the shaft assembly from the body.

8   Remove the condenser, contact set and leads from the baseplate.

9   Do not dismantle the advance mechanism other than for renewal of the small control springs. If wear has occurred, then the complete shaft assembly will have to be renewed. Any wear in the shaft bearings will necessitate renewal of the complete distributor.

10 Reassembly is a reversal of dismantling but observe the following:
   a)  Apply grease to the shaft bearing surfaces.
   b)  Fit the shaft thrust washer with raised pips towards the drive dog and the tongues of the drive dog parallel to and left of the rotor arm centre-line when the electrode end of the rotor arm is pointing vertically upwards. If a new shaft has been installed, it is supplied undrilled and it will have to be drilled in-line with the

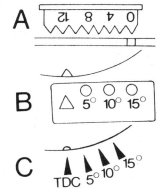

Fig. 4.8. Ignition timing marks (6 cylinder)
(Sec. 5)

A   Up to mid 1976
B   Mid 1976 on — manual gearbox

C   Mid 1976 on — automatic
     transmission

Fig. 4.9 Fitting sequence diagram
(6 cylinder distributor cap to
spark plugs) (Sec. 6)

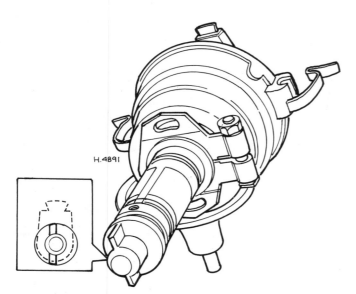

Fig. 4.10 Drive dog to rotor arm relationship (Sec. 8)

holes in the drive dog using a 3/16 in. (4.75 mm) drill at the same time pressing the shaft (at the cam end) and the drive dog towards each other. Stake the drive dog securing pin and then tap the end of the drive dog to flatten the pips on the thrust washer enough to provide the specified endfloat of 0.002 to 0.005 in. (0.0508 to 0.1270 mm).
c) Locate the baseplate so that the two prongs will fit either side of the screw hole below the cap clip and then press the baseplate down to engage it in the undercut of the body.

## 9  Coil polarity and testing

1   High tension current should be negative at the spark plug terminals. Check that the LT lead from the distributor connects with the negative (–) terminal on the coil.
2   1977 and later 4 cylinder models have a ballast resistor incorporated in the coil circuit.
3   Without special equipment, the best method of testing for a faulty coil is by substitution of a new unit. Before doing this however, check the security of the connecting leads and remove any corrosion which may have built up in the coil HT socket.

## 10 Spark plugs and HT leads

1   The correct functioning of the spark plugs is vital for the correct running and efficiency of the engine. The plugs fitted as standard are listed on the Specifications page.
2   At intervals of 6000 miles (9600 km) the plugs should be removed, examined and cleaned. If worn excessively, renew the plugs at 12,000 miles (19600 km). The condition of the spark plug will also tell much about the overall condition of the engine.
3   If the insulator nose of the spark plug is clean and white, with no deposits, this is indicative of a weak mixture, or too hot a plug. (A hot plug transfers heat away from the electrode slowly – a cold plug transfers it away quickly).
4   If the top and insulator nose is covered with hard black looking deposits, then this is indicative that the mixture is too rich. Should the plug be black and oily, then it is likely that the engine is fairly worn, as well as the mixture being too rich.
5   If the insulator nose is covered with light tan to greyish brown deposits, then the mixture is correct and it is likely that the engine is in

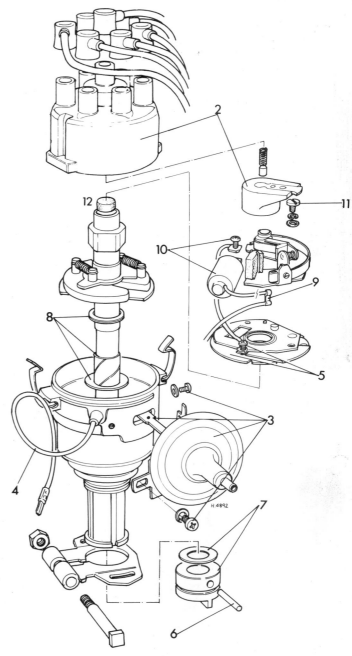

Fig. 4.11 Exploded view of the distributor
(6 cylinder type shown) (Sec. 8)

2   Cap and rotor arm
3   Vacuum unit
4   LT lead
5   Baseplate assembly
6   Drive dog to shaft pin
7   Drive dog and thrust washer
8   Shaft assembly with spacer and steel washer
9   Terminal plate
10  Condenser
11  Contact set screw
12  Lubrication pad

good condition.

6   If there are any traces of long brown tapering stains on the outside of the white portion of the plug, then the plug will have to be renewed, as this shows that there is a faulty joint between the plug body and the insulator, and compression is being allowed to leak away.

7   Plugs should be cleaned by a sand blasting machine, which will free them from carbon more thoroughly than cleaning by hand. The machine will also test the condition of the plugs under compression. Any plug that fails to spark at the recommended pressure should be renewed.

8   The spark plug gap is of considerable importance, as, if it is too large or too small the size of the spark and its efficiency will be seriously impaired. The spark plug gap should be set to 0.025 in. (0.65 mm) for the best results.

9   To set it, measure the gap with a feeler gauge, and then bend open, or close, the outer plug electrode until the correct gap is achieved. The centre electrode should never be bent as this may crack the insulation and cause plug failure, if nothing worse.

10   When replacing the plugs, remember to use new plug washers and replace the leads from the distributor in the correct firing order, number 1 cylinder being the one nearest the crankshaft pulley.

11   The plug leads require no attention other than being kept clean and wiped over regularly.

## 11  Fault diagnosis - ignition system

### Engine fails to start

1   If the engine fails to start and the car was running normally when it was last used, first check there is fuel in the fuel tank. If the engine turns over normally on the starter motor and the battery is evidently well charged, then the fault may be in either the high or low tension

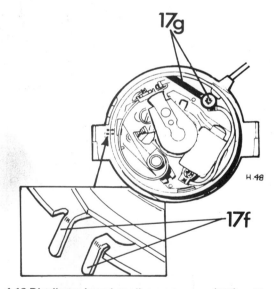

Fig. 4.12 Distributor baseplate alignment prongs (17f) and baseplate locking screw (17g) (Sec. 8)

circuits. First check the HT circuit. Note: If the battery is known to be fully charged; the ignition light comes on, and the starter motor fails to turn the engine check the tightness of the leads on the battery terminal and also the secureness of the earth lead to its connection to the body. It is quite common for the leads to have worked loose, even if they look and feel secure. If one of the battery terminal posts gets very hot when trying to work the starter motor this is a sure indication of a faulty connection to that terminal.

2   One of the commonest reasons for bad starting is wet or damp spark plug leads and distributor. Remove the distributor cap, if condensation is visible internally, dry the cap with a rag and also wipe over the leads. Replace the cap.

3   If the engine still fails to start, check that current is reaching the plugs by disconnecting each plug lead in turn at the spark plug end, and hold the end of the cable about 3/16th inch (4.8 mm) away from the cylinder block. Spin the engine on the starter motor.

4   Sparking between the end of the cable and the block should be fairly strong with a regular blue spark. (Hold the lead with rubber to avoid electric shocks). If current is reaching the plugs, then remove them and clean and regap them. The engine should now start.

5   If there is no spark at the plug leads, take off the HT lead from the centre of the distributor cap and hold it to the block as before. Spin the engine on the starter once more. A rapid succession of blue sparks between the end of the lead and the block indicate that the coil is in order and that the distributor cap is cracked, the rotor arm faulty, or the carbon brush in the top of the distributor cap is not making good contact with the spring on the rotor arm. Possibly the points are in bad condition. Clean and reset them as described in this Chapter.

6   If there are no sparks from the end of the lead from the coil, check the connections at the coil end of the lead. If it is in order start checking the low tension circuit.

7   Use a 12v voltmeter or a 12v bulb and two lengths of wire. With the ignition switch on and the points open test between the low tension wire to the coil (it is marked SW or +) and earth. No reading indicates a break in the supply from the ignition switch. Check the connections at the switch to see if any are loose. Refit them and the engine should run. A reading shows a faulty coil or condenser, or broken lead between the coil and the distributor.

8   Take the condenser wire off the points assembly and with the points open, test between the moving points and earth. If there now is a reading, then the fault is in the condenser. Fit a new one and the fault is cleared.

9   With no reading from the moving point to earth take a reading between earth and the CB or − terminal of the coil. A reading here shows a broken wire which will need to be replaced between the coil and distributor. No reading confirms that the coil has failed and must be replaced, after which the engine will run once more. Remember to refit the condenser wire to the points assembly. For these tests it is sufficient to separate the points with a piece of dry paper while testing with the points open.

### Engine misfires

10   If the engine misfires regularly, run it at a fast idling speed. Pull off each of the plug caps in turn and listen to the note of the engine. Hold the plug cap in a dry cloth or with a rubber glove as additional protection against a shock from the HT supply.

11   No difference in engine running will be noticed when the lead from the defective circuit is removed. Removing the lead from one of the good cylinders will accentuate the misfire.

12   Remove the plug lead from the end of the defective plug and hold it about 3/16th inch (4.8 mm) away from the block. Restart the engine. If the sparking is fairly strong and regular the fault must lie in the spark plug.

13   The plug may be loose, the insulation may be cracked, or the points may have burnt away giving too wide a gap for the spark to jump. Worse still, one of the points may have broken off. Either renew the plug, or clean it, reset the gap, and then test it.

14   If there is no spark at the end of the plug lead, or if it is weak and intermittent, check the ignition lead from the distributor to the plug. If the insulation is cracked or perished, renew the lead. Check the connections at the distributor cap.

15   If there is still no spark, examine the distributor cap carefully for tracking. This can be recognised by a very thin black line running between two or more electrodes or between an electrode and some other part of the distributor. These lines are paths which now conduct electricity across the cap thus letting it run to earth. The only answer is a new distributor cap.

16   Apart from the ignition timing being incorrect, other causes of misfiring have already been dealt with under the section dealing with the failure of the engine to start. To recap - these are that:

   a) the coil may be faulty giving an intermittent misfire;
   b) there may be damaged wire or loose connection in the low tension circuit;
   c) the condenser may be short circuiting;
   d) there may be a mechanical fault in the distributor (broken driving spindle or contact breaker spring).

17   If the ignition timing is too far retarded, it should be noted that the engine will tend to overheat, and there will be a quite noticeable drop in power. If the engine is overheating and the power is down and the ignition timing is correct, then the carburettor should be checked, as it is likely that this is where the fault lies.

# Chapter 5 Clutch

## Contents

## Specifications

| | |
|---|---|
| **Type** ... ... ... ... ... ... ... ... ... ... | Single dry plate, diaphragm spring, hydraulic operation |
| **Driven plate diameter** | |
| 4 cylinder ... ... ... ... ... ... ... ... ... | 8 in (203.0 mm) |
| 6 cylinder ... ... ... ... ... ... ... ... ... | 8.75 in (222.0 mm) |
| **Number of damper coil springs** ... ... ... ... ... ... | 6 |
| **Clutch release bearing** | |
| 4 cylinder ... ... ... ... ... ... ... ... ... | Carbon |
| 6 cylinder ... ... ... ... ... ... ... ... ... | Ball |
| **Master cylinder diameter** ... ... ... ... ... ... ... | 0.625 in (15.87 mm) |
| **Slave cylinder diameter** | |
| 4 cylinder ... ... ... ... ... ... ... ... ... | 1.125 in (28.57 mm) |
| 6 cylinder ... ... ... ... ... ... ... ... ... | 1.0 in (25.4 mm) |

| Torque wrench settings | lb/ft | Nm |
|---|---|---|
| *4 cylinder engine* | | |
| Slave cylinder bolts ... ... ... ... ... ... ... ... | 30 | 41 |
| Clutch pressure plate-to-flywheel bolts ... ... ... ... ... | 18 | 24 |
| Flywheel housing bolts ... ... ... ... ... ... ... ... | 30 | 41 |
| Flywheel housing-to-adaptor bolts ... ... ... ... ... ... | 18 | 25 |
| Primary drive cover screws ... ... ... ... ... ... ... | 20 | 28 |
| *6 cylinder engine* | | |
| Slave cylinder bolts ... ... ... ... ... ... ... ... | 30 | 41 |
| Diaphragm cover-to-flywheel bolts ... ... ... ... ... ... | 18 | 24 |
| Clutch release plate screws ... ... ... ... ... ... ... | 5 | 7 |
| Clutch cover plate-to-flywheel housing bolts ... ... ... ... | 6 | 8 |

## 1 General description

The clutch mechanism is of diaphragm spring type with a single driven plate. Actuation is hydraulic.

## 2 Maintenance

1 At the specified intervals, check the fluid level in the master cylinder reservoir and if necessary, top-up to the bottom of the filler neck using only recommended fluid.
2 No adjustment is required throughout the life of the driven plate.

## 3 Master cylinder - removal and refitting

1 Attach a bleed tube to the bleed nipple on the clutch slave cylinder and open the nipple. Remove the cap from the fluid reservoir and then pump the clutch pedal until all fluid has been expelled into a suitable container.
2 Disconnect the master cylinder pushrod from the clutch pedal.
3 Disconnect the hydraulic line from the master cylinder body.
4 Unscrew and remove the master cylinder flange nuts and withdraw the cylinder. The securing studs are mounted on a separate plate.
5 Refitting is a reversal of removal but bleed the system, as described in Section 7.

## 4 Master cylinder - overhaul

1 Clean the external surfaces of the assembly and detach the rubber dust excluding boot.
2 Extract the circlip and withdraw the pushrod complete with dished washer.
3 Withdraw the piston assembly.
4 Examine the surfaces of the piston and cylinder. If they are scored or show any 'bright' wear areas, the master cylinder must be renewed

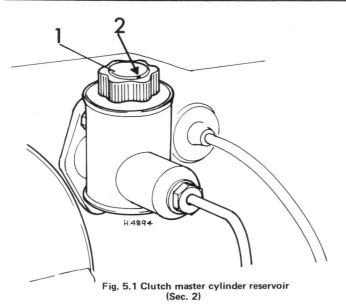

Fig. 5.1 Clutch master cylinder reservoir
(Sec. 2)

1   Cap                                        2   Breather holes

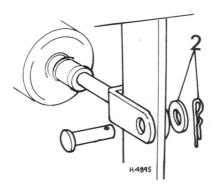

Fig. 5.2 Connection of clutch master cylinder pushrod to pedal arm
(Sec. 3)

2   Spring clip and washer

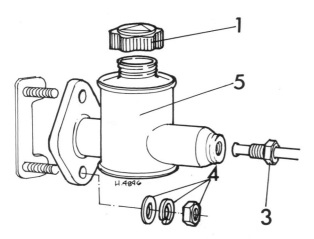

Fig. 5.3 Clutch master cylinder (Sec. 3)

1   Reservoir cap              4   Securing nuts
3   Union                      5   Reservoir

as a complete unit.

5   Where the components are in good order, remove and discard the
rubber seals and obtain a repair kit.

6   Reassembly is a reversal of dismantling but manipulate the seals
using the fingers only and dip each component in clean brake fluid
before assembling it. Note particularly that the larger diameter of the
spring enters the body first.

#### 5   Slave cylinder - removal and refitting

1   Drain the system by attaching a bleed tube to the slave cylinder
bleed nipple and after removing the reservoir cap, pumping the clutch
pedal to expel the fluid into a suitable container.

2   *On 4 cylinder cars,* disconnect the flexible hose by unscrewing the
union and locknut at the support bracket.

3   *On 6 cylinder cars,* unscrew the hollow bolt from the banjo union
and disconnect the flexible hose from the slave cylinder.

4   Unscrew and remove the two setscrews which secure the slave
cylinder to the flywheel housing, withdraw the cylinder leaving the
pushrod attached to the clutch release lever.

5   Refitting is a reversal of removal but bleed the system, as described
in Section 7.

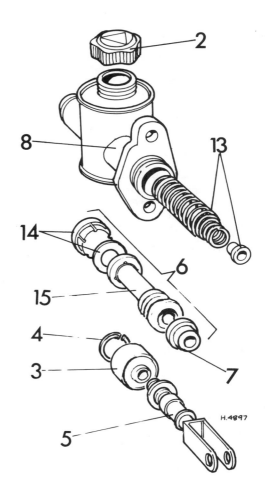

Fig. 5.4 Exploded view of clutch master cylinder (Sec. 4)

2   Reservoir cap              8    Body
3   Dust excluding boot        13   Spring and spring
4   Circlip                         retainer
5   Pushrod                    14   Main cup seal and
6   Piston assembly                 washer
7   Secondary cup seal         15   Piston

## 6   Slave cylinder - overhaul

1   Clean the external surfaces of the cylinder, release the retaining ring and remove the dust cover.
2   Extract the piston retaining circlip.
3   Extract the piston assembly either by tapping the cylinder body on a piece of wood, or by applying air from a tyre pump at the fluid inlet port.
4   Remove the return spring and bleed screw.
5   Check the piston and cylinder bore surfaces for scoring or 'bright' wear areas. If these are evident, renew the cylinder complete.
6   If the components are in good order, remove the rubber components and discard them and obtain a repair kit.
7   Reassembly is a reversal of dismantling but dip each part in clean hydraulic fluid before assembling and use only the fingers to manipulate the new seals into position. Note that the piston seal is fitted with its lip towards the small land of the piston and the return spring has its small end towards the piston.
8   There are small differences in design between the above cylinders used on 4 cylinder and 6 cylinder cars.

## 7   Hydraulic system - bleeding

1   Fill the clutch master cylinder reservoir with clean hydraulic fluid which has been stored in an airtight container and has remained unshaken for the preceding 24 hours.
2   Attach a bleed tube to the bleed screw on the slave cylinder and immerse the open end of the tube in a jar containing an inch or two of hydraulic fluid. Open the bleed screw one half a turn.
3   Have an assistant depress the clutch pedal fully, then tighten the bleed screw and allow the pedal to return unassisted. Repeat the operation until no air bubbles are seen being expelled from the end of the tube in the jar.
4   During the bleeding process, maintain the fluid level in the reservoir at least half-full and then finally top-up to the full mark when the operations are complete.

## 8   Clutch pedal - removal and refitting

1   Disconnect the clutch master cylinder pushrod from the clutch pedal. On later models also detach the pedal return spring.
2   Extract the self-tapping screw and plain washer which secure the shaft clip in position and then extract the spring clip from the clutch pedal end of the shaft.
3   Remove the insulation pad from the exterior top surface of the engine compartment bulkhead.
4   Extract the pivot shaft and remove the clutch pedal.
5   If the pedal shaft bushes are worn they can be extracted and new ones pressed in until they are just below the end faces of the pedal tubes.
6   Refitting is a reversal of removal but apply grease to the shaft bearing surfaces.

## 9   Clutch (4 cylinder) - removal, inspection and renovation

1   Removal of the flywheel housing and clutch is described in Chapter 1, Sections 9 and 28.
2   Due to the slow-wearing qualities of the clutch, it is not easy to decide when to go to the trouble of removing the gearbox in order to check the wear on the friction lining. The only positive indication that something needs doing is when it starts to slip or when squealing noises on engagement indicate that the friction lining has worn down to the rivets. In such instances it can only be hoped that the friction surfaces on the flywheel and pressure plate have not been badly worn or scored.
3   A clutch will wear according to the way in which it is used. Much intentional slipping of the clutch while driving - rather than the correct selection of gears - will accelerate wear. It is best to assume, however, that the friction disc will need renewal every 50 000 miles (80 000 km) at least and that it will be worth replacing it after 35 000 miles (56 000 km) if major overhaul is being carried out. The maintenance history of the car is obviously very useful in such cases.
4   Examine the surfaces of the pressure plate and flywheel for signs of scoring. If this is only light it may be left, but if very deep the pressure

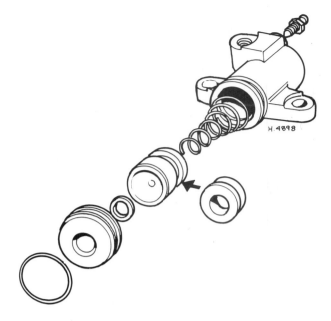

Fig. 5.5 Exploded view of 4 cylinder clutch slave cylinder (Sec. 6)

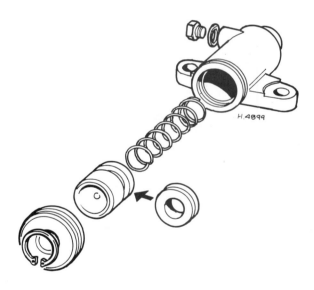

Fig. 5.6 Exploded view of 6 cylinder clutch slave cylinder (Sec. 6)

plate unit will have to be renewed. If the flywheel is deeply scored it should be taken off and advice sought from an engineering firm. Providing it may be machined completely across the face the overall balance of engine and flywheel should not be too severely upset. If renewal of the flywheel is necessary the new one will have to be balanced to match the original.
5   The friction plate lining surfaces should be at least 1/32 in. (0.8 mm) above the rivets, otherwise the disc is not worth putting back. If the lining material shows signs of breaking up or black areas where oil contamination has occured it should also be renewed. If facilities are readily available for obtaining and fitting new friction pads to the existing disc this may be done but the saving is relatively small compared with obtaining a complete new disc assembly which ensures that the shock absorbing springs and the splined hub are renewed also. The same applies to the pressure plate assembly which cannot be readily dismantled and put back together without specialised riveting tools and balancing equipment.

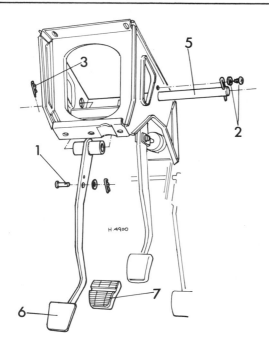

**Fig. 5.7 Clutch pedal components**

1  Pushrod clevis pin
2  Self-tapping screw
   and washer
3  Spring clip

5  Pivot shaft
6  Pedal arm
7  Pedal rubber

## 10 Clutch (6 cylinder) - removal, inspection and renovation

1   Removal of the clutch assembly is described in Chapter 1, Section 19.
2   For inspection and renovation, refer to paragraphs 2 to 5 of the preceding Section.

## 11 Clutch release bearing (4 cylinder) - renewal

1   This will normally be carried out at the same time as the clutch is overhauled.
2   If the engine/transmission is still in the car, remove the flywheel housing, as described in Chapter 1, Section 28, paragraphs 1 to 6.
3   Turn each of the clutch release bearing retaining clips through 90°

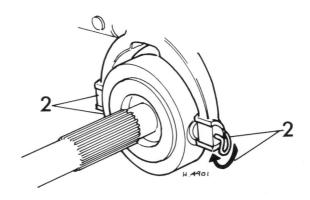

**Fig. 5.8 Carbon type release bearing (4 cylinder) (Sec. 11)**

2   Spring retaining clips

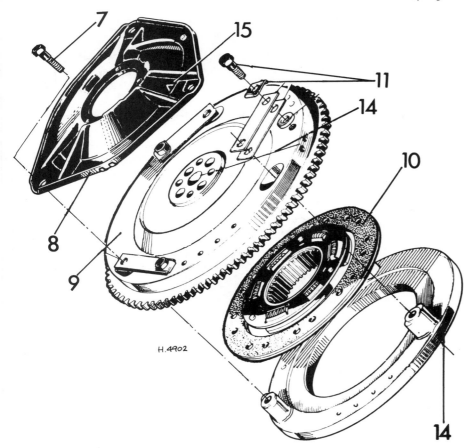

**Fig. 5.9 Clutch components (6 cylinder type) (Sec. 14)**

7   Diaphragm retaining bolt
8   Diaphragm cover
9   Flywheel
10  Driven plate
11  Driving strap bolts
14  Pressure plate mark (A) for flywheel alignment
15  Diaphragm cover alignment mark (A)

and remove the bearing from the withdrawal lever fork.

4   Refitting is a reversal of removal but always use new retaining springs.

## 12 Clutch release bearing (6 cylinder) - renewal

1   The clutch release bearing is accessible after removal of the clutch cover, as described in Chapter 1, Section 19, paragraphs 1 to 6.
2   Lift out the release bearing assembly and press the bearing from the throw-out plunger.
3   Refitting is a reversal of removal but apply grease to the lever and plunger socket.

## 13 Clutch (4 cylinder) - installation

1   With clean hands, locate the new driven plate on the flywheel so that the larger hub is away from the flywheel. The other side of the plate is normally marked FLYWHEEL SIDE.
2   A rod or stepped mandrel must now be used to centralise the driven plate before the clutch cover bolts are tightened more than finger-tight. The centralising tool must be able to pass through the splined hub of the driven plate and engage in the crankshaft spigot bush. As the tool is inserted the driven plate will be centralised and the cover bolts can then be tightened to their final specified torque.
3   Make sure that the clutch cover is correctly positioned on its

dowels.

4   Refer to Chapter 1, Section 62 and install the flywheel housing and other components.
5   Fill the primary drive reservoir with oil. To do this, remove the primary drive cover filler plug and inject 1½ pints (0.8 litre) of engine oil.

## 14 Clutch (6 cylinder) - installation

1   Locate the new driven plate on the clutch pressure plate so that the larger hub of the driven plate is away from the pressure plate (towards the flywheel). Some plates are marked FLYWHEEL SIDE (photo).
2   Locate the flywheel over the pressure plate so that the large dowel hole is to the right of the pressure plate 'A' mark, Fig. 5.9 (keys 14 and 15).
3   Install the diaphragm cover with the 'A' mark aligned to the pressure plate lug 'A' mark and then screw in the retaining bolts finger-tight.
4   Turn the assembly completely over and centralise the clutch driven plate to the flywheel then tighten the cover bolts just enough to nip the driven plate. As the assembly is fitted to the crankshaft, so the driven plate will automatically be centralised (photo).
5   Reverse the removal procedure (Chapter 1, Section 19) and finally tighten the clutch cover bolts to the specified torque after the bolts which secure the clutch release plate and also the flywheel to the crankshaft have first been tightened (photo).

14.1 Marking on clutch driven plate

14.4 Installing flywheel/clutch (6 cylinder) to crankshaft

14.5 Installing clutch release plate (6 cylinder)

## 15 Fault diagnosis - clutch

| Symptom | Reason/s |
| --- | --- |
| Judder when taking up drive | Loose engine mountings.<br>Worn or oil contaminated driven plate friction linings.<br>Worn splines on driven plate hub or input shaft.<br>Worn crankshaft spigot bush. |
| Clutch slip | Damaged or distorted pressure plate assembly.<br>Driven plate linings worn or oil contaminated. |
| Noise on depressing clutch pedal | Dry, worn or damaged clutch release bearing.<br>Excessive play in input shaft splines. |
| Noise as clutch pedal is released | Distorted driven plate.<br>Broken or weak driven plate hub cushion coil springs.<br>Distorted or worn input shaft.<br>Release bearing loose on fork. |
| Difficulty in disengaging clutch for gearchange | Fault in master cylinder or slave cylinder.<br>Air in hydraulic system.<br>Driven plate hub splines rusted on shaft. |

# Chapter 6 Manual gearbox and automatic transmission

*For modifications, and information applicable to later models, see Supplement at end of manual*

## Contents

## Specifications

### Manual gearbox

**No. of forward speeds** ... ... ... ... ... ... ...     4, all synchromesh

**Ratios**

| | |
|---|---|
| 1st ... ... ... ... ... ... ... ... ... ... | 3.29 : 1 |
| 2nd ... ... ... ... ... ... ... ... ... ... | 2.06 : 1 |
| 3rd ... ... ... ... ... ... ... ... ... ... | 1.38 : 1 |
| 4th ... ... ... ... ... ... ... ... ... ... | 1.00 : 1 |
| Reverse ... ... ... ... ... ... ... ... ... | 3.07 : 1 |

**Speedometer gear ratio** ... ... ... ... ... ... ...     6/15

**1st and 3rd speed gear endfloat** ... ... ... ... ...     0.006 to 0.008 in (0.15 to 0.20 mm)

**2nd speed gear endfloat** ... ... ... ... ... ... ...     0.005 to 0.008 in (0.13 to 0.20 mm)

**Laygear endfloat**

| | |
|---|---|
| 4 cylinder ... ... ... ... ... ... ... ... ... | 0.004 to 0.006 in (0.10 to 0.15 mm) |
| 6 cylinder ... ... ... ... ... ... ... ... ... | 0.002 to 0.003 in (0.05 to 0.08 mm) |

**Lubrication** ... ... ... ... ... ... ... ...     By engine oil

### Automatic transmission

**Type** ... ... ... ... ... ... ... ... ... ...     Borg-Warner 35 - three forward speeds and reverse

**Ratio range** ... ... ... ... ... ... ... ... ...     1 : 1 to 2 : 1

**Ratios**

| | |
|---|---|
| 1st ... ... ... ... ... ... ... ... ... ... | 2.39 : 1 |
| 2nd ... ... ... ... ... ... ... ... ... ... | 1.45 : 1 |
| 3rd ... ... ... ... ... ... ... ... ... ... | 1.00 : 1 |
| Reverse ... ... ... ... ... ... ... ... ... | 2.09 : 1 |

**Fluid capacity \*** ... ... ... ... ... ... ... ...     13 Imp pints (7.4 litres)

*\* At the time of draining, 5 Imp pints (3 litres) are retained in the torque converter.*

## Torque wrench settings

| | lb/ft | Nm |
|---|---|---|
| *Manual gearbox* | | |
| Drain plug ... ... ... ... ... ... ... ... ... ... | 20 | 27 |
| Remote control steady rod nut ... ... ... ... ... ... | 25 | 35 |
| Flywheel housing to adaptor ... ... ... ... ... ... | 23 | 32 |
| Gearbox to cylinder block bolts: | | |
|      5/16 UNF ... ... ... ... ... ... ... ... ... | 25 | 35 |
|      5/16 UNC ... ... ... ... ... ... ... ... ... | 12 | 16 |
|      3/8 UNF ... ... ... ... ... ... ... ... | 30 | 41 |
| Selector rod retaining plate screw ... ... ... ... ... | 16 | 22 |
| Input shaft drive gear nut ... ... ... ... ... ... | 120 | 166 |
| Input shaft bearing nut ... ... ... ... ... ... ... | 120 | 166 |
| Mainshaft nut (minimum) ... ... ... ... ... ... | 40 | 55 |
| Final drive pinion nut (left-hand thread) ... ... ... ... | 150 | 207 |
| Mainshaft bearing housing screw ... ... ... ... ... ... | 18 | 25 |
| Mainshaft locating plate screw ... ... ... ... ... ... | 15 | 21 |
| Mainshaft dowel bolt (6 cylinder) ... ... ... ... ... | 6 | 8 |
| Adaptor plate to cylinder block ... ... ... ... ... ... | 30 | 41 |
| Front cover screws ... ... ... ... ... ... ... ... | 18 | 24 |
| Clutch shaft nut (4 cylinder) ... ... ... ... ... ... | 60 | 83 |
| Clutch shaft bearing retainer screws (4 cylinder) ... ... | 15 | 20 |
| *Automatic transmission* | | |
| Chain cover to torque converter housing ... ... ... ... ... | 9 | 12 |
| Torque converter shaft nut ... ... ... ... ... ... | 120 | 166 |
| Input shaft nut ... ... ... ... ... ... ... ... | 30 | 41 |
| Driveplate to torque converter ... ... ... ... ... ... | 30 | 41 |
| Servo cover bolts ... ... ... ... ... ... ... | 8 | 11 |
| Crankcase to transmission casing ... ... ... ... ... | 30 | 41 |
| Converter housing to main casing ... ... ... ... ... ... | 10 | 14 |
| *Final drive* | | |
| Pinion nut ... ... ... ... ... ... ... ... ... | 150 | 207 |
| Differential cover: | | |
|      5/16 nuts ... ... ... ... ... ... ... ... ... | 18 | 25 |
|      7/16 nuts ... ... ... ... ... ... ... ... ... | 40 | 55 |
| Tightening 5/16 in studs into casing ... ... ... ... ... | 6 | 8 |
| Tightening 7/16 in studs into casing ... ... ... ... ... | 10 | 14 |
| Differential end cover setscrews ... ... ... ... ... ... | 18 | 25 |

# Part 1: Manual gearbox

## 1 General description

The manual gearbox fitted to both models is of four speed synchromesh type. Gear selection is by a floor-mounted lever and remote control rod. Lubrication is provided in common with the engine from the same engine sump supply.

## 2 Operations possible with gearbox still in car

The following operations can be carried out while the gearbox is still in the car.
1 Removal of front cover.
2 Gearshift control mechanism overhaul.
3 Gear selector mechanism and housing overhaul.

## 3 Gearbox - removal and installation

1 Removal of the gearbox is carried out in conjunction with the engine as a combined unit and separated from the engine after removal.
2 The procedures are fully described, according to engine type, in Chapter 1.

## 4 Front cover (4 cylinder gearbox) - removal and refitting

**If the gearbox is still in the car,** drain the engine oil and disconnect the speedometer cable.

### Gearbox in or out of car
1 Remove the stud and nuts and pull off the front cover.
2 Remove the joint gasket.
3 Extract the spring plate, the screwed bush and speedometer pinion.
4 Remove the endplate and the speedometer drive gear.
5 Refitting is a reversal of removal but use a new joint gasket and refill

the engine/gearbox with oil.

## 5 Front cover (6 cylinder gearbox) - removal and refitting

**If the gearbox is still in the car,** drain the engine oil, attach a hoist to the power unit and take its weight. Release the clips which secure the power steering pipes to the stud on the gearbox. Release the through-bolts which secure the left-hand mounting bracket to the front and rear left-hand mountings.

### Gearbox in or out of car
1 Remove the crankshaft pulley bolt and the pulley.
2 Remove the setscrew which secures the alternator also the four screws which retain the bracket to the gearbox casing.
3 Remove the left-hand mounting bracket.
4 Remove the gearbox front cover which is held in position by seven setscrews, one countersunk screw and a stud.
5 Peel off the cover gasket.
6 Installation is a reversal of removal but use a new gasket (photo).

## 6 Gearshift lever and remote control rods - removal and installation

1 Unscrew and remove the gear lever knob.
2 Raise the front of the car and support it under the right-hand front side jacking point.
3 From below the car, peel back the draught excluder and release the gearlever bayonet type securing cap.
4 Lift the gear lever assembly up into the draught excluder so that it clears the remote control mechanism and then extract the gearshift lever assembly from below the car. Detach the bayonet cap from the lever (photo).
5 To remove the remote control assembly, drive out the tension pin which retains the extension rod to the selector rod at the gearbox selector housing end (photo).
6 Remove the bolt which secures the remote control steady rod to

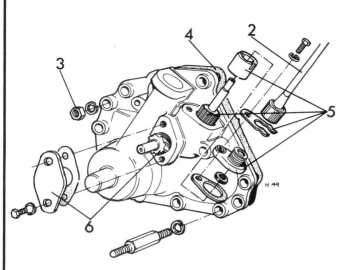

Fig. 6.1. Front cover assembly (4 cylinder gearbox) (Sec. 4)

2  Speedometer cable
3  Front cover nut
4  Joint gasket
5  Speedo driven gear and components
6  Speedo drive gear and end plate

Fig. 6.2. Front cover (6 cylinder gearbox) (Sec. 5)

1  Oil drain plug (engine/gearbox)
7  Front cover and gasket

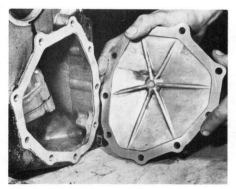

5.6 Installing gearbox front cover and gasket (6 cylinder)

6.4 Removing the gearshift lever from below the car

6.5 Removing the selector/extension rod tension pin

6.6 Remote control steady rod to selector housing bolt

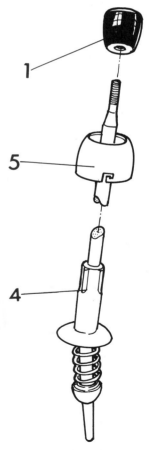

Fig. 6.3. Gear lever assembly (Sec. 6)
1  Knob
4  Lever
5  Bayonet type retainer

the selector housing (photo).

7   Disconnect the leads from the reversing lamp switch.

8   Remove the bolt which secures the remote control assembly to its mounting brackets and then withdraw the assembly downwards (photo).

9   Reassembly and installation are reversals of removal and dismantling. Apply grease to the gearshift lever operating surfaces. Make sure that the extension rod eye is the correct way up before attaching the extension rod to it.

6.8 Remote control assembly mounting bracket

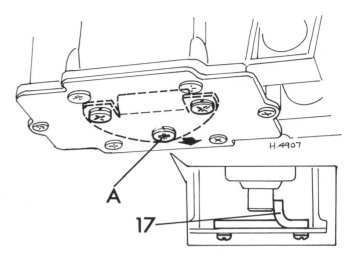

Fig. 6.4. Gearshift remote control assembly reverse lift plate adjustment screws (A), 17 reverse lift plate (Sec. 7) — models up to 1976

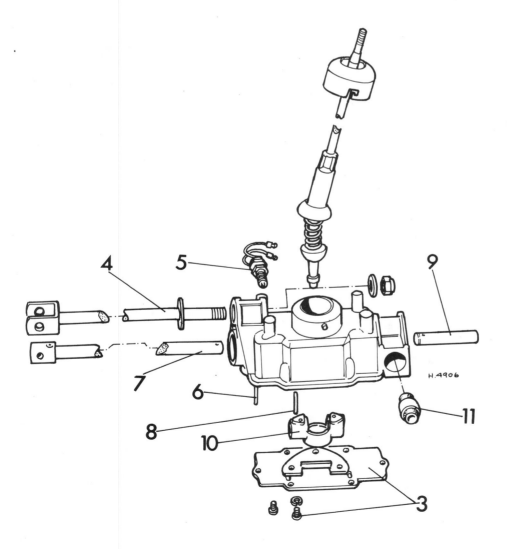

Fig. 6.5. Exploded view of gearshift remote control assembly (Sec. 7)

3   Bottom plate and reverse lift plate
4   Steady rod
5   Reversing lamp switch
6   Tension pin
7   Extension rod (crank uppermost to clear exhaust pipe)
8   Tension pin
9   Support rod
10  Extension rod eye
11  Mounting bush

## 7 Gearshift remote control assembly - overhaul

1  Remove the assembly as described in the preceding Section.
2  Secure the remote control assembly in a vice and remove the bottom cover and reverse light plates.
3  Remove the steady rod from the housing.
4  Remove the reverse light switch.
5  Move the extension rod eye to the rear and then drive out the tension pin which secures the extension rod to the eye.
6  Push the extension rod eye forwards and remove the tension pin which retains the support rod to the extension rod eye. Remove the extension rod.
7  Drive out the support rod and then lift out the extension rod eye.
8  If the mounting bushes are worn, they can be extracted and new ones fitted.
9  Reassembly is a reversal of dismantling but apply grease liberally to all friction surfaces and ensure that the cranked section of the extension rod is uppermost so that it will clear the exhaust system. Make sure that the extension rod eye is the correct way up before connecting the rod to it (see Fig. 6.5).
10  When the assembly has been installed on cars built up to 1976, carry out the following adjustment.
11  Slacken the three screws which secure the reverse lift plate to the bottom cover. Engage 3rd or 4th gear and push the reverse lift plate into contact with the gearshift lever stub. Use a screwdriver inserted at screw head 'A' to move the plate within the limits of the elongated holes in the cover (Fig. 6.4).
12  Tighten the screws and check for smooth selection of 3rd and 4th gears.
13  Adjustment of the reversing lamp switch should be checked. If necessary, release the switch locknut, select reverse gear and then with a battery and test lamp connected between the switch terminals, screw in the switch until the lamp lights. Screw the switch in a further half a turn and then tighten the locknut.

## 8 Gear selector mechanism and housing - oil seal renewal

**If the gearbox is still in the car,** drain the engine oil, and drive out the tension pin which secures the gearshift extension rod to the selector shaft. Remove the bolt which secures the remote control steady rod to the selector housing.

### Gearbox in or out of car
1  Remove the six nuts which secure the selector housing to the final drive housing and then pull the selector housing from its studs (photo).
2  Extract the circlip from the selector lever pivot and remove the pivot and the shaft. Drive out the old oil seal and install the new one, (see also next Section ) (photo).
3  Refitting the housing is a reversal of removal but use a new flange gasket and make quite sure that the selector levers have engaged positively with the lugs on the forks before tightening the housing bolts.

## 9 Gear selector mechanism - overhaul

1  Remove the selector housing, as described in the preceding Section.
2  Remove the circlip which secures the bellcrank lever pivot pin to the housing.
3  Withdraw the pivot pin and bellcrank levers, retaining the washers which are located between and on each side of the levers.
4  Withdraw the selector shaft.
5  Push the interlock spool locating pin into the spool and then remove the pin.
6  Renew any worn components and reassemble by reversing the dismantling procedure.

8.1 Removing selector housing

8.2 Selector assembly detail

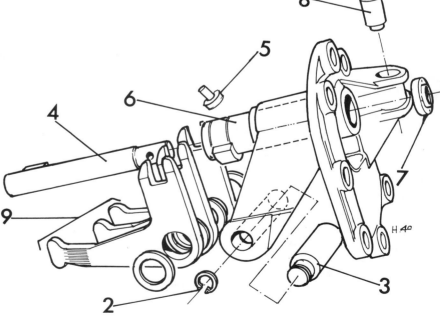

Fig. 6.6. Gear selector mechanism and housing (Sec. 8)

| | | |
|---|---|---|
| 2 Circlip | 5 Interlock spool locating pin | 7 Selector shaft oil seal |
| 3 Pivot pin | 6 Interlock spool | 8 Mounting bush |
| 4 Selector shaft | | 9 Bellcrank levers |

### 10 Gearbox - dismantling (general)

1   Purchase new gaskets, lockwasher and circlips in advance of
dismantling to save time. Observe strict cleanliness in all operations.
2   Unless suitable extractors or a press are available it is not
recommended that the major assemblies are dismantled but the work

should be left to your Leyland dealer.

### 11 Gearbox (4 cylinder) - dismantling into major assemblies

1   With the engine/gearbox removed from the car and the gearbox
separated from the engine, detach the final drive, as described in the

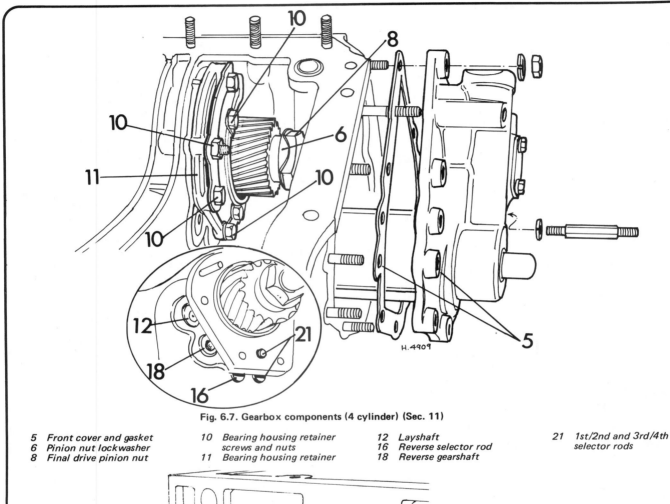

Fig. 6.7. Gearbox components (4 cylinder) (Sec. 11)

| | | |
|---|---|---|
| 5   Front cover and gasket | 10   Bearing housing retainer | 12   Layshaft |
| 6   Pinion nut lockwasher |     screws and nuts | 16   Reverse selector rod |
| 8   Final drive pinion nut | 11   Bearing housing retainer | 18   Reverse gearshaft |

21   1st/2nd and 3rd/4th
    selector rods

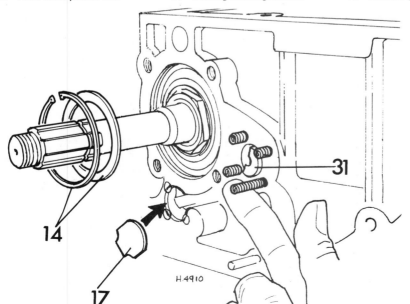

Fig. 6.8. Gearbox components (4 cylinder)
(Sec. 11)

14 Input shaft circlip and distance piece
17 Selector rod locating plate
31 Layshaft cut-away

following paragraphs:

2  Remove the setscrews which secure the end covers to the final drive housing and gearbox casing and pull off the covers.
3  Extract the differential bearing preload shims which are fitted beneath the cover at the clutch end.
4  Remove the single nut which secures the gear selector housing and also holds the final drive housing to the gearbox.
5  Unscrew and remove the remaining final drive housing to gearbox nuts, lift off the exhaust mounting bracket and the final drive housing complete with differential assembly.
6  Remove the gearbox front cover and gasket (nine nuts and a stud).
7  If the mainshaft is to be dismantled, flatten the final drive pinion nut lockwasher, move the synchro. sleeves to engage 1st and 3rd gears (preventing the mainshaft from turning) and then slacken the final drive pinion nut - *this has a left-hand thread.*
8  Move the synchro. sleeves back to disengage the gears.
9  Unlock and remove the bearing housing retainer screws and withdraw the retainer.
10  Drive out the layshaft from the gearbox casing and lift out the laygear and thrust washers.
11  Remove the circlip and distance piece which retain the input shaft.
12  Withdraw the input shaft from the gearbox casing.
13  Drive out the reverse selector rod so that it emerges from the rear of the casing. During this operation, cover the gearbox casing with a piece of cloth to prevent the interlock balls being thrown out and lost.
14  Extract the selector rod locating plate.
15  Push reverse gear shaft from the gearbox casing.
16  Remove reverse gear and extract reverse selector fork from the gearbox casing.
17  Drive out 1st/2nd and 3rd/4th selector fork rods and rest the selector forks in the bottom of the gearbox casing.
18  Remove the mainshaft assembly by first driving the shaft forward to clear the bearing housing from contact with the gearbox casing and then take the weight of the shaft and extract the selector forks. Turn the bearing housing to clear the front cover aperture and then remove the mainshaft assembly.
19  Extract the selector fork locating balls and springs (previously ejected) from the bottom of the gearbox casing.

**12  Mainshaft (4 cylinder) - overhaul**

1  If the final drive pinion nut has not already been released (see paragraph 7, of the preceding Section) remove it now, making sure that the pinion is gripped in a vice which is fitted with jaw protectors. Remove the final drive pinion.
2  Flatten the lockwasher and unscrew the nut (6) (Fig. 6.11) **which has a left-hand thread.**
3  Withdraw the 3rd/4th synchro. assembly complete with baulk rings.
4  Withdraw the shaft sleeve, 3rd speed gear and the interlocking thrust washer.
5  Remove 2nd speed gear and thrust washer.
6  Remove 1st/2nd synchro. unit complete with baulk rings.
7  Press the shaft from the bearing and remove reverse gear and 1st speed gear (photo).
8  If the bearing is worn, press it from its housing.
9  If the synchro. units are to be dismantled, push the hub from the sleeve taking care not to lose the springs or balls which will be ejected.
10  Check all components for wear, especially the synchro. baulk rings. Push them onto the gear cones and check that they engage before contacting the edge of the gear. If they do not, renew the hub and baulk ring.
11  If the bearing has been renewed, press it into its housing so that the projecting centre boss of the bearing faces towards the machined cut-away of the housing.
12  Reassemble the synchro. units. A worm drive clip or piston ring clamp will be found useful to retain the balls and springs to the hub and the assembly can then be tapped smartly into the sleeve and the clip or clamp removed.
13  Refit 1st speed gear and reverse gear to the shaft (photo).
14  Press the bearing housing onto the shaft.
15  Refit 1st/2nd synchro. unit complete with baulk rings, outer groove towards 2nd speed gear. This synchro. unit is smaller in diameter than the 3rd/4th synchro. unit (photo).
16  Refit the thrust washer and 2nd speed gear (photo).
17  Insert the sleeve into 3rd speed gear and position the interlocking

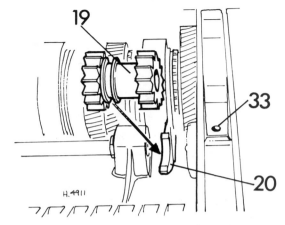

Fig. 6.9. Gearbox components (4 cylinder) (Sec. 11)

  19 Reverse gear
  20 Reverse selector fork
  33 Layshaft lubrication hole

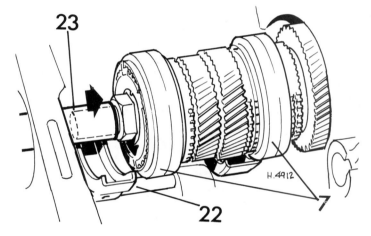

Fig. 6.10. Mainshaft (Sec. 12)

  7 Synchro sleeves
  22 Selector fork
  23 Drift

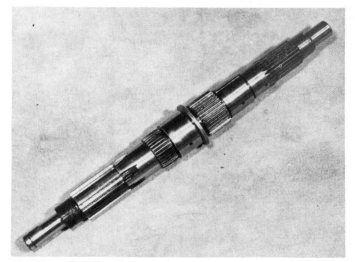

12.7 The mainshaft with gears removed

thrust washer onto the sleeve. Refit the complete assembly to the shaft (photo).
18 Refit 3rd/4th synchro. unit complete with baulk rings (photo).
19 Use a new lockwasher, apply thread locking fluid, tighten and lock

the nut (6) (Fig. 6.11). **This nut has a left-hand thread (photo).**
20 Install the final drive pinion, apply thread locking fluid, and fit the lockwasher and nut. This nut can be tightened and locked after the shaft has been fitted to the gearbox (photos).

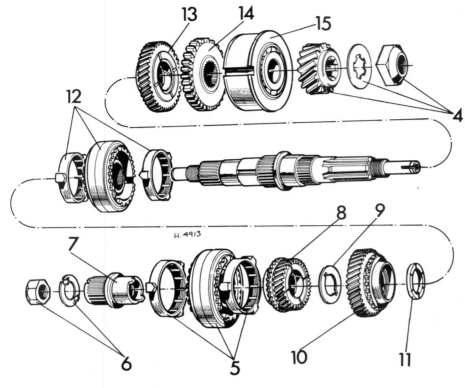

**Fig. 6.11. Mainshaft components (Sec. 12)**

4   Final drive pinion, nut and locking washer
5   3rd/4th synchro unit
6   Shaft nut and locking washer
7   Shaft sleeve
8   3rd speed gear
9   Thrust washer
10  2nd speed gear
11  Thrust washer
12  1st/2nd synchro unit
13  1st speed gear
14  Reverse gear
15  Bearing (6 cylinder type shown)

H.4913

12.13 Installing 1st. and reverse gears to mainshaft

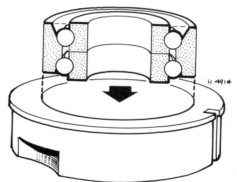

**Fig. 6.12. Correct installation of mainshaft bearing into its housing**

H.4914

12.15 Installing 1st/2nd synchro. unit to mainshaft

12.16 Fitting **thrust washer and 2nd.** speed gear to mainshaft

12.17 Installing 3rd speed gear assembly to mainshaft

12.18 Installing 3rd/4th synchro. unit to mainshaft

12.19 Fitting lockwasher and nut to mainshaft

12.20A Installing final drive pinion to mainshaft

12.20B Mainshaft assembled

## 13 Input shaft (4 cylinder) - overhaul

1   Extract the mainshaft spigot bearing from inside the input shaft.
2   Grip the shaft in a vice fitted with jaw protectors and after flattening the lockwasher, remove the bearing retaining nut (photo).
3   Press the shaft from the bearing.
4   Inspect all components for wear and renew as necessary.
5   To reassemble, press the input shaft into the bearing, refit the lockwasher and bearing retaining nut and tighten to specified torque. Lock the nut.
6   Fit the spigot bearing into the shaft.

## 14 Gearbox (4 cylinder) - reassembly

1   Insert the springs and balls into the selector forks. Retain them in position with pieces of dowel or tubing of suitable diameter.
2   Reverse the dismantling operations (13 to 18) in Section 11.
3   Fit the needle roller bearing into the input shaft.
4   Drive the input shaft bearing into the gearbox casing. If a new bearing has been installed, a distance piece must be selected from the sizes available until the circlip will just not enter its groove. Now select and install a distance piece of the next size down. Five selective size

13.2 Input shaft

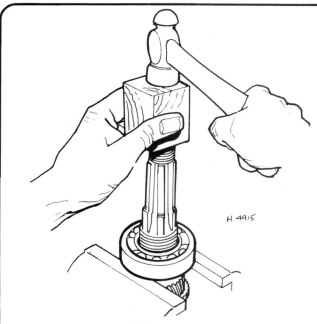

Fig. 6.13. Pressing input shaft from its bearing (Sec. 13)

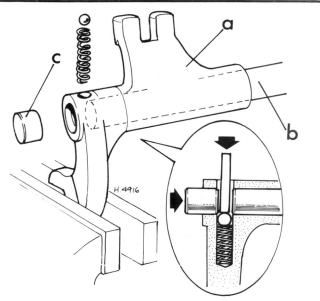

Fig. 6.14. Selector fork components (Sec. 14)

a   Fork          b   Selector rod          c   Temporary dowelling

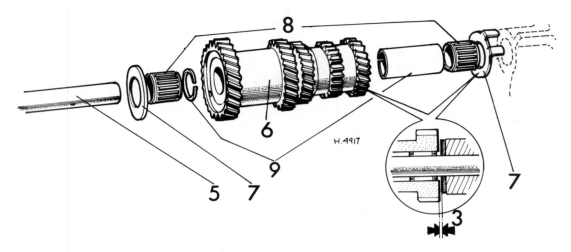

**Fig. 6.15. Laygear detail (Sec. 14)**

| | | |
|---|---|---|
| 3  Endfloat | 6  Laygear | 8  Needle roller bearings |
| 5  Layshaft *(being withdrawn)* | 7  Thrust washers | 9  Circlip and split sleeve |

distance pieces are available:

| | |
|---|---|
| 0.117 to 0.118 in. | 2.97 to 3.00 mm |
| 0.121 to 0.122 in. | 3.07 to 3.10 mm |
| 0.125 to 0.126 in. | 3.17 to 3.20 mm |
| 0.129 to 0.130 in. | 3.28 to 3.30 mm |
| 0.133 to 0.134 in. | 3.38 to 3.40 mm |

5   If the laygear has been renewed, always fit a new split sleeve and circlip, also new thrust springs.

6   Insert the layshaft into the casing so that the shaft cut-away is towards the clutch end and so positioned that it will locate in the adaptor plate.

7   Push the layshaft in so that it picks up the large thrust washer and the laygear and then select a small thrust washer of suitable thickness to provide a laygear endfloat of between 0.002 and 0.003 in. (0.05 and 0.08 mm). Feeler blades can be used to check this. Thrust washers are available in selective thicknesses as follows:

| | |
|---|---|
| 0.119 to 0.121 in. | 3.02 to 3.07 mm |
| 0.123 to 0.125 in. | 3.12 to 3.17 mm |
| 0.126 to 0.128 in. | 3.21 to 3.26 mm |
| 0.130 to 0.132 in. | 3.30 to 3.35 mm |
| 0.133 to 0.135 in. | 3.38 to 3.43 mm |

8   Drive the layshaft fully home.

9   Reverse the dismantling procedure (paragraphs 2 to 9 in Section 11) but make sure that the pinion and other nuts are all tightened to the specified torque.

10  Oil all gears and friction surfaces before reconnecting the gearbox to the engine.

## 15 Primary drive geartrain (4 cylinder) - overhaul

These components are accessible when the engine/transmission is still in position in the car provided that the flywheel housing is removed, as described in Chapter 1, Sections 9 and 28.

1   When withdrawing the flywheel housing, make sure that the special washer is still located on the front of the input shaft.

2   Remove the input shaft bearing from the flywheel housing.

3   Remove the clutch shaft and bearing from the housing, and then unlock and unscrew the shaft nut. Hold the shaft still in an old driven plate gripped in the jaws of a vice to do this.

4   Remove the distance piece and oil thrower.

5   Press the clutch shaft from its bearing.

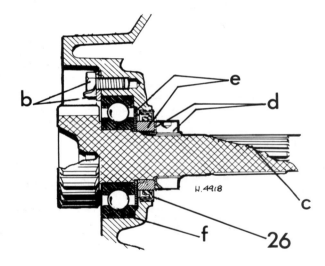

**Fig. 6.16. Sectional view of clutch shaft components (4 cylinder gearbox) (Sec. 15)**

| | | |
|---|---|---|
| b  Bearing retainer nut and locking washer | e  Distance piece and oil thrower | |
| c  Clutch shaft | f  Shaft bearing | |
| d  Shaft nut and locking washer | 26  Oil seal | |

6   Extract and renew the clutch shaft oil seal.

7   Examine the idler gear needle bearings and renew them if necessary.

8   Reassembly is a reversal of dismantling but the endfloat of the idler gear must be checked in relation to its bearing cap. This can be carried out using a dial gauge or feeler blades and where necessary adjusting the thickness of the thrust washers to give an endfloat of between 0.004 and 0.006 in. (0.10 and 0.15 mm). Thrust washers are available in the following thicknesses:

| | |
|---|---|
| 0.128 to 0.129 in. | 3.25 to 3.28 mm |
| 0.130 to 0.131 in. | 3.30 to 3.33 mm |
| 0.132 to 0.133 in. | 3.35 to 3.38 mm |
| 0.134 to 0.135 in. | 3.40 to 3.43 mm |

9   Make sure the idler gear is installed with its marked face outwards and tighten all nuts and bolts to the specified torque.

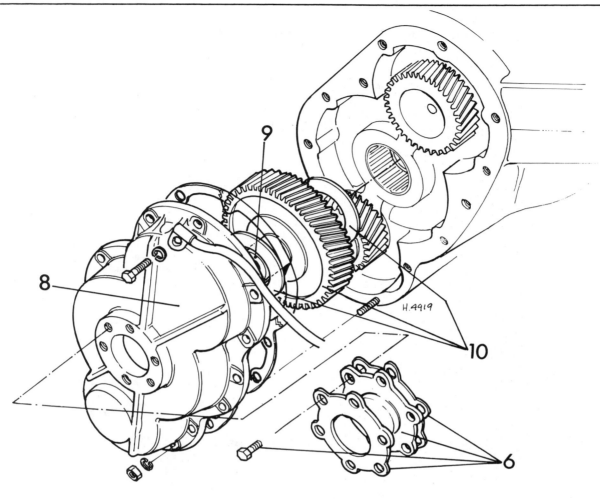

**Fig. 6.17. Idler gear (4 cylinder) (Sec. 15)**

6  Idler bearing cap

8  Primary drive cover

9  Outward facing reference mark

10  Idler gear and thrust washers

## 16 Gearbox (6 cylinder) - dismantling into major assemblies

1  With the gearbox separated from the engine, pull out the idler gear and retrieve the thrust washers.
2  Remove the engine oil filter assembly and the oil pump connector. A special socket will be required to unscrew the latter.
3  Remove the gearbox front cover and the two external bolts which secure the oil pump and then withdraw the pump.

4  Remove the setscrews which secure the side covers to the final drive housing and gearbox casing and pull off the covers. Remove any differential bearing preload shims fitted beneath the cover at the clutch end (photos).
5  Remove the nuts which secure the gear selector housing and the final drive housing to the gearbox and then unscrew and remove the remaining nuts which hold the final drive housing to the gearbox.
6  Lift off the exhaust mounting bracket and pull the final drive housing away complete with the differential assembly (photo).

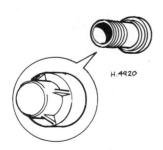

Fig. 6.18. Oil pump connector (6 cylinder gearbox) and special socket for removing it (Sec. 16)

16.4A Removing a final drive housing side cover

16.4B Removing a differential bearing pre-load shim (clutch end only)

7  Remove the speedometer angle drive unit and unscrew and remove the speedometer drive pinion.
8  Extract the circlip which secures the speedometer drive tension pin retaining cap to the mainshaft.
9  Lift off the speedometer drive tension pin retaining cap but do not extract the roll pin and then pull the drive gear from the mainshaft (photo).
10  Flatten the final drive pinion nut lockwasher and push the synchro. sleeves to engage 1st and 3rd gears so that the mainshaft will not turn (photo).
11  Unscrew the final drive pinion nut (left-hand thread).
12  Flatten the input shaft nut lockwasher and slacken the nut. Disengage the gears by moving the synchro. sleeves back to their original position.

13  Remove the mainshaft bearing retainer.
14  Drive out the layshaft, so that it emerges from the clutch end of the gearbox, leaving the laygear in position.
15  Drive out the reverse idler gear shaft.
16  Flatten the locking tab of the selector rod retaining plate screw and remove the screw, washer and plate.
17  Drive out the three selector rods and remove the selector forks, taking care to retrieve the balls and springs which will be ejected.
18  Remove reverse idler gear.
19  Remove the mainshaft locating bolt and then extract the shaft from the crankshaft pulley end of the gearbox.
20  Remove the nut, (previously loosened see paragraph 12) and extract the lockwasher and gear from the input shaft.
21  Extract the input shaft retaining circlip and then drive the input shaft assembly into the gearbox interior using a soft-faced mallet.
22  The laygear and thrust washers can now be lifted from the gearbox.
23  Extract the two circlips which retain the input shaft gear needle roller bearing to the gear casing and drive out the bearing (photo).
24  If required, the idler spigot bearing bush can be driven out by inserting a drift through the idler gear needle roller bearing.
25  Extract the idler gear needle roller bearing inner circlip and then remove the idler gear bearing from the gearbox casing complete with its outer circlip (photo).

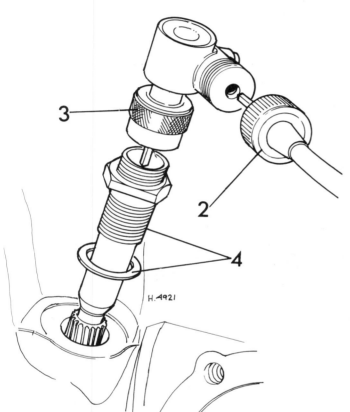

Fig. 6.19. Speedo drive cable (2), angle drive unit (3) and drive pinion (4) (6 cylinder gearbox) (Sec. 16)

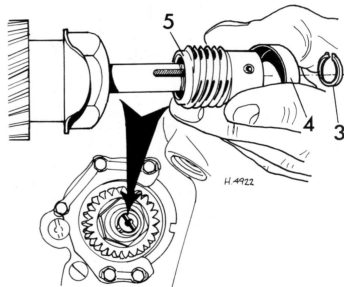

Fig. 6.20. Speedo drive gear circlip (3), tension pin retaining cap (4) and drive gear (5) on mainshaft (6 cylinder gearbox) (Sec. 16)

16.6 Lifting the final drive assembly from the gearbox casing

16.9 Removing speedometer drive gear from mainshaft

16.10 Unscrewing final drive pinion nut (LH thread)

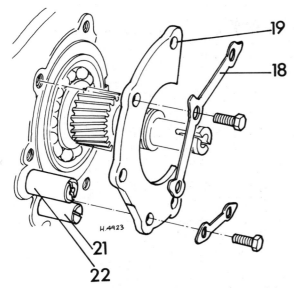

Fig. 6.21. Mainshaft bearing retainer (6 cylinder gearbox) (Sec. 16)

18 Lockplate   19 Retainer   21 Layshaft   22 Reverse idler gearshaft

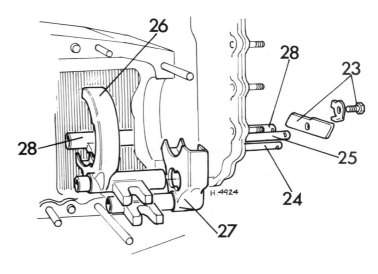

Fig. 6.22. Selector rod components (6 cylinder gearbox) (Sec. 16)

23 Selector rod retaining plate   26 1st/2nd selector fork
24 1st/2nd selector rod           27 3rd/4th selector fork
25 3rd/4th selector rod           28 Reverse selector rod and fork

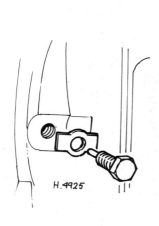

Fig. 6.23. Mainshaft retaining plate and bolt (6 cylinder gearbox) (Sec. 16)

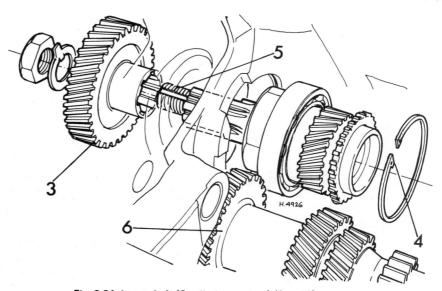

Fig. 6.24. Input shaft (6 cylinder gearbox) (Sec. 16)

3 Shaft gear   4 Circlip   5 Input shaft   6 Laygear

16.25 Extracting idler gear inner needle roller bearing circlip

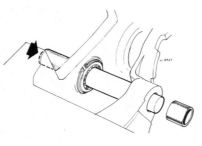

Fig. 6.25. Driving out the spigot bearing bush (6 cylinder gearbox) (Sec. 16)

16.23 Extracting input shaft needle roller bearing circlip

### 17 Mainshaft (6 cylinder) - overhaul

This is carried out in a similar way to that described in Section 12.

### 18 Input shaft (6 cylinder) - overhaul

This is carried out in a similar way to that described in Section 13.

### 19 Gearbox (6 cylinder) - reassembly

1   If a new idler bearing is being installed, fit the outer circlip and then drive the bearing into the gearbox casing from the outside. Fit the inner circlip.

2   If a new spigot bearing is being installed for the idler gear, drive it in flush with the gearbox casing and then ream it with a 7/8 in. (22.225 mm) reamer lubricated with paraffin (photo).

3   Install the inner circlip into the input shaft gear bearing housing and drive the new needle roller bearing into position. Fit the outer circlip.

4   Install the needle roller bearings into the laygear (photo).

5   Insert the springs and balls into the selector forks and retain them with suitable rods or dowelling.

6   Locate the reverse idler gear in the bottom of the gearbox casing together with the laygear and its large thrust washer but do not fit any of these components yet (photo).

7   Drive the input shaft assembly into the gearbox casing (photo).

8   Fit the thickest possible circlip to the input shaft from the three selective sizes (photo):

| | |
|---|---|
| 0.060 in. (1.54 mm) | coloured black |
| 0.062 in. (1.59 mm) | coloured orange |
| 0.064 in. (1.64 mm) | coloured blue |

9   Align the groove on the mainshaft bearing housing with the dowel bolt locating hole in the gearbox casing and drive the mainshaft assembly into position (photos).

10  Install the dowel bolt (photo).

11  Insert the layshaft so that it picks up the large thrust washer and laygear. Select and fit a smaller thrust washer to give a laygear endfloat of between 0.002 and 0.003 in. (0.05 and 0.08 mm). Small thrust washers are available in the following thicknesses (photo):

| | |
|---|---|
| 0.119 to 0.121 in. | (3.02 to 3.07 mm) |
| 0.123 to 0.125 in. | (3.12 to 3.17 mm) |
| 0.126 to 0.128 in. | (3.21 to 3.26 mm) |
| 0.130 to 0.132 in. | (3.30 to 3.35 mm) |
| 0.133 to 0.135 in. | (3.38 to 3.43 mm) |

12  Refit the reverse idler gear shaft.

13  Now refit the selector rods, forks, detent springs and balls. To do this, first locate the reverse fork and only just insert the selector rod into it, then insert the spring and ball into the fork. Depress the spring and ball and fully insert the selector rod. It is not possible to insert or depress the detent ball and spring in the other two selector forks once they are in position and therefore they must be installed and a short piece of tapered rod or dowel used to retain the balls and springs in their depressed state. Install the 1st/2nd and 3/4th selector forks together as they interlock with each other. Make sure that the detent balls and springs are in position and held depressed by the temporary rods without allowing the balls and springs to be displaced. The selector rods must have their slots at the crankshaft pulley end of the gearbox and take care that the mainshaft assembly is not pushed out of position as the bearing retainer plate has not yet been fitted (photos).

14  Refit the mainshaft bearing housing retainer plate and bend up the locking plate tabs (photo).

15  Fit the selector rod retaining plate and lock it (photo).

16  Move the selector forks to lock two gears at the same time and then tighten the final drive pinion nut to the specified torque. If a torque wrench is not available to record such a high reading, use a box spanner and a two foot bar, tightening fully. Lock the nut, by bending the washer up on three sides (photo).

19.2 Idler gear spigot bearing installed and reamed

19.4 Installing laygear needle roller bearing

19.6 Laygear and reverse idler gear located in gearbox pending installation of shafts

19.7 Installing input shaft

19.8 Fitting input shaft circlip

19.9A Mainshaft bearing housing groove

19.9B Installing mainshaft assembly

19.10 Installing mainshaft bearing dowel bolt

19.11 Laygear and large thrust washer

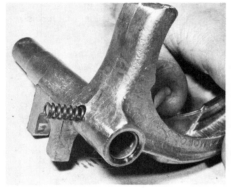

19.13A Inserting detent spring into 1st/2nd selector fork

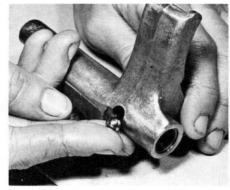

19.13B Inserting detent ball into 1st/2nd selector fork

19.13C Using tapered rod to hold detent components depressed

19.13D Tapered rod fully inserted into selector fork

19.13E Installing 1st/2nd and 3rd/4th selector forks interconnected

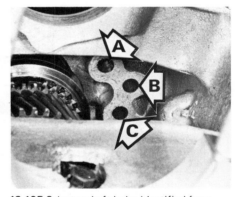

19.13F Selector shaft holes identified from interior of gearbox
A  3rd/4th      B  1st/2nd      C  Reverse

19.14 Mainshaft bearing housing retainer plate

19.15 Selector rod retaining plate

19.16 Final drive pinion nut locked in position

19.17 Input shaft gear nut locked in position

17 Refit the input shaft gear with a new lock washer and nut. Tighten to torque and lock (photo).
18 Move the selector forks to the neutral mode.
19 Reverse the operations described in Section 16, paragraphs 1 to 9.
20 Make sure that all other nuts and screws are tightened to the specified torque and oil the internal components of the gearbox before connecting it to the engine.

## 20 Primary drive geartrain (6 cylinder) - overhaul

These components are accessible when the engine/transmission is still in position in the car provided that the flywheel and clutch are removed, as described in Section 19, of Chapter 1.

1  **If the engine/transmission is still in the car,** withdraw the idler gear and from the rear face of the gear, insert two 5/16 in. (8.0 mm) bolts. Refit the idler gear complete with thrust washer.
To the temporary bolts fit a piece of flat steel bar (suitably drilled and cranked), to lock the idler gear while the input shaft nut is slackened.

2  **If the transmission is out of the car,** lock the mainshaft to prevent it turning by selecting 1st and 3rd gears simultaneously.

3  Release the input shaft gear retaining nut after flattening the lockplate and withdraw the crankshaft primary gear and thrust washer (photos).

4  Remove the idler gear and its thrust washer (photo).

5  Remove the input shaft gear and the temporary idler gear locking tool (if fitted).

6  Renew any worn components.

7  Reassembly is a reversal of dismantling but tighten the input shaft nut to the specified torque and then lubricate all components with engine oil.

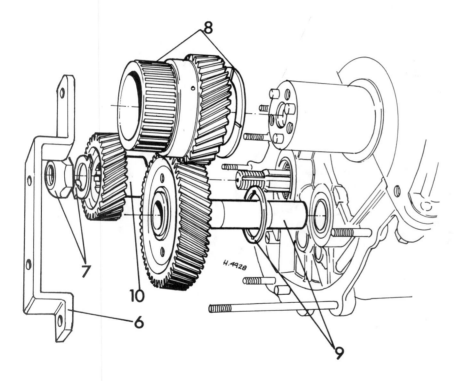

Fig. 6.26. Idler gear (6 cylinder)
(Sec. 20)

6    Temporary locking bar
7    Input gear nut and locking washer
8    Crankshaft primary gear and thrust washer
9    Idler gear and thrust washer
10   Input shaft gear

20.3A Primary gear train (6 cylinder)

20.3B Crankshaft primary gear and thrust washer

20.4 Removing idler gear

**21 Fault diagnosis - manual gearbox**

| Symptom | Reason/s |
| --- | --- |
| Weak or ineffective synchromesh | Synchronising cones worn, split or damaged.<br>Baulk ring synchromesh dogs worn or damaged. |
| Jumps out of gear | Broken gearchange fork rod spring.<br>Gearbox coupling dogs badly worn.<br>Selector fork rod groove badly worn. |
| Excessive noise | Incorrect grade of oil in gearbox or oil level too low.<br>Bush or needle roller bearings worn or damaged.<br>Gear teeth excessively worn or damaged.<br>Laygear thrust washers worn allowing excessive end play. |
| Excessive difficulty in engaging gear | Clutch pedal adjustment incorrect (see Chapter 5). |

## Part 2: Automatic transmission

### 22 General description

Borg-Warner automatic transmissions have been fitted to medium and large sized cars for many years and the popular model 35 was modified allowing it to be fitted to the front wheel drive cars. In the original design it takes the place of the clutch and gearbox and is mounted in the usual position behind the engine. However, as with front wheel drive models where the manual gearbox is fitted underneath the engine, so is this automatic transmission.

From Fig. 6.28 it will be noted that the torque converter is not mounted in line with the gear train but fitted above it. The torque developed by the engine is transmitted to the gear train by a special type of chain. With this layout there is a division between the engine and the automatic transmission unit so that the engine oil is retained in the engine and normal automatic transmission fluid in the automatic transmission and differential unit. This is of course a deviation from normal Leyland transverse unit design.

Due to the complexity of the automatic transmission unit, if performance is not up to standard or overhaul is necessary, it is imperative that this be left to your local main agents who will have all the special equipment and knowledge for fault diagnosis and rectification. The successful overhaul of an automatic transmission unit requires the use of many very special tools and the content of this Chapter is therefore confined to supplying general information and any service information that will be of practical use to the owner.

### 23 Maintenance

1  The most important item of regular maintenance is to keep the fluid level topped-up with clean fluid of the specified type.
2  Fluid level checks should be carried out in the following way. Drive the car for a minimum of five miles (8 km) to bring the fluid to normal operating temperature.
3  Position the car on level ground and fully apply the handbrake. Select 'P' and allow the engine to idle for two or three minutes. While the engine is idling, move the selector lever through its complete range and then select 'P'.
4  With the engine still idling, withdraw the dipstick, wipe it clean, re-insert it and withdraw it for the second time and read off the fluid level.
5  If neccessary, add fluid to bring the level to the 'HIGH' mark on the dipstick. The difference between the 'LOW' and 'HIGH' marks is 1 Imp. pint (0.6 litres).
6  Draining and refilling the automatic transmission unit is not specified as a routine maintenance operation.
7  Periodically wipe the external surfaces of the transmission casing free from oil and dirt and check the security of all nuts and bolts.

### 24 Speed selector cable - adjustment

1  Should the automatic gearbox fail to respond to a selector position, first check the fluid level and then carry out the following test.
2  With the engine idling in 'N', select 'D' and release the handbrake.

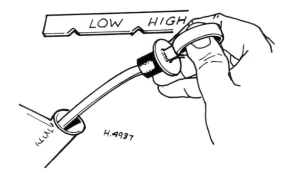

**Fig. 6.27. Combined dipstick/fluid filler tube (automatic transmission) (Sec. 23)**

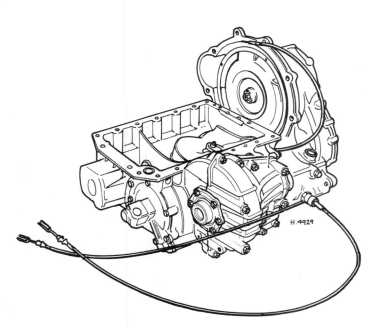

**Fig. 6.28. Automatic transmission unit (Sec. 22)**

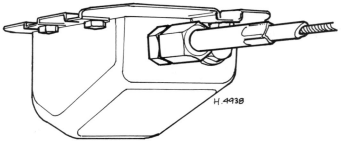

**Fig. 6.29. Speed selector outer cable and locknut (automatic transmission) (Sec. 24)**

Drive forward by accelerating and then push the selector lever to 'N'. Disconnection of the drive should be felt immediately.

3   Repeat the operation in reverse using 'R' and 'N'.

4   Any malfunction may be due to faulty selector cable adjustment which should be rectified as follows:

Switch off the engine, position the selector lever in '1'. Slacken the outer cable adjuster locknut and push the outer cable fully into the selector lever housing. Retighten the locknut and re-check the speed selection throughout the range.

## 25 Front and rear brake bands - adjustment

1   This adjustment should only be carried out when any fault may be the result of incorrect setting of one or both brake bands as detailed in 'Fault diagnosis' (Section 28).

2   Drain the automatic transmission.

3   Remove the servo cover and gasket.

4   Release the now accessible front band adjusting screw locknut and tighten the adjusting screw to 8 lb/ft (11 Nm). Now unscrew the adjusting screw by between 1 and 1¼ turns. Retighten the locknut.

5   Where the rear band requires adjustment, unhook the piston return spring from the servo casing and release the adjusting screw locknut. Tighten the adjusting screw to 10 lb/in. only. Unscrew the adjusting screw by between 2 and 2½ turns. Retighten the locknut. Refit the piston return spring.

6   Refit the servo cover and a new gasket and refill the automatic transmission to the correct level.

## 26 Primary drive chain - removal and installation

1   *On 4 cylinder engines,* the automatic transmission primary drive chain is accessible with the engine/transmission still in the car but the transmission fluid will have to be drained first.

2   *On 6 cylinder engines,* the engine/transmission must be removed from the car.

3   Remove the primary chain cover and gasket.

4   Flatten the lockwashers and unscrew and remove the nut on the input shaft and the nut on the torque converter sprockets. To prevent the torque converter sprocket turning, place a wedge between the sprocket and the front pump suction boss.

5   Pull the sprockets and chain off their shafts simultaneously, leaving the input shaft bearing and spacer in position.

6   Installation is a reversal of removal but tighten all nuts and bolts to the specified torque.

**Note:** *On 4 cylinder engined cars, if the work is being carried out with the engine in the car, in order to fit a torque wrench to the input shaft nut, the following preliminary operations will have to be performed.*

   a)  *Support the engine on a jack.*
   b)  *Extract the engine right-hand front mounting through bolt.*
   c)  *Remove the engine right-hand rear mounting bracket.*
   d)  *Disconnect the engine earth lead.*
   e)  *Disconnect the fuel inlet pipe from the fuel pump.*
   f)  *Disconnect the servo hose from the manifold.*
   g)  *Raise the engine slightly.*

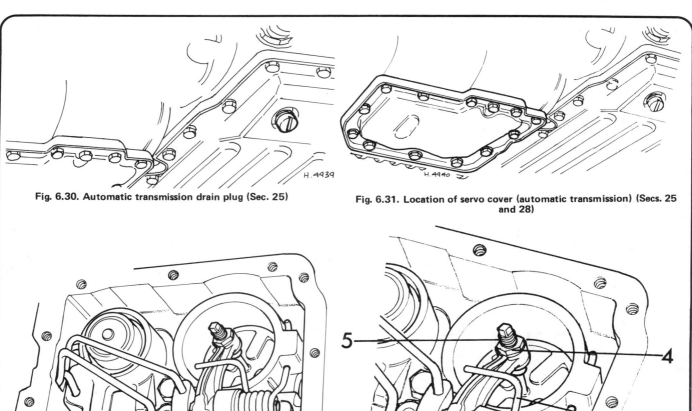

Fig. 6.30. Automatic transmission drain plug (Sec. 25)

Fig. 6.31. Location of servo cover (automatic transmission) (Secs. 25 and 28)

Fig. 6.32. Front band adjuster screw (4) and locknut (3) (automatic transmission) (Sec. 25)

Fig. 6.33. Rear band adjuster screw locknut (4) and adjuster screw (5) and piston return spring (3), automatic transmission (Sec. 25)

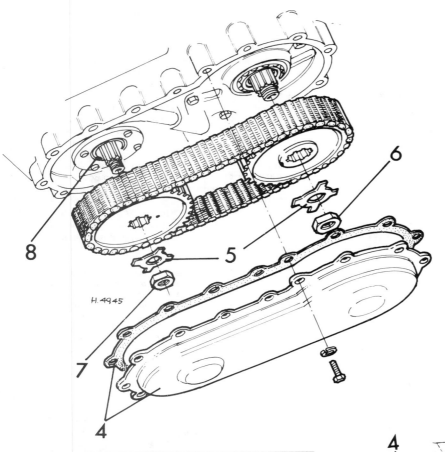

H.4945

**Fig. 6.34. Primary drive chain and
sprockets (automatic transmission)
(Sec. 26)**

4   *Chain cover and gasket*
5   *Lockwashers*
6   *Torque converter shaft nut*
7   *Input shaft nut*
8   *Input shaft spacer and bearing*

## 27 Automatic transmission - removal and installation

1   This is carried out as a combined unit together with the engine, as
described in Chapter 1.

## 28 Final drive pinion - removal and installation

1   This operation will be required if the crownwheel in the final
drive unit (see Chapter 8) is renewed as both components must be
renewed as a matched pair.
2   Remove the engine/transmission from the car and separate the
transmission from the engine all as described in Chapter 1 according
to engine type.
3   Remove the driveplate from the torque converter. The bolts are
accessible through the starter motor aperture.
4   Remove the primary drive chain (Section 26, this Chapter).
5   Remove the front and rear servos and struts. To do this unbolt the
valve body and servo covers (see Fig. 6.31). Release the rear servo
and rear clutch tubes and hang them over the casing. Remove the front
servo tube and then extract the two screws and withdraw the front
brake band strut. Finally, remove the centre support dowel bolt and
sealing washer, remove the two screws and withdraw the rear servo
assembly and rear brake band strut.
6   Disconnect the parking pawl operating rod.
7   Remove the torque converter housing (note the three internal
bolts which secure the housing to the main casing), extracting the
input shaft spacer as it is withdrawn.
8   Remove the differential unit, as described in Chapter 8.
9   Remove the geartrain assembly and front and rear brake bands
from the transmission casing.
10 Withdraw the extension housing and release the governor pressure
tube from its seal in the extension housing and then remove the housing
and gasket.
11 Remove the governor retaining circlips from the shaft taking great
care not to damage the sealing surfaces of the shaft during the operation.

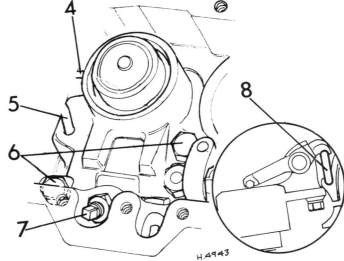

H.4943

**Fig. 6.35. Automatic transmission front servo tubes (4 and 5), front
servo assembly screws (6), front brake band adjusting screw (7), front
servo arm strut (8) (Sec. 28)**

Turn the governor to bring the weight to the bottom, pull the assembly
from the shaft and retrieve the locating ball.
12 Flatten the tabs on the pinion nut lockwasher which are accessible
through the differential housing aperture. On later models, the nut is
staked into a shaft detent.
13 Engage the parking pawl and unscrew the pinion nut which has a
left-hand thread.
14 Extract the final drive pinion from the output shaft. A special tool
will normally be needed to extract this by engaging with the pinion
end flange. However, as the purpose of removal is almost certain to be

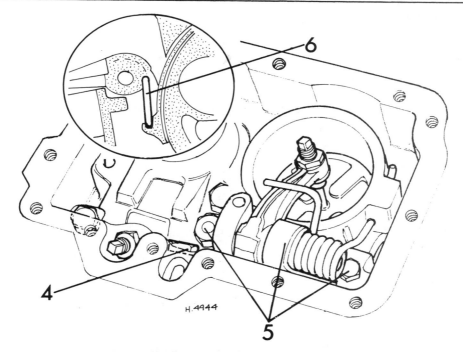

Fig. 6.36. Automatic transmission rear servo centre support dowel bolt (4), rear servo and securing screws (5), rear servo arm strut (6) (Sec. 28)

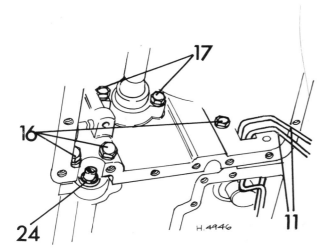

Fig. 6.37. Torque converter housing interior view (Sec. 28)

11 Rear clutch and servo tubes
16 Internal securing bolts
17 End sealing plate bolts
24 'O' ring seal for governor pressure tube

for renewal in conjunction with the crownwheel, a clip or clamp can be applied to the pinion as a pressure point for engagement of a two or three-legged puller.

15 Installation of the final drive pinion is largely a reversal of the removal operation but observe the following points:

(a) Tighten the pinion nut to a torque of 160 lbf ft (217 Nm) and lock or stake it according to type.

(b) Retain the governor locating ball in position with a dab of petroleum jelly (Vaseline) and make sure that the governor is fitted so that its small cover plate is towards the final drive pinion.

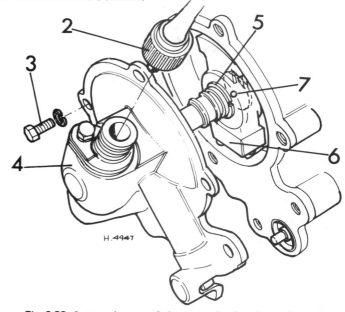

Fig. 6.38. Automatic transmission extension housing and governor components (Sec. 28)

2 Speedometer drive cable
3 Setscrew
4 Extension housing
5 Governor circlip
6 Governor
7 Locating ball

(c) Locate the strut on the rear servo arm with a dab of petroleum jelly and tighten the retaining screws to 15 lb/ft (20 Nm).

(d) Locate the strut on the front servo arm with a dab of petroleum jelly and tighten the retaining screws to 15 lb/ft (20 Nm).

For 'Fault diagnosis - automatic transmission' see next page

**29 Fault diagnosis - automatic transmission**

| Symptom | Reason/s |
|---|---|
| Engine will not start in 'N' or 'P' | Flat battery.<br>Fault in circuit.<br>Incorrect selector cable adjustment.<br>Faulty inhibitor switch. |
| Engine starts in positions other than 'N' or 'P' | Incorrect selector cable adjustment.<br>Faulty inhibitor switch. |
| Severe bump when selecting 'D' or 'R' | Idling speed too high.<br>Faulty downshift valve or cable adjustment. |
| Poor acceleration and low maximum speed | Incorrect fluid level.<br>Incorrect selector cable adjustment. |
| Delayed or no 1 to 2 shift | Incorrect front brake band adjustment. |
| Delayed or no 2 to 3 shift | Incorrect front brake band adjustment. |
| No 3 to 2 downshift or engine braking | Incorrect front brake band adjustment. |
| Drag in 'R' | Incorrect front brake band adjustment. |
| Drag in 'D' or '2' | Incorrect rear brake band adjustment. |
| No 2 to 1 downshift or engine braking | Incorrect rear brake band adjustment. |
| Slip on take off in 'R' and no engine braking in '1' | Incorrect rear brake band adjustment. |

*The most likely causes of faulty operation are incorrect oil level and linkage adjustment. Any other faults or mal-operation of the automatic transmission unit must be due to internal faults and should be rectified by your Leyland dealer. An indication of a major internal fault may be gained from the colour of the oil which under normal conditions should be transparent red. If it becomes discoloured or black then burned clutch or brake bands must be suspected.*

# Chapter 7 Driveshafts

*For modifications, and information applicable to later models, see Supplement at end of manual*

## Contents

## Specifications

| | |
|---|---|
| **Type** ... ... ... ... ... ... ... ... ... ... | Hardy Spicer solid shaft with one constant velocity (CV) joint and one sliding joint. Shafts are of unequal length and not interchangeable |

### Torque wrench settings

| | lb/ft | Nm |
|---|---|---|
| Driveshaft (hub) nut ... ... ... ... ... ... ... ... | 150 | 203 |
| Suspension lower swivel pin nut ... ... ... ... ... ... | 40 | 55 |
| Suspension upper swivel pin nut ... ... ... ... ... ... | 40 | 55 |
| Trackrod-end balljoint nut ... ... ... ... ... ... ... | 35 | 48 |

## 1 General description

1 Drive is transmitted from the final drive differential unit to the front roadwheels by means of two driveshafts of unequal length. The driveshafts are of solid shaft type incorporating constant velocity joints, one of which is of sliding type.

2 Owners of 2200 cars with manual gearbox built before 1978 should be aware of a modification to be carried out by dealers under manufacturers' instruction in an effort to reduce driveshaft wear which has been found to be exceptionally rapid on these cars. Essentially, the engine mountings are moved to the rear by 1½ in (38.1 mm) in order to reduce the driveshaft angle under certain road and steering conditions. At the same time, the condition of the driveshafts will be examined and new ones installed if necessary.

3 The above condition, and the modification required, does not apply to any 1800 model, nor to 2200 models equipped with automatic transmission.

## 2 Driveshafts - maintenance and inspection

No regular maintenance is required but inspect the rubber boots frequently for splits or deterioration and renew them if necessary, as described in Section 4.

## 3 Driveshaft - removal and installation

1 Insert a piece of wood approximately 1½ in. wide x 5/8 in. thick (40.0 x 16.0 mm) between the suspension upper arm and the rebound rubber, see Chapter 11.

2 Slacken the front roadwheel nuts.

3 Raise the front of the car and support it on a stand placed under each front side jacking point.

4 Remove the roadwheels.

5 *On 4 cylinder cars*, slacken the 'U' bolt which secures the exhaust pipe, remove the bracket from the differential housing and push the bracket down the pipe.

6 *On all cars*, release the driveshaft from the final drive, using the tool and method described in Chapter 1, Section 22, paragraph 36.

7 Extract the split pin from the hub nut and remove the nut. In order to prevent the shaft turning, have an assistant apply the footbrake hard as the nut is unscrewed.

8 Using a soft-faced mallet, drive the shaft from the drive flange splines and then extract the split collar. Alternatively, use a three-legged puller with the centre screw applied to the end of the driveshaft.

9 Disconnect the trackrod-end from the steering arm.

10 Disconnect the upper and lower suspension balljoints from the suspension arms and withdraw the driveshaft assembly.

11 Extract the water shield and the bearing spacer and then press the shaft out of the inner bearing.

12 Commence installation by fitting the inner bearing onto the driveshaft tight against the flange then fit the bearing spacer.

13 Position the water shield approximately ¼ in. (6.0 mm) onto the shaft and then pack the area between the shield and the bearing with grease.

14 Clean all the old grease from inside the hub and pack the area between the water shield and the oil seal with grease.

15 Push the driveshaft into the final drive (differential unit) with sufficient force to lock the shaft into its retaining ring. Check that it is properly locked by pulling it gently.

16 Reconnect the suspension and trackrod-end balljoints.

17 Pull the driveshaft into the hub either using a suitable puller or by fitting pieces of tubing as distance pieces and screwing on the shaft nut. Fit the split collar after the driveshaft is fully seated.

18 Tighten all bolts and nuts to specified torque and in the case of the shaft nut, turn it to the next hole (not backwards) if necessary to align the slot in the castellated nut. Use a new split pin.

## 4 Driveshaft flexible boots - renewal

1 If a split or hole in a driveshaft boot has been overlooked for any length of time, then the joint must be dismantled and thoroughly cleaned before renewing the boot (see Sections 5 or 6).

2 Remove the driveshaft, as described in the preceding Section.

*Outer boot*

3 Cut through the circular band which retains the constant velocity

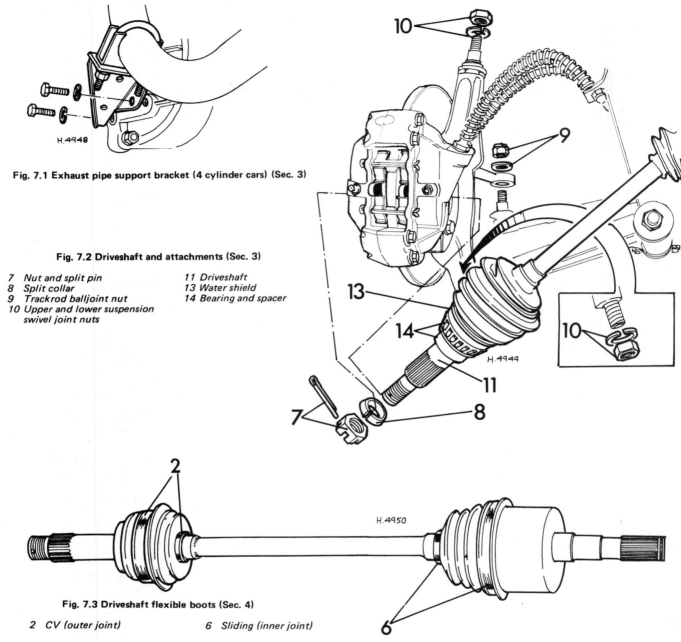

Fig. 7.1 Exhaust pipe support bracket (4 cylinder cars) (Sec. 3)

Fig. 7.2 Driveshaft and attachments (Sec. 3)

7   Nut and split pin          11  Driveshaft
8   Split collar               13  Water shield
9   Trackrod balljoint nut     14  Bearing and spacer
10  Upper and lower suspension
    swivel joint nuts

Fig. 7.3 Driveshaft flexible boots (Sec. 4)

2   CV (outer joint)          6  Sliding (inner joint)

joint boot in position. Peel back the boot and expose the joint.
4   Hold the driveshaft upright and using a soft-faced mallet strike the
edge of the constant velocity joint until it releases from the driveshaft.
5   Extract the boot from the driveshaft.

*Inner boot*
6   Cut through the circular bands which secure the boot to the
driveshaft and the sliding joint.
7   Extract the boot from the driveshaft.
8   Wipe away as much grease as possible from the joints and from the
outside of the driveshaft.
9   Locate the new boots on the driveshaft and then fit the driveshaft
to the inner member of the constant velocity joint. Use a soft-faced
mallet and compress the jump ring on the driveshaft to facilitate entry
of the shaft into the inner member.
10  Now pack each joint with the correct quantity of lubricant which
is:

*Sliding (inner) joint - 150 cc of Shell Tivella 'A' grease*
*CV (outer) joint - 52 cc of Duckhams Bentone Q5795*
11  Secure the **boots using new bands** (if available) or two or three turns

of soft iron wire.
12  Install the driveshaft as described in the preceding Section.

___

**5   Driveshaft CV (outer) joint - overhaul**

1   Remove the driveshaft (Section 3).
2   Remove the CV joint flexible boot (Section 4).
3   Tilt and swivel the inner member of the joint and the ball cage in
the outer member until the balls can be prised from the cage.
4   Swivel the inner member and the ball cage into alignment with the
joint axis and then rotate the cage until its two large windows coincide
with two of the lands in the joint outer member.
5   Withdraw the inner member and cage from the outer member.
6   Swivel the inner member into alignment with the axis of the ball
cage so that two lands of the inner member coincide with the two large
windows in the ball cage and then withdraw the inner member from the
chamfered bore side of the ball cage.
7   Clean and examine all components and renew any that are worn.
8   Reassembly is a reversal of dismantling but note that the inner

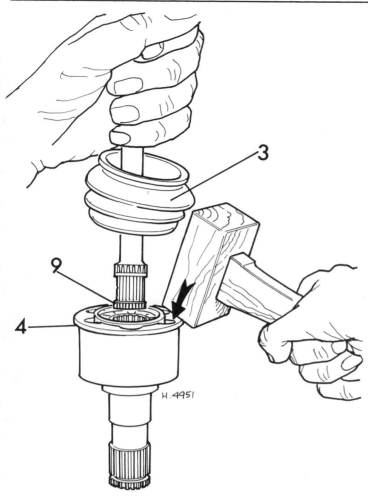

Fig. 7.4 Separating CV joint from driveshaft (striking point arrowed) (Sec. 4)

3   Flexible bout      4   CV joint      9   Jump ring

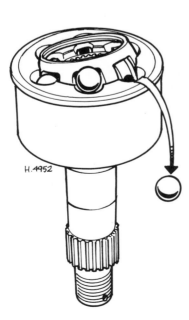

Fig. 7.5 Removing balls from CV joint (Sec. 5)

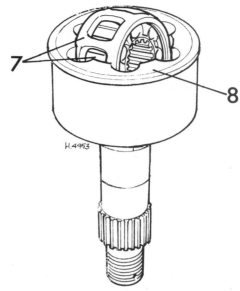

Fig. 7.6 Removing inner member from CV joint (Sec. 5)

7   Inner member and          8   Outer member
    ball cage

Fig. 7.7 Removing inner member from chamfered side of ball cage of CV joint (Sec. 5)

9   Lands in alignment with large      10 Inner member
    windows

member and cage must be fitted into the outer member with the chamfered bore side of the cage at the blind end of the outer member and the lugs on the inner member at the open end of the outer member.
9   Pack the joint with lubricant, as described in Section 4 and then fit the driveshaft to the inner member using a soft-faced mallet.

## 6   Driveshaft sliding (inner) joint - overhaul

1   Remove the driveshaft (Section 3).
2   Remove the sliding joint flexible boot (Section 4).
3   Remove and discard the retaining ring from the lip of the sliding joint and withdraw the driveshaft from the sliding joint outer member. This ring is only used to prevent the joint being pulled apart during the building of the car and it can be discarded. Replacement of the ring is not necessary.
4   Remove the jump ring from the driveshaft and withdraw the sliding joint inner member and ball cage assembly.
5   Prise the balls from the ball cage.
6   Rotate the joint inner member inside the ball cage until the lands on the inner member coincide with the grooves inside the ball cage and then withdraw the inner member.

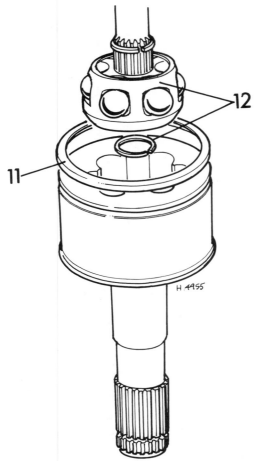

Fig. 7.8 Driveshaft sliding joint components (Sec. 6)

11 Retaining ring (disposable)
12 Jump ring and inner member

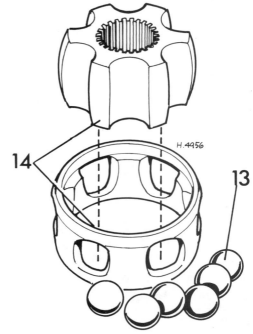

Fig. 7.9 Sliding joint inner member and ball cage (Sec. 6)

13 Balls
14 Lands and groove in alignment to permit separation
   of components

7    Clean and examine all components and renew any that are worn.
8    Reassembly is a reversal of dismantling but note that the inner member and ball cage assembly must be fitted to the driveshaft so that the long tapered end of the ball cage faces towards the CV joint end of the driveshaft.
9    Lubricate the joint, as described in Section 4.

**7    Fault diagnosis - driveshafts**

| Symptom | Reason/s |
| --- | --- |
| Vibration | Driveshafts bent. |
| | Driveshafts out of balance. |
| | Worn or 'dry' joints. |
| | Roadwheels/tyres need balancing. |
| 'Clunk' on taking up drive or on deceleration | Worn driveshaft splines. |
| | Loose hub nut. |
| | Loose roadwheel nuts. |

# Chapter 8 Final drive and differential

## Contents

## Specifications

| Type ... ... ... ... ... ... ... ... ... ... | Helical gears and differential, integral with gearbox |
|---|---|

**Ratios**

| | | | | | | | | |
|---|---|---|---|---|---|---|---|---|
| Manual gearbox ... ... ... ... ... ... ... | 3.72 : 1 |
| Automatic transmission ... ... ... ... ... ... | 3.83 : 1 |
| Differential bearing preload ... ... ... ... ... ... | 0.003 to 0.005 in (0.08 to 0.13 mm) |

| Torque wrench settings | lb/ft | Nm |
|---|---|---|
| Crownwheel bolts ... ... ... ... ... ... ... ... | 55 to 60 | 76 to 83 |
| Differential end cover setscrews ... ... ... ... ... | 18 | 25 |
| Differential cover nuts: | | |
| Small (5/16 in) ... ... ... ... ... ... ... | 18 | 25 |
| Large (7/16 in) ... ... ... ... ... ... ... | 40 | 55 |

## 1 General description

The final drive is integral with the gearbox or automatic transmission and comprises helical gears and the differential.

The ratio differs between the units used on manual or automatic transmission.

Lubrication is provided by the engine/gearbox oil in the case of manual gearbox cars or from the transmission fluid in the case of automatic transmission cars.

## 2 Differential end cover oil seals - renewal

1 This operation can be carried out without removing the power unit from the car.
2 Drain the engine/gearbox oil or the automatic transmission fluid as applicable.
3 Jack-up the front of the car and support securely on axle-stands.
4 Remove the roadwheel.
5 Disconnect the front suspension upper and lower swivel pins by removing the nuts. Using the tool described in Chapter 1, Section 22 release the driveshaft from the differential. Support the inner end of the driveshaft and reconnect the suspension upper swivel pin temporarily.
6 Clean away any dirt or oil from the differential end covers.
7 If the oil seal on the end cover at the clutch (or torque converter end) is being renewed, remove the cover securing bolts and withdraw the cover carefully retaining the shims fitted against the thrust face of the bearing.
8 If the oil seal is being renewed on the crownwheel side, remove the exhaust steady bracket from the final drive housing flange before unbolting the end cover (photo).
9 Lever the old oil seal from the end cover and carefully drive in a new one.
10 Clean away all trace of old gasket and locate a new one making sure that the cut-outs in both the cover and gasket are in alignment.
11 Return the shims to their original location and install the cover again ensuring that the cut-outs in the cover are in alignment with the oil holes in the differential housing.
12 Tighten the cover bolts to the specified torque.
13 Complete the installation of the driveshaft by reversing the removal operations.

2.8 Exhaust mounting bracket on final drive housing

## 3 Final drive housing and differential - removal and installation

1 Remove the engine/transmission from the car, as described in Chapter 1.
2 Remove the end covers from the final drive housing, carefully retaining the shims located under the cover at the clutch (or torque converter) end.
3 *On cars fitted with a manual gearbox,* remove the single nut which secures the gearshift housing and the final drive housing to the gearbox.
4 *On all cars,* remove the remaining nuts which secure the final drive housing to the gearbox.
5 Remove the exhaust mounting bracket.

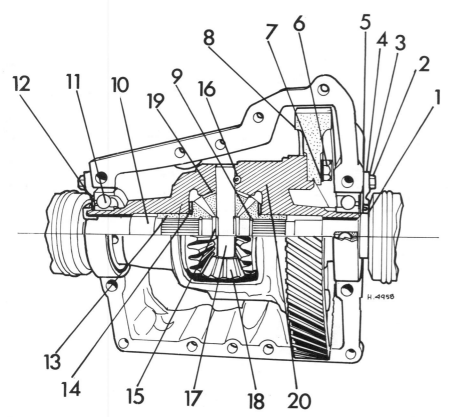

Fig. 8.1 Sectional view of the final drive
unit

1 End cover oil seal
2 End cover setscrew
3 Lock washer
4 End cover
5 Gasket
6 Crownwheel bolt
7 Lock washer
8 Crownwheel
9 Driveshaft retaining circlip
10 Driveshaft
11 Differential cage bearing
12 Pre-load shims
13 Differential gear
14 Washer
15 Distance piece
16 Tension pin
17 Pinion centre pin
18 Differential pinion
19 Washer
20 Differential case

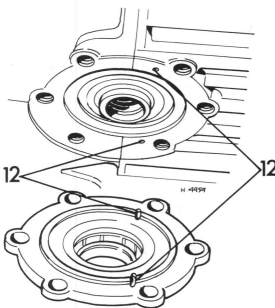

Fig. 8.2 Differential end covers showing oil cut-outs and holes (12)
(Sec. 2)

3.6 View of final drive unit

6    Pull off the final drive housing and lift out the differential assembly
(photo).
7    Installation is a reversal of removal. Should the final drive unit not
seat fully on the transmission casing, this will probably be due to the
crownwheel not meshing with the final drive pinion. To overcome
this, just turn either gearwheel slightly. *On manual gearbox cars,* check
that the selectors engage with the gearbox fork assemblies.
8    Tighten all bolts to their specified torque and make sure that the
shims are returned to their original position under the end cover at the
clutch (or torque converter) end of the final drive housing.

### 4    Final drive unit - dismantling and reassembly

1    Remove the unit, as described in the preceding Section.
2    Mark the relative position of the crownwheel to the differential
cage.
3    Flatten the tabs of the lockwashers and remove the bolts which
secure the crownwheel to the cage.
4    Lift the crownwheel from the cage.
5    Pull the bearings from the differential cage using a suitable bearing
extractor.
6    Drive out the tension pins which retain the differential pinion pin
and then remove the pin.
7    Remove the pinions and thrust washers.
8    Remove the differential gears and washers.
9    Clean and examine all components for wear or damage and renew

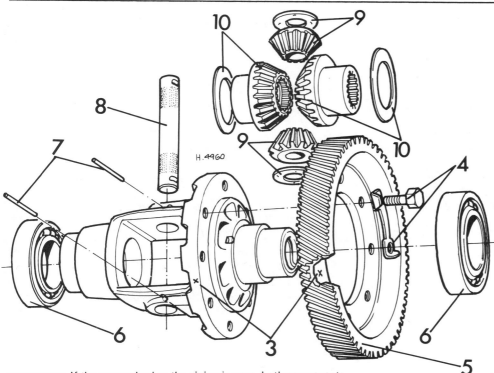

Fig. 8.3 Final drive components (Sec. 4)

3  Crownwheel and cage alignment marks
4  Crownwheel lockwashers and bolts
5  Crownwheel
6  Differential cage bearings
7  Tension pins
8  Pinion pin
9  Pinions and thrust washers
10 Differential gears and washers

as necessary. If the crownwheel or the pinion is worn, both components must be renewed as a matched pair. Removal of the pinion is described in Chapter 6, Sections 11 ot 16 for cars with a manual gearbox and Section 28 for cars having automatic transmission.

10 Commence reassembly by fitting new circlips into the retaining grooves in the differential gears.

11 Install the differential gears and washers, the pinions and thrust washers using new tension pins.

12 Install the bearings to the differential cage. Apply pressure to the bearing centre tracks only and make sure that the numbers on the bearings face away from the cage.

13 Bolt the crownwheel to the differential cage using new locking tabs. If the original crownwheel is being refitted, make sure that the marks made before dismantling are in alignment.

14 Refit the differential unit into the gearbox casing.

15 *If the original differential cage bearings have been refitted,* bolt on the end covers, using new gaskets and making sure that the original shims are returned to their location under the end cover at the clutch (or torque converter) end of the final drive housing.

16 *If new differential cage bearings have been fitted,* only tighten the final drive housing securing nuts enough to just hold the unit to the gearbox so that it can be slightly displaced when the end cover is fitted at the clutch (or torque converter) end of the housing. Install and bolt on the end cover and a new gasket at the crownwheel end. Fit the opposite end cover without its gasket or any shims and tighten the bolts evenly just enough for the cover to nip the bearing outer track. Using feeler blades, measure the gap between the flange of the end cover and the casing and record the reading. Calculate the shim pack required by employing the formula (a − b) + c = d when —

(a) *is average thickness of cover gasket (compressed) 0.008 in. (0.20 mm)*

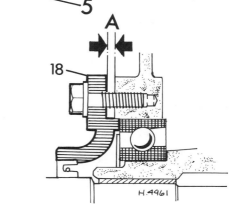

Fig. 8.4 Differential bearing pre-load calculation diagram (Sec. 4)

A  Cover to flange clearance              18 Cover

(b) *clearance measured (A) (Fig. 8.4) between cover and casing.*
(c) *pre-load required 0.004 in. (0.10 mm)*
(d) *thickness of bearing shim pack required.*

Shims are available in the following thicknesses:
0.0015 in. (0.004 mm)
0.0025 in. (0.06 mm)

Refit the end covers and tighten all bolts and nuts to the specified torque.

## 5  Fault diagnosis - final drive and differential

| Symptom | Reason/s |
| --- | --- |
| Oil leaks | Faulty end cover oil seals.<br>Faulty end cover gaskets.<br>End covers incorrectly installed (oil holes not in alignment). |
| Noisy operation | General wear in components.<br>Incorrect bearing preload. |

# Chapter 9 Braking system

*For modifications, and information applicable to later models, see Supplement at end of manual*

## Contents

## Specifications

### Type ... ... ... ... ... ... ... ... ...
Lockheed dual circuit, hydraulic. Disc front, drum rear. Servo assistance. Handbrake mechanical to rear wheels.

### Discs
| | |
|---|---|
| Diameter ... ... ... ... ... ... ... ... ... | 10.64 in (270.0 mm) |
| Total pad area ... ... ... ... ... ... ... | 26.4 in$^2$ (170 cm$^2$) |
| Swept area ... ... ... ... ... ... ... ... | 222.72 sq in (1436.9 sq cm) |
| Minimum pad friction material thickness ... ... ... ... | 1/16 in (1.6 mm) |

### Drums
| | |
|---|---|
| Diameter ... ... ... ... ... ... ... ... ... | 9 in (229.0 mm) |
| Shoe lining ... ... ... ... ... ... ... ... | 9 x 1.75 in (229.0 x 44.5 mm) |
| Swept area ... ... ... ... ... ... ... ... | 95.92 sq in (618.8 sq cm) |
| Wheel cylinder diameter ... ... ... ... ... ... | 0.563 in (14.29 mm) |

### Master cylinder
| | |
|---|---|
| Type ... ... ... ... ... ... ... ... ... | Tandem incorporating pressure differential warning actuator |
| Diameter ... ... ... ... ... ... ... ... ... | 0.813 in (20.64 mm) |

### Vacuum servo
| | |
|---|---|
| Type ... ... ... ... ... ... ... ... ... | Lockheed 65LR direct acting |

### Torque wrench settings
| | lb/ft | Nm |
|---|---|---|
| Disc caliper bolts ... ... ... ... ... ... ... ... | 55 | 76 |
| Disc dust shield to hub bolts ... ... ... ... ... ... | 15 | 21 |
| Disc to drive flange bolts ... ... ... ... ... ... | 45 | 62 |
| Master cylinder mounting nuts ... ... ... ... ... ... | 17 | 23 |
| Pressure differential actuator end plugs ... ... ... ... ... | 18 | 25 |
| Pressure differential switch ... ... ... ... ... ... | 3 | 4 |
| Front driveshaft (hub) nut ... ... ... ... ... ... | 150 | 207 |
| Roadwheel nut ... ... ... ... ... ... ... ... | 45 | 62 |
| Rear hub nut ... ... ... ... ... ... ... ... | 60 | 83 |
| Rear backplate nuts ... ... ... ... ... ... ... | 20 | 28 |
| Bleed screws ... ... ... ... ... ... ... ... | 5 | 7 |
| Brake pedal bracket to servo ... ... ... ... ... ... | 15 | 21 |
| Steering column to brackets ... ... ... ... ... ... | 15 | 21 |
| Steering intermediate shaft to column ... ... ... ... ... | 20 | 27 |

## 1 General description

The braking system is of four wheel hydraulic type having discs at the front and drums at the rear.

Servo assistance is provided to a tandem type master cylinder and the hydraulic system is of dual circuit type. Each circuit comprises two of the four pistons in each of the front disc calipers and one rear brake wheel cylinder on the opposite side of the car.

A self-resetting pressure differential warning actuator is incorporated in the hydraulic system to provide a warning should the pressure drop in one circuit. No adjustment is required to either front or rear brakes which are self-adjusting.

The handbrake operates through mechanical linkage to the rear brake shoes.

## 2  Disc pads - inspection and renewal

1   At the intervals specified in 'Routine maintenance', jack-up the front of the car and remove the roadwheels.
2   Inspect the thickness of the friction material. If this has worn down to 1/16 in (1.6 mm) then the pads must be renewed (photo).
3   To do this, flatten the ends of the retaining pins and extract them.
4   Remove the anti-rattle springs and then grip each of the pads in turn with a pair of pliers and extract them from the caliper.
5   Brush out any accumulated dust and dirt taking care not to inhale it.
6   In order to accommodate the increased thickness of the new pads, the caliper pistons should be depressed evenly and equally into their cylinders using a short piece of wood or flat metal bar. As the pistons are pressed in, the fluid level in the master cylinder will rise and fluid will be displaced so either draw off some fluid from the reservoir using an old hydrometer or alternatively fit a bleed tube to the caliper bleed nipple and submerge its open end in a jar containing a little hydraulic fluid. Release the bleed nipple and as the pistons are depressed, fluid will be expelled into the jar. Retighten the bleed nipple.
7   Install the new disc pads making sure that the friction surface is against the disc. No anti-squeal shims are fitted (photo).
8   Install the anti-rattle springs (longer legs to centre) and push in the new retaining pins supplied with the new pads. Bend up the ends of the pins (photo).
9   Apply the footbrake hard several times to bring the pads into contact with the discs, refit the roadwheels and lower the car.
10  Check and top-up the master cylinder reservoir to the correct level using clean fluid. Discard any fluid which was bled from the system earlier.
11  Always fit new disc pads in complete axle sets - never renew one side only.

## 3  Brake shoes - inspection and renewal

1   At the intervals specified in 'Routine maintenance', slacken the rear roadwheel nuts, release the handbrake and jack-up the rear of the car. Support the car under the rear suspension body bracket.
2   Remove the roadwheel and withdraw the grease retaining cap.
3   Extract the split pin and retainer from the hub nut. Unscrew and remove the nut and special washer. On the left-hand side of the car, the nut has a left-hand thread and on the right-hand side of the car it has a right-hand thread (photo).
4   Pull the hub/drum assembly from the stub axle. If it is tight, tap it off gently using a soft-faced mallet or employ a suitable extractor (photo).
5   After very high mileages or if the interior of the drum has become grooved (due to neglect to renew linings before the rivets contact the friction surface), then it is possible that the action of the automatic adjuster may cause the shoes to lock the drum onto the axle and prevent its removal. In these circumstances, access to the automatic adjuster will have to be obtained by drilling a hole in the brake drums. The hole should be drilled in accordance with the diagram (Fig. 9.1) and then a thin screwdriver inserted and the lever lifted to release the automatic adjuster mechanism. On reassembly, the hole should be sealed with a rubber plug.
6   With the brake drum removed, brush away all dust from the shoes and drum interior, taking care not to inhale it. If the linings are in good condition, the drum can be refitted but if they are worn down or nearly down to the rivets, renew the shoes on an exchange basis. It is not worth attempting to reline shoes yourself. If there is any evidence of oil leakage, this must be rectified before installing the new shoes and it will probably be due to a faulty wheel cylinder (see Section 7) or hub oil seal (see Chapter 11).
7   To renew the shoes, release the shoe steady spring and dished washer from the trailing shoe. To do this, grip the slotted dished washer with a pair of pliers, depress it and turn it through 90°. It can then be withdrawn from the 'T' shaped head of the steady post and the spring

2.2 Checking disc pad wear

2.7 Installing a disc pad

2.8 Installing disc pad anti-rattle springs and pins

3.3 Removing rear hub washer

3.4 Removing a rear brake drum

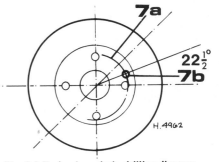

Fig. 9.1 Brake drum hole drilling diagram for release of automatic adjuster (Sec. 3)

7a Drilling arc
7b 5/16 in. (8.0 mm) hole

removed.

8  Ease the trailing shoe from its anchorages and extract the shoe upper return spring (photo).

9  Disengage and withdraw the cross lever and its spring.

10  Use a pair of pliers to release the lower return spring and remove the

trailing shoe.

11  Remove the steady spring and washer from the leading shoe, turn the shoe so that the handbrake cable can be released from its lever and then withdraw the leading shoe.

12  Place an elastic band or a piece of wire round the wheel cylinder pistons to prevent them falling out and do not touch the footbrake pedal while the shoes and drum are withdrawn.

13  Lay the new shoes on the bench in their correct installation attitude noting carefully the relative positions of the leading and trailing ends of the shoes (the greater or smaller areas of exposed shoe web not covered by the friction lining).

14  Transfer the automatic adjuster mechanism to the inside face of the

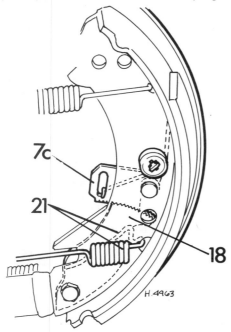

Fig. 9.2 Rear shoe automatic adjuster lever (7c), adjuster mechanism (18) and bottom return spring (21) (Sec. 3)

3.8 View of right-hand rear brake assembly

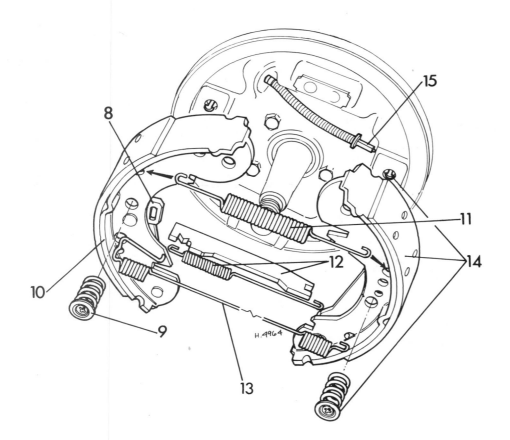

Fig. 9.3 Rear brake components (LH side) (Sec. 3)

8  Adjuster lever
9  Shoe steady dished washer
10  Trailing shoe
11  Upper shoe return spring
12  Cross lever and spring
13  Lower return spring
14  Leading shoe and steady post and spring
15  Handbrake cable

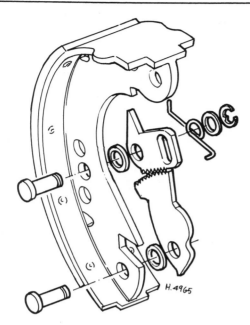

Fig. 9.4 Trailing shoe and automatic adjuster components (Sec. 3)

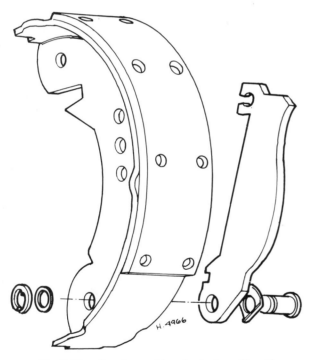

Fig. 9.5 Leading shoe and handbrake lever (Sec. 3)

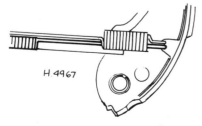

Fig. 9.6 Correct position of cross lever spring below the brake shoe lower return spring (Sec. 3)

new trailing shoe. Fit the pivot pins after applying a smear of high melting point grease to them.

15 Set the mechanism to the minimum adjustment position by lifting the release lever and moving the adjuster lever towards the friction lining.

16 Transfer the handbrake lever to the inside face of the leading shoe. Smear the pivot pin with high melting point grease and make sure that the spring washer has its concave side to the lever.

17 Apply a smear of high melting point grease to the shoe contact points of the brake backplate, the wheel cylinder and lower shoe anchorage and the cross lever.

18 Fit the lower return spring to the trailing shoe making sure that the inside end is over the automatic adjuster lever.

19 Install the shoes, the cross lever (making sure that its return spring is below the shoe lower return spring), the upper return spring and the steady springs and dished washers.

20 Install the brake drum, tightening the hub nut to the specified torque. If necessary, in order to insert the split pin, overtighten the nut slightly, never back it off.

21 Fit the roadwheel and then repeat the operations on the opposite wheel. Never renew one set of brake shoes only, always renew them as complete axle sets.

22 When the car has been lowered to the ground, apply the footbrake several times to operate the automatic adjuster mechanism and then check and top-up, if necessary, the master cylinder reservoir.

## 4 Front disc - inspection, removal and refitting

1 When a considerable mileage has been covered, or if the disc pads have not been renewed and have worn below the specified minimum thickness, check the disc for distortion or run-out and grooving.

2 Light scoring or grooving is normal and should be ignored. Heavy scoring or deep grooving will necessitate renewal of the disc.

3 Jack-up the front of the car and remove the roadwheel and disc pads. Using either a dial gauge or feeler blades against a fixed point, turn the hub/disc assembly and check that any run-out does not exceed 0.008 in (0.2 mm) otherwise the disc will have to be renewed.

4 To renew the disc, slacken the front roadwheel nuts and the driveshaft nut **before** jacking up the front of the car.

5 Remove the caliper, as described in Section 6 and tie it up out of the way to avoid straining the hoses.

6 Remove the driveshaft nut and the split collar.

7 Pull the driving flange/disc assembly from the driveshaft. If it is tight, use a suitable puller.

8 Grip the disc in a vice fitted with jaw protectors and remove the bolts which secure the disc to the driving flange.

9 If required, the disc brake shield can be removed after extracting the two securing bolts.

10 Refitting is a reversal of removal, but tighten all bolts and nuts to the specified torque.

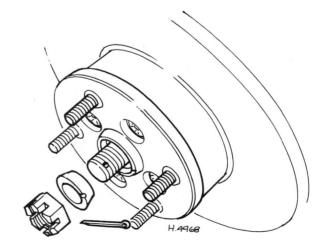

Fig. 9.7 Front driveshaft nut and split collar (Sec. 4)

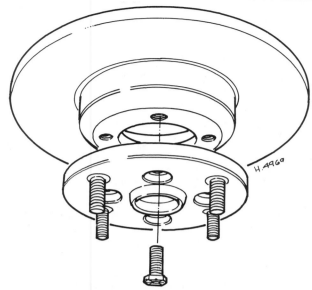

Fig. 9.8 Front disc and driving flange (Sec. 4)

**5  Rear brake drum and backplate - inspection, removal and refitting**

1  Removal of the rear brake drum is described in Section 3.
2  With the drum removed, inspect the interior friction surface for
grooves. If these are evident, renew the drum. Internal calipers will be
required to check for ovality, a condition which can occur after a high
mileage and must be rectified by renewal of the drum.
3  To remove the rear brake backplate, first withdraw the shoe
assembly (see Section 3).
4  Compress the clip which retains the handbrake cable to the
backplate and then draw the cable through the backplate.
5  Disconnect the hydraulic brake line from the wheel cylinder and
plug the line to prevent loss of fluid.
6  Remove the three bolts which retain the backplate to the radius
arm and withdraw the backplate.
7  The wheel cylinder can be removed after extracting the securing
circlip.
8  Refitting is a reversal of removal but remember to bleed the
hydraulic system, as described in Section 9.

**6  Front disc caliper - removal, overhaul and refitting**

1  Jack-up the front of the car, support it securely and remove the
roadwheel.
2  Extract the disc pads (Section 2).
3  Disconnect the hydraulic hoses making sure that they are identified
for correct reconnection. Unscrew the union on the rigid pipelines and
plug or cap their ends to prevent loss of fluid. Then unscrew and
remove the nuts and lockwashers from the ends of the flexible hoses
to release them from their body support brackets.
4  Unscrew and remove the two bolts which secure the caliper to the
swivel hub. Remove the caliper and unscrew the flexible hoses from it.
5  Clean all dirt from the external surfaces of the unit and drain any
brake fluid from it.
6  Place a thin piece of wood between the pistons and depress two
pistons on the same side with the fingers. Now apply air pressure from
a foot pump at one of the fluid entry holes while placing a finger over
the other hole. One of the pistons will be ejected and can be removed.
7  Apply air pressure at the other fluid entry hole, placing the finger
over the hole previously blocked and eject the second piston. Identify
both pistons in respect of their cylinders by using a piece of masking
tape. Clean components only with methylated spirit or hydraulic fluid.
8  From the two empty cylinders, prise the wiper seal and retainer and
the piston seal, use a blunt probe to prevent scratching the cylinder
bores. Should either piston or cylinder surface show signs of scoring or
'bright' wear areas, then the caliper must be renewed complete.
9  Obtain the appropriate repair kit and fit the new seals and retainer,

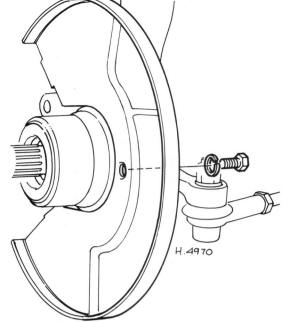

Fig. 9.9 Disc shield and securing bolts (Sec. 4)

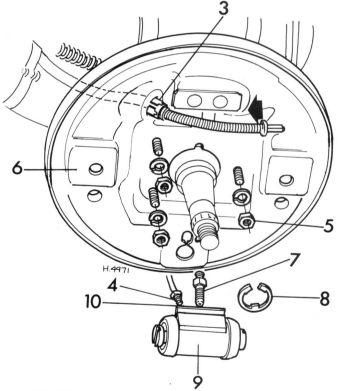

Fig. 9.10 Rear brake backplate attachments (Sec. 5)

3  Handbrake cable clip
4  Fluid pipe union
5  Nut
6  Backplate
7  Bleed screw
8  Wheel cylinder retaining circlip
9  Wheel cylinder
10  Gasket

using the fingers only to manipulate them into position.
10  Dip each piston in brake fluid and insert it squarely into its original
cylinder bore.
11  Holding the two pistons, just serviced, in the depressed position,
eject the other two pistons in a similar manner to that just described.
Install new seals and inspect the piston and cylinder surfaces for scoring

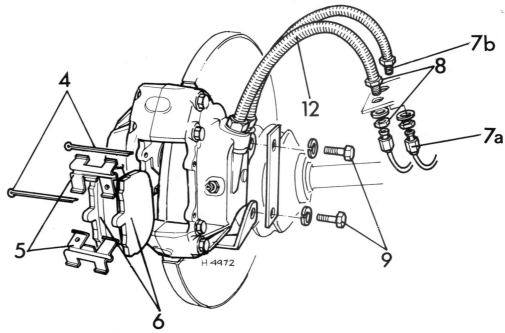

**Fig. 9.11 Disc caliper and attachments (Sec. 6)**

4 Pad pins
5 Anti-rattle clips
6 Pads

7a Fluid line union
7b Flexible hose nut
   and lockwasher

8 Secondary hose
   and union

9 Caliper securing bolts

**Fig. 9.12 Exploded view of a rear wheel cylinder (Sec. 7)**

2 Dust excluding boots
3 Piston and spring

9 Seals (flat face towards
   piston)

or 'bright' wear areas, renewing the complete unit if evident.
12 Refitting is a reversal of removal but on completion, bleed the hydraulic system, as described in Section 9.

## 7 Rear wheel cylinder - overhaul

1   Removal of the rear wheel cylinder is described in Section 5.

2   Clean the external surfaces of the cylinder and then peel off the dust cover from each end of the cylinder body.
3   Withdraw the pistons and the coil spring.
4   Discard the rubber seals and dust covers, wash the components in methylated spirit or clean hydraulic fluid and examine the surfaces of the pistons and cylinder bores for scoring or 'bright' wear areas. If these are evident, renew the wheel cylinder complete.
5   If the components are in good condition, obtain a repair kit and fit new seals, using the fingers only to manipulate them into position. Dip each piston/seal assembly in clean hydraulic fluid and enter it into the cylinder body making sure that the coil spring is located between the pistons.
6   Refit the cylinder, shoe assembly and drum and then bleed the hydraulic system, as described in Section 9.

## 8 Master cylinder - removal, overhaul and refitting

1   Jack-up the front of the car and remove the roadwheels.
2   Attach a bleed tube to each of the **inboard** bleed screws on one caliper. Release the bleed screw one turn and expel the fluid by pumping the footbrake pedal until the master cylinder reservoir is empty.
3   Pull the electrical connector plug from the pressure differential switch which is located between the master cylinder and the servo unit (Fig. 9.13).
4   Disconnect the fluid pipes from the master cylinder body.
5   Remove the master cylinder from the servo unit by unscrewing and removing the two securing nuts and washers.
6   Clean all dirt from the external surfaces of the master cylinder.
7   Unscrew and remove the pressure differential switch.
8   Secure the master cylinder in a vice fitted with jaw protectors and unscrew and remove the two shouldered screws which secure the fluid reservoir. Withdraw the reservoir from the master cylinder body.
9   Extract the two reservoir sealing rings.
10  Extract the circlip from the end of the cylinder bore.
11  Withdraw the primary piston and return spring.
12  Using a copper or brass rod, insert it into the cylinder and depress the secondary piston so that the stop pin can be extracted from the secondary piston fluid feed port.
13  Withdraw the secondary piston and spring either by shaking them

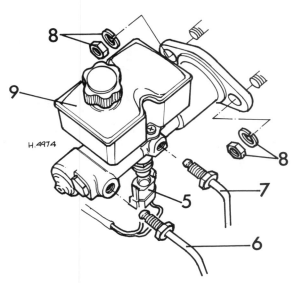

**Fig. 9.13 Brake master cylinder connections (Sec. 8)**

5  *Pressure differential switch plug*   7  *Primary fluid line*
6  *Secondary fluid line*               8  *Securing nuts*
                                     9  *Reservoir*

out or by applying air pressure to the secondary outlet port.

14 Unscrew and remove the end plug and washer but do not prise off the distance piece from the end plug spigot.

15 Extract the pressure differential assembly, either by shaking it from the body or by applying air pressure to the secondary outlet port.

16 Wash all components in methylated spirit or clean hydraulic fluid and examine the surfaces of the pistons and cylinder bore for scoring or 'bright' wear areas. Where these are evident renew the complete master cylinder.

17 If the components are in good condition, discard all seals and obtain the appropriate repair kit.

18 Fit new 'O' ring seals to the pressure warning piston.

19 Install a shim washer to the primary and secondary pistons.

20 Using the fingers only, manipulate the two identical piston seals into place on the primary and secondary pistons (lip facing away from washer).

21 Of the two remaining seals contained in the repair kit, fit the thinner one to the secondary piston (lip towards primary spring seat). Fit the thicker one to the primary piston (lip towards piston seal).

22 Fit the shorter return spring and cup to the secondary piston, dip the assembly into clean hydraulic fluid and insert it into the master cylinder body. Take care not to trap the seal lip.

23 Depress the secondary piston and insert the stop pin after the head of the piston has been seen to pass the feed port.

24 Install the return spring and cup to the primary piston, dip the assembly into clean hydraulic fluid and insert it into the master cylinder body. Take care not to trap the seal lips. Refit the retaining circlip.

25 Insert the pressure differential piston into its bore and then fit a new sealing washer to the end plug and screw it in, tightening it to

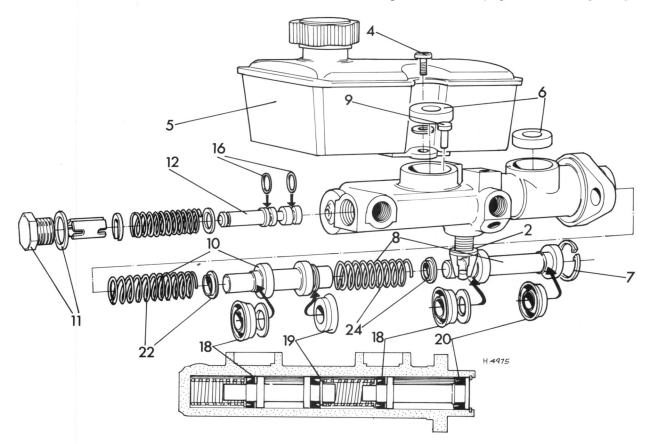

**Fig. 9.14 Exploded view of the brake master cylinder (Sec. 8)**

| | | | |
|---|---|---|---|
| 2  *Pressure differential switch* | 8  *Primary piston and spring* | 16  *'O' ring seals* | 22  *Secondary piston return* |
| 4  *Reservoir screws* | 9  *Stop pin* | 18  *Piston seals* |     *spring and cup* |
| 5  *Reservoir* | 10  *Secondary piston and spring* | 19  *Secondary piston seal* | 24  *Primary piston return* |
| 6  *Seals* | 11  *End plug and washer* | 20  *Primary piston seal* |     *spring and cup* |
| 7  *Circlip* | 12  *Pressure differential piston* | | |

specified torque.

26  Install new reservoir seals (round edge first).

27  Install the reservoir, tightening the shouldered securing screws to the specified torque.

28  Fit the pressure differential warning switch.

29  Refitting the master cylinder is a reversal of removal but on completion, bleed the hydraulic system, as described in Section 9.

## 9  Hydraulic system - bleeding

1  Gather together a supply of clean hydraulic fluid (which has been kept stored in an airtight container and has remained unshaken for the preceding 24 hours), three bleed tubes and two or three glass jars.

2  Raise the front of the car and support it securely. Remove the front roadwheels.

3  Top-up the fluid reservoir on the master cylinder.

4  Fit a bleed tube to each of the inboard bleed screws on one of the front calipers.

5  Fit a bleed tube to the rear brake wheel cylinder which is on the same side of the car as the caliper just mentioned.

6  Pour sufficient hydraulic fluid into the jars so that the ends of the bleed tubes are submerged.

7  Open the rear brake screw one turn and then have an assistant depress the brake pedal fully and rapidly to the floor. Allow the pedal to return to its stop by quickly lifting the foot.

8  Repeat this operation until hydraulic fluid is seen being expelled from the end of the bleed tube free from air bubbles. Close the bleed screw (pedal depressed), using a spanner of short length and not over-tightening it.

9  Top-up the reservoir with clean fluid, always discard fluid which has been bled from the system. Never let the level in the reservoir fall below the half full mark during the bleeding operations.

10  Now open the two inboard bleed screws on the front caliper. Depress the foot pedal repeatedly until no air bubbles are seen emerging from the ends of the bleed tubes and then tighten the bleed screws while the foot pedal is fully depressed. Top-up the master cylinder fluid reservoir.

11  Remove one of the bleed tubes from the caliper and apply it to the outboard bleed screw. Submerge its end in the fluid in the bleed jar, release the screw one turn and then have an assistant depress the foot pedal repeatedly until no more air bubbles emerge from the end of the tube. Retighten the bleed screw (pedal depressed).

12  Top-up the master cylinder reservoir and then re-open the rear bleed screw. Bleed as previously described and when the fluid emerges free from air bubbles, tighten the bleed screw.

13  Repeat all the foregoing bleeding operations on the brakes on the opposite side of the car.

14  Finally remove the bleed tubes, discard the fluid which has been bled from the system and top-up the master cylinder reservoir to the correct level with clean fluid from a sealed container.

## 10  Flexible hoses - inspection, removal and refitting

1  Inspect the condition of the flexible hydraulic hoses. If they are swollen, perished or chafed, they must be renewed.

2  To remove a flexible hose, hold the flats on its end-fitting in an open ended spanner and unscrew the union nut which couples it to the rigid brake line.

3  Disconnect the flexible hose from the rigid line and support bracket and then unscrew the hose from the caliper or wheel cylinder circuit as the case may be.

4  Refitting is a reversal of removal. The flexible hoses may be twisted not more than one quarter turn in either direction if necessary to provide a 'set' to ensure that they do not rub or chafe against any adjacent component.

5  Bleed the hydraulic system on completion.

6  Hydraulic pipe and hose end fittings and unions are used incorporating both UNF and metric threads. It is vital that replacements are fitted which have the correct compatible threads. Metric fittings are identified with the letter M. Always screw a hydraulic line fitting in by hand pressure initially to verify the thread type and **note that a metric flexible hose will have a gap between its end face and the component into which it is screwed.** This is because it seals against the bottom of the fluid port. **Never use a copper sealing**

washer with a metric hose or attempt to force the end fitting flush by excessive tightening.

## 11  Rigid brake lines - inspection, removal and refitting

1  At regular intervals wipe the steel brake pipes clean and examine them for signs of rust or denting caused by flying stones.

2  Examine the securing clips which are plastic coated to prevent wear to the pipe surface. Bend the tongues of the clips if necessary to ensure that they hold the brake pipes securely without letting them rattle or

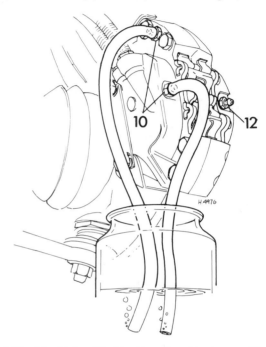

**Fig. 9.15a. Bleed tubes fitted to disc caliper bleed screws (Sec. 9)**

*10  Inner bleed screws*          *12  Outboard bleed screw*

**Fig. 9.15b. Bleed tube fitted to rear wheel cylinder (Sec. 9)**

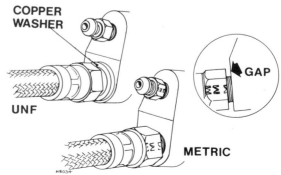

**Fig. 9.16. UNF and metric brake hydraulic hose connections**

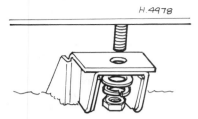

Fig. 9.17 Attachment of rear seat (Sec. 12)

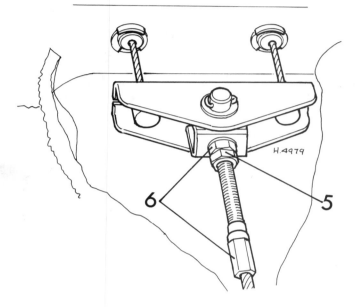

Fig. 9.18 Handbrake cable equaliser (Sec. 12)

5   Locknut

6   Adjuster nut and
    hexagon

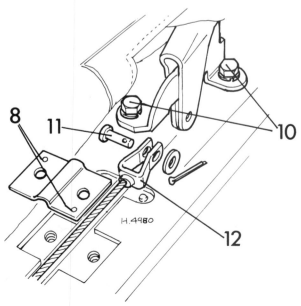

Fig. 9.19 Handbrake front cable attachment to lever (Sec.13)

8   Guide plate rivets          11  Clevis pin
10  Handbrake lever bolts       12  Clevis fork

vibrate.
3    Check that the pipes are not touching any adjacent components or rubbing against any part of the vehicle. Where this is observed, bend the pipe gently away to clear.
4    Although the pipes are plated any section of pipe may become rusty through chafing and should be renewed. Brake pipes are available to the correct length and fitted with end unions from most Leyland dealers and can be made to pattern by many accessory suppliers. When installing the new pipes use the old pipes as a guide to bending and do not make any bends sharper than is necessary. Refer also to paragraph 6, Section 10.
5    The system will of course have to be bled when the circuit has been reconnected.

## 12 Handbrake - adjustment

1    This is not a routine operation and the rear brakes, having automatic adjusters, will normally keep the handbrake fully adjusted also automatically.
2    Where there is excessive movement of the handbrake lever as well as excessive free-movement of the footbrake pedal, then faulty operation of the self-adjusting mechanism must be suspected. Where the mechanism is in good order, then the handbrake cable has probably stretched and the following adjustment should be carried out.
3    Remove the rear seat to gain access to the cable equaliser.
4    Set the handbrake lever three notches ('clicks') from the fully off position.
5    Raise the rear of the car and support it under the rear side jacking points.
6    Turn each rear roadwheel. It should just be possible to turn them against the binding action of the brakes.
7    If they turn freely without any indication of binding then the cable is slack and must be adjusted at the equaliser by turning the adjuster nut after releasing the locknut.
8    When the binding condition has been obtained, fully release the handbrake lever and check that the rear roadwheels rotate freely without any tendency to bind.
9    Tighten the locknut at the equaliser and refit the rear seat.

## 13 Handbrake cables - renewal

1    Remove the front passenger seat and the rear seat.
2    If a centre console is fitted, remove it (Chapter 12).
3    Remove the front seat belt anchorages from between the front seats.
4    Remove the rear door seal and carpet retainer.
5    Remove the two rear screws which secure the front door seal and carpet retainer. Pull the carpet from under the front retainer and the seat belt reel. Lift the carpet and prop it against the driver's seat.
6    Drill out the pop rivets from the guide plate and remove the plate.
7    Release the locknut which secures the front cable and disconnect the trunnion of the equaliser from the cable threaded portion.
8    Remove the bolts which secure the handbrake lever to the floor.
9    Remove the clevis pin which secures the clevis fork to the handbrake lever.
10   Extract the front handbrake cable from between the guide plates and the floor.
11   To remove a rear handbrake cable, first remove the rear brake drum (Section 2) and shoe assembly.
12   Remove the clip which secures the cable to the radius arm.
13   Pull the cable out of the retaining clip on the suspension cross tube.
14   Compress the retaining clip and pull the handbrake cable through the brake backplate.
15   Remove the rear seat and then holding the balance lever, pull the inner cable from the slot in the equaliser.
16   Extract the clip from the outer cable and then withdraw the complete cable assembly from beneath the car.
17   Refitting of the cables is a reversal of removal but apply grease to the clevis pins and adjust the handbrake on completion, as described in the preceding Section.

## 14 Brake pedal (manual gearbox) - removal and refitting

1    This is carried out in a similar manner to that described for the

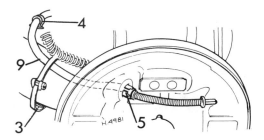

Fig. 9.20 Handbrake rear cable attachment (Sec. 13)

3  Radius arm clip                5  Backplate clip
4  Suspension cross-tube clip     9  Handbrake cable

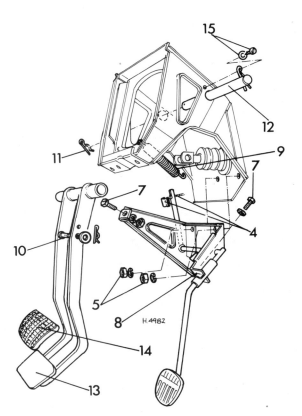

Fig. 9.21 Brake and accelerator pedal attachments (automatic transmission) (Sec. 15)

4  Accelerator cable and spring     9  Brake pedal return spring
   clip                           10  Clevis pin
5  Accelerator pedal bracket      11  Spring pin
   to servo stud nuts             12  Pedal shaft
7  Setscrew                       13  Pedal assembly
8  Accelerator pedal bracket      14  Pedal rubber
                                  15  Self-tapping screw

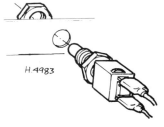

Fig. 9.22 Brake stop lamp switch and locking nuts (Sec. 17)

clutch pedal in Chapter 5, Section 8.

## 15 Brake pedal (automatic transmission) - removal and refitting

1  Remove the parcels tray (Chapter 12).
2  Remove the steering column assembly (Chapter 11).
3  Remove the demister duct on the driver's side.
4  Disconnect the accelerator cable from the pedal arm after pulling off the spring clip (Chapter 3, Section 13).
5  Remove the accelerator pedal bracket from the studs on the brake servo unit.
6  Pull the carpet down from behind the pedals and remove the insulation pad from the outside top surface of the engine compartment rear bulkhead.
7  Remove the setscrew which secures the accelerator pedal bracket to the body and pedal bracket.
8  Withdraw the accelerator pedal bracket assembly.
9  Disconnect the brake pedal return spring.
10 Remove the clevis pin which secures the pushrod to the brake pedal.
11 Remove the self-tapping screw and plain washer which retain the shaft and extract the spring from the opposite end of the shaft.
12 Push the shaft through the pedal and withdraw the pedal.
13 Renewal of the pedal shaft bushes can be carried out by pressing the old ones out and the new ones in until they are just below the end face of the tube.
14 Refitting is a reversal of removal but apply grease to all friction surfaces.

## 16 Pedal bracket - removal and refitting

1  Remove the parcels tray.
2  On manual gearbox cars, disconnect the steering column and lower it but leaving it still attached to the intermediate shaft (see Chapter 11).
3  On automatic transmission cars, the steering column must be removed from the car.
4  Release the strap which secures the cables to the pedal bracket.
5  Disconnect the speedometer cable from the back of the speedometer and withdraw the cable through the pedal bracket.
6  Disconnect the cables from the brake stop lamp switch.
7  Disconnect the choke control cable from the carburettor and withdraw the cable through the pedal bracket hole.
8  If a radio is fitted, pull the aerial (antenna) lead from the back of the radio and withdraw it through the pedal bracket.
9  Carry out the operations described in paragraphs 4 to 8 and 10 of the preceding Section.
10 On manual gearbox cars, remove the clevis pin which connects the pushrod to the clutch pedal, also remove the nuts which secure the clutch master cylinder.
11 On automatic transmission cars, remove the nuts which secure the blanking plate.
12 Remove the two screws which secure the top of the pedal bracket to the body and withdraw the pedal bracket assembly.
13 Remove the brake stop lamp switch and detach the brake pedal return spring.
14 Disconnect the pedals from the bracket, as described in Sections 14 or 15 according to type.
15 Refitting is a reversal of removal but make sure that the accelerator pedal return spring is hard against the pedal lever and under the panel.

## 17 Brake stoplamp switch - adjustment

1  This is easier to adjust if the parcels tray is first removed.
2  Switch on the ignition and release the switch locknuts. Adjust the position of the switch by turning the nuts until the stoplamps go out, then turn the nuts a further half turn to move the switch closer to the pedal arm and lock the nuts. Switch off the ignition.

## 18 Vacuum servo unit - description

1  A vacuum servo unit is fitted into the brake hydraulic circuit in series with the master cylinder, to provide assistance to the driver when the brake pedal is depressed. This reduces the effort required by the

driver to operate the brakes under all braking conditions.

2   The unit operates by vacuum obtained from the induction manifold and comprises basically a booster diaphragm and non-return valve. The servo unit and hydraulic master cylinder are connected together so that the servo unit piston rod acts as the master cylinder pushrod. The driver's braking effort is transmitted through another pushrod to the servo piston and its built in control system. The servo unit piston does not fit tightly into the cylinder, but has a strong diaphragm to keep its edges in constant contact with the cylinder wall, so assuring an air tight seal between the two parts. The forward chamber is held under vacuum conditions created in the inlet manifold of the engine and, during periods when the brake pedal is not in use, the controls open a passage to the rear chamber so placing it under vacuum conditions as well. When the brake pedal is depressed, the vacuum passage to the rear chamber is cut off and the chamber opened to atmospheric pressure. The consequent rush of air pushes the servo piston forward in the vacuum chamber and operates the main pushrod to the master cylinder.

3   The controls are designed so that assistance is given under all conditions and, when the brakes are not required, vacuum in the rear chamber is established when the brake pedal is released. All air from the atmosphere entering the rear chamber is passed through a small air filter.

4   Under normal operating conditions the vacuum servo unit is very reliable and does not require overhaul except at very high mileages. In this case it is far better to obtain a service exchange unit, rather than repair the original unit.

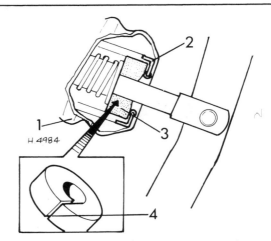

Fig. 9.23 Servo air filter (Sec. 20)

1   Dust excluder
2   Retainer
3   Filter
4   Cut made in filter to ease installation

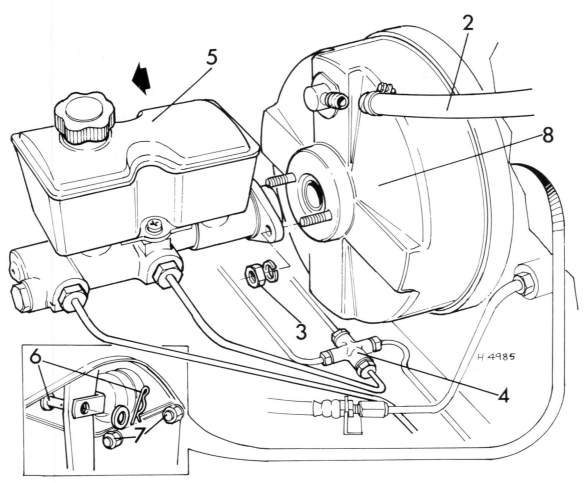

Fig. 9.24 Vacuum servo unit and master cylinder mounting (Sec. 21)

2   Vacuum hose from inlet manifold
3   Master cylinder mounting nuts
4   Four way union
5   Fluid reservoir
6   Clevis pin and spring pin
7   Servo to brake pedal bracket nuts
8   Vacuum servo unit

5  It is emphasised, that the servo unit assists in reducing the braking effort required at the foot pedal and in the event of its failure, the hydraulic braking system is in no way affected except that the need for higher pedal pressures will be noticed.

## 19 Vacuum servo hose and non-return valve - renewal

1  Disconnect the vacuum hose from both the servo unit and the inlet manifold and remove it.
2  Observe the angle of the nozzle of the non-return valve and then pull the valve from its sealing grommet. A flat blade inserted between the valve and the grommet will help in levering the valve out.
3  Pull the grommet from the servo housing gripping it securely with a pair of pliers so that it does not fall inside the unit.
4  Refitting is a reversal of removal but apply a little rubber grease or brake fluid to facilitate entry of the valve into the grommet.

## 20 Vacuum servo air filter - renewal

1  At the intervals specified in 'Routine maintenance', pull back the boot from around the brake pushrod.

2  Withdraw the retainer and pull out the filter. If this is in one piece, it can be cut from the pushrod.
3  To save disconnecting the pushrod, cut the new filter as shown in Fig. 9.23 and install it. Refit the retainer and the boot.

## 21 Vacuum servo unit - removal and installation

1  Disconnect the lead from the pressure differential switch which is located between the master cylinder and the servo unit.
2  Disconnect the hose from the servo unit.
3  Remove the nuts which secure the master cylinder to the servo unit.
4  Slacken the union at the four way connector which connects the feed pipe from the master cylinder.
5  Pull the master cylinder gently downwards and forwards to clear the servo studs. Retighten the union and support the master cylinder to avoid straining the connecting pipes.
6  Disconnect the pushrod from the brake pedal.
7  Remove the four nuts which secure the servo unit to the brake pedal bracket and then pull the servo unit from the engine bulkhead.
8  Installation is a reversal of removal but the hydraulic system may need bleeding if air has entered at the released union.

## 22 Fault diagnosis - braking system

| Symptom | Reason/s |
|---|---|
| Pedal travels almost to floorboards before brakes operate | Brake fluid level too low. Caliper leaking. Master cylinder leaking (bubbles in master cylinder fluid). Brake flexible hose leaking. Brake line fractured. Brake system unions loose. Rear automatic adjusters seized. |
| Brake pedal feels springy | New linings not yet bedded in. Brake discs or drums badly worn or cracked. Master cylinder securing nuts loose. |
| Brake pedal feels spongy and soggy | Caliper or wheel cylinder leaking. Master cylinder leaking (bubbles in master cylinder reservoir). Brake pipe line or flexible hose leaking. Unions in brake system loose. Air in hydraulic system. |
| Excessive effort required to brake car | Pad or shoe linings badly worn. New pads or shoes recently fitted — not yet bedded-in. Harder linings fitted than standard causing increase in pedal pressure. Linings and brake drums contaminated with oil, grease or hydraulic fluid. Servo unit inoperative or faulty. |
| Brakes uneven and pulling to one side | Linings and discs or drums contaminated with oil, grease or hydraulic fluid. Tyre pressures unequal. Radial ply tyres fitted at one end of the car only. Brake caliper loose. Brake pads or shoes fitted incorrectly. Different type of linings fitted at each wheel. Anchorages for front suspension or rear suspension loose. Brake discs or drums badly worn, cracked or distorted. |
| Brakes tend to bind, drag or lock-on | Air in hydraulic system. Wheel cylinders or calipers seized. Handbrake cables too tight. |

# Chapter 10 Electrical system

*For modifications, and information applicable to later models, see Supplement at end of manual*

## Contents

## Specifications

| System type | ... ... ... ... ... ... ... ... ... | 12 volt, negative earth | |
|---|---|---|---|

| Battery | ... ... ... ... ... ... ... ... ... | 55, 66 or 68 (option) amp hr at 20 hr rate | |
|---|---|---|---|

### Alternator

| | | Lucas 18ACR | AC Delco |
|---|---|---|---|
| Type ... ... ... ... ... ... ... ... ... ... | | Lucas 18ACR | AC Delco |
| Output (at 14V, 6000 alternator rev/min) ... ... ... | | 43 amp | 45 amp |
| Minimum brush length (protruding from moulding) ... ... ... | | 0.2 in (5.0 mm) | 0.4 in (10.0 mm) |

### Starter motor

| Type ... ... ... ... ... ... ... ... ... ... | Pre-engaged M35J or 2M100 |
|---|---|
| Armature endfloat ... ... ... ... ... ... ... | 0.01 in (0.25 mm) |
| Minimum brush length ... ... ... ... ... ... ... | 0.375 in (10.0 mm) |

### Windscreen wipers

| Motor type ... ... ... ... ... ... ... ... | Lucas 14 WA |
|---|---|
| Minimum brush length ... ... ... ... ... ... ... | 0.18 in (4.7 mm) |
| Armature endfloat ... ... ... ... ... ... ... | 0.002 to 0.008 in (0.05 to 0.2 mm) |

### Fuses

(1)   16 amp. Heater motor circuit
(2)   8 amp. Wiper and washer circuit
(3)   8 amp. Side, tail and rear number plate on right-hand side of car, also panel lamps and cigar lighter lamp
(4)   8 amp. Side and tail lamps on left-hand side of car
(5)   16 amp. Hazard warning flasher circuit, brake failure circuit, cigar lighter, interior lamps
(6)   16 amp. Horn, headlamp flasher switch
(7)   8 amp. Seatbelt switch and warning circuit, rear window heater switch and warning lamp, direction indicator flashers, reversing lamps, stop lamps
(8)   16 amp. Rear window demist relay and rear window demist unit

### Bulbs

| | Wattage | Number |
|---|---|---|
| Headlamp (bulbs) ... ... ... ... ... ... ... ... | 60/65 | GLB 472 |
| Headlamp (sealed beam): | | |
| Outer ... ... ... ... ... ... ... ... ... ... | 60/37.5 | GLU 105 |
| Inner ... ... ... ... ... ... ... ... ... ... | 50 | GLU 103 |
| Front parking lamp ... ... ... ... ... ... ... | 4 | BSF 233 |
| Direction indicator lamp ... ... ... ... ... ... ... | 21 | GLB 382 |
| Side repeater lamp ... ... ... ... ... ... ... | 5 | GLB 501 |
| Stop/tail lamp ... ... ... ... ... ... ... ... | 21/5 | GLB 380 |
| Tail lamp ... ... ... ... ... ... ... ... ... | 5 | GLB 207 |

## Bulbs

| | Wattage | Number |
|---|---|---|
| Reversing lamp ... ... ... ... ... ... ... ... ... | 21 | GLB 382 |
| Rear number plate lamp ... ... ... ... ... ... ... | 5 | GLB 501 |
| Panel warning lamps ... ... ... ... ... ... ... ... | 2.2 | GLB 504 |
| Switch illumination and seatbelt warning lamps ... ... | 2 | BFS 281 |
| Cigar lighter lamp ... ... ... ... ... ... ... ... | 2.2 | BFS 643 |
| Automatic transmission selector index lamp ... ... ... | 2 | BFS 281 |
| Interior lamps ... ... ... ... ... ... ... ... | 6 | GLB 254 |
| Heater indicator lamp ... ... ... ... ... ... ... | 1.2 | GLB 286 |
| Side repeater lamp ... ... ... ... ... ... ... | 5 | GLB 501 |

## Torque wrench settings

| | lb/ft | Nm |
|---|---|---|
| Alternator mounting bolts ... ... ... ... ... ... ... | 20 | 28 |
| Alternator pulley: | | |
|    Lucas ... ... ... ... ... ... ... ... ... | 25 | 35 |
|    AC Delco ... ... ... ... ... ... ... ... | 50 | 69 |
| Starter motor securing bolts ... ... ... ... ... ... | 30 | 41 |
| Starter motor tie-bolts ... ... ... ... ... ... ... | 8 | 11 |
| Seatbelt bracket bolts ... ... ... ... ... ... ... | 18 | 25 |

## 1 General description

The electrical system is of 12 volt negative earth type. The battery supplies a steady current to the ignition system and for the operation of the electrical accessories.

The alternator maintains the charge in the battery and the voltage regulator which is incorporated in the alternator, adjusts the charging rate according to the demands of the engine.

A pre-engaged type starter motor is fitted to all models.

## 2 Battery - removal and refitting

1 The battery is located within the engine compartment on the right-hand side.
2 To remove the battery first disconnect the lead from the negative (−) terminal followed by the positive (+) one.
3 Detach the battery holding down clamp bolts and lift the battery from its platform. Take care not to spill electrolyte on the bodywork or the paint will be damaged.
4 Refitting is a reversal of removal but make sure that the lead terminals and battery posts are clean and making a sound metal-to-metal contact. Finally smear the terminals with petroleum jelly as a protection against corrosion.

## 3 Battery - maintenance and inspection

1 Keep the top of the battery clean by wiping away dirt and moisture.
2 Remove the plugs or lid from the cells and check that the electrolyte level is just above the separator plates. If the level has fallen, add only distilled water until the electrolyte level is just above the separator plates.
3 As well as keeping the terminals clean and covered with petroleum jelly, the top of the battery, and especially the top of the cells, should be kept clean and dry. This helps prevent corrosion and ensures that the battery does not become partially discharged by leakage through dampness and dirt.
4 Once every three months, remove the battery and inspect the battery securing bolts, the battery clamp plate, tray and battery leads for corrosion (white fluffy deposits on the metal which are brittle to touch). If any corrosion is found, clean off the deposits with ammonia and paint over the clean metal with an anti-rust/anti-acid paint.
5 At the same time inspect the battery case for cracks. If a crack is found, clean and plug it with one of the proprietary compounds marketed for this purpose. If leakage through the crack has been excessive then it will be necessary to refill the appropriate cell with fresh electrolyte as detailed later. Cracks are frequently caused to the top of battery cases by pouring in distilled water in the middle of winter *after* instead of *before* a run. This gives the water no chance to mix with the electrolyte and so the former freezes and splits the battery case.
6 If topping up the battery becomes excessive and the case has been inspected for cracks that could cause leakage, but none are found, the battery is being over-charged and the voltage regulator within the alternator must be at fault.

7 With the battery on the bench at the three monthly interval check, measure its specific gravity with a hydrometer to determine the state of charge and condition of the electrolyte. There should be very little variation between the different cells and if a variation in excess of 0.25 is present it will be due to either:
   a) *Loss of electrolyte from the battery at some time caused by spillage or a leak, resulting in a drop in the specific gravity of electrolyte when the deficiency was replaced with distilled water instead of fresh electrolyte.*
   b) *An internal short circuit caused by buckling of the plates or a similar malady pointing to the likelihood of total battery failure in the near future.*
8 The specific gravity of the electrolyte for fully charged conditions at the electrolyte temperature indicated, is listed in Table A. The specific gravity of a fully discharged battery at different temperatures of the electrolyte is given in Table B.

### Table A

*Specific Gravity - Battery Fully Charged*

*1.268 at 100° F or 38° C electrolyte temperature*
*1.272 at  90° F or 32° C electrolyte temperature*
*1.276 at  80° F or 27° C electrolyte temperature*
*1.280 at  70° F or 21° C electrolyte temperature*
*1.284 at  60° F or 16° C electrolyte temperature*
*1.288 at  50° F or 10° C electrolyte temperature*
*1.292 at  40° F or   4° C electrolyte temperature*
*1.296 at  30° F or −1° C electrolyte temperature*

### Table B

*Specific Gravity - Battery Fully Discharged*

*1.098 at 100° F or 38° C electrolyte temperature*
*1.102 at  90° F or 32° C electrolyte temperature*
*1.106 at  80° F or 27° C electrolyte temperature*
*1.110 at  70° F or 21° C electrolyte temperature*
*1.114 at  60° F or 16° C electrolyte temperature*
*1.118 at  50° F or 10° C electrolyte temperature*
*1.122 at  40° or   4° C electrolyte temperature*
*1.126 at  30° F or −1° C electrolyte temperature*

## 4 Battery - electrolyte replenishment

1 If the battery is in a fully charged state and one of the cells maintains a specific gravity reading which is 0.25 or more lower than the others, and a check of each cell has been made with a voltage meter to check for short circuits (a four to seven second test should give a steady reading of between 1.2 to 1.8 volts), then it is likely that electrolyte has been lost from the cell with the low reading at some time.
2 Top up the cell with a solution of 1 part sulphuric acid to 2.5 parts of water. If the cell is already fully topped up draw some electrolyte out of it with an hydrometer.
3 When mixing the sulphuric acid and water **never add water to sulphuric acid** - always pour the acid slowly onto the water in a glass container. **If water is added to sulphuric acid it will explode.**

4   Continue to top-up the cell with the freshly made electrolyte and then recharge the battery and check the hydrometer readings.

## 5   Battery - charging

1   In winter time when heavy demand is placed upon the battery, such as when starting from cold, and much electrical equipment is continually in use, it is a good idea to occasionally have the battery fully charged from an external source at the rate of 3.5 or 4 amps (see Section 7).
2   Continue to charge the battery at this rate until no further rise in specific gravity is noted over a four hour period.
3   Alternatively, a trickle charger at the rate of 1.5 amps can be safely used overnight.
4   Specially rapid 'boost' charges which are claimed to restore the power of the battery in 1 to 2 hours are most dangerous as they can cause serious damage to the battery plates.

## 6   Alternator - general description and maintenance

1   Briefly, the alternator comprises a rotor and stator. Current is generated in the coils of the stator as soon as the rotor revolves. This current is three-phase alternating which is then rectified by positive and negative silicon diodes and the level of voltage required to maintain the battery charge is controlled by a regulator unit.
2   Maintenance consists of occasionally wiping away any oil or dirt which may have accumulated on the outside of the unit.
3   No lubrication is required as the bearings are grease sealed for life.
4   Check the drivebelt tension periodically to ensure that its specified deflection is correctly maintained as described in Chapter 1, Section 85.

## 7   Alternator - special precautions

Take extreme care when making circuit connections to a vehicle fitted with an alternator and observe the following. When making connections to the alternator from a battery always match correct polarity. Before using electric-arc welding equipment to repair any part of the vehicle, disconnect the connector from the alternator and disconnect the positive battery terminal. Never start the car with a battery charger connected. Always disconnect both battery leads before using a mains charger. If boosting from another battery, always connect in parallel using heavy cable.

Never pull off a battery lead while the engine is running as a means of stopping it. If working under the bonnet and the engine must be stopped, pull the coil HT lead or LT lead from the distributor.

## 8   Alternator - testing in position in the car

1   Prior to testing, check that the drivebelt is correctly tensioned and that all connections are secure.
2   Disconnect the brown cable with the eyelet from the terminal on the starter motor solenoid.
3   Connect an ammeter between the brown cable and the terminal on the starter motor solenoid.
4   Connect a voltmeter across the battery terminals.
5   Run the engine up to 6000 rev/min and hold it there. The ammeter reading should stabilise.
6   If the ammeter reads zero, the alternator has an internal fault and must be overhauled.
7   If the ammeter reads below 10 amps and the voltmeter reads between 13.6 and 14.4 volts and if the battery is in a low state of charge when checked with an hydrometer, remove the alternator and take it for further performance testing at your local auto-electrical engineers. The specified output should be 43 amps at 14 volts at an engine speed of 6000 rev/min.
8   If an ammeter reading of below 10 amps and a voltmeter reading below 13.6 volts is obtained, then the integral voltage regulator in the alternator is faulty and must be renewed.
9   The voltage regulator is also at fault if the ammeter reads above 10 amps and the voltmeter above 14.4 volts.

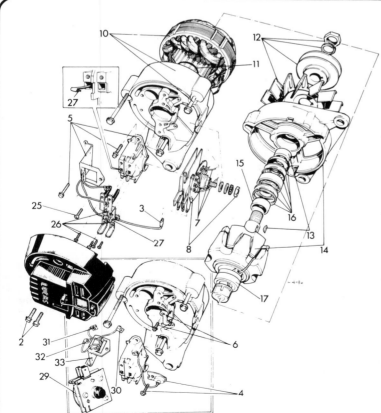

### Fig. 10.1a. Exploded view of the Lucas alternator

  2  Alternator end cover and screws
  3  Lead to rectifier terminal
  4  Surge protection diode
  5  Brush box/regulator assembly
  6  Rectifier earthing link and screw
  7  Stator cable connections to rectifier
  8  Rectifier retaining nut
 10  Slip ring end bracket and stator
 11  Slip ring end bracket 'O' ring seal
 12  Fan pulley and nut
 13  Rotor shaft key and distance piece
 14  Rotor and drive-end bracket
 15  Distance piece
 16  Drive-end bracket bearing assembly
 17  Slip rings
 25  Regulator to brushbox screw
 26  Brush terminal strips and screws
 27  Brush leaf spring
 29  Rectifier
 30  Field (F) terminal green lead, fits under inner bush
       retaining plate
 31  Positive (+) terminal yellow lead connects to
       outside of outer bush retaining plate
 32  Battery positive (B+) red lead connects to
       middle positive heat sink plate side spade connector of
       rectifier
 33  Regulator

## 9 Alternator - removal and refitting

1 Disconnect the battery negative terminal.
2 Release the alternator adjustment strap bolts and the alternator mounting bolts and push the alternator in towards the engine so that the drivebelt can be slipped from its pulley.
3 Remove the adjustment strap bolt and the alternator mounting bolts, lift the unit from its mounting bracket and disconnect the connector plug from the rear .
*On 4 cylinder models,* access to the mounting bolts is facilitated if the water pump pulley is first removed and the power steering pump (if fitted), unbolted and moved upwards.
4 Refitting is a reversal of removal but tension the drivebelts, as described in Chapter 1, Section 85.

## 10 Alternator - overhaul

1 Due to the need for special testing equipment and the possibility of damage being caused to the alternator diodes if incorrect testing methods are adopted, it is recommended that overhaul be limited to renewal of the brushes if they have worn below their specified limit. Where other faults occur, an exchange unit should be obtained.

### Lucas alternator
2 With the alternator removed from the car, withdraw the end cover (two screws).
3 Record the wiring colours and sequence to the rectifier spade terminals and disconnect the leads.
4 Remove the screw which retains the surge protection diode to the end bracket.
5 Remove the brush box (two screws) and the regulator (one screw) from the end bracket.
6 If the slip rings are burned or discoloured, polish them with fine grade glass paper (not emery).
7 Remove the brushes, noting the leaf spring which is fitted at the side of the inner brush.
8 Reassembly is a reversal of dismantling but make quite sure that the internal terminal connections are correctly made to the regulator.

### AC Delco alternator
9 The brush assembly can be removed after extracting the insulated securing screw. Make sure that the new brushes slide freely in their guides.

### All alternators
10 When exchanging or renewing an alternator, remove the pulley as this will be required for the new unit. On Lucas types, grip the pulley in a vice fitted with jaw protectors and unscrew the retaining nut. On AC Delco types, the rotor shaft can be held still by inserting an Allen key in the end of the shaft while the pulley nut is unscrewed.

## 11 Starter motor - general description

1 Two types of starter motor may be encountered and the motor fitted to your car should be identified before commencing overhaul, as described in Sections 13 or 14.
2 The method of engagement on the pre-engaged starter is that the drive pinion is brought into mesh with the starter ring gear before the main starter current is applied.
3 When the ignition is switched on, current flows from the battery to the solenoid which is mounted on the top of the starter motor body. The plunger in the solenoid moves inward so causing a centrally pivoted lever to move in such a manner that the forked end pushes the drive pinion into mesh with the starter ring gear. When the solenoid plunger reaches the end of its travel, it closes an internal contact and full starting current flows to the stator field coils. The armature is then able to rotate the crankshaft so starting the engine.
4 A special one way clutch is fitted to the starter drive pinion so that when the engine just fires and starts to operate on its own, it does not drive the starter motor.

## 12 Starter motor - removal and refitting

1 Raise the bonnet and disconnect the lead from the battery negative terminal.
2 Peel back the rubber cover from the starter solenoid terminal. Disconnect the cable from this terminal (Fig. 10.2).
3 Disconnect the Lucar type connector from the solenoid.
4 Unscrew and remove the two starter motor securing bolts and withdraw the motor. On 4 cylinder models, a spacer plate is fitted.
5 Refitting is a reversal of removal.

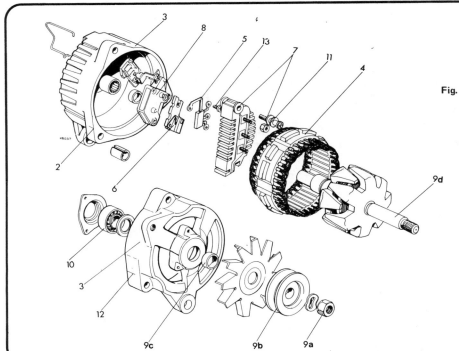

**Fig. 10.1b. Exploded view of AC Delco alternator**

2 Alignment marks
3 Slip ring end bracket
4 Stator windings
5 Diode trio
6 Brush assembly
7 Rectifier bridge and screws
8 Regulator
9a Pulley nut
9b Pulley and fan
9c Spacer
9d Rotor shaft
10 Bearings
11 Stator lead nuts
12 Drive end frame
13 Diode trio bolt

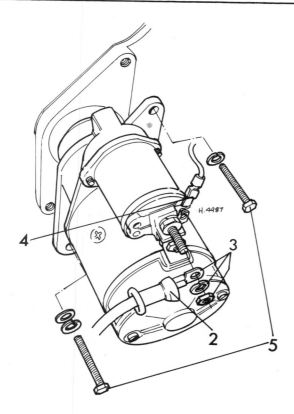

**Fig. 10.2. Starter motor connections (Sec. 12)**

2   *Flexible terminal cover*        4   *Lucar type connector*
3   *Terminal nut and washer*        5   *Starter motor retaining bolts*

## 13 Starter motor (type M35J) - overhaul

1   With the starter motor removed, as previously described, disconnect the link between the solenoid 'STA' terminal and the motor terminal.
2   Detach the solenoid from the drive end bracket (two nuts).
3   Lift the solenoid plunger and return spring from the engagement lever.
4   Remove the rubber sealing block from the drive end bracket.
5   Remove the retaining ring from the engagement lever pivot pin and withdraw the pin.
6   Unscrew the drive end bracket bolts and remove the bracket.
7   Remove the sealing cover (if fitted) from the engagement lever.
8   Remove the armature end cap from the commutator end bracket.
9   Extract the split pin from the end of the armature shaft and remove the shim washers and thrust plate.
10   Remove the armature complete with its internal thrust washers.
11   Release the commutator end bracket (four screws) and then detach the bracket from the yoke.
12   Disengage the field brushes from the brush box and lift away the commutator end bracket.
13   Using a piece of tubing, tap the thrust collar to expose the jump ring. Extract the jump ring and withdraw the starter drive from the armature shaft.
14   Detach the spring ring to release the engagement lever, the thrust washers and the spring from the roller clutch drive.
15   Inspect all components for wear. If the armature shaft bushes require renewal, press them out or screw in a ½ in tap. Before inserting the new bushes, soak them in engine oil for 24 hours.
16   If the brushes have worn below the minimum specified length, renew them by cutting the end bracket brush leads from the terminal post. File a groove in the head of the terminal post and solder the new brush leads into the groove. Cut the field winding brush leads about ¼ in (6.4 mm) from the joint of the field winding. Solder the new brush leads to the ends of the old ones. Localise the heat from the field windings.
17   Check the field windings for continuity using a torch battery and test bulb. If the windings are faulty, removal of the pole shoe screws

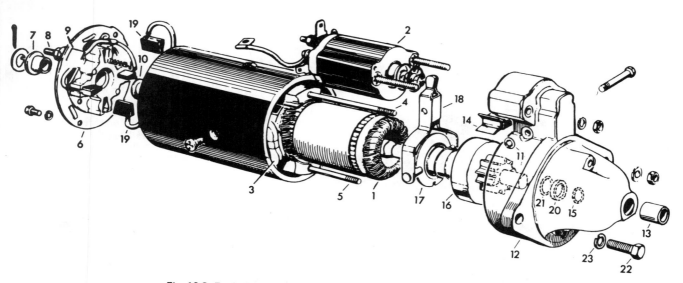

**Fig. 10.3. Exploded view of type M35J starter motor (Sec. 13)**

1   *Armature*
2   *Solenoid*
3   *Field coil*
4   *Pole piece and long stud*
5   *Pole piece and short stud*
6   *Commutator end bracket bush*
7   *Commutator end bracket bush*
8   *Field terminal*
9   *Terminal insulating bush*
10   *Thrust plate*
11   *Pivot pin retaining clip*
12   *Drive end bracket*
13   *End bracket bush*
14   *Grommet*
15   *Jump ring*
16   *Roller clutch drive*
17   *Bearing bush*
18   *Lever and pivot assembly*
19   *Brush*
20   *Thrust collar*
21   *Shim*
22   *Fixing bolt*
23   *Lock washer*

should be left to a service station having a pressure screwdriver as they are very tight.

18 Check the insulation of the armature by connecting a test bulb, torch battery and using probes placed on the armature shaft and each commutator segment in turn. If the test bulb lights at any position then the insulation has broken down, and the armature must be renewed. Discoloration of the commutator should be removed by polishing it with a piece of glass paper (not emery cloth). Do not undercut the insulation.

19 Reassembly is a reversal of dismantling but apply grease to the moving parts of the engagement lever and the outer surface of the roller clutch housing. Make sure that the thrust plate and shim washers are prevented from rotating by correct installation of the split pin. Check that the armature endfloat does not exceed 0.01 in (0.25 mm) otherwise the armature shaft thrust washers must be changed.

### 14 Starter motor (type 2M100) - overhaul

1   Slacken the nut which secures the connecting link to the solenoid terminal 'STA'.
2   Remove the two screws which secure the solenoid to the drive-end bracket.
3   Lift the solenoid plunger upwards and separate it from the engagement lever. Extract the return spring, spring seat and dust excluder from the plunger body.
4   Withdraw the block from between the drive end bracket and the starter motor yoke.
5   Remove the armature end cap from the commutator end bracket.
6   Chisel off some of the claws from the armature shaft spire nut so that the nut can be withdrawn from the shaft.
7   Remove the two tie-bolts and then withdraw the commutator end cover and starter motor yoke from the drive-end bracket.
8   Separate the commutator end cover from the starter motor yoke, at the same time disengaging the field coil brushes from the brush box to facilitate separation.
9   Withdraw the thrust washer from the armature shaft.
10  Remove the spire nut from the engagement lever pivot pin and then extract the pin from the drive-end bracket.
11  Withdraw the armature and roller clutch drive assembly from the drive-end bracket.
12  Using a piece of tubing, drive back the thrust collar to expose the jump ring on the armature shaft. Remove the jump ring and withdraw the thrust collar and the roller clutch.
13  Remove the spring ring and release the engagement lever, thrust

washers and spring from the roller-clutch drive.
14  Remove the dust excluding seal from the bore of the drive-end bracket.
15  Carry out the inspection and test procedure given in paragraphs 15 to 18 of the preceding Section.
16  Reassembly is a reversal of dismantling but apply grease to the moving parts of the engagement lever, the outer surface of the roller clutch housing and to the lips of the drive-end bracket dust seal. Install a new spire nut to the armature shaft positioning it to give the specified shaft endfloat. Measure this endfloat by inserting feeler blades between the face of the spire nut and the flange of the commutator end bush.

### 15 Fuses

1   The fuse box is located within the engine compartment on the right-hand side (Fig. 10.5).
2   The electrical circuits which are protected are given in Specifications at the beginning of this Chapter.
3   Always renew a 'blown' fuse with one of similar rating. If the fuse blows immediately it is renewed, find and rectify the fault before renewing the fuse again.
4   The radio is protected by a line fuse. Access to this fuse is obtained by pushing in both ends of the fuse holder, twisting and releasing.
5   Additional accessories which are fitted and which are to be 'off' when the ignition is switched off should be connected to fuse contacts 1, 2, 7 or 8.
6   Two spare fuses are located in the fuse box cover. On early models with a heated rear window No 8 fuse is 25A to protect it.

### 16 Relays

1   The relays used in the car electrical circuit control the following equipment:
    *Direction indicators, hazard warning lamps, heated rear window, seat belt warning lamp, starter motor solenoid switch.*
2   The relays for the direction indicator, hazard warning and seat belt warning lamps are located below the instrument panel, to one side of the steering column according to whether the car is left-hand or right-hand drive.
3   In the event of faulty operations of the indicator or hazard warning lamps, first check the fuses and then the individual lamp bulbs.
4   The relays for the heated rear window and the starter motor switch are located in the heater plenum chamber. To reach them, raise the

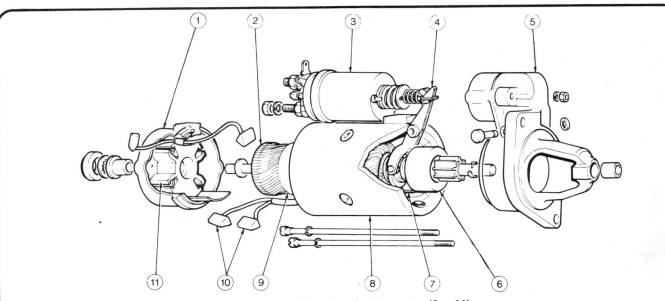

Fig. 10.4. Exploded view of type 2M100 starter motor (Sec. 14)

| 1 | Commutator end bracket | 4 | Engagement lever | 7 | Pole shoe | 10 | Brush |
|---|---|---|---|---|---|---|---|
| 2 | Commutator | 5 | Drive end bracket | 8 | Yoke | 11 | Brush box moulding |
| 3 | Solenoid | 6 | Drive assembly | 9 | Armature | | |

bonnet and remove the right-hand air intake grille by turning each of the securing screws one half turn. Identify the particular relay by means of its connecting wiring. The heated rear window relay has green/slate, black, and green/yellow wires attached to it while the starter relay has brown/red, white/red, black, and brown leads attached. Pull the relay from its clip and detach the multi-connector.

### 17 Fuel, temperature and battery voltage gauges - fault diagnosis

1   Due to the need for special equipment, it is not possible to test the gauges or transmitter units except by substitution of new components.
2   However, the following symptoms will indicate possible causes of malfunction.
3   If the fuel contents and the water temperature gauges both start to give false readings at the same time, then the voltage stabiliser on the

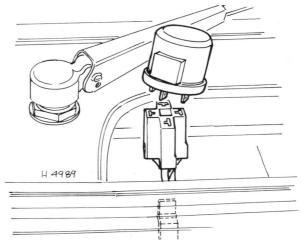

Fig. 10.6. Relays for the heated rear window and starter motor solenoid switch are housed in the heater plenum chamber

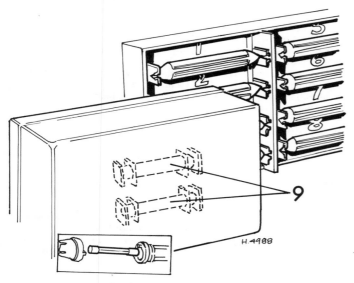

Fig. 10.5. The fuse box (Sec. 15)

9   Inset shows in-line fuse for radio

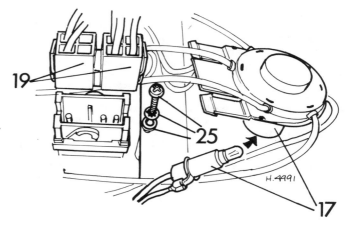

Fig. 10.8. Instrument opticell (17), multi-connectors (19), fascia panel screws (25) (Sec. 18)

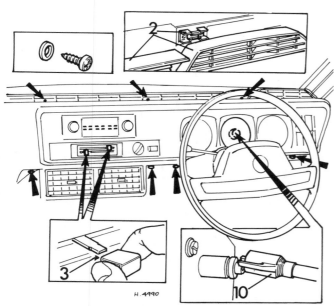

Fig. 10.7. Fascia components (Sec. 18)

2   Side vents and clips        10   Speedometer cable
3   Control knob clip                  connection

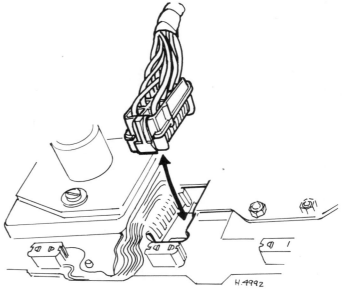

Fig. 10.9. Instrument cluster  multi-connector (Sec. 18)

instrument panel may be at fault.

4  If the battery voltage indicator shows a reading of less than 10V and the battery is known to be in a fully charged state, the gauge is probably faulty.

5  Always check all the instrument and transmitter leads and connections for security before taking further steps to rectify a fault.

6  The fuel and temperature gauges may take up to two minutes to reach their normal readings.

7  Removal of the gauges and voltage stabiliser is described in Section 18 of this Chapter.

8  Removal of the fuel tank transmitter and the water temperature switch is described in Chapters 2 and 3 respectively.

## 18 Instruments - removal and installation

1  Disconnect the lead from the battery negative terminal.

2  Pull the side vents and moulding to the rear to unclip them from the fascia top rail.

3  Through the holes in the heater control knobs, insert a probe, depress the spring clip and detach the knobs.

4  Withdraw the driver's ashtray from its holder and then remove the two screws which secure the ashtray holder to the underside of the fascia.

5  Remove the four screws and release the cowl from the steering column.

6  Release the fascia surround lower edge from the fascia support rail by removing the four screws.

7  Release the fascia surround upper edge from the fascia top rail by removing the three screws.

8  Reach behind the fascia and disconnect the speedometer cable from the speedometer head by depressing the locking lever.

9  Pull the fascia surround slightly to the rear to disengage its locating studs from the fascia support rail and then disconnect the bulb holder from the seat belt warning lamp and the cigar lighter wires.

10  If the car is equipped with a radio, disconnect all the leads from it.

11  If the car is equipped with a clock, disconnect the leads from its rear face.

12  Withdraw the bulb holder from the instrument opticell (see Section 19) and detach the opticell from the fascia support.

13  Now hold the fascia surround so that the instruments are facing upwards, compress the locking tabs and disconnect all the multi-connector plugs from the switches.

14  Disconnect the multi-connector from the back of the instrument cluster and then withdraw the fascia surround complete with instruments from the car.

15  Separate the instrument cluster from the fascia surround (six screws).

16  The individual instruments can now be removed after extracting the lens and instrument casing screws.

17  The instrument voltage stabiliser can be removed by unplugging it from the rear of the printed circuit board.

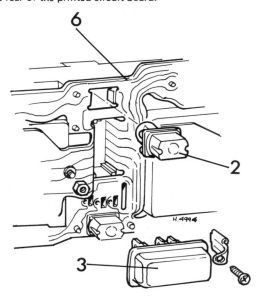

Fig. 10.10. Rear view of instrument cluster (Sec. 18)

| | | |
|---|---|---|
| 2  Bulb holder | 3  Instrument voltage stabiliser | 6  Printed circuit |

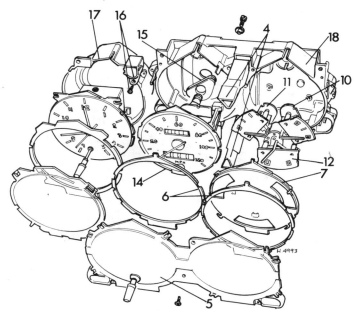

Fig. 10.11. Exploded view of the instrument cluster (Sec. 18)

| | | |
|---|---|---|
| 4  Lighting tubes | 12  Battery condition indicator | |
| 5  Lens | 14  Speedometer | |
| 6  Bezel | 15  Speedometer mounting rubber | |
| 7  Face plate and glass | 16  Bulb holder | |
| 10  Water temperature gauge | 17  Clock housing | |
| 11  Fuel contents gauge | | |

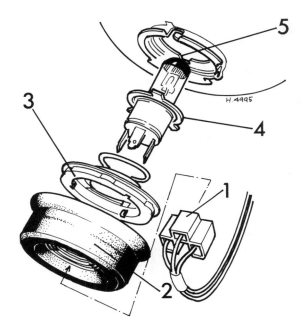

Fig. 10.12. Bulb type headlamp components (4 lamp system) (Sec. 19)

| | |
|---|---|
| 1  Connector plug | 4  Bulb unit |
| 2  Dust excluder | 5  Reflector seating notch |
| 3  Retainer | |

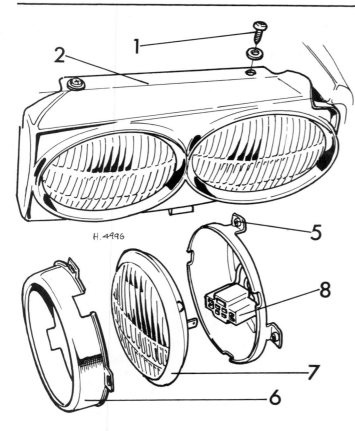

Fig. 10.13a. Sealed beam type headlamp components
(Sec. 19) (4 lamp system)

| | | | |
|---|---|---|---|
| 1 | Securing screw | 6 | Retaining rim |
| 2 | Headlamp finisher | 7 | Sealed beam unit |
| 5 | Retaining rim screws | 8 | Multi-pin connector |

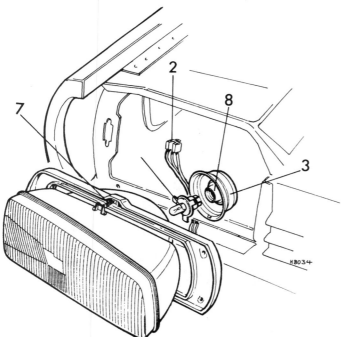

Fig.10.13b. Headlamp unit (2 lamp system) (Sec. 19)

| | | | |
|---|---|---|---|
| 2 | Plug | 8 | Bulb holder |
| 3 | Seal | 9 | Bulb (halogen type) |
| 7 | Screw ball and nylon socket | | |

18 Installation is a reversal of removal but remember to wipe finger marks from the lens inner face before fitting and note that the multi-connector which connects to the back of the instrument cluster has locking tabs of different widths to ensure correct installation.

### 19 Bulbs - renewal

*Headlamps (4 lamp system)*
1   Semi-sealed (bulb type) or sealed-beam lamp units may be encountered.
2   *To renew a bulb,* open the bonnet and pull the connecting plug

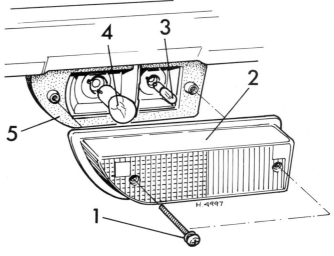

Fig. 10.14. Front parking and direction indicator lamp (Sec. 19)

| | | | |
|---|---|---|---|
| 1 | Lens screw | 4 | Direction indicator bulb |
| 2 | Lens | 5 | Seal |
| 3 | Parking lamp bulb | | |

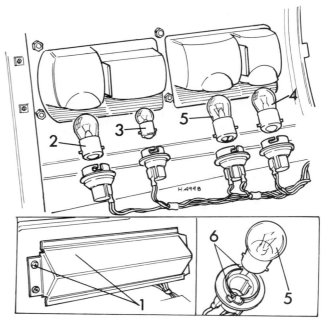

Fig. 10.15. Rear lamp cluster (Sec. 19)

| | | | |
|---|---|---|---|
| 1 | Protective cover | 4 | Direction indicator bulb |
| 2 | Reversing lamp bulb | 5 | Stop/tail bulb |
| 3 | Tail lamp bulb | 6 | Stop/tail lamp bulb holder |

from the bulb and then detach the rubber seal. Press in and turn the retaining cover in an anticlockwise direction and withdraw it. Remove the bulb unit.
3   Do not touch this type of bulb with the fingers and if inadvertently touched, clean it thoroughly by wiping it with a rag moistened in methylated spirit.
4   Refitting is a reversal of removal but make sure that the spigot on the bulb unit engages correctly in the reflector seating.
5   *To renew a sealed beam unit,* remove the headlamp finisher (two screws) from the front of the grille.
6   Unscrew the three retaining screws two complete turns, rotate the lamp rim in a clockwise direction and remove it.
7   Pull the sealed beam unit forward and disconnect the multi-pin socket.
8   Installation is a reversal of removal. **Note:** With either type of headlamp, do not touch the adjustment screws (see Section 20) when renewing a bulb or sealed beam unit or the headlamp alignment will be altered.

### Headlamps - 2 lamp (trapezoidal) system
9   Raise the bonnet and disconnect the multi-wiring plug from the rear of the bulb. Depress and rotate the bulb holder and remove it from the lamp unit. Do not handle the bulb with the fingers. If you do, then it must be cleaned with methylated spirit before operation. The lamp unit can be removed from the car by jarring its adjusting screw ball ends out of their nylon sockets.

### Front parking and direction indicator lamps
10  Access to these bayonet fixing type bulbs is obtained after removal of the lens (two screws).

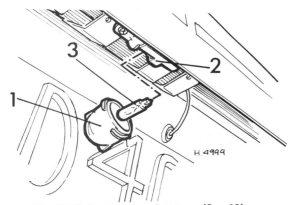

**Fig. 10.16. Rear number plate lamp (Sec. 19)**

1  *Lens*     2  *Retaining lugs*   3  *Capless type bulb*

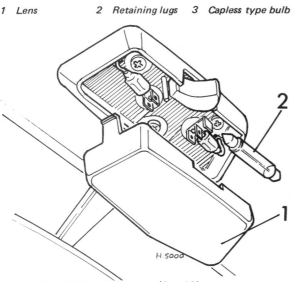

**Fig. 10.17. Interior lamp (Sec. 19)**

1  *Lens*                    2  *Festoon type bulb*

### Rear lamp cluster
11  Access to these bulb holders is obtained from inside the luggage compartment.
12  Remove the protecting cover (two screws) and then turn each individual bulb holder clockwise to release it.
13  Note that the stop/tail bulb (twin filament) has offset pins and its bulb holder will also only fit into the lamp unit one way.

### Rear number plate lamp
14  To gain access to the bulb, press and turn the lens to release it from the lamp base. The bulb is of capless type and is simply pulled from its holder.

### Interior lamp
15  Slightly depress one end of the plastic lens and remove it from the lamp base. Extract the festoon type bulb from its retaining clips.
16  On some models an additional interior lamp is installed and the lens and bulb are removed in a similar way to that just described in the preceding paragraph.

### Cigar lighter bulb
17  Access to this bulb will necessitate removal of the radio (see Section 28) or blanking plate if a radio is not fitted (Fig. 10.19).
18  Squeeze the sides of the cigar lighter bulb hood and withdraw it. Extract the bulb holder from the hood and then remove the bayonet type bulb.

### Panel and warning lamps
19  These bulbs, with the exception of the ones for the seat belt and heater indicator lamps, are accessible by reaching up under the instrument panel. If necessary, remove the ashtray assembly to provide more room to work (Fig. 10.20).
20  Press the bulb holder sideways gently to free it and then pull it from the instrument housing. Renew the capless type bulb simply by pulling it from its holder. Check that the printed circuit contacts are correctly seated before refitting the holder.
21  The bulbs for the heater indicator and seat belt warning lamps are only accessible after removing the radio or radio position blanking plate (see Section 28) (Fig. 10.21).
22  Switches and heater controls are illuminated from a single light source by means of fibre opticells (see Section 18, paragraph 12 of this Chapter). To renew the bulb, hold the opticell and pull the bulb holder from its housing. The bulb is of bayonet fixing type (Fig. 10.22).
23  The switch 'ON' warning lamp bulb can be renewed after pressing the two retainers together and pulling the connector plug from the

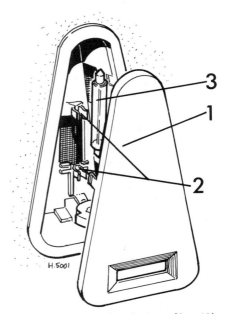

**Fig. 10.18. Supplementary interior lamp (Sec. 19)**

1  *Lens*    2  *Bulb Holder Clips*    3  *Festoon bulb*

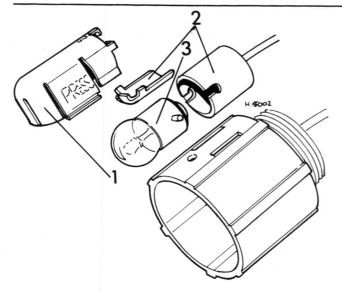

Fig. 10.19. Cigar lighter bulb holder hood (1), holder (2), bulb (3), (Sec. 19)

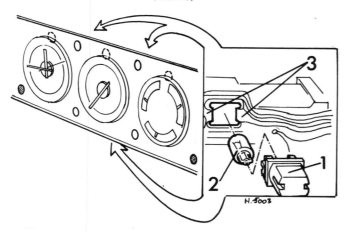

Fig. 10.20. Location of panel lamps and warning lamp bulbs (Sec. 19)

1   Bulb holder                3   Printed circuit contacts
2   Capless type bulb

back of the switch. The bulb is of capless type.

### Automatic transmission speed selector lamps
24 To reach these bulbs, prise the top finisher from the rear console. Lift the gaiter up the seat belt anchorages. Remove the rear console (four screws).
25 Unscrew the knob from the selector lever and remove the centre console (three screws).
26 Pull the nacelle from the selector mechanism.
27 To renew the bayonet fixing type bulb in the nacelle lamp, raise the lamp body and withdraw the bulb holder.
28 To renew the bulb in the selector lamp, move the selector lever to '1' and remove the bulb holder.

### Glovebox lamp
29 This bulb is of festoon type and is simply prised from its clips.

### Engine compartment lamp
30 The bulb is renewed in a similar manner to that described for the rear number plate lamp.

### Radiator grille lamp (Wolseley marque only)
31 Insert a finger through the air intake grille on each side of the lamp and press the lamp retaining clips together. Pull the badge from the lamp body and then remove the bayonet fixing type bulb from its holder.

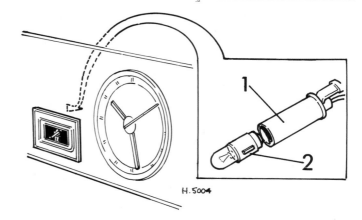

Fig. 10.21. Seatbelt warning lamp (Sec. 19)

1   Bulb holder                  2   Bulb

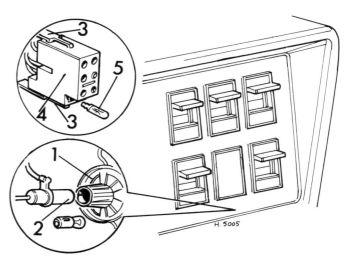

Fig. 10.22. Switch illumination (Sec. 19)

| 1 | Distribution cell | 2 | Bulb holder | 4 | Connector |
|---|---|---|---|---|---|
| | | 3 | Retainers | 5 | Capless bulb |

### 20 Headlamps - adjustment

1 The headlamps may be of two or four lamp system, depending upon the car model. On the four lamp system, all four lamps are illuminated when main beam is selected but the two inner lamps extinguish when the beam is dipped.
2 It is recommended that headlamp beams are set on an optical beam setter at a service station but in an emergency, temporary adjustment can be made by turning the adjuster screws which are accessible from within the engine compartment.

### 21 Steering column combination switch - removal and refitting

1 Disconnect the lead from the battery negative terminal.
2 Remove the steering wheel, as described in Chapter 11.
3 Release the strap which secures the switch wiring harness to the steering column and then disconnect the multi-pin connectors.
4 Slacken the switch clamp screw and withdraw the switch assembly from the steering column.
5 The wiper/washer switch can be detached from the mounting plate of Lucas type switches if the two securing rivets are drilled out.
6 When refitting the combination switch, locate the switch lug in the

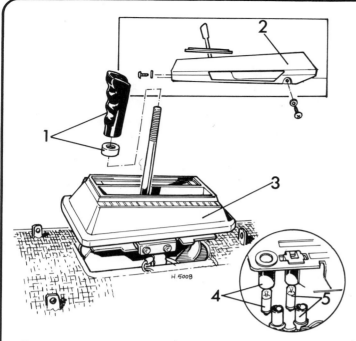

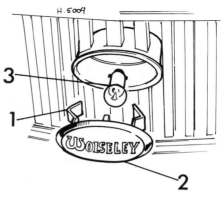

Fig. 10.26. Radiator grille badge (Sec. 19)

1  Badge retaining    2  Badge         3  Bulb
   clips

Fig. 10.23. Automatic transmission speed selector illumination
(Sec. 19)

1  Control lever     2  Centre console   4  Nacelle lamp
   knob             3  Nacelle          5  Selector lamp

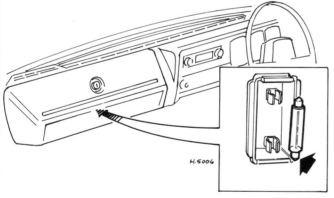

Fig. 10.24. Glovebox lamp (Sec. 19)

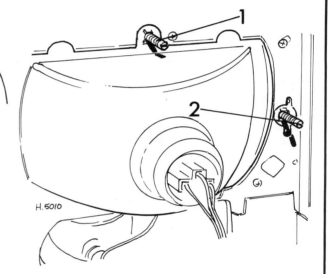

Fig. 10.27. Two headlamp (bulb type) adjustment screws
(Sec. 20)

1  Vertical adjustment              2  Horizontal adjustment

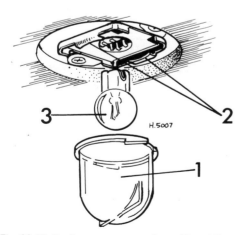

Fig. 10.25. Engine compartment lamp (Sec. 19)

1  Lens          2  Retaining clips for  3  Bulb
                    lens

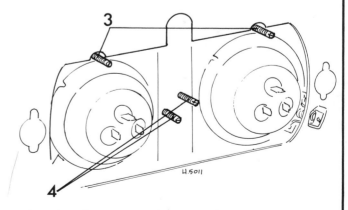

Fig. 10.28. Four headlamp (sealed beam) adjustment screws
(Sec. 20)

3  Vertical adjustment              4  Horizontal adjustment

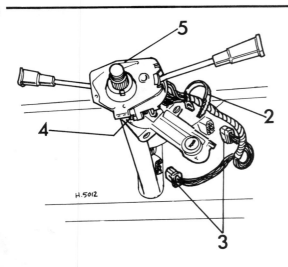

Fig. 10.29. Steering column combination switch (Sec. 21)

2  Harness strap
3  Multi-pin connector
4  Switch clamp screw
5  Switch assembly

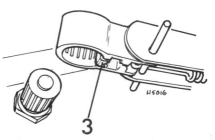

Fig. 10.30. Lighting switch (Sec. 23)

3  Retaining clips
4  Optic fibre light holder
5  Switch

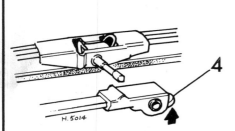

Fig. 10.31. Wiper blade to arm attachment (Sec. 24)

4  Retaining lever

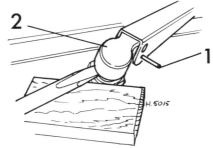

Fig. 10.32. Removal of a wiper arm (Sec. 24)

1  Temporary pin
2  Arm

Fig. 10.33. Wiper arm to driving spindle clip (3) (Sec. 24)

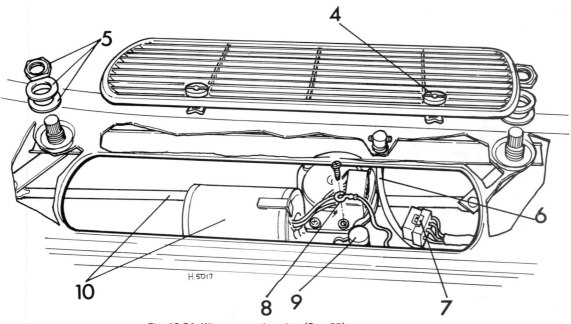

Fig. 10.34. Wiper motor location (Sec. 25)

4  Air intake grille clips
5  Drive spindle nuts and washers
6  Washer jet tube
7  Multi-connector plug
8  Earth lead
9  Rubber mounting bush
10  Wiper motor and linkage

slot of the steering column. Check that the striker dog on the nylon switch centre is in line with and adjacent to the direction indicator switch stalk.

## 22 Ignition/starter switch - removal and refitting

1   Extract the screws and withdraw the shroud from the steering column. There is no need to disconnect or remove the choke control.
2   Remove the nuts and bolts which retain the column to the pedal bracket.
3   Remove the pinch bolt which retains the upper end of the steering column and lower the column.
4   Remove the small retaining screw and withdraw the ignition/starter switch from the steering column lock. Disconnect the wiring multi-pin plug.
5   Removal of the steering column lock is described in Chapter 11, Section 23.
6   Refitting is a reversal of removal.

## 23 Lighting switch - removal and refitting

1   Remove the front ashtray and the ashtray holder (two screws).
2   Press the two retainers on the multi-pin connector together and then pull the connector from the back of the switch.
3   Withdraw the opticell light holder from the switch body.
4   Push the switch from the fascia panel.
5   Refitting is a reversal of removal.

## 24 Wiper blades and arms - removal and refitting

1   The wiper blades should be renewed as soon as they no longer wipe the windscreen cleanly. To remove a blade, lift the small retaining lever and pull the blade pivot pin from the hole in the arm.
2   To remove a wiper arm, open the bonnet, lift the wiper arm slightly and insert a pin through the holes in the arm to take the load of the spring. Lever the arm from its driving spindle using a long screwdriver and a block of wood as a fulcrum point.
3   Refitting is a reversal of removal but when installing the arm to the spindle splines, do not press it fully home to engage its retaining clip until the alignment of the arm/blade assembly to the lower edge of the windscreen frame has been checked and, if necessary, adjusted.

## 25 Wiper motor and linkage - removal and refitting

1   Open the bonnet and remove both wiper arms.
2   Remove the air intake grille from the driver's side by turning each retaining clip through one half a turn.
3   Unscrew the nuts from the wiper arm driving spindles, remove flat washers and rubber grommets.
4   Disconnect the windscreen washer tube located just above the wiper motor.
5   Disconnect the multi-connector plug from the motor.
6   Disconnect the earth lead from the wiper motor gear cover.
7   Extract the flexible mounting bush and then lower the motor and linkage into the heater air intake chamber. Move it towards the driver's side first, then in the opposite direction and finally tilt it upwards and extract it from the grille aperture.
8   Refitting is a reversal of removal but only tighten the wiper spindle nuts until four threads are exposed above the nut. Install the wiper arms after the motor has been operated and switched off so that it has parked automatically.

## 26 Wiper motor and linkage - overhaul

1   With the wiper motor and linkage removed, as described in the preceding Section, unscrew the nut which secures the driving link arm to the motor drive spindle.
2   Prise the link arm from the tapered splined shaft.
3   Remove the motor from the frame (three screws).
4   Remove the gear cover from the motor (four screws).
5   Withdraw the drive gear and the shaft assembly.

6   If the linkage requires attention, prise off the rubber spacer from the wiper drive pivot assembly. Remove the retaining clip and disconnect the link arm from the wiper drive spindle. Note the nylon washer located between the arms of the linkage. Drill out the retaining rivets and detach the drive spindle assemblies from the frame.
7   Renew any worn components. If the motor is worn or faulty, it is best exchanged for a new one as individual parts are unlikely to be available.
8   Commence reassembly by fitting the wave washer to the shaft of the drive gear.
9   Liberally grease the shaft and gear and insert the gear into the motor housing so that the parked position marked on the gear faces the driving pinion.
10  Install the gear cover and then fit the driving link arm onto the splined shaft so that it is parallel with the mounting frame.
11  If the driving spindles have been renewed, then they should be re-riveted to the frame. Apply graphite based grease to all friction and pivot points.

## 27 Windscreen washer and jets

1   The electrically operated washer pump and fluid reservoir are located within the engine compartment. Always keep the reservoir

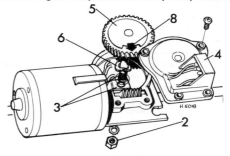

Fig. 10.35. Wiper motor driveshaft nut (2), link arm (3), gear cover (4) drive gear/shaft assembly (6), wave washer (8), parked position (8) (Sec. 26)

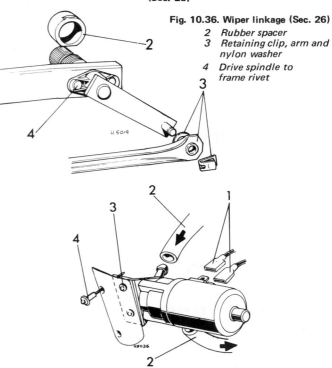

Fig. 10.36. Wiper linkage (Sec. 26)

2   Rubber spacer
3   Retaining clip, arm and nylon washer
4   Drive spindle to frame rivet

Fig. 10.37a. Windscreen washer pump

1   Electrical leads
2   Inlet and outlet fluid pipes
3   Mounting pop rivet
4   Mounting pop rivet

filled to its correct level with a mixture of clean water and washer fluid. The addition of this fluid will help to prevent the water freezing during cold weather.

2  Regularly inspect the security of all washer tubes and electrical leads. If the pump fails to operate, it cannot be repaired but must be renewed as a complete unit. Before doing this, check that the circuit fuse (no. 2) has not 'blown' or that the jets are not clogged or the reservoir empty. Drill out the pump mounting rivets to remove it.

3  The washer jets are accessible after removal of the under-bonnet air intake grilles. Each jet is secured by a wing nut and has a rubber washer above and a felt washer below its mounting platform.

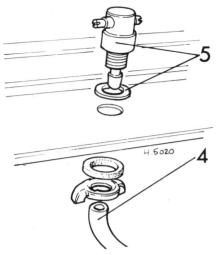

Fig. 10.37b. Washer jet tube (4) and jet assembly (5) (Sec. 27)

## 28  Radio (Leyland type) - removal and refitting

1  Disconnect the lead from the battery negative terminal.
2  Pull off the radio control knobs.
3  Remove the two retaining nuts and withdraw the fascia board or panel.
4  Withdraw the radio finisher and push the radio backwards (towards the front of the car) and remove the heater air distribution bulb.
5  Extract the radio mounting plate, pull the radio forward (towards the rear of the car) and disconnect the earth lead from the right-hand side.
6  The radio can now be pulled from its aperture sufficiently far to disconnect the power supply and aerial leads.
7  Refitting is a reversal of removal.

## 29  Radios and tape players (aftermarket type) - fitting (general)

This Section describes the installation of in-car entertainment (ICE) equipment which was not fitted as standard or as an option by the car manufacturer during production of the car.

A radio or tape player is an expensive item to buy; and will only give its best performance if fitted properly. It is useless to expect concert hall performance from a unit that is suspended from the dashpanel on string with its speaker resting on the back seat or parcel shelf! If you do not wish to do the installation yourself there are many in-car entertainment specialists' who can do the fitting for you.

Make sure the unit purchased is of the same polarity as the vehicle. Ensure that units with adjustable polarity are correctly set before commencing installation.

It is difficult to give specific information with regard to fitting, as final positioning of the radio/tape player, speakers and aerial is entirely a matter of personal preference. However, the following paragraphs give guidelines to follow, which are relevant to all installations.

*Radios*

Most radios are a standardised size of 7 inches wide, by 2 inches deep - this ensures that they will fit into the radio aperture provided in most cars. Alternatively, a special console can be purchased which will fit between the dashpanel and the floor. These consoles can also be used for additional switches and instrumentation if required. The following points should be borne in mind before deciding exactly where to fit the unit.

a)  *The unit must be within easy reach of the driver wearing a seat belt.*
b)  *The unit must not be mounted in close proximity to an electric tachometer, the ignition switch and its wiring, or the flasher unit and associated wiring.*
c)  *The unit must be mounted within reach of the aerial lead, and in such a place that the aerial lead will not have to be routed near the components detailed in the preceding paragraph 'b'.*
d)  *The unit should not be positioned in a place where it might cause injury to the car occupants in an accident; for instance, under the dashpanel above the driver's or passengers' legs.*
e)  *The unit must be fitted really securely.*

Some radios will have mounting brackets provided together with instructions; others will need to be fitted using drilled and slotted metal strips, bent to form mounting brackets - these strips are available from most accessory stores. The unit must be properly earthed, by fitting a separate earth lead between the casing of the radio and the vehicle frame.

Use the radio manufacturer's instructions when wiring the radio

into the vehicle's electrical system. If no instructions are available refer to the relevent wiring diagram to find the location of the radio 'feed' connection in the vehicle's wiring circuit. A 1-2 amp 'in-line' fuse must be fitted in the radio's 'feed' wire - a choke may also be necessary (see next Section).

The type of aerial used, and its fitted position is a matter of personal preference, In general the taller the aerial, the better the reception. It is best to fit a fully retractable aerial - especially, if a mechanical car-wash is used or if you live in an area where cars tend to be vandalised. In this respect electric aerials which are raised and lowered automatically switching the radio on or off are convenient, but are more likely to give trouble than the manual type.

When choosing a site for the aerial the following points should be considered:

a)  *The aerial lead should be as short as possible - this means that the aerial should be mounted at the front of the vehicle.*
b)  *The aerial must be mounted as far away from the distributor and HT leads as possible.*
c)  *The part of the aerial which protrudes beneath the mounting point must not foul the roadwheels, or anything else.*
d)  *If possible the aerial should be positioned so that the coaxial lead does not have to be routed through the engine compartment.*
e)  *The plane of the panel on which the aerial is mounted should not be so steeply angled that the aerial cannot be mounted vertically (in relation to the 'end-on' aspect of the vehicle). Most aerials have a small amount of adjustment available.*

Having decided on a mounting position, a relatively large hole will have to be made in the panel. The exact size of the hole will depend upon the specific aerial being fitted, although, generally, the hole required is of ¾ inch diameter. On metal bodied cars, a 'tank-cutter' of the relevant diameter is the best tool to use for making the hole. This tool needs a small diameter pilot hole drilled through the panel, through which, the tool clamping bolt is inserted. When the hole has been made the raw edges should be de-burred with a file and then painted, to prevent corrosion.

Fit the aerial according to the manufacturer's instructions. If the aerial is very tall, or if it protrudes beneath the mounting panel for a considerable distance it is a good idea to fit a stay between the aerial and the vehicle frame. This stay can be manufactured from the slotted and drilled metal strips previously mentioned. The stay should be securely screwed or bolted in place. For best reception it is advisable to fit an earth lead between the aerial body and the vehicle frame.

It will probably be necessary to drill one or two holes through bodywork panels in order to feed the aerial lead into the interior of the car. Where this is the case ensure that the holes are fitted with rubber grommets to protect the cable, and to stop possible entry of water.

Positioning and fitting of the speaker depends mainly on its type. Generally, the speaker is designed to fit directly into the aperture already provided in the car (usually in the shelf behind the rear seats, or in the top of the dashpanel). Where this is the case, fitting the speaker is just a matter of removing the protective grille from the aperture and screwing or bolting the speaker in place. Take great care not to damage the speaker diaphragm whilst doing this. It is a good idea to fit a 'gasket' between the speaker frame and the mounting panel in order to prevent vibration - some speakers will already have such a gasket fitted.

If a 'pod' type speaker was supplied with the radio, the best acoustic results will normally be obtained by mounting it on the shelf behind the rear seat. The pod can be secured to the mounting panel with self-tapping screws.

When connecting a rear mounted speaker to the radio, the wires should be routed through the vehicle beneath the carpets or floor mats - preferably through the middle, or along the side of the floorpan, where they will not be trodden on by passengers. Make the relevant connections as directed by the radio manufacturer.

By now you will have several yards of additional wiring in the car; use PVC tape to secure this wiring out of harm's way. Do not leave electrical leads dangling. Ensure that all new electrical connections are properly made (wires twisted together will not do) and completely secure.

The radio should now be working, but before you pack away your tools it will be necessary to 'trim' the radio to the aerial. Follow the radio manufacturer's instructions regarding this adjustment.

## Tape players

Fitting instructions for both cartridge and cassette stereo tape players are the same and in general the same rules apply as when fitting a radio. Tape players are not usually prone to electrical interference like radio - although it can occur - so positioning is not so critical. If possible the player should be mounted on an 'even-keel'. Also, it must be possible for a driver wearing a seat belt to reach the unit in order to change, or turn over, tapes.

For the best results from speakers designed to be recessed into a panel, mount them so that the back of the speaker protrudes into an enclosed chamber within the vehicle (eg; door interiors or the trunk cavity).

To fit recessed type speakers in the front doors first check that there is sufficient room to mount the speaker in each door without it fouling the latch or window winding mechanism. Hold the speaker against the skin of the door, and draw a line, around the periphery of the speaker. With the speaker removed draw a second 'cutting' line, within the first, to allow enough room for the entry of the speaker back, but at the same time providing a broad seat for the speaker flange. When you are sure that the 'cutting-line' is correct, drill a series of holes around its periphery. Pass a hacksaw blade through one of the holes and then cut through the metal between the holes until the centre section of the panel falls out.

De-burr the edges of the hole and then paint the raw metal to prevent corrosion. Cut a corresponding hole in the door trim panel - ensuring that it will be completely covered by the speaker grille. Now drill a hole in the door edge and a corresponding hole in the door surround. These holes are to feed the speaker leads through - so fit grommets. Pass the speaker leads through the door trim, door skin and out through the holes in the side of the door and door surround. Refit the door trim panel and then secure the speaker to the door using self-tapping screws. Note: if the speaker is fitted with a shield to prevent water dripping on it, ensure that this shield is at the top.

'Pod' type speakers can be fastened to the shaft behind the rear seat, or anywhere else offering a corresponding mounting point on each side of the car. If the 'pod' speakers are mounted on each side of the shelf behind the rear seat, it is a good idea to drill several large diameter holes through to the luggage boot beneath each speaker - this will improve the sound reproduction. 'Pod' speakers sometimes offer a better reproduction quality if they face the rear window - which then acts as a reflector - so it is worthwhile experimenting before finally fixing the speakers.

## 30 Radios and tape players - suppression of interference (general)

To eliminate buzzes, and other unwanted noises, costs very little and is not as difficult as sometimes thought. With a modicum of common sense and patience and following the instructions in the following paragraphs, interference can be virtually eliminated. (Reference should be made to Figs. 10.38 to 10.43).

The first cause for concern is the generator. The noise this makes over the radio is like an electric mixer and the noise speeds up when

you rev up (if you wish to prove the point, you can remove the fanbelt and try it). The remedy for this is simple; connect a 1.0 mf - 3.0 mf capacitor between earth, probably the bolt that holds down the generator base, and the *large* terminal on the alternator. This is most important, for if you connect it to the small terminal, you will probably damage the generator permanently.

A second common cause of electrical interference is the ignition system. Here a 1.0 mf capacitor must be connected between earth and the SW or + terminal on the coil. This may stop the tick, tick, tick sound that comes over the speaker. Next comes the spark itself.

There are several ways of curing interference from the ignition HT system. One is to use carbon film HT leads and the more successful method is to use resistive spark plug caps of about 10,000 ohm to 15,000 ohm resistance. If, due to lack of room, these cannot be used, an alternative is to use 'in-line' suppressors. If the interference is not too bad, you may get away with only one suppressor in the coil to distributor line. If the interference does continue (a 'clacking' noise) then 'doctor' all HT leads.

At this stage it is advisable to check that the radio is well earthed, also the aerial and to see that the aerial plug is pushed well into the set and that the radio is properly trimmed (see preceding Section). In addition, check that the wire which supplies the power to the set is as short as possible and does not wander all over the car. At this stage it is a good idea to check that the fuse is of the correct rating. For most sets this will be about 1 to 2 amps.

At this point the more usual causes of interference have been suppressed. If the problem still exists, a look at the causes of interference may help to pinpoint the component generating the stray electrical discharges.

The radio picks up electromagnetic waves in the air; now some are made by regular broadcasters, and some, which we do not want, are made by the car. The home made signals are produced by stray electrical discharges floating around the car. Common producers of these signals are electric motors, ie, the windscreen wipers, electric screen washers, electric window winders, heater fan or an electric aerial if fitted. Other sources of interference are flashing turn signals and instruments. The remedy for these cases is shown for an electric motor whose interference is not too bad and for instrument suppression. Turn signals are not normally suppressed. In recent years, radio manufacturers have included in the line (live) of the radio, in addition to the fuse, an 'in-line' choke.

All the foregoing components are available from radio stores or accessory stores. If you have an electric clock fitted this should be suppressed by connecting a 0.5 mf capacitor directly across it as shown.

If after all this, you are still experiencing radio interference, first assess how bad it is, for the human ear can filter out unobtrusive unwanted noises quite easily, but if you are still adamant about eradicating the noise, then continue.

As a first step, a few "experts" seem to favour a screen between the radio and the engine. This is OK as far as it goes - literally! - for the whole set is screened anyway and if interference can get past that then a small piece of aluminium is not going to stop it.

A more sensible way of screening is to discover if interference is coming down the wires. First, take the live lead; interference can get between the set and the choke (hence the reason for keeping the wires short). One remedy here is to screen the wire and this is done by buying screened wire and fitting that. The loudspeaker lead could be screened also to prevent "pick-up" getting back to the radio - although this is unlikely.

Without doubt, the worst source of radio interference comes from the ignition HT leads, even if they have been suppressed. The ideal way of suppressing these is to slide screening tubes over the leads themselves. As this is impractical, we can place an aluminium shield over the majority of the lead areas. In a vee- or twin-cam engine this is relatively easy but for a straight engine, the results are not particularly good.

Now for the really impossible cases, here are a few tips to try out. Where metal comes into contact with metal, an electrical disturbance is caused which is why good clean connections are essential. To remove interference due to overlapping or butting panels you must bridge the join with a wide braided earth strap (like that from the frame to the engine/transmission). The most common moving parts that could create noise and should be strapped are, in order of importance:

a) *Silencer to frame.*
b) *Exhaust pipe to engine block and frame.*
c) *Air cleaner to frame.*
d) *Front and rear bumpers to frame.*

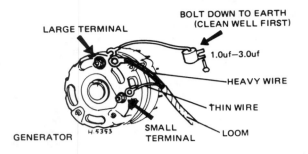

LARGE TERMINAL

BOLT DOWN TO EARTH
(CLEAN WELL FIRST)

1.0uf—3.0uf

HEAVY WIRE

THIN WIRE

GENERATOR

SMALL TERMINAL

LOOM

Fig. 10.38. The correct way to connect a capacitor to the alternator

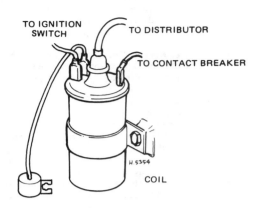

TO IGNITION SWITCH

TO DISTRIBUTOR

TO CONTACT BREAKER

COIL

Fig. 10.39. The capacitor must be connected to the ignition switch side of the coil

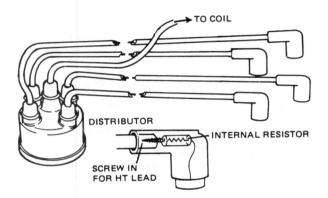

TO COIL

DISTRIBUTOR

INTERNAL RESISTOR

SCREW IN FOR HT LEAD

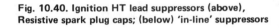

Fig. 10.40. Ignition HT lead suppressors (above), Resistive spark plug caps; (below) 'in-line' suppressors

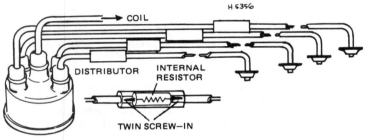

COIL

DISTRIBUTOR

INTERNAL RESISTOR

TWIN SCREW—IN

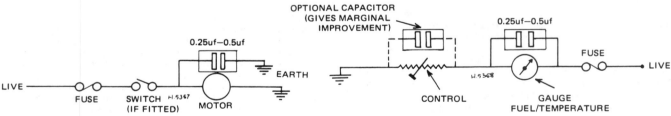

OPTIONAL CAPACITOR (GIVES MARGINAL IMPROVEMENT)

0.25uf—0.5uf

0.25uf—0.5uf

LIVE

FUSE

SWITCH (IF FITTED)

MOTOR

EARTH

CONTROL

GAUGE FUEL/TEMPERATURE

FUSE

LIVE

Fig. 10.41. Correct method of suppressing electric motors

Fig. 10.42. Method of suppressing gauges and their control units

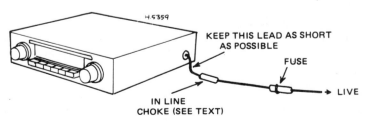

KEEP THIS LEAD AS SHORT AS POSSIBLE

FUSE

LIVE

IN LINE CHOKE (SEE TEXT)

Fig. 10.43. All 'in-line' choke should be fitted into the live supply lead as close to the unit as possible

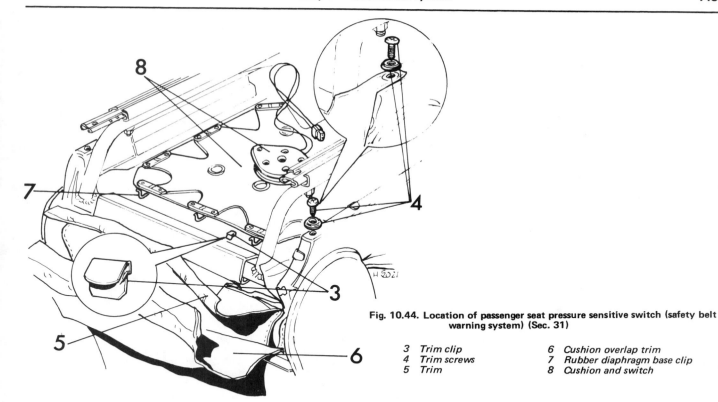

Fig. 10.44. Location of passenger seat pressure sensitive switch (safety belt warning system) (Sec. 31)

| | |
|---|---|
| 3  Trim clip | 6  Cushion overlap trim |
| 4  Trim screws | 7  Rubber diaphragm base clip |
| 5  Trim | 8  Cushion and switch |

e)  Steering column to frame.
f)  Bonnet and boot lids to frame.

These faults are most pronounced when (1) the engine is idling, (2) labouring under load. Although the moving parts are already connected with nuts, bolts, etc, these do tend to rust and corrode, thus creating a high resistance interference source.

If you have a "ragged" sounding pulse when mobile, this could be wheel or tyre static. This can be cured by buying some anti-static powder and sprinkling it liberally inside the tyres.

If the interference takes the shape of a high pitched screeching noise that changes its note when the car is in motion and only comes now and then, this could be related to the aerial, especially if it is of the telescopic or whip type. This source can be cured quite simply by pushing a small rubber ball on top of the aerial (yes, really!) as this breaks the electric field before it can form; but it would be much better to buy yourself a new aerial of a reputable brand. If, on the other hand, you are getting a loud rushing sound every time you brake, then this is brake static. This effect is most prominent on hot dry days and is cured only by fitting a special kit, which is quite expensive.

In conclusion, it is pointed out that it is relatively easy, and therefore cheap, to eliminate 95 per cent of all noise, but to eliminate the final 5 per cent is time and money consuming. It is up to the individual to decide if it is worth it. Please remember also, that you cannot get concert performance out of a cheap radio.

Finally, players and eight track players are not usually affected by noise but in a very bad case, the best remedies are the first three suggestions plus using a 3 - 5 amp choke in the "live" line and in incurable cases screen the live and speaker wires.

**Note:** if your car is fitted with electronic ignition, then it is not recommended that either the spark plug resistors or the ignition coil capacitor be fitted as these may damage the system. Most electronic ignition units have built-in suppression and should therefore, not cause interference.

## 31 Seat belt warning system

1   A warning system is fitted to all models which causes an indicator lamp to illuminate should the ignition be switched on when either the front seats are occupied but the seat belts are not fastened.
2   An audible warning is also given under these conditions by the clicking of the flasher unit.
3   If a heavy parcel is placed upon the front passenger seat then the seat belt should be fastened to prevent the warning system being actuated.
4   Access to the pressure sensitive switch under the passenger's seat is obtained after removing the seat and the seat lower trim clips.

## 32 Fault diagnosis - electrical system

| Symptom | Reason/s |
|---|---|
| Starter fails to turn engine | Battery discharged. |
| | Battery defective internally. |
| | Battery terminal leads loose or earth lead not securely attached to body. |
| | Loose or broken connections in starter motor circuit. |
| | Starter motor switch or solenoid faulty. |
| | Starter brushes badly worn, sticking, or brush wires loose. |
| | Commutator dirty, worn or burnt. |

| Symptom | Reason/s |
|---|---|
| | Starter motor armature faulty. |
| | Field coils earthed. |
| Starter turns engine very slowly | Battery in discharged condition. |
| | Starter brushes badly worn, sticking or brush wires loose. |
| | Loose wires in starter motor circuit. |
| Starter spins but does not turn engine | Pinion or flywheel gear teeth broken or worn. |
| | Battery discharged. |
| Starter motor noisy or excessively rough engagement | Pinion or flywheel gear teeth broken or worn. |
| | Starter motor retaining bolts loose. |
| Battery will not hold charge for more than a few days | Battery defective internally. |
| | Electrolyte level too low or electrolyte too weak due to leakage. |
| | Plate separators no longer fully effective. |
| | Battery plates severely sulphated. |
| | Fan belt slipping. |
| | Battery terminal connections loose or corroded. |
| | Alternator not charging. |
| | Short in lighting circuit causing continual battery drain. |
| | Regulator unit not working correctly. |
| Ignition light fails to go out, battery runs flat in a few days | Fan belt loose and slipping or broken. |
| | Alternator brushes worn, sticking, broken or dirty. |
| | Alternator brush springs weak or broken. |
| | Internal fault in alternator. |

**Failure of individual electrical equipment to function correctly is dealt with alphabetically, item-by-item, under the headings listed below**

### Horn

| | |
|---|---|
| Horn operates all the time | Horn push either earthed or stuck down. |
| | Horn cable to horn push earthed. |
| Horn fails to operate | Blown fuse. |
| | Cable or cable connection loose, broken or disconnected. |
| | Horn has an internal fault. |
| Horn emits intermittent or unsatisfactory noise | Cable connections loose. |
| | Horn incorrectly adjusted. |

### Lights

| | |
|---|---|
| Lights do not come on | If engine not running, battery discharged. |
| | Wire connections loose, disconnected or broken. |
| | Light switch shorting or otherwise faulty. |
| Lights come on but fade out | If engine not running battery discharged. |
| | Light bulb filament burnt out or bulbs or sealed beam units broken. |
| | Wire connections loose, disconnected or broken. |
| | Light switch shorting or otherwise faulty. |
| Lights give very poor illumination | Lamp glasses dirty. |
| | Lamps badly out of adjustment. |
| Lights work erratically - flashing on and off, especially over bumps | Battery terminals or earth connection loose. |
| | Lights not earthing properly. |
| | Contacts in light switch faulty. |

### Wipers

| | |
|---|---|
| Wiper motor fails to work | Blown fuse. |
| | Wire connections loose, disconnected or broken. |
| | Brushes badly worn. |
| | Armature worn or faulty. |
| | Field coils faulty. |
| Wiper motor works very slowly and takes excessive current | Commutator dirty, greasy or burnt. |
| | Armature bearings dirty or unaligned. |
| | Armature badly worn or faulty. |
| Wiper motor works slowly and takes little current | Brushes badly worn. |
| | Commutator dirty, greasy or burnt. |
| | Armature badly worn or faulty. |
| Wiper motor works but wiper blades remain static | Wiper motor gearbox parts badly worn. |

**Wiring diagram - Special headlamp circuit**

When the headlamps flash on dipped beam and/or line fuses are fitted in the headlamp main beam circuits use the circuit diagram below in conjunction with the wiring diagram on page 146

| | | | |
|---|---|---|---|
| 1 | Headlamp main RH | 5 | Headlamp dip LH |
| 2 | Headlamp main LH | 6 | Headlamp flasher switch |
| 3 | Line fuse 8A | 7 | Headlamp dipswitch |
| 4 | Headlamp dip RH | 8 | Main beam warning lamp |

**Cable colour code**

| | | | | | | | | | |
|---|---|---|---|---|---|---|---|---|---|
| B | Black | LG | Light green | P | Purple | U | Blue |
| G | Green | N | Brown | R | Red | W | White |
| K | Pink | O | Orange | S | Slate | Y | Yellow |

When a cable has two colour code letters the first denotes the main colour and the second denotes the tracer colour

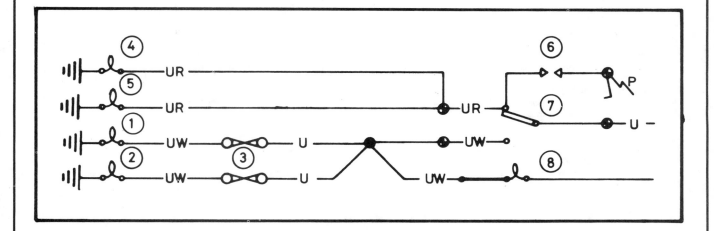

# Key to the wiring diagram

Several of the components listed in this key may not be included in the specification of all models. Models exported to certain countries or territories may have special fitments to conform to the mandatory requirements or legislation of those countries.

| | | | |
|---|---|---|---|
| 1 | Direction indicator lamp - front LH | 43 | Lighting switch |
| 1a | Direction indicator repeater lamp LH | 44 | Brake failure test switch/warning light |
| 2 | Fog lamps | 45 | Panel lamp illumination switch |
| 3 | Parking lamp - front LH | 46 | Panel lamp dimmer resistance |
| 4 | Direction indicator lamp - front RH | 47 | Heater fan motor |
| 4a | Direction indicator repeater lamp RH | 48 | Radio |
| 5 | Parking lamp - front RH | 49 | Ignition warning light |
| 5a | Radiator grille badge lamp | 50 | Hazard warning switch |
| 6 | Headlamp - dip beams | 51 | Direction indicator flasher unit |
| 6a | Headlamp - main beams | 52 | Voltage stabilizer - instruments |
| 7 | Windscreen wiper motor | 53 | Stop lamp switch |
| 8 | Starter motor | 54 | Seat belt warning flasher unit |
| 9 | Starter solenoid | 55 | Cigar lighter unit |
| 10 | Alternator | 56 | Cigar lighter illumination |
| 11 | Windscreen washer pump | 57 | Opticell unit bulb - fibre optics illumination |
| 12 | Battery | 58 | Fuel gauge |
| 13 | Direction indicator warning light | 59 | Coolant temperature gauge |
| 14 | Radiator cooling fan motor | 60 | Oil pressure warning light |
| 15 | Door switches - front | 61 | Seat belt warning light |
| 16 | Door switches - rear | 62 | Split brake system differential switch |
| 17 | Luggage compartment lamp switch | 63 | Stop lamps |
| 18 | Starter solenoid relay | 64 | Seat belt switch - passengers |
| 19 | Direction indicator switch | 65 | Seat belt switch - drivers |
| 20 | Headlamp dipswitch | 66 | Heated rear window unit |
| 21 | Headlamp flasher switch | 67 | Hazard warning light |
| 22 | Windscreen wiper/washer switch | 68 | Headlamp main beam warning light |
| 23 | Radiator cooling fan thermostat | 69 | Printed circuit - instrument panel |
| 24 | Interior lamps - rear | 70 | Panel illumination lamps |
| 25 | Automatic gearbox safety switch | 71 | Reverse lamp - LH |
| 26 | Ignition/starter switch | 72 | Direction indicator lamp rear RH |
| 27 | Horn push | 73 | Reverse lamp - RH |
| 28 | Fusebox | 74 | Automatic gearbox quadrant illumination |
| 29 | Clock | 75 | Glovebox lamp |
| 30 | Roof lamp - front | 76 | Direction indicator lamp - rear LH |
| 31 | Luggage compartment lamp | 77 | Rear parking lamp - LH |
| 32 | Horns | 78 | Number plate lamps |
| 33 | Hazard warning flasher unit | 79 | Rear parking lamp - RH |
| 34 | Heated rear window relay | 80 | Reverse lamp switch |
| 35 | Engine compartment lamp switch | 81 | Seat switch - passengers |
| 36 | Ignition coil | 82 | Glovebox lamp switch |
| 37 | Heater fan switch | 83 | Battery condition indicator gauge |
| 38 | Line fuse | 84 | Fuel gauge tank unit |
| 39 | Engine compartment lamp | 85 | Coolant temperature gauge |
| 40 | Heated rear window switch/warning light | 86 | Oil pressure switch |
| 41 | Fog lamp switch | | |
| 42 | Distributor | | |

## Cable colour code

| B | Black | N | Brown | S | Slate | Y | Yellow |
|---|---|---|---|---|---|---|---|
| G | Green | O | Orange | U | Blue | LG | Light green |
| K | Pink | P | Purple | W | White | R | Red |

When a cable has two colour code letters the first denotes the main colour and the second denotes the tracer colour

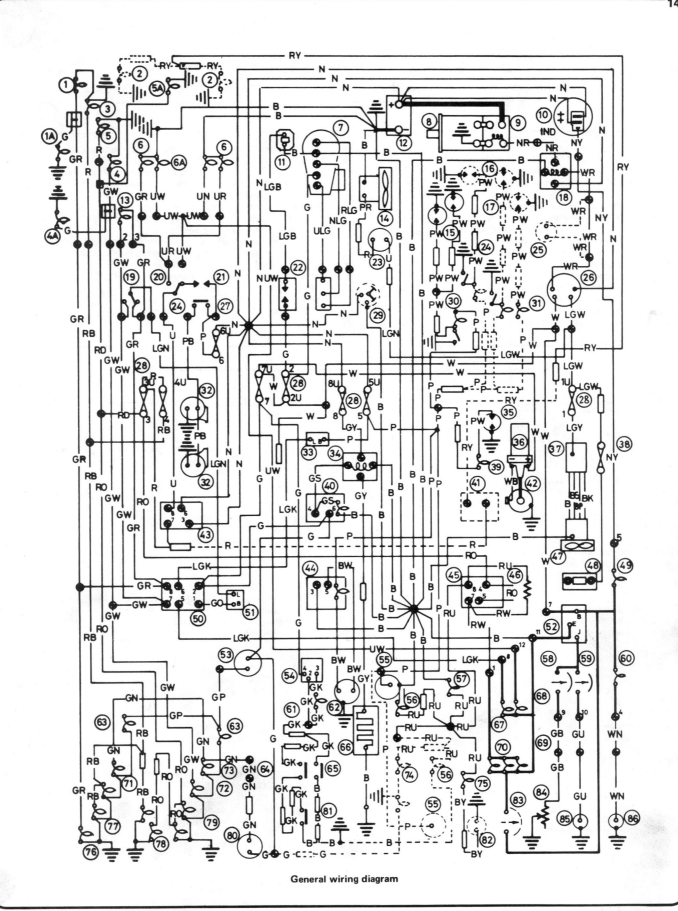

**General wiring diagram**

# Chapter 11 Suspension and steering

*For modifications, and information applicable to later models, see Supplement at end of manual*

## Contents

## Specifications

### Front suspension

Type ... ... ... ... ... ... ... ... ... ...    Independent Hydragas system, operating through upper and lower suspension arms

### Rear suspension

Type ... ... ... ... ... ... ... ... ... ...    Independent Hydragas system, operating through trailing arms
Nominal toe-in (each wheel) ... ... ... ... ...    0° 30' (0.15 in — 4.0 mm) *
Camber ... ... ... ... ... ... ... ... ...    1° ± 0° 30' negative *
* These angles are set in production and are non-adjustable

### Steering angles

Front wheel alignment ... ... ... ... ... ... ...    Parallel ± 1/16 in (1.6 mm)
Camber ... ... ... ... ... ... ... ... ...    0° 30' positive ± 0° 30'
Castor ... ... ... ... ... ... ... ... ...    1° 30' positive ± 0° 30'
Steering axis inclination ... ... ... ... ... ...    11°
Steering lock angle of outer wheel with inner wheel at 20° ... ...    19° 11'

### Steering gear

Type ... ... ... ... ... ... ... ... ...    Rack and pinion (power option on 1800 models, standard on 2200)
Steering wheel diameter ... ... ... ... ... ...    15.75 in (400.0 mm)
No. of turns of steering wheel (lock-to-lock) ... ... ...    4.57 (manual) 3.26 (power)
Turning circle ... ... ... ... ... ... ...    37 ft 10 in (11.52 m)
Track:
    Front ... ... ... ... ... ... ... ...    58.0 in (147.3 cm)
    Rear ... ... ... ... ... ... ... ...    57.4 in (145.82 cm)
Wheelbase ... ... ... ... ... ... ... ...    105.0 in (266.7 cm)
Ground clearance ... ... ... ... ... ... ...    6.45 in (16.40 cm)

### Wheels

Type (standard) ... ... ... ... ... ... ... ...    Ventilated disc 4½ JFH x 14
Denovo (option) ... ... ... ... ... ... ...    105.0 mm x 350.0 mm

### Tyres

Standard ... ... ... ... ... ... ... ...    185/70SR - 14 radial   (special option 175/70SR - 14 radial)
Denovo (option) ... ... ... ... ... ... ...    195 mm - 65 mm SR  - 350
Tyre pressures, Standard (cold):
    Normal - Front ... ... ... ... ... ... ...    23 lb sq in (1.6 kg sq cm)
    Rear ... ... ... ... ... ... ... ...    21 lb sq in (1.5 kg sq cm)
    Fully laden or high speed - Front ... ... ... ...    26 lb sq in (1.8 kg sq cm)
    Rear ... ... ... ... ...    24 lb sq in (1.7 kg sq cm)
Tyre pressures, Special option (cold):
    Normal - Front ... ... ... ... ... ...    27 lb sq in (1.9 kg sq cm)
    - Rear ... ... ... ... ... ...    25 lb sq in (1.8 kg sq cm)
    Fully laden or high speed - Front ... ... ...    30 lb sq in (2.1 kg sq cm)
    - Rear ... ... ... ...    28 lb sq in (2.0 kg sq cm)

## Torque wrench settings

| | lb/ft | Nm |
|---|---|---|
| **Front suspension** | | |
| Hub nut ... ... ... ... ... ... ... ... ... ... | 200 | 272 |
| Bump rubber to bracket ... ... ... ... ... ... ... ... | 30 | 41 |
| Bump rubber bracket to valance ... ... ... ... ... ... ... | 15 | 21 |
| Suspension arm swivel pin nuts ... ... ... ... ... ... | 40 | 55 |
| Suspension arm swivel housings ... ... ... ... ... ... | 70 | 97 |
| Upper arm pivot bolt ... ... ... ... ... ... ... ... | 120 | 166 |
| Lower arm pivot bolt ... ... ... ... ... ... ... ... | 50 | 69 |
| Lower arm rear bush to body ... ... ... ... ... ... ... | 15 | 21 |
| | | |
| **Rear suspension** | | |
| Hub nut ... ... ... ... ... ... ... ... ... ... | 60 | 83 |
| Cross-tube mounting setscrews | | |
| To body ... ... ... ... ... ... | 37 | 51 |
| To cross-tube ... ... ... ... ... ... | 20 | 28 |
| Radius arm pivot nut ... ... ... ... ... ... ... | 160 | 221 |
| Rebound strap bracket bolts ... ... ... ... ... ... ... | 44 | 61 |
| Bump rubber to radius arm nut ... ... ... ... ... ... ... | 20 | 28 |
| Reaction rubber to body screws ... ... ... ... ... ... ... | 20 | 28 |
| | | |
| **Steering** | | |
| Steering wheel nut ... ... ... ... ... ... ... ... | 35 | 48 |
| Steering arm to hub bolts ... ... ... ... ... ... ... | 35 | 48 |
| Trackrod-end balljoint taper pin nut ... ... ... ... ... ... | 35 | 48 |
| Steering rack to trunnion bolts ... ... ... ... ... ... | 38 | 53 |
| Rack trunnion to body bolts ... ... ... ... ... ... ... | 20 | 28 |
| Intermediate shaft pinch bolt ... ... ... ... ... ... ... | 20 | 28 |
| Power steering reservoir setscrew ... ... ... ... ... ... | 35 | 48 |
| Trackrod to steering rack ... ... ... ... ... ... ... | 40 | 55 |
| Trackrod-end locknuts ... ... ... ... ... ... ... | 35 | 48 |
| Roadwheel nuts ... ... ... ... ... ... ... ... | 45 | 62 |

## 1 General description

The suspension system is independent on all four wheels utilising the Hydragas system. The fluid chambers in the front and rear Hydragas units on the same side of the car are interconnected. Each Hydragas displacer unit comprises a nitrogen-filled spherical chamber and a displacer chamber between which is located a two way valve to provide the necessary suspension damping. The space above the flexible separator in the upper chamber is charged with nitrogen to provide the springing effect. The space between the separator and the diaphragm is filled with fluid and is at a higher pressure than that of the nitrogen. This pressure differential has the effect of compressing the nitrogen and lifting the separator from the bottom of the spherical chamber and causing the fluid and gas pressures to equalise. When a front wheel is on a ridge and a rear wheel is in a hollow, the compression of the front diaphragm in the Hydragas unit displaces fluid which is transferred through the interconnecting pipe to the rear displacer chamber on the same side of the car. As this displaced fluid is accommodated by the opening of the rear displacer chamber, the fluid pressure in the system will not overcome the damper valve and so the nitrogen springs are not deflected. Movement of the body is therefore restricted to a minimum.

When a front wheel hits a bump with the rear wheel still on level ground, fluid is displaced and both front and rear nitrogen springs are displaced.

When both front and rear roadwheels hit bumps simultaneously, the compression of the front and rear disphragms increases the fluid pressure making it pass through the damper valves, thus compressing the nitrogen springs. Under these conditions, fluid flow through the interconnecting pipe is minimal. The fluid used in the Hydragas suspension system is of a special mixture and no substitute must be used.

The Hydragas displacer units transmit their action in the case of the front wheels, through upper and lower suspension arms which are connected to the swivel hub of the driveshaft. With the rear units, movement is transmitted through radius arms attached to cross-tubes.

The steering is of rack and pinion type, differing in design according to whether manual or power-assisted steering is fitted. The steering column incorporates an intermediate shaft fitted with two universal joints.

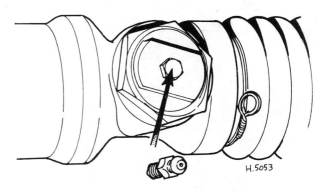

Fig. 11.1. Steering rack grease point (Sec. 2)

## 2 Suspension and steering - maintenance

1 No maintenance is required to the Hydragas suspension system.
2 At the intervals specified in 'Routine Maintenance' remove the plug from the top of the steering rack pinion housing and screw in a grease nipple instead. Apply a grease gun and give five or six strokes only. Remove the grease nipple and refit the plug.
3 If the car is equipped with power steering, regularly check the fluid level in the reservoir. To do this, switch off the engine, remove the combined filler cap/dipstick. Top-up if necessary to the appropriate 'Full' mark according to oil temperature using engine oil (photo).
4 Periodically check the power steering pump belt tension, as described in Chapter 1, Section 85.

## 3 Suspension overhaul - precautions

1 Prior to dismantling any part of the suspension system, if such work

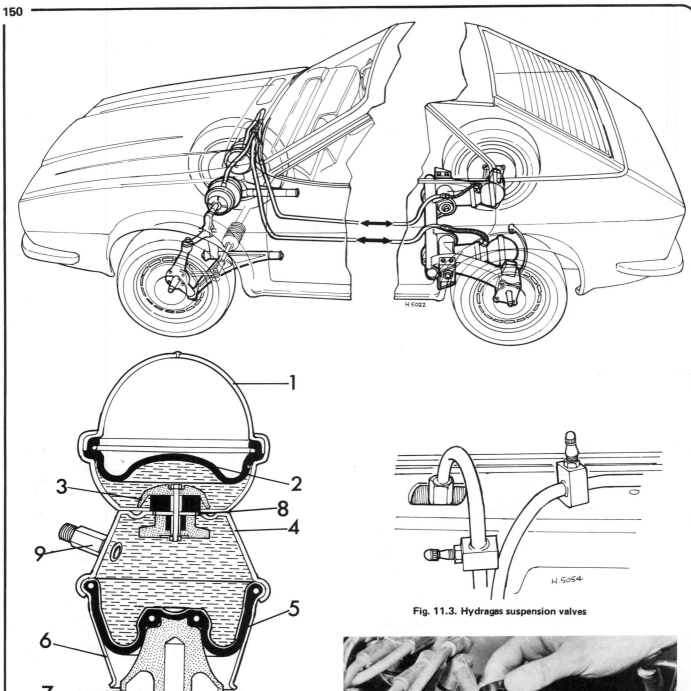

Fig. 11.2. Hydragas system layout and sectional view of a displacer unit

1  Nitrogen filled chamber
2  Separator
3  Two-way damper valve
4  Displacer chamber
5  Diaphragm
6  Displacer strut
7  Piston
8  Bleed hole
9  Adaptor

Fig. 11.3. Hydragas suspension valves

2.3 Checking power steering pump oil level

Fig. 11.4. Front suspension components

1 Displacer unit
2 Spacer
3 Spring
4 Dust cover
5 Ball pin
6 Socket
7 Locknut
8 Special washer
9 Bolt
10 Pivot bush
11 Upper arm
12 Bump/rebound bracket
13 Bump rubber
14 Rebound rubber
15 Locknut
16 Slotted washer
17 Buffer washer
18 Bush
19 Special washer
20 Arm rear bush
21 Special washer
22 Lower arm
23 Driveshaft
24 Water shield
25 Oil seal
26 Taper roller bearing
27 Bearing spacer
28 Oil seal
29 Swivel hub
30 Lockwasher
31 Shims
32 Ball pin
33 Housing
34 Dust cover
35 Nut and lockwasher
36 Steering arm
37 Hollow dowels
38 Brake disc
39 Roadwheel stud
40 Hub flange
41 Split collar
42 Nut
43 Bolt

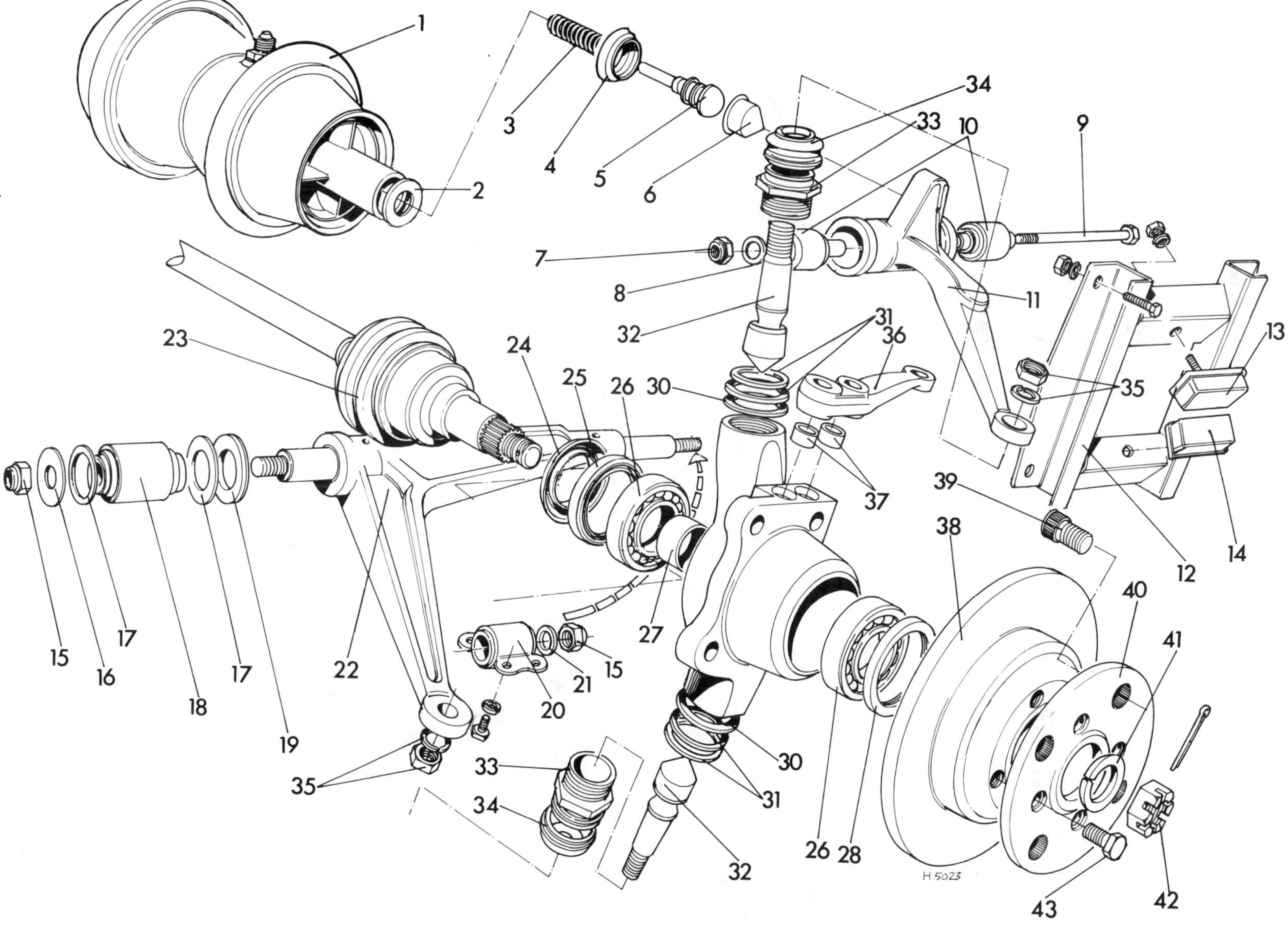

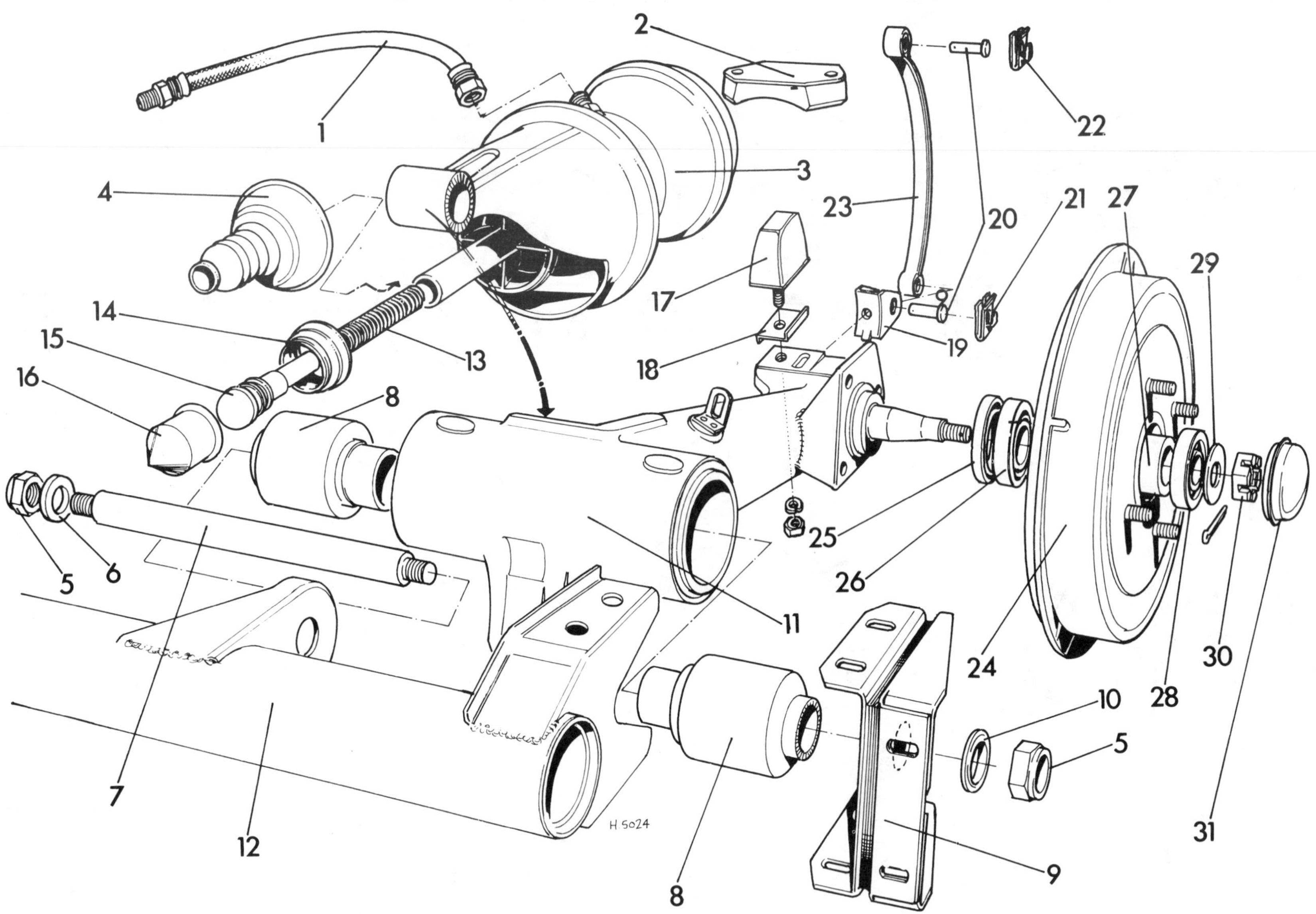

Fig. 11.5. Rear suspension components

1 Flexible hose
2 Reaction rubber
3 Displacer unit
4 Boot
5 Locknut
6 Special washer
7 Pivot shaft
8 Bush
9 Mounting rubber
10 Special washer
11 Radius arm
12 Cross-tube
13 Spring
14 Dust cover
15 Ball pin
16 Socket
17 Bump rubber
18 Locating plate
19 Clevis pin
20 Clevis pin
21 Retaining clip
22 Retaining clip
23 Rebound strap
24 Brake drum
25 Oil seal
26 Hub bearing
27 Spacer
28 Bearing
29 Special washer
30 Nut
31 Cap

Rebound strap bracket

H 5624

will entail disconnection of the Hydragas system, then it will have to be first depressurised, then recharged, after the work has been completed. This can only be carried out by your Leyland dealer or a service station having the necessary equipment. On no account touch the Hydragas system valves or the system will be rendered inoperative or at least, the trim level upset (see Section 18).

2   In order that suspension overhaul work can be carried out at home, it is quite safe to drive from and to your nearest dealer with the system depressurised, provided the road surface is reasonable and the road speed is kept below 30 mph (50 km/h). The action of the suspension bump rubbers will provide the necessary temporary suspension characteristics.

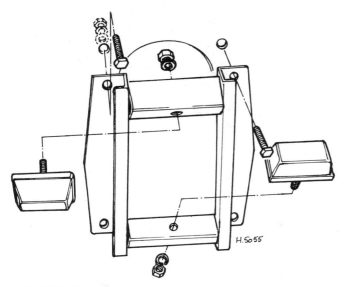

**Fig. 11.6. Front suspension bump and rebound rubbers (Sec. 4)**

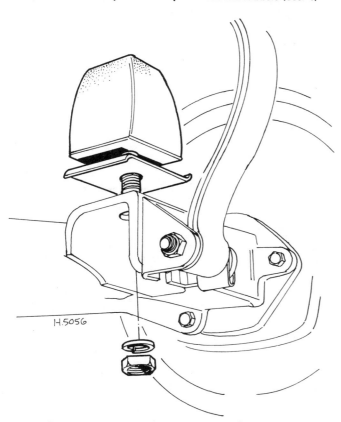

**Fig. 11.7. Rear suspension bump rubber (Sec. 4)**

### 4   Suspension bump rubbers - renewal

1   Jack-up and support the appropriate side of the car and remove the roadwheel.

*Front bump and rebound rubbers*
2   Remove the setscrew which is secured by the nut on the inside of the engine compartment valance and which in turn retains the bump bracket.
3   Remove the three setscrews which secure the bracket to the valance and then slide the bracket along the suspension upper arm. Remove the bump and rebound rubbers which are retained by pegs.

*Rear bump rubber*
4   Remove the nut which secures the bump rubber to the radius arm. Separate the rubber from the locating plate noting the position of the plate lips.
5   Refitting is a reversal of removal but tighten all nuts and bolts to the specified torque.

### 5   Rear suspension rebound strap and reaction rubber - renewal

1   *To renew the rebound strap,* jack-up both the car and the radius arm so that any tension is released from the strap. Remove the spring clips and the clevis pins.
2   Refitting is a reversal of removal but the side of the strap marked 'REAR FACE' must be towards the rear of the car.
3   *To renew the reaction rubber,* the system will have to be depressurised on one side. The rubber can then be unbolted from the floor (Fig. 11.9).
4   Refitting the new reaction rubber is a reversal of removal but make sure that the flat side of the rubber faces towards the front of the car. Tighten the retaining bolts to the specified torque and have the system recharged by your dealer.

### 6   Front suspension upper arm - removal, overhaul and refitting

1   Have your dealer depressurise the appropriate side of the Hydragas system.
2   Raise the car and support it securely. Remove the roadwheel.
3   Disconnect the swivel balljoint from the suspension upper arm using an extractor or wedges. As the balljoint is disconnected, support the suspension under the lower arm. On 6 cylinder cars, remove the alternator if automatic transmission is fitted.

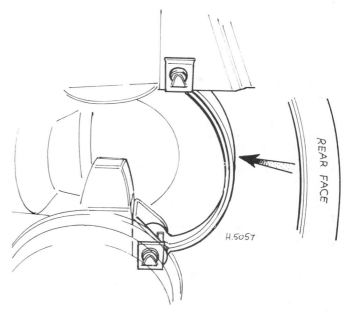

**Fig. 11.8. Rear suspension rebound strap (Sec. 5)**

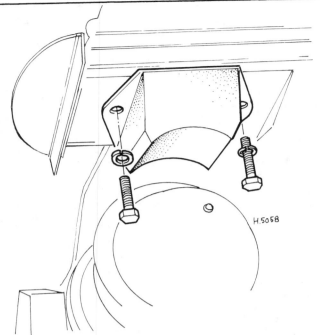

Fig. 11.9. Rear suspension reaction rubber (Sec. 5)

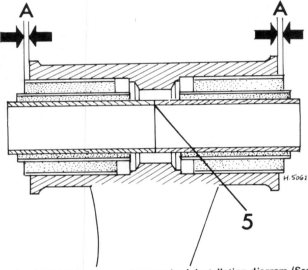

Fig. 11.11. Front suspension arm bush installation diagram (Sec. 6)

5   Arm centre line

A = 0.068 to 0.078 in
(1.72 to 1.97 mm)

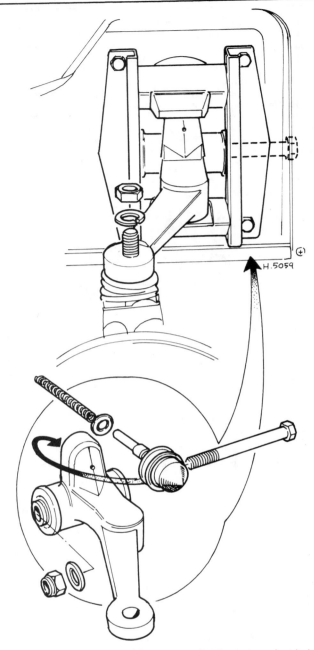

Fig. 11.10. Attachment of front suspension lower arm pivot bolt
(Sec. 6)

4   Remove the bump and rebound bracket, as described in Section 4.
5   Remove the locknut and special washer from the end of the suspension arm pivot bolt which projects into the engine compartment. Tap the threaded end of the pivot bolt with a soft-faced mallet so that its opposite end can be gripped and withdrawn into the car interior.
6   Withdraw the suspension arm complete with knuckle joint. The latter may be levered out if required. On six cylinder cars having automatic transmission, a spacing washer is fitted to the knuckle joint spigot.
7   Renewal of the suspension arm bushes is best left to your dealer but where pressing facilities are available, press them out using a suitable mandrel. During this operation, the flexible bushes will probably separate from the outer sleeves as pressure is applied to the inner sleeves. The outer sleeves can be removed afterwards after splitting them with a sharp cold chisel. Press the new bushes into the suspension arm by applying pressure to their outer sleeves. When the end faces of the inner sleeves are together in the centre of the arm, then there should be a projection of the outer sleeve on each side of the arm as

shown in Fig. 11.11.
8   Commence refitting the suspension upper arm by packing the knuckle joint with specified grease.
9   Apply graphite grease to the knuckle joint spigot.
10  Install the suspension arm but only tighten the pivot bolt locknut finger-tight.
11  Jack-up the suspension until the upper arm is horizontal and then tighten the pivot bolt locknut to the specified torque.
12  On completion, have your dealer recharge the Hydragas system.

### 7   Front suspension lower arm - removal, overhaul and refitting

1   Raise the front of the car and support it securely. Remove the roadwheel (photo).
2   Slacken the locknuts on the suspension lower arm pivot bushes.
3   Disconnect the suspension arm from the lower swivel balljoint pin.
4   From the front pivot bush of the suspension arm, remove the

locknut and special washer. Remove the buffer washer from the boss of the bush.

5   Support the lower arm and remove the four screws which secure the rear pivot bush to the body.

6   Withdraw the lower arm out of the front pivot bush and extract the inner buffer washer and the special washer.

7   Remove the locknut and washer which secure the rear bush and withdraw the bush from the arm.

8   Renewal of the suspension lower arm front bush can be carried out using a length of threaded studding, two nuts, washers and suitable distance pieces to withdraw it. Pull the new bush into position until its face is flush with the mounting bracket. The rear pivot bush is renewed as an assembly.

9   Refitting the suspension arm is a reversal of removal but make sure that the special washer on the front pivot bush has its chamfered face towards the suspension arm.

10 Tighten the locknuts and rear bush retaining screws only finger-tight until with a jack under the suspension lower arm and the weight of the car on the suspension they can be tightened to specified torque in the following order: (i) front bush locknut, (ii) rear bush to body screws, (iii) rear bush locknut.

## 8   Front suspension swivel balljoints - removal and refitting

1   Raise the front of the car, support it adequately and remove the front roadwheel. Remove the brake caliper and tie it up.

2   *If the upper swivel balljoint* is to be removed, place a supporting jack under the suspension lower arm and then remove the ball pin nut and washer and disconnect the balljoint from the suspension arm using a separator or two wedges.

3   Lower the jack under the suspension arm and disconnect the balljoint from the upper arm.

4   Flatten the locktab and unscrew the balljoint housing from the swivel hub.

5   *If the lower swivel balljoint* is to be removed, then first slacken the suspension lower arm pivot locknuts, otherwise the operations are similar to those described for the upper joint.

6   Before installing a new balljoint to the swivel hub, thoroughly clean out the seating in the hub. Install the new balljoint to the hub but not including the locking washer or any shims. Tighten until the ball pin is just nipped but is still free to swivel without any endplay. Now measure the gap between the housing and the swivel hub using feeler blades. From this dimension subtract between 0.009 and 0.013 in. (0.23 and 0.33 mm). The resulting dimension must be equalled by the thickness of the locking washer and shim pack to provide the balljoint with the necessary preload. To meet this requirement, shims are available in the following thicknesses: 0.002 in (0.05 mm); 0.003 in (0.08 mm); 0.005 in (0.13 mm); 0.010 in (0.25 mm); 0.030 in (0.75 mm).

7   Assemble the shims and locking washer and then screw in the balljoint swivel housing to the specified torque. Bend up the tab of the locking washer. Reconnect and tighten the ball pin nuts.

8   Tighten the suspension lower arm nuts when the weight of the car is on the arm.

7.1 One side of the front suspension

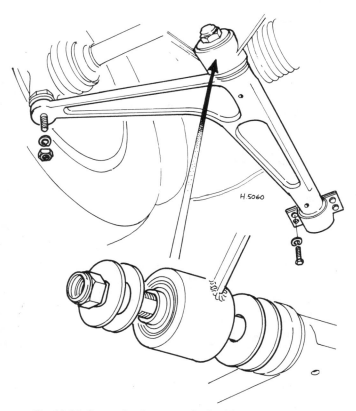

Fig. 11.12. Suspension lower arm bush and washer arrangement (Sec. 7)

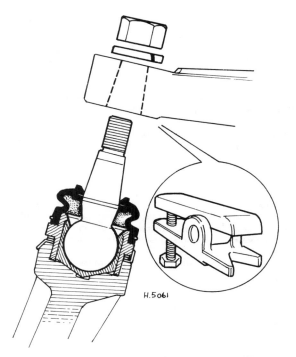

Fig. 11.13. Sectional view of suspension upper swivel balljoint and suitable balljoint separator (Sec. 8)

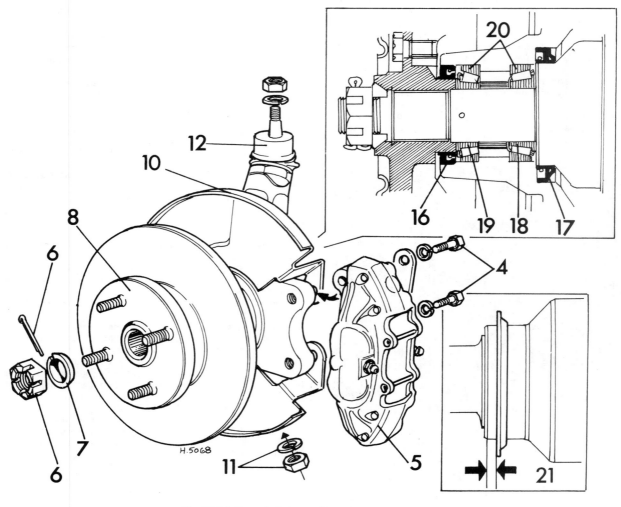

**Fig. 11.14. Front hub details (Sec. 9)**

| | | | |
|---|---|---|---|
| 4 Caliper bolts | 8 Hub flange | 16 Inner oil seal | 19 Inner bearing |
| 5 Caliper | 10 Disc shield | 17 Outer oil seal | 20 Bearing outer tracks |
| 6 Hub nut | 11 Lower swivel nut | 18 Outer bearing | 21 Location of water shield |
| 7 Split collar | 12 Upper swivel balljoint | | |

## 9 Front hub bearings - removal and refitting

1   As the hub nut and roadwheel nuts are very tight, slacken these nuts before jacking-up the front of the car and supporting it securely on axle stands.

2   Unbolt the caliper and tie it up out of the way to prevent strain on the flexible hoses.

3   From the end of the driveshaft, remove the hub nut and split collar.

4   Tap the end of the driveshaft from the drive flange assembly using a soft-faced mallet or alternatively use a two or three-legged puller applying pressure from the centre screw to the end of the driveshaft.

5   Disconnect the trackrod-end balljoint from the steering arm.

6   Remove the disc dust shield.

7   Disconnect the suspension lower arm from the ball pin of the swivel joint.

8   Disconnect the suspension upper arm from the ball pin of the swivel joint.

9   Withdraw the hub assembly and pull off the water shield from the driveshaft.

10  Extract the inner and outer oil seals, the bearing races and the bearing spacer.

11  Using a soft metal drift, drive out the inner and outer bearing races from the hub.

12  Refitting is a reversal of removal but if both front wheel bearings

are being renewed, do not mix the components of the bearing sets as they are matched in production. Always use new oil seals and pack the bearings with fresh grease.

13  Locate a new water shield at a position ¼ in (6.0 mm) onto the hub.

14  Tighten all bolts and nuts to specified torque.

## 10 Rear hub bearings - removal and refitting

1   Remove the brake drum, as described in Chapter 9, Section 3.

2   If the race of the inner bearing is found to be retained on the hub shaft, remove it using a suitable puller.

3   Extract the oil seal, drive out the inner track of the inner bearing and remove the spacer.

4   Drive out the inner race of the outer bearing.

5   Drive out the bearing outer tracks from the hub.

6   Refitting is a reversal of removal but observe the following:

   a) Pack the bearings with specified grease.

   b) The bearing spacer must be installed so that its narrower internal diameter is adjacent to the outer bearing.

   c) The oil seal must be fitted flush with the housing.

   d) Do not fill the hub cap with grease.

   e) Tighten nuts to the specified torque.

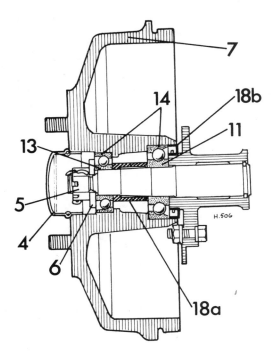

**Fig. 11.15. Sectional view of a rear hub (Sec. 10)**

| | | | |
|---|---|---|---|
| 4 | Dust cap | 13 | Outer bearing |
| 5 | Hub nut | 14 | Bearing outer tracks |
| 6 | Special washer | 18a | Bearing spacer |
| 7 | Brake drum | 18b | Oil seal |
| 11 | Inner bearing | | |

## 11 Front displacer unit - removal and installation

1  Have your dealer depressurise the Hydragas system.
2  Remove the front suspension upper arm (Section 6).
3  Unscrew the interconnecting pipe union from the displacer unit.
4  Withdraw the displacer unit from its location in the body.
5  The knuckle joint can be levered from the upper arm.
6  Installation is a reversal of removal but observe the following points:
    *a)  Pack the knuckle joint with specified grease.*
    *b)  Make sure that the special washer is fitted to the knuckle joint on automatic 6 cylinder cars only.*
    *c)  Ensure that the interconnecting pipe is centrally placed in the body aperture after it is connected.*

## 12 Rear displacer unit - removal and installation

1  Have your dealer depressurise the Hydragas system on the side of the car being overhauled.
2  Jack-up the rear of the car, support it securely and remove the roadwheel.
3  Disconnect the hose from the displacer unit (photo).
4  Remove the locknut and special washer from the inner end of the radius arm pivot shaft and support the radius arm assembly.
5  Remove the two setscrews which secure the cross-tube mounting rubber to the body. The jack may have to be lowered slightly in order to obtain access to the front setscrew. Withdraw the mounting rubber and pivot shaft from the radius arm so that the displacer can be released.
6  Installation is a reversal of removal but observe the following points:
*Initially only tighten the mounting rubber to body and cross-tube screws finger-tight, then support the radius arm in such a position that dimension 'A' is as specified in Fig. 11.17. Now hold the displacer unit hard against its reaction rubber and tighten the radius*

12.3 A rear displacer unit

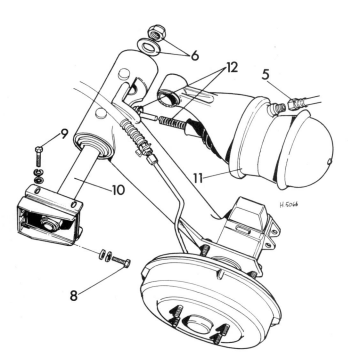

**Fig. 11.16. Rear suspension attachment (Sec. 12)**

| | | | |
|---|---|---|---|
| 5 | Flexible hose | 9 | Cross tube mounting rubber bolt |
| 6 | Radius arm pivot shaft nut | 10 | Radius arm/pivot shaft |
| 8 | Cross tube mounting rubber bolt | 11 | Displacer unit |
| | | 12 | Knuckle joint |

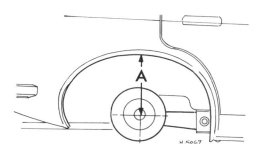

**Fig. 11.17. Radius arm setting diagram (Sec. 12)**

*A  =  11.2 in (285.0 mm)*

*arm pivot nut. Force a wedge between the cross-tube and the out-board end of the radius arm and then tighten the mounting rubber-to-cross-tube setscrews followed by the mounting rubber-to-body setscrews.*

7   Have your dealer re-charge the Hydragas system.

### 13  Rear displacer knuckle joint and boot - removal and refitting

1   Have your dealer depressurise the Hydragas system.
2   Jack-up the rear of the car and support it securely on axle stands.
3   Hold the radius arm in the full rebound position (use a wedge between bump rubber and the body).
4   Pull the boot from the lip of the cup, pull the ball from the cup and extract the knuckle ball and spring from the displacer strut. Extract the cup from the bore of the radius arm.
5   Pull the boot from the displacer unit and strut.
6   Refitting is a reversal of removal.
7   Have the Hydragas system re-charged and the body trim height adjusted.

### 14  Displacer rigid connecting pipe - removal and refitting

1   Have your dealer depressurise the Hydragas system.
2   Working beneath the car, disconnect the pipe union at the front displacer unit.
3   Remove the fuel pipe (pump to carburettor).
4   Remove the fuel pump.
5   *If the left-hand displacer pipe* is being removed, remove the exhaust pipe clamp. Remove the rear roadwheel and support the radius arm in its normal static position, using a jack positioned under the brake drum. The exhaust pipe can now be removed.
6   *With either pipe,* disconnect the union from the rear displacer flexible hose. If a restrictor washer is fitted between the pipe and the hose, discard it if a new pipe is to be installed.
7   Support the cross-tube mounting with a jack and remove the two screws which secure the mounting bracket to the body. Now lower the cross-tube.
8   Unclip the displacer from the underside of the body and remove the rubbers.
9   Detach any pipe clips and pull the displacer connecting pipe down from between the cross-tube and the body and then with the help of an assistant, withdraw the pipe from the engine compartment, passing it between the steering rack and the body.
10  Refitting the pipe is a reversal of removal but only use the restrictor washer if the original pipes are being installed.
11  Have the Hydragas system recharged and the body trim height adjusted by your dealer.

### 15  Displacer flexible hose - removal and refitting

1   Have your dealer depressurise the Hydragas system.
2   Hold the flats of the hose hexagon in an open-ended spanner and unscrew the rigid pipe union.
3   Disconnect the flexible and rigid pipes and then unscrew the flexible hose from the displacer unit.
4   Refitting the hose is a reversal of removal.
5   Have the Hydragas system re-charged and the body trim height checked by your dealer.
6   A restrictor washer is used on early units; discard this when a new hose is being installed.

### 16  Rear suspension radius arm - removal, overhaul and refitting

1   Have your dealer depressurise the Hydragas system.
2   Jack-up the rear of the car and support it on stands.
3   Disconnect the flexible hose from the displacer unit. Plug the open end of the hose.
4   Disconnect the brake pipe and flexible hose at the radius arm bracket. Plug the hose.
5   Remove the brake drum, as described in Chapter 9, Section 3.
6   Remove the strap which retains the handbrake cable to the radius arm.

7   Remove the three nuts and their special bolts which secure the brake backplate to the radius arm.
8   Withdraw the complete brake assembly, pass it over the radius arm and support it on blocks underneath the body.
9   Remove the locknut and special washer from the inner end of the pivot shaft.
10  Support the centre of the radius arm, remove the spring clip and clevis pin and detach the rebound strap from the radius arm bracket.
11  Remove the two setscrews which secure the mounting rubber to the body, also the four setscrews which secure it to the cross-tube.
12  Release the mounting rubber and the pivot shaft from the mounting

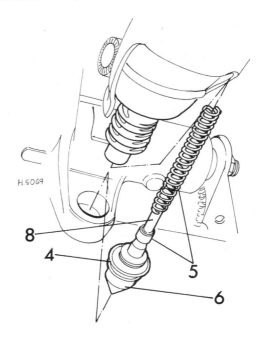

**Fig. 11.18. Rear displacer unit knuckle joint assembly (Sec. 13)**

4   *Boot*                              6   *Cup*
5   *Knuckle ball and spring*          8   *Balljoint spigot*

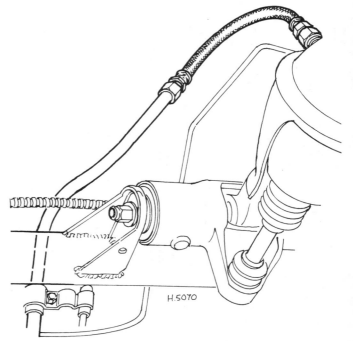

**Fig. 11.19. Rear displacer unit flexible hose (Sec. 15)**

tube brackets and withdraw the radius arm. Detach the mounting rubber and pivot shaft from the radius arm.

13 The displacer unit, the knuckle joint spring, the knuckle joint, the rebound strap bracket and the bump rubber can all be removed from the radius arm if required.

14 The radius arm bushes can be renewed as described for front suspension arms in Section 6, paragraph 7. Make sure that the new bushes are pressed in flush with the radius arm.

15 Refitting is a reversal of removal but apply graphite grease to the knuckle joint spigot and screw the inner pivot nut and mounting rubber screws finger tight until the radius arm has been jacked-up to provide a dimension 'A' as shown in Fig. 11.17. All nuts, screws and bolts should then be tightened to their specified torque wrench settings.

16 Bleed the brake hydraulic circuit and have the Hydragas system recharged and the body trim height checked and adjusted by your dealer.

## 17 Rear suspension cross tube end mountings - removal and refitting

1 Have your dealer depressurise the Hydragas system.

2 Jack-up the rear of the car, support it securely and remove the rear roadwheels.

3 Disconnect the exhaust pipe front strap from the cross-tube mounting.

4 Disconnect the exhaust pipe rear strap from the tailpipe and support the pipe.

5 Disconnect the flexible hoses from the rear displacer units.

6 Remove the locknuts and special washers from the inner ends of the pivot shafts.

7 Release the handbrake cables from their clips on the cross-tube.

8 On one side of the car remove the screws which secure the cross-tube mountings to the body and to the cross-tube itself.

9 Free the mounting rubber and pivot shaft from the cross-tube bracket.

10 Move the radius arm on one side of the car clear of the cross-tube and support the arm on a block or axle stand.

11 Support the cross-tube at its centre point, preferably on a trolley jack.

12 Repeat the operations described in paragraphs 8, 9 and 10 on the opposite side of the car.

13 Lower the cross-tube jack and withdraw the assembly from beneath the car.

14 Refitting is a reversal of removal, but before tightening the cross-tube mounting nuts and the radius inner pivot nuts, set the radius arm as shown in Fig. 11.17. Hold the displacer units hard against their reaction rubber pads while tightening the radius arm inner pivot nuts.

15 Have the Hydragas system recharged and the body trim height checked by your dealer.

## 18 Body trim height - adjustment

1 To ensure correct operation of the suspension, good roadholding and positive steering, it is important that the correct body trim height is maintained at all times.

2 This is a job for your dealer who will have the necessary equipment to increase or decrease the pressure in the Hydragas system using the two valves shown in Fig. 11.3.

3 When the car is standing (without occupants) on a level surface with tyres correctly inflated the body trim height is correct when the dimension 'A' measured between the hub centre and the wheel arch is as specified in Fig. 11.22.

## 19 Trackrod-ends - removal and refitting

1 Where 'lost motion' is observed at the steering wheel or when movement or shake can be felt at the trackrod-end balljoint if the trackrod is gripped and moved up and down, then the trackrod-end must be renewed.

2 Disconnect the trackrod-end ball pin from the eye of the steering arm using a suitable extractor or forked wedges.

3 Holding the trackrod-end quite still in an open ended spanner, release the locknut. Unscrew the trackrod-end and count the number of threads between the end of the trackrod and the face of the locknut to

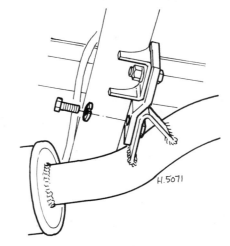

Fig. 11.20. Exhaust front mounting (Sec. 17)

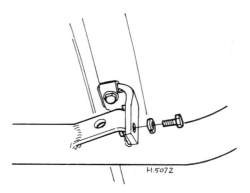

Fig. 11.21. Exhaust rear mounting (Sec. 17)

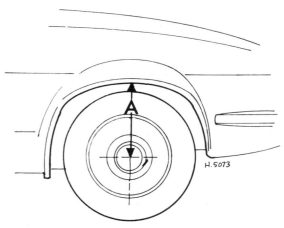

Fig. 11.22. Body trim height diagram (Sec. 18)

*A = 14.5 (± 0.25 in (368.3 (± 6.0) mm)*
*Variation from side to side must not exceed 0.39 in (10.0 mm)*

give an approximate setting position on refitting.

4 Screw on the new trackrod-end and reconnect it to the steering eye. Check the front wheel alignment, as described in Section 28.

5 Should the steering arms be removed, note the locating dowels and tap the arms upwards to release them after withdrawing the bolts (Fig. 11.23).

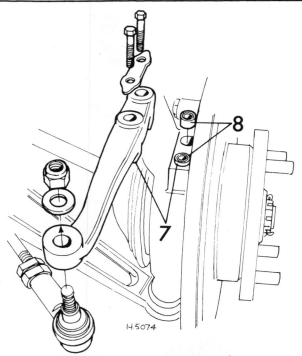

**Fig. 11.23. Steering arm attachment to swivel hub showing hollow locating dowels (7 and 8) (Sec. 19)**

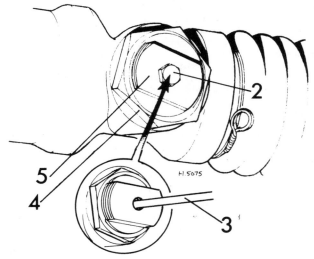

**Fig. 11.24. Centralising steering rack (Sec. 21)**

| | |
|---|---|
| 2  Screw | 4  Locknut |
| 3  Dowel | 5  Threaded plug |

## 20 Steering gear bellows - renewal

1    Should the bellows on the rack housing split or become perished, they must be renewed. If the bellows have been in a faulty condition for some time then the rack assembly should be removed, dismantled, cleaned and lubricated with fresh grease.

2    To remove the bellows, first disconnect the trackrod-end balljoint pins from the eyes of the steering arms, then holding the trackrod-end quite still in an open ended spanner, release the locknut.

3    Unscrew the trackrod-end and count the number of threads between the end of the trackrod and the face of the locknut. Record this as it will give an approximate position for installation of the trackrod-ends during reassembly.

4    Cut the retaining wires or remove the clips from the bellows and remove them from the trackrods.

5    Refitting is a reversal of removal but on completion, check the front wheel alignment (Section 28).

## 21 Steering gear (manual) - removal, overhaul and refitting

1    Remove the pinch bolt which secures the intermediate shaft to the pinion.

2    Pull back the carpet for access to the bulkhead cover plate and seal.

3    Raise the front of the car and support it securely on stands and remove the roadwheel from the side opposite to the steering wheel.

4    Disconnect the trackrod-end ball pins from the eyes of the steering arms.

5    Remove the four bolts which secure the rack to the mounting trunnions and then ease the rack assembly downwards to disengage the pinion from the intermediate shaft. Now move the rack to full lock on the passenger side, turn the rack housing so that the pinion moves rearwards and withdraw the complete assembly from between the body and the exhaust pipe.

6    Release the trackrod-end locknuts and unscrew and remove the trackrod-ends and the locknuts from the trackrods.

7    Remove the bellows from the rack housing.

8    Flatten the lockwasher tabs and unscrew and remove the tie rod/balljoint assemblies from each end of the rack.

9    Release the rack housing plunger plug locknut and unscrew the plug. Extract the plunger spring.

10   Remove the pinion seal and unscrew the pinion bearing retainer.

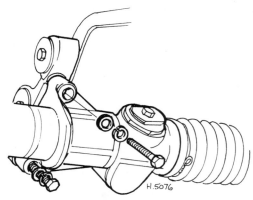

**Fig. 11.25. Steering rack to trunnion bolts (pinion end) (Sec. 21)**

11   Extract the pinion assembly by gripping the pinion in the jaws of a vice fitted with jaw protectors and carefully tapping the rack from the pinion.

12   Extract the rack from the pinion end of the rack housing.

13   Remove the plunger from the rack housing.

14   If required, the bearing can be driven from the pinion housing and the bearing pressed from the pinion shaft after removing its securing circlip.

15   The rack bush can be extracted after releasing its retaining staking.

16   Clean all components and renew any which are worn.

17   Reassembly is a reversal of dismantling but observe the following:

   a) *Centralise the rack by inserting a dowel into the plunger plug hole and moving the rack until the dowel engages in the hole drilled in the rack. Remove the dowel and tighten the plug until the rack is just held. Now unscrew the plug 1/8th of a turn and tighten the locknut. Turn the pinion one half a turn in each direction to test for stiffness.*

   b) *Tighten the trackrod to rack nut to 40 lb/ft (55 Nm) and then bend up the locking plate tabs on three flats of the nut.*

   c) *Inject 2 oz (56 g) of specified grease into the pinion housing, followed by the same amount at the ends of the racks which will eventually be covered by the flexible bellows.*

18   Refitting the rack assembly to the car should be carried out in the following way. Set the steering wheel in the straight-ahead position (spokes horizontal) and offer up the rack and pinion assembly having first centralised the rack by inserting a dowel into the plunger plug hole. Push the intermediate shaft onto the pinion so that the pinch bolt hole and the pinion groove are in alignment.

19   Tighten the rack to trunnion bolts at the pinion end first, then

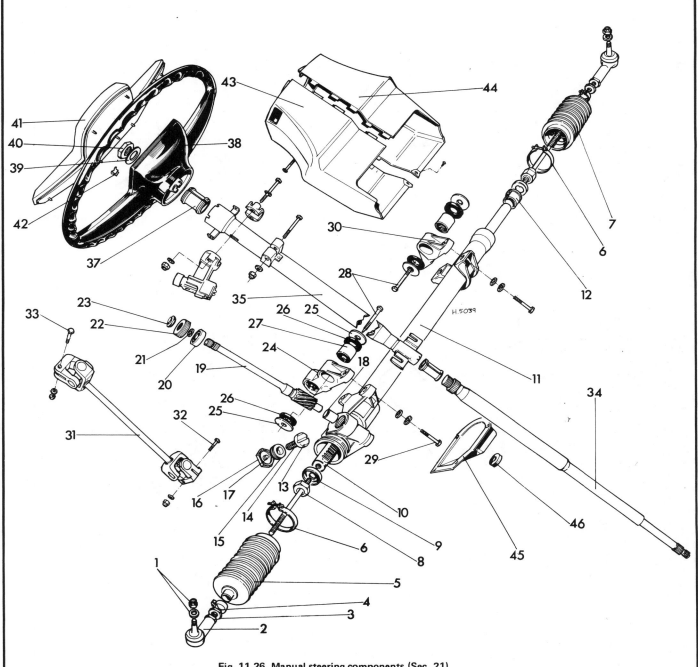

**Fig. 11.26. Manual steering components (Sec. 21)**

| | | | |
|---|---|---|---|
| 1 Nut and washer | 12 Bush | 23 Oil seal | 34 Steering shaft |
| 2 Trackrod end | 13 Plunger | 24 Trunnion | 35 Steering column |
| 3 Locknut | 14 Spring | 25 Plain washer | 36 Bottom bush |
| 4 Clip | 15 Plug | 26 Buffer | 37 Top bush |
| 5 Rack bellows | 16 Locknut | 27 Bush | 38 Steering wheel |
| 6 Clip | 17 Screw | 28 Bolt | 39 Lockwasher |
| 7 Bellows | 18 Bush | 29 Bolt | 40 Nut |
| 8 Trackrod | 19 Pinion | 30 Trunnion | 41 Crash pad |
| 9 Locking washer | 20 Bearing | 31 Intermediate shaft | 42 Clip |
| 10 Rack | 21 Circlip | 32 Pinch bolt | 43 Cowl |
| 11 Rack housing | 22 Retaining ring | 33 Pinch bolt | 44 Cowl |
| | | | 45 Cover plate |
| | | | 46 Seal |

release the bolts which secure the other trunnion to the bodyframe and tighten the rack to trunnion bolts, finally tighten the trunnion to bodyframe bolts.

20 Make sure that the sealing strip between the cover plate and body is in good order.

21 Check the front wheel alignment, as described in Section 28.

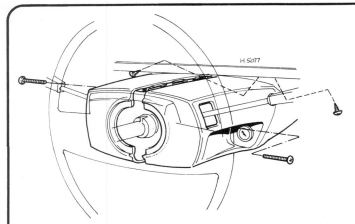

Fig. 11.27. Steering column cowl attachment (Sec. 22)

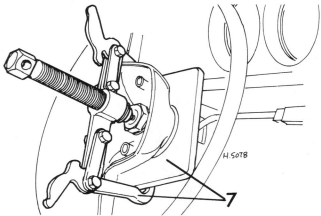

Fig. 11.28. Using a puller to extract the steering wheel (Sec. 22)

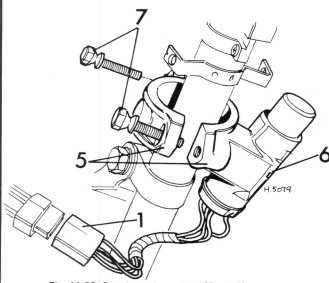

Fig. 11.29. Steering column lock (Sec. 23)

| 1 | Ignition switch connector | 6 | Switch |
|---|---|---|---|
| 5 | Lock assembly | 7 | Shear bolts |

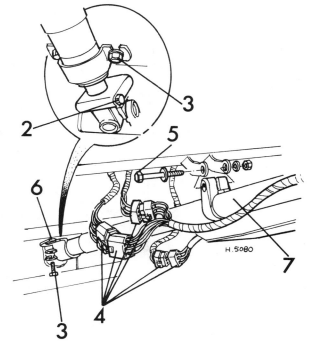

Fig. 11.30. Steering column attachment (Sec. 24)

| 2 | Pinch bolt | 5 | Column clamp bolt |
|---|---|---|---|
| 3 | Lower bracket screw | 6 | Lower bracket |
| 4 | Combination switch connector plugs | 7 | Steering column |

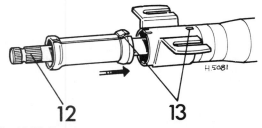

Fig. 11.31. Steering column bottom bush (Sec. 24)

*12 Steering shaft*　　　　　　　*13 Bush projecting tab and column slot*

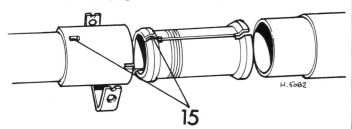

Fig. 11.32. Steering column upper bush (Sec. 24)

*15 Bush projecting tab and column slot*

## 22 Steering wheel - removal and refitting

1   Set the steering in the 'straight-ahead' position and prise the crash pad from the steering wheel spokes.
2   Remove the two securing screws and withdraw the left-hand cowl. Remove the right-hand cowl. If the cowls are difficult to remove, the steering column upper clamp will have to be released and the column gently depressed.
3   Turn the ignition key to unlock the column lock and then unscrew and remove the steering wheel nut and washer.
4   Mark the relationship of the steering wheel to the steering shaft and then screw the steering wheel nut on again but only two or three threads.
5   If the steering wheel will not pull off by hand pressure, use a suitable two or three-legged puller but protect the lower edge of the steering wheel hub by inserting a thin wooden or metal plate to act as a leverage point for the claws of the puller.
6   Refitting is a reversal of removal but make sure that the slots and dog of the switch bush engage correctly with the switch and wheel hub. Align the wheel to the shaft using the marks made before removal with the roadwheels in the 'straight-ahead' position.
7   Tighten the steering wheel nut to the specified torque.
8   The lip of the steering column cowl should be just above the boss of the steering wheel. If adjustment is required, slacken the steering column bottom bracket and clamp bolts, and move the column up or down as necessary. Retighten the bolts.

## 23 Steering column lock/switch - removal and installation

1   Disconnect the multi-connector from the ignition switch and release the cable retaining clip.
2   Release the steering column cowls and move them to each side.
3   Centre-punch the heads of the shear type bolts which secure the lock assembly to the steering column. Drill out the bolts completely or drill holes to accept bolt extractors.
4   Remove the lock and clamp plate.
5   The ignition/starter switch can be removed from the column lock after withdrawal of the small retaining screw.
6   When installing the new lock assembly, centralise the lock body over the slot in the outer column, fit the clamp plate and screw in the shear bolts only a little more than finger-tight. Check the operation of the lock and switch at all key positions and then tighten the bolts until their heads break off.

## 24 Steering column - removal, overhaul and refitting

1   Withdraw the left-hand steering column cowl and tie it to one side.
2   Remove the pinch bolt which secures the steering shaft to the intermediate shaft.
3   Disconnect the steering column lower clamp by slackening one clamp screw and removing the other one.
4   Disconnect the combination switch connector plugs.
5   Unscrew and remove the column upper clamp pinch bolt, extract the bottom bracket from the bolt and withdraw the column complete with steering wheel into the car interior.
6   Remove the steering wheel, combination switch and lock assembly.
7   Grip the steering column carefully in a vice fitted with jaw protectors.
8   Pull the inner shaft from the top of the outer column. The bush at the base of the column will be destroyed during this operation.
9   Extract the top bush and then prise up the retaining tag and withdraw the bottom bush.
10  Renew the bushes and any other worn components.
11  Apply graphite grease to the grooves of the new steering column bushes.
12  Insert the shaft into the column so that it projects about 3 in (76.0 mm) from the lower end of the column.
13  Open the bottom bush so that it will pass over the splines of the shaft and then drive it into the outer column (chamfered end first). Make sure that one of the projections of the bush engages in the slot in the outer column. Bend down the bush retaining tag but do not let it foul the inner shaft.
14  Install the column upper bush in a similar manner to the lower one.

15  Finally adjust the position of the shaft so that it projects 3.45 in (88.0 mm) above the outer column.

## 25 Steering gear (power assisted) - removal, overhaul and refitting

1   Remove the pinch bolt which secures the intermediate shaft to the pinion on the rack housing.
2   Raise the front of the car and support it securely.
3   Remove the roadwheel from the steering column side of the car.
4   Remove the suspension lower arm (Section 7) also from the steering column side.
5   Disconnect the trackrod-ends from the steering arms.
6   Disconnect the fluid return hose from the rack pipe.
7   Disconnect the feed hose union, catching the small amount of oil which will be released.
8   Remove the bolt which secures the rack mounting trunnion to the body on the front passenger's side.
9   Remove the two bolts which secure the rack housing to the trunnion on the driver's side.
10  Lower the rack assembly onto the exhaust pipe then lift it and withdraw it from the driver's side of the car. Detach the trunnion end housing.
11  Clean the external surfaces of the rack housing and then disconnect all the pipes from the valve housing. Identify the pipes before removing them (see Fig. 11.34).
12  Unscrew and remove the trackrod-ends and their locknuts.
13  Remove the bellows.
14  Bend up the lockplate tabs and unscrew the trackrods from each end of the rack.
15  Release the plunger plug locknut, unscrew the plug and extract the spring.
16  Mark the relative position of the valve housing to the rack and then unbolt and remove the housing complete with pinion/valve assembly. Tap the pinion/valve assembly from the valve housing.
17  Extract the circlip from the top of the housing and then remove the backing washer and seal. Detach the seal from the valve.
18  Using a small punch, unscrew the nut which secures the rack end housing. Pull the end housing from the rack housing and extract the 'O' ring seal, the shim and the oil seal (Fig. 11.35).
19  Remove the protecting sleeve and withdraw the pipe adaptor from the rack housing. Extract the rack, the plunger and the sleeve which fits against the seal.
20  To extract the seal from the rack housing, insert a screwdriver through the adaptor hole so that it passes between the seal and the stop and tip the seal sideways.
21  To remove the rack piston and seal assembly, withdraw the circlip exercising great care not to scratch the surface of the rack. Extract the shims which may be located between the circlip and piston. Withdraw the piston, 'O' ring seal and second circlip.
22  Press the pinion bearing from the housing.
23  If the bush in the end housing is to be renewed, cut it with a fine saw blade and then drive it out.
24  Clean, and examine all components and renew any that are worn. Renew seals as a matter of routine. Reassembly is a reversal of

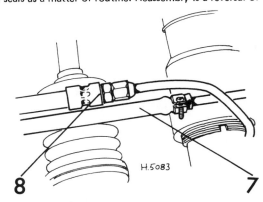

H.5083

**Fig. 11.33. Power assisted steering rack housing hose connections (Sec. 25)**

7   *Return hose*                              8   *Feed hose union*

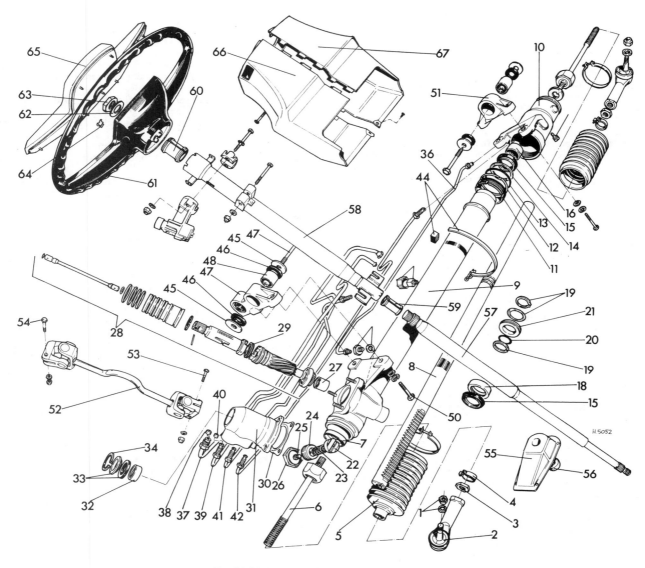

**Fig. 11.34. Power steering components**

| | | | | | | | |
|---|---|---|---|---|---|---|---|
| 1 | Nut and washer | 18 | Sleeve | 35 | Adaptor and seal | 52 | Intermediate shaft |
| 2 | Trackrod end | 19 | Shim circlip | 36 | Pipe (interconnecting) | 53 | Pinch bolt |
| 3 | Locknut | 20 | 'O' ring | 37 | Pipe (oil return) | 54 | Pinch bolt |
| 4 | Clip | 21 | Piston/ring assembly | 38 | Outlet port insert | 55 | Cover plate |
| 5 | Bellows | 22 | Rack damper plunger | 39 | Pipe (oil feed) | 56 | Seal |
| 6 | Trackrod | 23 | Spring | 40 | Insert (inlet port) | 57 | Steering shaft |
| 7 | Locking washer | 24 | Plug | 41 | Pipe to rack housing | 58 | Steering column |
| 8 | Rack | 25 | Screw | 42 | Pipe to end housing | 59 | Bottom bush |
| 9 | Rack housing | 26 | Locknut | 43 | Adaptor | 60 | Top bush |
| 10 | End housing | 27 | Needle bearing | 44 | Clip and insulator | 61 | Steering wheel |
| 11 | End housing nut | 28 | Valve/pinion assembly | 45 | Plain washer | 62 | Lockwasher |
| 12 | Spring ring | 29 | Valve seal | 46 | Buffer washer | 63 | Nut |
| 13 | 'O' ring | 30 | Gasket | 47 | Trunnion | 64 | Clip |
| 14 | Shim | 31 | Valve housing | 48 | Bush | 65 | Crash pad |
| 15 | Seal | 32 | Needle bearing | 49 | Bolt | 66 | Cowl |
| 16 | Bush | 33 | Seal and washer | 50 | Bolt | 67 | Cowl |
| 17 | Locating peg | 34 | Circlip | 51 | Trunnion | | |

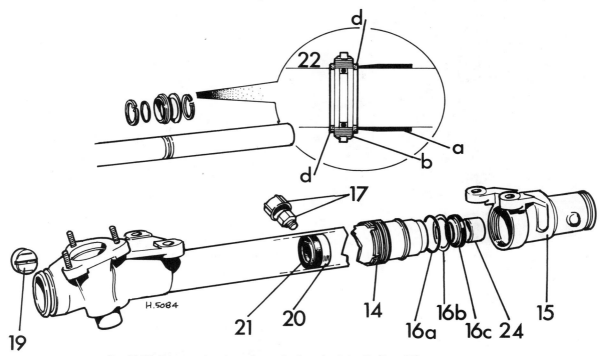

Fig. 11.35. Power assisted steering rack piston/seal details (Sec. 25)

| | | | |
|---|---|---|---|
| 14 | End housing nut | 16c | Oil seal |
| 15 | End housing | 17 | Pipe adaptor |
| 16a | 'O' ring | 18 | Rack |
| 16b | Shim | 19 | Plunger |

| | | | |
|---|---|---|---|
| 20 | Sleeve | 22a | Protective sleeve (tool) |
| 21 | Seal | 22b | Circlip |
| 22 | Sectional view of rack | 22c | Piston with 'O' ring seal |
| | piston/seal assembly | 22d | Circlip |

dismantling, but observe the following:

25 Fit the rack housing seal complete with backing ring (taper into seal) onto the rack.

26 Install the sleeve onto the rack so that the flange is furthest from the seal.

27 Fit the piston circlips using a new 'O' ring seal. Shims must be fitted between the piston and a circlip to provide an endfloat not exceeding 0.010 in (0.25 mm).

28 Align the hole in the sleeve with the countersunk hole in the rack housing and insert the rack assembly carefully into the housing. Make sure that the end housing securing nut is against the ring.

29 Align the hole in the sleeve with the one in the rack housing and screw in the pipe adaptor.

30 Pack the space round the pinion teeth with 2 oz (56 g) of specified grease.

31 Adjust the rack plunger by first centralising the rack by inserting a dowel in the plunger plug hole and moving the rack until the dowel engages in the hole in the rack. Remove the dowel and tighten the plunger plug until the rack is just held. Unscrew the plug 1/8th of a turn and tighten the plug locknut. Check for binding by turning the pinion one half a turn in each direction.

32 Tighten the trackrod to rack nuts to 80 lb/ft (108 Nm) and bend down the lockplate tabs on three flats of the nut.

33 Apply 2 oz (56 g) of specified grease to the rack end joints which will eventually be covered by the flexible bellows.

34 Screw on the trackrod-ends and their locknuts an equal amount onto each trackrod.

35 Check and adjust the front wheel alignment.

36 Refill and bleed the power steering system as described in Section 27.

## 26 Power steering pump - removal, overhaul and refitting

1 Disconnect the flow and return pipes from the pump.

2 Slacken the pump mounting and adjustment link bolts, push the pump sufficiently to one side to release the drive belt from the pump pulley (photo).

3 Remove the link and mounting bracket setscrews and withdraw the

pump from its mounting bracket.

4 Remove the pulley retaining nut. The easiest way to prevent the pulley turning during this operation is to fit an old drivebelt to the

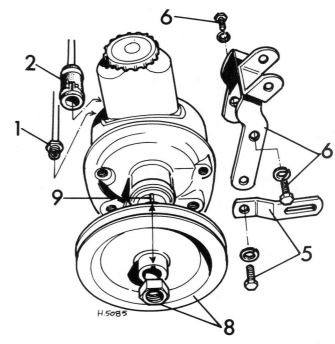

Fig. 11.36. Power steering pump (Sec. 26)

| | | | |
|---|---|---|---|
| 1 | Reservoir union | 6 | Mounting bracket and |
| 2 | Return hose | | setscrews |
| 5 | Adjuster link | 8 | Pulley nut |
| | | 9 | Woodruff key |

26.2 Location of power steering pump (drive belt removed)

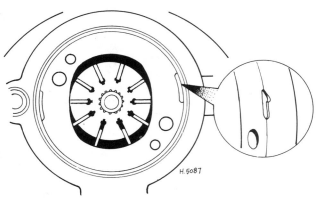

Fig. 11.37. Power steering pump vane installation diagram (Sec. 26)

H.5087

Fig. 11.38. Exploded view of the power steering pump (Sec. 26)

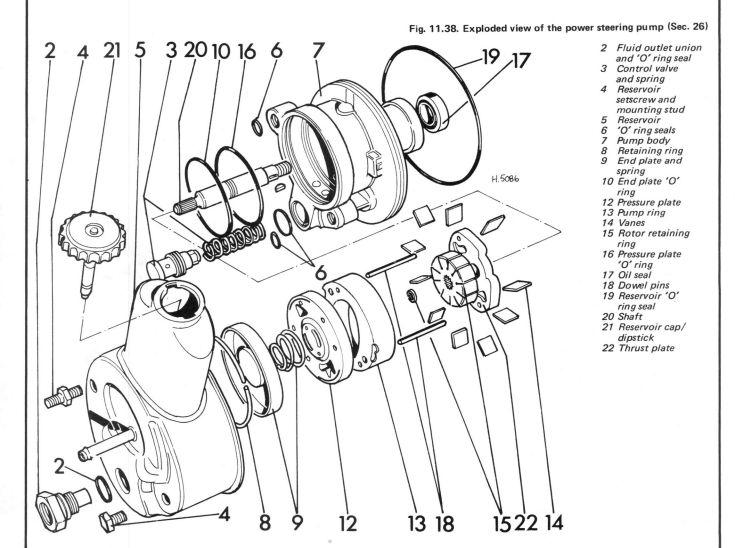

H.5086

2   Fluid outlet union
    and 'O' ring seal
3   Control valve
    and spring
4   Reservoir
    setscrew and
    mounting stud
5   Reservoir
6   'O' ring seals
7   Pump body
8   Retaining ring
9   End plate and
    spring
10  End plate 'O'
    ring
12  Pressure plate
13  Pump ring
14  Vanes
15  Rotor retaining
    ring
16  Pressure plate
    'O' ring
17  Oil seal
18  Dowel pins
19  Reservoir 'O'
    ring seal
20  Shaft
21  Reservoir cap/
    dipstick
22  Thrust plate

pulley groove and then to grip the belt as close to the pulley as possible in the jaws of a vice.

5   Extract the drive key from the pulley shaft.

6   Clean the external surfaces of the pump. If the pump has seen service over a high mileage, it will probably be more economical to obtain a new pump rather than overhaul the old, well worn unit. However, where the repair kit and parts are available, first unscrew the outlet pipe union and extract the 'O' ring seal.

7   Withdraw the control valve assembly and the spring from the outlet union hole in the pump housing.

8   Remove the setscrew and mounting stud which secure the reservoir to the pump. Rock the reservoir back and forth to break the adhesion of the 'O' ring seal and withdraw the reservoir. Remove the single large and three small 'O' ring seals from the face of the pump housing.

9   Secure the pump in the jaws of a vice and then insert a pin punch through the small hole in the pump housing to release the retaining ring. The use of a screwdriver at the same time will help to prise the ring from its seat.

10  Rock the end plate in the pump housing to release the adhesion of the 'O' ring seal and then withdraw the end plate and spring from the pump housing. Extract the end plate 'O' ring seal.

11  Tap the pulley end of the pump shaft gently to free the pressure plate from its 'O' ring seal. Withdraw the pressure plate, the pump ring and the shaft assembly from the pump housing.

12  Withdraw the ten vanes from their slots in the pump rotor.

13  Remove the pump rotor and thrust plate from the shaft by extracting the retaining ring.

14  Remove the pressure plate 'O' ring from its groove in the pump housing and the shaft seal, taking care not to damage the bearing.

15  Clean and examine all components for wear. Renew any that are worn. Renew all seals as a matter of routine.

16  Reassembly is a reversal of removal but observe the following points:

   a)  Dip all parts in clean engine oil before assembly.
   b)  The thrust plate must be installed to the shaft so that the cavity in the plate is towards the rotor end of the shaft.
   c)  Fit the rotor to the shaft so that the countersunk side of the rotor is next to the pressure plate.
   d)  Install the dowel pins into clean holes in the pump body. Any oil left in the holes can cause the pump casing to crack due to hydraulic pressure being created as the pins are driven in.
   e)  Install the pump ring so that the half arrow on its periphery is at the end plate end of the pump housing and facing towards the relief valve.
   f)  Install the vanes in the rotor slots so that their rounded edges are next to the pump ring.
   g)  The end plate should be pressed onto its 'O' ring in the pump housing only far enough to permit installation of the end plate retaining ring and the ends of this ring must be adjacent to the removal hole.
   h)  The spring on the flow control valve must be inserted first when the valve assembly is installed.
   j)  Tighten the outlet union and reservoir setscrew to a torque of 35 lb/ft (47 Nm).

17  Refit the key and pulley to the pump shaft making sure that the pulley boss is away from the pump.

18  Refit the pump by reversing the removal operations. Tighten the drivebelt to give a total deflection at the mid-point of the longest run of the belt of ½ in (12.5 mm).

19  Refill the pump reservoir with engine oil and then bleed the system, as described in the next Section.

## 27  Power steering system - bleeding

1   Check that the pump reservoir is half filled with oil.

2   Disconnect the LT lead which runs to the contact breaker (white/black) from the terminal on the coil, to prevent the engine firing.

3   Operate the starter motor for five seconds, then top-up the reservoir again to the half full level.

4   Centralise the steering, reconnect the LT lead, start the engine and let it idle.

5   Open the throttle slightly and watch the reservoir oil level. Top-up immediately if it falls.

6   Drive the car forwards or backwards just enough to be able to turn the steering to the left and then to the right, but without attaining full lock in either case.

7   Again centralise the steering, switch off the engine and top-up the reservoir level to the full mark, using clean engine oil.

## 28  Front wheel alignment and steering angles

1   Accurate front wheel alignment is essential for good steering and slow tyre wear. Before considering the steering angle, check that the tyres are correctly inflated, that the front wheels are not buckled, the hub bearings are not worn or incorrectly adjusted and that the steering linkage is in good order, without slackness or wear at the joints.

2   Wheel alignment consists of four factors:
   *Camber,* is the angle at which the front wheels are set from the vertical when viewed from the front of the car. Positive camber is the amount (in degrees) that the wheels are tilted outwards at the top from the vertical.
   *Castor,* is the angle between the steering axis and a vertical line when viewed from each side of the car. Positive castor is when the steering axis is inclined rearward.
   *Steering axis* inclination is the angle, when viewed from the front of the car, between the vertical and an imaginary line drawn between the upper and lower suspension armswivels.
   *Front wheel tracking.* This normally gives the front roadwheels a toe-in or toe-out but in the case of cars covered by this manual, the front roadwheels should be set parallel.

3   All steering angles, other than front wheel alignment, are set in production and cannot be altered.

4   To check front wheel alignment, place the car on level ground with the tyres correctly inflated and the front roadwheels in the straight-ahead position.

5   Remove the plug from the plunger screw on the rack housing, insert a dowel and move the steering until the dowel engages in the hole in the rack. The steering is now centralised.

6   If the trackrod-ends have been removed, set them at a datum point by releasing their locknuts and the bellows outer clips and turning each trackrod until the roadwheels are parallel. This can best be checked by laying a length of steel rod or wood along the side of the car. When it touches all four sidewalls of the front and rear tyres, then the front wheels will be approximately parallel with each other.

7   Obtain or make a tracking gauge. One may be easily made from tubing, cranked to clear the sump and bellhousing, having an adjustable nut and setscrew at one end.

8   Using the gauge, measure the distance between the two inner wheel rims at hub height at the rear of the wheels.

9   Rotate the wheels (by pushing the car backwards or forwards) through 180° (half a turn) and again using the gauge, measure the distance at hub height between the two inner wheel rims at the front of the roadwheels.

10  The two measurements should be the same to give a parallel characteristic.

11  Where this is not the case, turn each trackrod an equal amount and when adjustment is correct and has been re-checked, tighten the trackrod-end locknuts making sure that the trackrod-ends are in their correct attitude (centre of their arcs of travel).

12  Check that the steering rack bellows are not twisted and tighten the securing clips.

13  Remove the gauge, the rack dowel pin and refit the rack plug.

## 29  Roadwheels and tyres

1   Whenever the roadwheels are removed it is a good idea to clean the insides of the wheels to remove accumulations of mud and in the case of the front ones, disc pad dust.

2   Check the condition of the wheel for rust and repaint if necessary.

3   Examine the wheel stud holes. If these are tending to become elongated or the dished recesses in which the nuts seat have worn or become overcompressed, then the wheel will have to be renewed.

4   With a roadwheel removed, pick out any embedded flints from the tread and check for splits in the sidewalls or damage to the tyre carcass generally.

5   Where the depth of tread pattern is 1 mm or less, the tyre must be renewed.

6   Rotation of the roadwheels to even out wear is a worthwhile idea if the wheels have been balanced off the car. Include the spare wheel in

the rotational pattern.

   With radial tyres it is recommended that the wheels are moved between front and rear on the same side of the car only.

7   If the wheels have been balanced on the car then they cannot be moved round the car as the balance of wheel, tyre and hub will be upset. In fact their exact stud fitting positions must be marked before removing a roadwheel so that it can be returned to its original 'in balance' state.

8   It is recommended that wheels are re-balanced halfway through the life of the tyres to compensate for the loss of tread rubber due to wear.

9   Finally, always keep the tyres (including the spare) inflated to the recommended pressures and always replace the dust caps on the tyre valves. Tyre pressures are best checked first thing in the morning when the tyres are cold.

## 30 Fault diagnosis - suspension and steering

| Symptom | Reason/s |
|---|---|
| **Steering feels vague, car 'wanders' and 'floats' at speed** | |
| General wear or damage | Tyre pressures uneven. |
| | Steering gear balljoints badly worn. |
| | Suspension geometry incorrect. |
| | Steering mechanism free play excessive. |
| | Front suspension and rear suspension pick-up points out of alignment. |
| **Stiff and heavy steering** | |
| Lack of maintenance or accident damage | Tyre pressures too low. |
| | Front wheel alignment incorrect. |
| | Suspension geometry incorrect. |
| | Steering gear incorrectly adjusted too tightly. |
| | Steering column badly misaligned. |
| **Wheel wobble and vibration** | |
| General wear or damage | Wheel nuts loose. |
| | Front wheels and tyres out of balance. |
| | Steering balljoints badly worn. |
| | Hub bearings badly worn. |
| | Steering gear free play excessive. |

# Chapter 12 Bodywork and fittings

*For modifications, and information applicable to later models, see Supplement at end of manual*

## Contents

## 1 General description

The body and underframe is of all steel welded construction. All models are of four door type and differences between 4 and 6 cylinder versions and the different marques concern trim, accessory detail, radiator grilles and motifs.

In order to prevent distortion of the body, it is most important that the jacking and towing procedures described in the 'Routine Maintenance' Section at the front of this manual are at all times observed.

## 2 Maintenance - bodywork and underframe

1 The general condition of a car's bodywork is the one thing that significantly affects its value. Maintenance is easy but needs to be regular and particular. Neglect, particularly after minor damage, can lead quickly to further deterioration and costly repair bills. It is important also to keep watch on those parts of the car not immediately visible, for instance the underside, inside all the wheel arches and the lower part of the engine compartment.

2 The basic maintenance routine for the bodywork is washing - preferably with a lot of water, from a hose. This will remove all the loose solids which may have stuck to the car. It is important to flush these off in such a way as to prevent grit from scratching the finish. The wheel arches and underbody need washing in the same way to remove any accumulated mud which will retain moisture and tend to encourage rust. Paradoxically enough, the best time to clean the underbody and wheel arches is in wet weather when the mud is thoroughly wet and soft. In very wet weather the underbody is usually cleaned of large accumulations automatically, and this is a good time for inspection.

3 Periodically it is a good idea to have the whole of the underside of the car steam cleaned, engine compartment included, so that a thorough inspection can be carried out to see what minor repairs and renovations are necessary. Steam cleaning is available at many garages and is necessary for removal of accumulation of oily grime which sometimes is allowed to cake thick in certain areas near the engine, gearbox and back axle. If steam facilities are not available, there are one or two excellent grease solvents available which can be brush applied. The dirt can then be simply hosed off.

4 After washing paintwork, wipe off with a chamois leather to give an unspotted clear finish. A coat of clear protective wax polish will give added protection against chemical pollutants in the air. If the paintwork sheen has dulled or oxidised, use a cleaner/polisher combination to restore the brilliance of the shine. This requires a little effort, but is usually caused because regular washing has been neglected. Always check that the door and ventilator opening drain holes and pipes are completely clear so that water can drain out. Bright work should be treated the same way as paintwork. Windscreens and windows can be kept clear of the smeary film which often appears if a little ammonia is added to the water. If they are scratched, a good rub with a proprietary metal polish will often clear them. Never use any form of wax or other body or chromium polish on glass.

## 3 Maintenance - upholstery and carpets

1 Mats and carpets should be brushed or vacuum cleaned regularly to keep them free of grit. If they are badly stained remove them from the car for scrubbing or sponging and make quite sure they are dry before replacement. Seats and interior trim panels can be kept clean by a wipe over with a damp cloth. If they do become stained (which can be more apparent on light coloured upholstery) use a little liquid detergent and a soft nail brush to scour the grime out of the grain of the material. Do not forget to keep the head lining clean in the same way as the upholstery. When using liquid cleaners inside the car do not over-wet the surfaces being cleaned. Excessive damp could get into the seams and padded interior causing stains, offensive odours or even rot. If the inside of the car gets wet accidentally it is worthwhile taking some trouble to dry it out properly particularly where carpets are involved. Do not leave oil or electric heaters inside the car for this purpose.

## 4 Minor bodywork damage - repair

*See photo sequence on pages 174 and 175.*

### Repair of minor scratches in the car's bodywork

If the scratch is very superficial, and does not penetrate to the metal of the bodywork, repair is very simple. Lightly rub the area of the scratch with a paintwork renovator, or a very fine cutting paste, to remove loose paint from the scratch and to clear the surrounding bodywork of wax polish. Rinse the area with clean water.

Apply touch-up paint to the scratch using a thin paintbrush, continue to apply thin layers of paint until the surface of the paint in the scratch is level with the surrounding paintwork. Allow the new paint at least two weeks to harden; then, blend it into the surrounding paintwork by rubbing the paintwork, in the scratch area with a paintwork renovator, or a very fine cutting paste. Finally apply wax polish. Where the scratch has penetrated, right through to the metal of the bodywork, causing the metal to rust, a different repair technique is required. Remove any loose rust from the bottom of the scratch with a penknife, then apply rust inhibiting paint to prevent the formation of rust in the future. Using a rubber or nylon applicator fill the scratch with bodystopper paste. If required, this paste can be mixed with cellulose thinners to provide a very thin paste which is ideal for filling narrow scratches. Before the stopper-paste in the scratch hardens, wrap a piece of smooth cotton rag around the top of a finger. Dip the finger in cellulose thinners and then quickly sweep it across the surface of the stopper-paste in the scratch; this will ensure that the surface of the stopper-paste is slightly hollowed. The scratch can now be painted over as described earlier in this Section.

## Repair of dents in the car's bodywork

When deep denting of the car's bodywork has taken place, the first task is to pull the dent out, until the affected bodywork almost attains its original shape. There is little point in trying to restore the original shape completely, as the metal in the damaged area will have stretched on impact and cannot be reshaped fully to its original contour. It is better to bring the level of the dent up to a point which is about 1/8 inch (3 mm) below the level of the surrounding bodywork. In cases where the dent is very shallow anyway, it is not worth trying to pull it out at all.

If the underside of the dent is accessible, it can be hammered out gently from behind, using a mallet with a wooden or plastic head. Whilst doing this, hold a suitable block of wood firmly against the impact from the hammer blows and thus prevent a large area of bodywork from being 'belled-out'.

Should the dent be in a section of the bodywork which has a double skin or some other factor making it inaccessible from behind, a different technique is called for. Drill several small holes through the metal inside the dent area - particularly in the deeper sections. Then screw long self-tapping screws into the holes just sufficiently for them to gain a good purchase in the metal. Now the dent can be pulled out by pulling on the protruding heads of the screws with a pair of pliers.

The next stage of the repair is the removal of the paint from the damaged area, and from an inch or so of the surrounding 'sound' bodywork. This is accomplished most easily by using a wire brush or abrasive pad on a power drill, although it can be done just as effectively by hand using sheets of abrasive paper. To complete the preparations for filling, score the surface of the bare metal with a screwdriver or the tang of a file, or alternatively, drill small holes in the affected area. This will provide a really good 'key' for the filler paste.

To complete the repair see the Section on filling and respraying.

## Repair of rust holes or gashes in the car's bodywork

Remove all paint from the affected area and from an inch or so of the surrounding 'sound' bodywork, using an abrasive pad or a wire brush on a power drill. If these are not available a few sheets of abrasive paper will do the job just as effectively. With the paint removed you will be able to gauge the severity of the corrosion and therefore decide whether to replace the whole panel (if this is possible) or to repair the affected area. Replacement body panels are not as expensive as most people think and it is often quicker and more satisfactory to fit a new panel than to attempt to repair large areas of corrosion.

Remove all fittings from the affected area except those which will act as a guide to the original shape of the damaged bodywork (eg. headlamp shells etc.). Then, using tin snips or a hacksaw blade, remove all loose metal and any other metal badly affected by corrosion. Hammer the edges of the hole inwards in order to create a slight depression for the filler paste.

Wire brush the affected area to remove the powdery rust from the surface of the remaining metal. Paint the affected area with rust inhibiting paint; if the back of the rusted area is accessible treat this also.

Before filling can take place it will be necessary to block the hole in some way. This can be achieved by the use of one of the following materials: Zinc gauze, Aluminium tape or Polyurethane foam.

Zinc gauze is probably the best material to use for a large hole. Cut a piece to the approximate size and shape of the hole to be filled, then

position it in the hole so that its edges are below the level of the surrounding bodywork. It can be retained in position by several blobs of filler paste around its periphery.

Aluminium tape should be used for small or very narrow holes. Pull a piece off the roll and trim it to the approximate size and shape required, then pull off the backing paper (if used) and stick the tape over the hole; it can be overlapped if the thickness of one piece is insufficient. Burnish down the edges of the tape with the handle of a screwdriver or similar, to ensure that the tape is securely attached to the metal underneath.

Polyurethane foam is best used where the hole is situated in a section of bodywork of complex shape, backed by a small box section (eg; where the sill panel meets the rear wheel arch - most cars). The unusual mixing procedure for this foam is as follows: Put equal amounts of fluid from each of the two cans provided in the kit, into one container. Stir until the mixture begins to thicken, then quickly pour this mixture into the hole, and hold a piece of cardboard over the larger apertures. Almost immediately the polyurethane will begin to expand, gushing out of any small holes left unblocked. When the foam hardens it can be cut back to just below the level of the surrounding bodywork with a hacksaw blade.

## Bodywork repairs - filling and respraying

Before using this Section, see the Sections on dent, deep scratch, rust hole, and gash repairs.

Many types of bodyfiller are available, but generally speaking those proprietary kits which contain a tin of filler paste and a tube of resin hardener are best for this type of repair. A wide, flexible plastic or nylon applicator will be found invaluable for imparting a smooth and well contoured finish to the surface of the filler.

Mix up a little filler on a clean piece of card or board - use the hardener sparingly (follow the maker's instructions on the packet) otherwise the filler will set very rapidly.

Using the applicator, apply the filler paste to the prepared area; draw the applicator across the surface of the filler to achieve the correct contour and to level the filler surface. As soon as a contour that approximates the correct one is achieved, stop working the paste - if you carry on too long the paste will become sticky and begin to 'pick-up' on the applicator. Continue to add thin layers of filler paste at twenty-minute intervals until the level of the filler is just 'proud' of the surrounding bodywork.

Once the filler has hardened, excess can be removed using a metal plane or Dreadnought file. From then on, progressively finer grades of abrasive paper should be used, starting with a 40 grade production paper and finishing with 400 grade 'wet-and-dry' paper. Always wrap the abrasive paper around a flat rubber, cork, or wooden block - otherwise the surface of the filler will not be completely flat. During the smoothing of the filler surface the 'wet-and-dry' paper should be periodically rinsed in water. This will ensure that a very smooth finish is imparted to the filler at the final stage.

At this stage the 'dent' should be surrounded by a ring of bare metal, which in turn should be encircled by the finely 'feathered' edge of the good paintwork. Rinse the repair area with clean water until all of the dust produced by the rubbing-down operation is gone.

Spray the whole repair area with a light coat of grey primer - this will show up any imperfections in the surface of the filler. Repair these imperfections with fresh filler paste or bodystopper, and once more smooth the surface with abrasive paper. If bodystopper is used, it can be mixed with cellulose thinners to form a really thin paste which is ideal for filling small holes. Repeat this spray and repair procedure until you are satisfied that the surface of the filler, and the feathered edge of the paintwork are perfect. Clean the repair area with clean water and allow to dry fully.

The repair area is now ready for spraying. Paint spraying must be carried out in a warm, dry, windless and dust free atmosphere. This condition can be created artificially if you have access to a large indoor working area, but if you are forced to work in the open, you will have to pick your day very carefully. If you are working indoors, dousing the floor in the work area with water will 'lay' the dust which would otherwise be in the atmosphere. If the repair area is confined to one body panel, mask off the surrounding panels; this will help to minimise the effects of a slight mis-match in paint colours. Bodywork fittings (eg;

chrome strips, door handles etc.,) will also need to be masked off. Use genuine masking tape and several thicknesses of newspaper for the masking operation.

Before commencing to spray, agitate the aerosol can thoroughly, then spray a test area (an old tin, or similar) until the technique is mastered. Cover the repair area with a thick coat of primer; the thickness should be built up using several thin layers of paint rather than one thick one. Using 400 grade 'wet-and-dry' paper, rub down the surface of the primer until it is really smooth. While doing this, the work area should be thoroughly doused with water, and the 'wet-and-dry' paper periodically rinsed in water. Allow to dry before spraying on more paint.

Spray on the top coat, again building up the thickness by using several thin layers of paint. Start spraying in the centre of the repair area and then, using a circular motion, work outwards until the whole repair area and about 2 inches of the surrounding original paintwork is covered. Remove all masking material 10 to 15 minutes after spraying on the final coat of paint.

Allow the new paint at least 2 weeks to harden fully; then, using a paintwork renovator or a very fine cutting paste, blend the edges of the new paint into the existing paintwork. Finally, apply wax polish.

## 5 Major body damage - repair

Where serious damage has occurred or large areas need renewal due to neglect, it means certainly that completely new sections or panels will need welding in and this is best left to professionals. If the damage is due to impact it will also be necessary to completely check the alignment of the body shell structure. Due to the principle of construction the strength and shape of the whole can be affected by damage to a part. In such instances the services of a Leyland agent with specialist checking jigs are essential. If a body is left misaligned it is first of all dangerous as the car will not handle properly and secondly uneven stresses will be imposed on the steering, engine and transmission, causing abnormal wear or complete failure. Tyre wear may also be excessive.

## 6 Maintenance - hinges and locks

1 Oil the hinges of the bonnet, boot and doors with a drop or two of light oil periodically. A good time is after the car has been washed.
2 Oil the bonnet release, the catch pivot pin and the safety catch pivot pin periodically.
3 Do not over lubricate door latches and strikers. Normally a little oil on the rotary cam spindle alone is sufficient.

## 7 Doors - tracing rattles and their rectification

1 Check first that the door is not loose at the hinges and that the latch is holding the door firmly in position. Check also that the door lines up with the aperture in the body.
2 If the hinges are loose or the door is out of alignment it will be necessary to reset the hinge positions, as described in Section 12.
3 If the latch is holding the door properly it should hold the door tightly when fully latched and the door should line up with the body. If it is out of alignment it needs adjustment. If loose, some part of the lock mechanism must be worn out and requires renewal.
4 Other rattles from the door would be caused by wear or looseness in the window winder, the glass channels and sill strips or the door buttons and interior latch release mechanism.

## 8 Windscreen and backlight glass - removal and refitting

1 Where a windscreen is to be replaced then if it is due to shattering, the fascia air vents should be covered before attempting removal. Adhesive sheeting is useful to stick to the outside of the glass to enable large areas of crystallised glass to be removed.
2 Where the screen is to be removed intact or is of laminated type then an assistant will be required. First release the rubber surround from the bodywork by running a blunt, small screwdriver around and under the rubber weatherstrip both inside and outside the car. This

operation will break the adhesive of the sealer originally used. Take care not to damage the paintwork or catch the rubber surround with the screwdriver. Remove the windscreen wiper arms and interior mirror and place a protective cover on the bonnet.
3 Have your assistant push the inner lip of the rubber surround off the flange of the windscreen body aperture. Commence pushing the glass at one of the upper corners. Once the rubber surround starts to peel off the flange, the screen may be forced gently outwards by careful hand pressure. The second person should support and remove the screen complete with rubber surround and bright trim as it comes out.
4 Remove the bright trim from the rubber surround.
5 Before fitting a windscreen, ensure that the rubber surround is completely free from old sealant and glass fragments, and has not hardened or cracked. Fit the rubber surround to the glass and apply a bead of suitable sealant between the glass outer edge and the rubber.
6 Cut a piece of strong cord greater in length than the periphery of the glass and insert it into the body flange locating channel of the rubber surround.
7 Apply a thin bead of sealant to the face of the rubber channel which will eventually mate with the body.
8 Offer the windscreen to the body aperture and pass the ends of the cord, previously fitted and located at bottom centre into the vehicle interior.
9 Press the windscreen into place, at the same time have an assistant pulling the cords to engage the lip of the rubber channel over the body flange.
10 Remove any excess sealant with a paraffin soaked rag and fit the bright trim.
11 Removal and installation of the rear window glass is carried out in an identical manner but (if fitted) disconnect the leads to the heating element in the glass.

## 9 Front door lock - removal and refitting

1 Wind the door glass fully up.
2 Remove the two screws from the armrest, turn the armrest to the vertical position and pull it from the door.
3 Unscrew the knob from the sill lock plunger (photo).
4 Prise the insert from the window regulator handle, extract the screw and remove the handle (photos).
5 Remove the door lock remote control handle bezel (one screw) (photo).
6 Insert a flat blade between the door interior trim and the door and release one or two press stud type fasteners. Using the fingers, prise the remaining press studs and trim panel from the door (photo).
7 Lift the trim panel from the door.
8 Detach the waterproof sheet from the internal face of the door.
9 Remove the screw which retains the glass rear channel to the door panel. Move the lower end of the channel forward to provide access to the lock linkage.
10 Remove the screw which secures the remote control to the door inner panel. Slide the control to the rear to release it from the door panel.
11 Unclip and remove the remote control link from the door and lock.
12 Unclip and remove the door lock link from the lock cylinder assembly.
13 Disconnect the nylon connecting link from the ball end of the door exterior handle (photo).
14 Remove the four screws which hold the lock assembly to the door and with the lock in its locked position, withdraw it into the door cavity, then remove it through the large aperture in the door interior panel.
15 Unclip and detach the lock cylinder assembly and the sill plunger links from the lock.
16 Refitting is a reversal of removal but adjust the nylon connecting link attached to the ball end of the door exterior handle so that with the lock in the unlocked state, the lower end of the locking lever is just clear of the lock trigger plate when the nylon link is aligned to the ball end.

## 10 Rear door lock - removal and refitting

1 This is very similar to the procedure described in the preceding Section except, of course, that a lock cylinder is not incorporated in

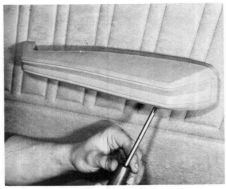
9.2A Extracting an arm rest securing screw

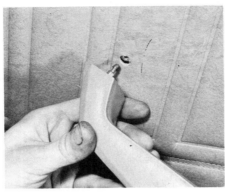
9.2B Removing an arm rest

9.3 Interior door lock plunger

9.4A Removing insert from window regulator handle

9.4B Removing window regulator handle

9.5 Door lock interior remote control handle beze

9.6 Interior door trim panel press stud

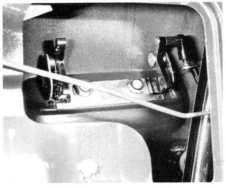
9.13 View of door exterior handle from within door cavity

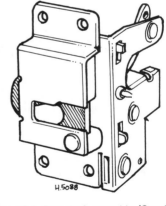
Fig. 12.1. Door lock assembly (Sec. 9)

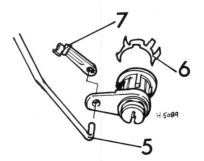
Fig. 12.2. Lock cylinder assembly (Sec. 9)

5   Link
6   Lock retainer
7   Link clip

11.5 Window regulator unit securing screws

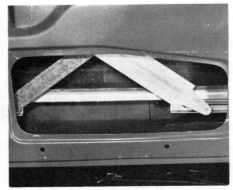
11.6 Door window glass lifting channel slides

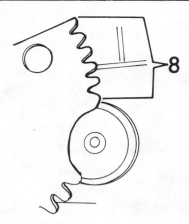

**Fig. 12.3. Window regulator setting prior to installation (Sec. 11)**

*8   Six teeth showing above pinion*

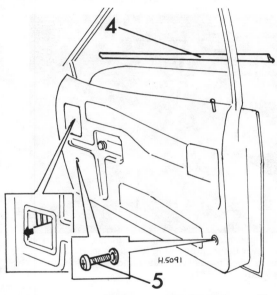

**Fig. 12.4. Front door glass guides and securing screws (Sec. 13)**

*4   Sealing strip*                          *5   Lower securing screws*

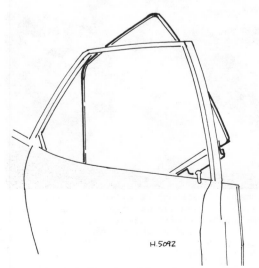

**Fig. 12.5. Method of glass removal from front door (Sec. 13)**

the system.

## 11  Front window regulator - removal and refitting

1   Raise the glass to the fully closed position.
2   Remove the door interior trim panel, as described in Section 9.
3   Remove the waterproof sheet from the internal face of the door.
4   Wedge the glass in the fully closed position by using two pieces of wood.
5   Remove the four screws which secure the regulator unit to the door panel, push the regulator inwards and forwards to disconnect it from the slides of the glass lifting channels (photo).
6   Withdraw the regulator through the large aperture in the door inner panel (photo).
7   Commence refitting by winding the regulator until six teeth are visible above the pinion housing (fully raised position) and then reverse the removal operations.
8   Engage the regulator arms in the slides in the following order: (i) door inner panel slide, (ii) glass channel rear slide, (iii) glass channel front slide.
9   Prior to fully tightening the regulator unit screws, wind the window down slightly and adjust the position of the glass within its guides.

## 12  Rear window regulator - removal and refitting

1   Wind the window glass fully down.
2   Remove the door interior trim panel, as described in Section 9.
3   Remove the waterproof sheet from the internal face of the door.
4   Support the glass and remove the four screws which retain the regulator unit.
5   Push the regulator unit inwards and to the rear to disengage it from the glass channel.
6   Withdraw the regulator unit through the large aperture in the door panel.
7   Refitting is a reversal of removal but engage the regulator arms in the slides in the following order: (i) glass channel front slide, (ii) glass channel rear slide, (iii) door inner panel slide.

## 13  Front door glass - removal and refitting

1   Wind the glass down to its lowest position, remove the door interior trim panel, as described in Section 9, and remove the waterproof sheet.
2   Pull the glass outer sealing strip upwards to release it from the clips on the sill.
3   Remove the two screws and release the lower ends of the door glass guides from the door inner panel.
4   Position the glass inside the door so that the guides are between the glass and the door outer panel.
5   Push the glass forward and disconnect the glass lifting channel from the front arm of the regulator then move it to the rear and disconnect the channel from the rear arm of the regulator.
6   Withdraw the glass upwards towards the outer side of the door, at the same time tilting it as shown in Fig. 12.5.
7   The channels can be driven from the glass using a hammer and a small block of hardwood.
8   Refitting is a reversal of removal but position the lifting channel as indicated in the diagram (Fig. 12.6).

## 14  Rear door glass - removal and refitting

1   The operations are similar to those described for the front door glass in the preceding Section, except that the rivet which secures the top of the glass rear guide to the top of the door must be drilled out.
2   Pull the top of the guide forward to release it from the fixed glass rubber. Rotate the guide so that its upper mounting bracket is pointing towards the door and withdraw the guide. The door sill will need prising open slightly to ease withdrawal.
3   Withdraw the fixed glass and its rubber surround in a forward direction from the door.
4   Withdraw the main glass panel upwards and towards the inner side of the door after disengaging the regulator arms from the glass channels.
5   Refitting is a reversal of removal but position the lifting channel on

This sequence of photographs deals with the repair of the dent and paintwork damage shown in this photo. The procedure will be similar for the repair of a hole. It should be noted that the procedures given here are simplified — more explicit instructions will be found in the text

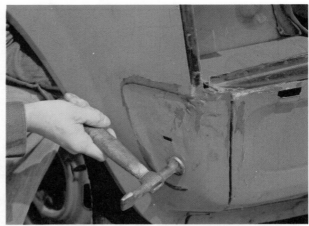

In the case of a dent the first job — after removing surrounding trim — is to hammer out the dent where access is possible. This will minimise filling. Here, the large dent having been hammered out, the damaged area is being made slightly concave

Now all paint must be removed from the damaged area, by rubbing with coarse abrasive paper. Alternatively, a wire brush or abrasive pad can be used in a power drill. Where the repair area meets good paintwork, the edge of the paintwork should be 'feathered', using a finer grade of abrasive paper

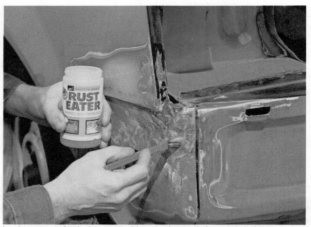

In the case of a hole caused by rusting, all damaged sheet-metal should be cut away before proceeding to this stage. Here, the damaged area is being treated with rust remover and inhibitor before being filled

Mix the body filler according to its manufacturer's instructions. In the case of corrosion damage, it will be necessary to block off any large holes before filling — this can be done with aluminium or plastic mesh, or aluminium tape. Make sure the area is absolutely clean before ...

... applying the filler. Filler should be applied with a flexible applicator, as shown, for best results; the wooden spatula being used for confined areas. Apply thin layers of filler at 20-minute intervals, until the surface of the filler is slightly proud of the surrounding bodywork

Initial shaping can be done with a Surform plane or Dreadnought file. Then, using progressively finer grades of wet-and-dry paper, wrapped around a sanding block, and copious amounts of clean water, rub down the filler until really smooth and flat. Again, feather the edges of adjoining paintwork

The whole repair area can now be sprayed or brush-painted with primer. If spraying, ensure adjoining areas are protected from over-spray. Note that at least one inch of the surrounding sound paintwork should be coated with primer. Primer has a 'thick' consistency, so will find small imperfections

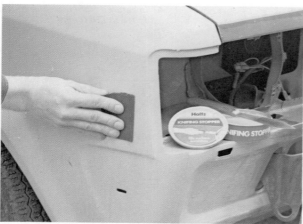

Again, using plenty of water, rub down the primer with a fine grade wet-and-dry paper (400 grade is probably best) until it is really smooth and well blended into the surrounding paintwork. Any remaining imperfections can now be filled by carefully applied knifing stopper paste

When the stopper has hardened, rub down the repair area again before applying the final coat of primer. Before rubbing down this last coat of primer, ensure the repair area is blemish-free — use more stopper if necessary. To ensure that the surface of the primer is really smooth use some finishing compound

The top coat can now be applied. When working out of doors, pick a dry, warm and wind-free day. Ensure surrounding areas are protected from over-spray. Agitate the aerosol thoroughly, then spray the centre of the repair area, working outwards with a circular motion. Apply the paint as several thin coats

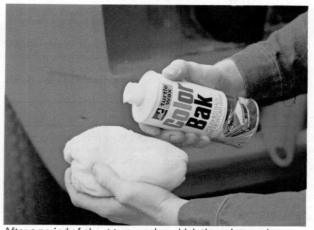

After a period of about two weeks, which the paint needs to harden fully, the surface of the repaired area can be 'cut' with a mild cutting compound prior to wax polishing. When carrying out bodywork repairs, remember that the quality of the finished job is proportional to the time and effort expended

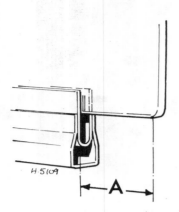
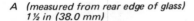

**Fig. 12.6. Lifting channel installation diagram (front door glass) (Sec. 13)**

*A    (measured from rear edge of glass)*
*1½ in (38.0 mm)*

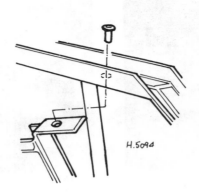

**Fig. 12.7. Rear door glass guide securing rivet (Sec. 14)**

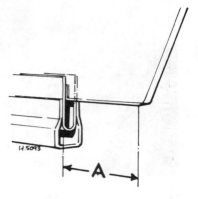

**Fig. 12.8. Rear door glass lifting channel installation diagram (Sec. 14)**

*A    (measured from rear edge of glass)*
*1 1/8 in (28.0 mm)*

the glass in accordance with the diagram and insert a new pop rivet at the top of the rear guide (Fig. 12.8).

## 15 Front door - removal and installation

1    Remove the door internal trim panel, as described in Section 9.
2    Open the door fully and support its lower edge on jacks or blocks with pads of rag to prevent damage to the paintwork. Mark the position of the hinge plates on the door.
3    Remove the six nuts and two plates and lift the door from the hinge plates.
4    If the hinges are to be removed, mark their position on the body pillars.
5    To remove the lower hinge, protect the threads on the door check stud, support the hinge plate and drive the stud from it.
6    Fully open the hinge and drive the door check plate forwards so that its second detent groove engages with the detent roller. Pull the checkplate and spring from the hinge.
7    Drive the hinge lower pin downwards and remove it.
8    Drive the hinge upper pin upwards and remove it.
9    The fixed plates of the hinges are secured to the body by welding and if worn or distorted they will have to be renewed by your dealer or a body repair shop.
10 Reassembly and installation are reversals of dismantling and removal but align the doors within and flush with, the body shell before finally tightening the hinge nuts. If essential, shims can be used under the hinge plates if the door panel is lower than the surrounding body panels.

## 16 Rear door - removal and installation

1    The procedure is similar to that described for a front door in the preceding Section, except that the door glass front guide must be moved aside (one screw) to gain access to the hinge nuts.

## 17 Bonnet - removal and installation

1    Open the bonnet and support it in the fully open position.
2    Remove the bonnet lock striker (two bolts).
3    Remove the sound insulating pad after extracting the securing clips.
4    Have an assistant support the bonnet and then unscrew the bolts which attach the support struts to the bonnet.
5    If an engine compartment lamp is fitted, the leads must be disconnected at the snap-connectors.
6    Mark the position of the hinge plates on the underside of the bonnet and then remove the hinge securing screws. Lift the bonnet from the

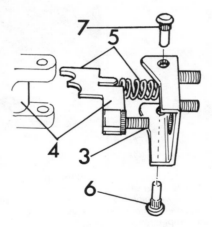

**Fig. 12.9. Door lower hinge components (Sec. 15)**

| | |
|---|---|
| 3   Door check stud | 5   Check plate and spring |
| 4   Door check plate groove | 6   Hinge lower pin |
|      and roller | 7   Hinge upper pin |

car (photo).
7    Installation is a reversal of removal.

## 18 Bonnet lock - removal and refitting

1    Release the radiator from the bonnet lock platform (two bolts) to provide access to the lock (Fig. 12.10).
2    Disconnect the lock remote control cable from the lock lever (Fig. 12.11).
3    Unbolt the lock assembly and withdraw it downwards from the lock platform.
4    If the cable is to be removed or renewed, disconnect the outer cable from its clip on the bonnet lock platform and draw the cable through its three plastic clips (Fig. 12.12).
5    Disconnect the inner cable from the bonnet release hand control (one bolt) and detach the outer cable clip from the hand control mounting bracket (Fig. 12.13).
6    Withdraw the cable assembly into the interior of the car.
7    Refitting is a reversal of removal but before tightening the lock bolts, close the bonnet to centralise the lock in relation to the striker. The latter can be adjusted to ensure correct bonnet closure if the locknut is released and the centre screw turned (Fig. 12.14).

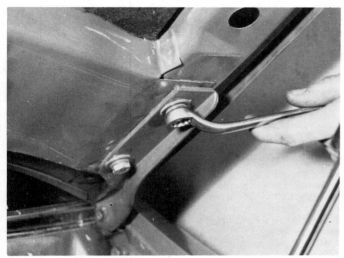

17.6 Removing a bonnet hinge bolt

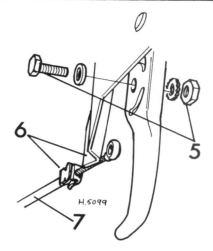

Fig. 12.13. Bonnet release hand control (Sec. 18)

5   Cable securing bolt and nut          7   Outer cable
6   Outer cable clip and bracket

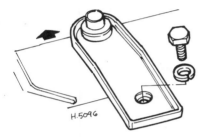

Fig. 12.10. Radiator top support bracket (Sec. 18)

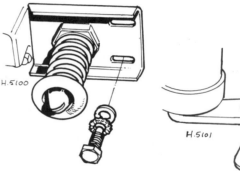

Fig. 12.14. Bonnet lock
striker (Sec. 18)

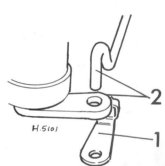

Fig. 12.15. Luggage boot lock
link clip (1) and link (2)
(Sec. 19)

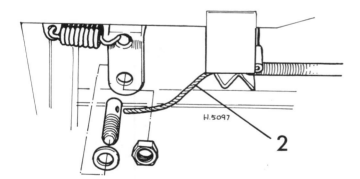

Fig. 12.11. Bonnet lock cable (2) and connection (Sec. 18)

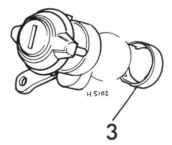

Fig. 12.16. Luggage boot lock cylinder assembly (Sec. 19)

3   Retaining clip

### 19 Luggage boot lid lock - removal and refitting

1   Open the lid fully and remove the clip which secures the lock link
to the lever on the cylinder assembly.
2   Disconnect the link from the lever.
3   Unbolt (four screws) the lock from inside the boot lid.
4   To remove the lock cylinder assembly, prise open the retaining clip
and release it from the shoulder on the lock body. Withdraw the
cylinder lock from the outside.
5   Refitting is a reversal of removal but note that the lugs on the lock
cylinder body are of different widths to ensure that it can only be
installed one way.

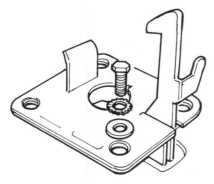

Fig. 12.12. Bonnet lock assembly (Sec. 18)

**20 Front wheel arch liner - removal and refitting**

1   In the interest of body protection, liners are fitted under the front wings. Unless they are removed at reasonably regular intervals and the undersurface of the wing given a coat of protective paint, these components may, in fact, have the opposite effect and actually increase the rate of corrosion due to the build up of wet mud behind them.
2   Jack-up the front of the car, support it securely and remove the roadwheels.
3   Extract the screws which secure the liners to the valance.
4   Pull the front of the liner from the wing and then using a flat lever prise it from the turned-over edge of the wing.
5   Refitting is a reversal of removal but insert the rear of the liner first under the wheel arch.
6   On cars built after 1975, a pop rivet is used to secure the liner to the rear of the valance instead of a self-tapping screw.

**21 Front parcels shelf - removal and refitting**

1   Release the fresh air vent control from the parcels shelf (two screws).
2   Disconnect the leads from the loudspeaker and remove it from the parcels tray (four screws).
3   Remove the two screws which attach the lower edge of the parcels tray to the heater.
4   Remove the two bolts which secure the parcels tray to the side brackets and dashpanel brackets.
5   Release the parcels tray from the underside of the fascia support, (two screws).

6   Remove the fresh air vents and withdraw the parcels tray.
7   Refitting is a reversal of removal.

**22 Rear parcels shelf - removal and refitting**

1   This operation is carried out by compressing the tangs (accessible from within the luggage boot) of the nine securing buttons, withdrawing the buttons and the shelf liner.

**23 Rear seat armrest - removal and refitting**

1   Remove the nut and washers from the rear seat cushion clip and remove the cushion.
2   Remove the two screws and drill out the two pop rivets which secure the bottom of the rear seat squab. Lower the squab and release it from the body brackets.
3   Remove the six retaining screws and withdraw the armrest from the rear of the squab.
4   Refitting is a reversal of removal.

**24 Front seat - removal and refitting**

1   Prior to removing the passenger seat, disconnect the seat belt switch lead at the plug.
2   Remove the four screws and release the seat slides from the floor. Remove the seat.
3   Refitting is a reversal of removal but note that the large flat washers are located under the carpet.

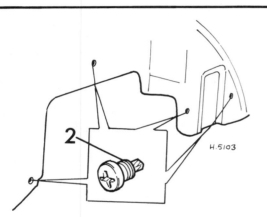
Fig. 12.17. Location of front wheel arch liner screws (2) (Sec. 20)

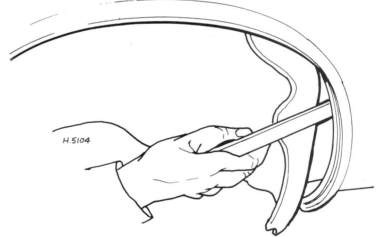
Fig. 12.18. Method of removing front wheel arch liner (Sec. 20)

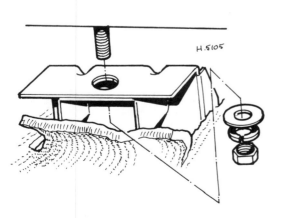
Fig. 12.19. Method of anchoring rear seat (Sec. 23)

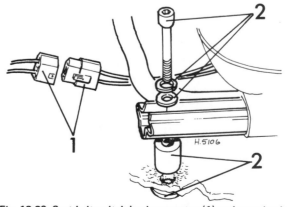
Fig. 12.20. Seat belt switch lead connector (1) and securing bolt and washers on passenger side (2) (Sec. 24)

## 25 Face level ventilators - removal and refitting

1   Remove the two screws which secure the centre of the front parcels shelf to the underside of the fascia.
2   Pull down the centre of the parcels shelf enough to be able to extract the face level ventilator.
3   Refitting is a reversal of removal.

## 26 Heating and ventilation system - description

1   Heat for the system is provided from the engine coolant.
2   Air is delivered to the car interior and to the windscreen and to fresh air outlets in the centre of the fascia panel.
3   Fresh air is either drawn in from outside or recirculated according to the setting of the controls.
4   Air extraction slots are provided, one at each side of the rear window.
5   Fresh air vents are provided, one at each end of the front parcels shelf, these operate quite independently of the heating system.
6   Air from the heating and ventilating system is boosted by a three speed blower fan which operates in conjunction with the position of the air control lever.
7   The heater control panel incorporates two levers, the upper one controlling the air distribution and the lower one the temperature.
8   The air distribution lever settings are as follows:

*O   Heater off, air intake closed.*
*R   Recirculated air, blower operates at slow speed.*
*1   Fresh air intake, blower operates at slow speed.*
*2   Fresh air intake, blower operates at normal speed.*
*3   Fresh air intake, blower operates at fast speed.*

9   The temperature control lever operates from **cold** on the extreme left to **maximum heat** on the extreme right and may be set in any position in conjunction with the desired setting of the air distribution lever.
10  Access to components of the heater unit can only be obtained after removal of the complete unit.

## 27 Heater/ventilation unit - removal and installation

1   Disconnect the lead from the battery negative terminal.
2   Drain the cooling system (Chapter 2).
3   Disconnect the flexible coolant hoses from the nozzles on the heater unit. Be prepared for some loss of coolant.
4   *On cars with automatic transmission,* remove the rear and front consoles.
5   Remove the radio (Chapter 10) or blanking plate if a radio is not fitted.
6   Remove the front parcels shelf (Section 21).
7   Remove the windscreen demister ducts.

8   Disconnect all heater and switch leads, identifying them for correct reconnection.
9   Release the drain pipe from the base of the heater casing.
10  Support the heater unit and remove the screw which secures the heater bracket to the bulkhead. Note the location of the earth lead from the radio under this screw.
11  Lift the heater from its bulkhead brackets and rest it on the floorpan centre tunnel.
12  Identify the heater control cables and their heater connecting points and then release the inner cables and their outer cable clips from the heater.
13  Remove the heater assembly from the car.
14  Installation is a reversal of removal. Refill the cooling system.

## 28 Heater - dismantling and reassembly

1   With the heater unit removed from the car, pull the electrical leads through the grommet on the air inlet box. Remove the securing screws and withdraw the air inlet box.
2   Drill out the three pop rivets which secure the upper casing to the lower casing, also the rivet which retains the pipe bracket to the upper casing. Remove the clips which secure the two halves of the casing together.
3   Separate the casings and lift out the blower motor. Pull the fan from the motor shaft.
4   If the matrix is to be removed, lift off the face level flap, raise the air mixing flap and disconnect the operating link from the lever.
5   Withdraw the seal from the matrix casing and then, holding the pipe bracket and pipes push the pipes up through the heater casing and extract the matrix from the casing.
6   A fault in either the motor or matrix is best rectified by installation of a new component but if the matrix is blocked it is worthwhile reverse flushing it or using a reliable cleansing agent. If the matrix is leaking, do not waste your time trying to solder it but obtain a new or reconditioned unit.
7   Reassembly is a reversal of dismantling, but observe the following points:

   *a)   Fit new pipe seals in the matrix.*
   *b)   Make sure that the rubber mounting strips are stuck securely to the motor casing.*
   *c)   Install the fan so that 3/16 in (5.0 mm) of the shaft projects through the fan hub.*
   *d)   Locate the motor so that its tag engages with the lower half of the heater casing.*
   *e)   Pop rivet the upper and lower casings together.*

## 29 Fan motor resistor - removal and refitting

1   Two types of heater motor resistor may be encountered.

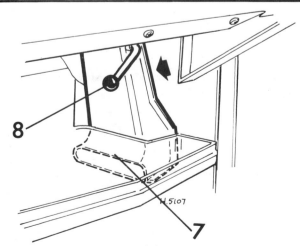

Fig. 12.21. Knee level vents (7) and operating lever (8) (Sec. 26)

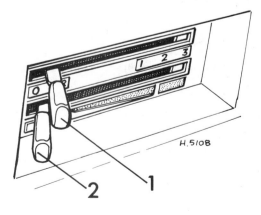

Fig. 12.22. Heater controls (Sec. 26)

*1   Air distribution*          *2   Temperature*

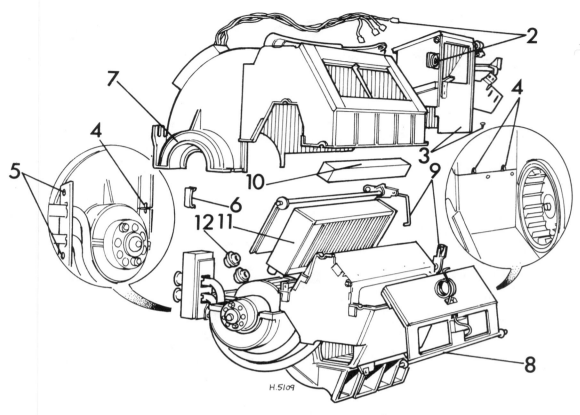

**Fig. 12.23. Exploded view of the heater (Sec. 28)**

| | | | |
|---|---|---|---|
| 2  Leads and grommet | 5  Pipe bracket pop | 7  Top casing | 10  Packing seal |
| 3  Air inlet box screws | rivets | 8  Face level flap | 11  Matrix |
| 4  Casing pop rivets | 6  Casing clip | 9  Air bleed flap and link | 12  Pipe seals |

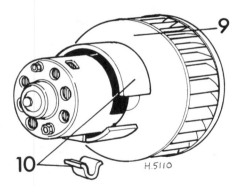

**Fig. 12.24. Heater blower motor housing (9) and rubber mounting strip and tag (10) (Sec. 28)**

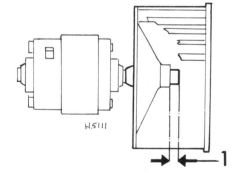

**Fig. 12.25. Heater fan to motor shaft installation diagram (Sec. 28)**

*1   =   3/16 in (5.0 mm)*

## External type

2   Access to this type of resistor is obtained by opening the bonnet and then removing the air intake grille on the passenger side after turning the retaining clips through half a turn.

3   Mark the wires and then disconnect them from the resistor. Extract the resistor securing screw.

## Internal type

4   Access to this type of resistor can be obtained in the following way without having to drain the heater assembly or cooling system.

5   Remove the front parcels tray, and the front and rear consoles (where fitted).

6   Detach the demister ducts from the heater and plenum chamber.

7   Remove either the radio blanking plate or the radio.

8   Disconnect the leads from the heater blower switch (marking them carefully for correct reconnection) also those from the blower motor.

9   Slacken the clips which secure the heater hoses to the pipe stubs but do not disconnect the hoses, only slide the clips along the pipes.

10 Pull the drain tube from the base of the heater unit.

11 Support the weight of the heater and extract the screw which holds the heater bracket to the bulkhead.

12 Free the insulation pad from around the bracket and then lift the heater from its mountings and rest it on the floor pan.

13 Prise out the pad from the top face of the heater assembly followed by the resistor unit.

14 Refitting in both cases is a reversal of removal.

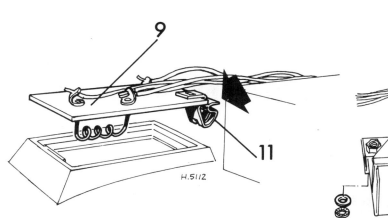

**Fig. 12.26a. Heater blower motor internal type resistor unit (Sec. 29)**

9   *Resistor*                 11  *Retaining clip*

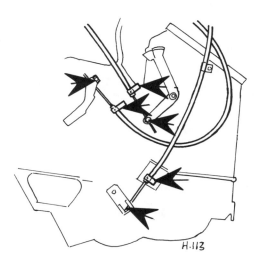

**Fig. 12.27. Control cable connections at heater (Sec. 30)**

*Cables, clips and trunnion screws (arrowed)*

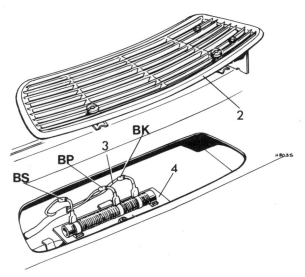

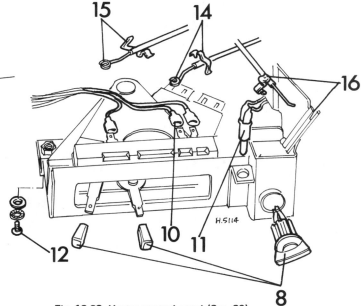

**Fig. 12.28. Heater control panel (Sec. 30)**

| | | | |
|---|---|---|---|
| 8 | *Control lever knobs* | 14 | *Air control and blower cable* |
| 10 | *Blower switch leads* | 15 | *Heat control cable* |
| 11 | *Bulb holder* | 16 | *Air distribution control cable* |
| 12 | *Panel securing screws* | | |

---

**30 Heater controls and cables - removal and refitting**

1   Disconnect the battery.

2   Remove the front parcels shelf.

3   Detach the heater face level ventilator (right-hand side air duct).

4   Identify each control cable and note to where it is connected on the heater unit.

5   Disconnect the inner cables from the trunnion at the heater and the outer cables from their clips.

6   Unhook the air distribution control cable from the heater. Pull the air distribution control knob and the temperature control knob so that the clips in the knobs can be depressed and the knobs withdrawn from their levers.

7   Remove the radio or blanking plate as applicable.

8   Disconnect the leads from the blower switch noting carefully their sequence for reconnection.

9   Detach the heater control panel bulb and then remove the two screws which retain the remote control lever assembly to the underside of the fascia.

10 Remove the control lever and cable assembly, passing it down the steering column.

11 Disconnect the individual cables from the control unit.

12 Refitting is a reversal of removal but before fully tightening the inner cable trunnion screws at the heater, check their operation over their full arc of travel and adjust the position of the inner cable or the outer cable clip, as necessary.

**Fig. 12.26b. Heater blower motor external resistor unit (Sec. 29)**

| | |
|---|---|
| 2 | *Air intake grille* |
| 3 | *Leads* |
| 4 | *Resistor* |
| BS | *Black/Slate* |
| BP | *Black/Purple* |
| BK | *Black/Pink* |

# Chapter 13 Supplement:
# Revisions and information on later models

## Contents

## 1 Introduction

This Supplement mainly covers the modifications and changes made to later Princess 2 models equipped with the six-cylinder 'E' Series engine, although certain of the procedures outlined are also applicable to earlier models.

In order to use the Supplement to the best advantage, it is suggested that it is referred to before the main Chapters of this manual to ensure that any relevant information can be absorbed into the original procedures described in Chapters 1 to 12.

## 2 Specifications

*Engine (6-cylinder 'E' Series)*
**Valve clearances (cold)***

| | |
|---|---|
| Inlet.............................................................................. | 0.35 to 0.40 mm (0.014 to 0.016 in) |
| Exhaust.......................................................................... | 0.45 to 0.50 mm (0.018 to 0.020 in) |

*\* Adjust by changing shims only if clearance less than 0.30 mm (0.012 in) at routine service check*

*Cooling system*
**Thermostat** ................................................................... 82°C (180°F)

*Fuel system*
**Fast idle speed** ................................................................ 1200 rpm

**Fuel octane rating**................................................................ 97 RON (4 star)

*Electrical system*
**In-line fuses**

| | |
|---|---|
| Radio.......................................................................... | 1.5A |
| Headlamp main beam.......................................................... | 8A |
| Rear fog lamps................................................................ | 10A |

*Bodywork and fittings*
**Max. roof rack load** ....................................................... 132 lb (60 kg)

*\* Adjust by changing shims only if clearance less than 0.30 mm (0.012 in) at routine service check*

## 3  Engine

### *Oil level - checking*

1   In order to avoid a false reading when checking the engine oil level, make sure that the moulded handle of the dipstick is horizontal, with the word 'OIL' readable from the spark plug side of the engine.
2   Make sure that the oil level is read off from the upward facing side of the dipstick.

## 4  Manual gearbox and automatic transmission

### *Rotary type inhibitor switch (automatic transmission)*

1   On later models a rotary type adjustable reversing/starter inhibitor switch is fitted to the automatic transmission.
2   If the switch must be removed for any reason or is to be disconnected pending removal of the transmission, pull back the carpet below the heater unit and disconnect the switch leads at their connecting plugs. Push the grommet out of the floor and pass the switch leads out of the vehicle interior.
3   Raise the vehicle so that the switch is accessible from under the right-hand side.
4   Release the switch wiring harness from its clips, remove the switch fixing bolt and remove the switch. The leads are soldered to the switch terminals.
5   Refitting is a reversal of removal, but observe the following points:

(a) *Align the neutral marks on the switch*
(b) *If this type of switch has not been previously used, fit a spacer*

(supplied with the switch) between the switch and the
transmission casing
(c) *Screw in the switch fixing bolt finger tight*

6   Set the transmission in neutral and then connect a test lamp/battery across the start (S) terminal leads. Rotate the switch until the test lamp goes out, then turn it in the opposite direction until the lamp lights and continue in that direction until the lamp just goes out. Mark these two 'lights-out' positions of the switch, and then turn the switch to a point mid-way between them.
7   Tighten the switch screw.
8   Check that the lamp lights up only when the speed selector lever is moved to the 'P' and 'N' positions.
9   Transfer the test lamp circuit to the reverse (R) terminals of the switch and check that the lamp lights only when the selector lever is in the 'R' position.
10  Reconnect the switch leads.

### *Downshift cable (automatic transmission) - adjustment*

11  Connect a tachometer and have the engine idling at 750 rpm while at normal operating temperature.
12  Adjust the cable threaded end fitting at the carburettor to give an inner cable stop clearance (A) of 1.5 mm (0.059 in) as shown in Fig. 13.2.
13  Now depress the accelerator pedal fully and check that full throttle is obtained and that the inner cable stop-to-end fitting clearance (B) is 44.5 mm (1.75 in) as shown in Fig. 13.3.

### *Downshift cable (automatic transmission) - renewal*

14  Disconnect the cable from the linkage at the carburettor end.
15  Unscrew the outer end fitting from the transmission casing.

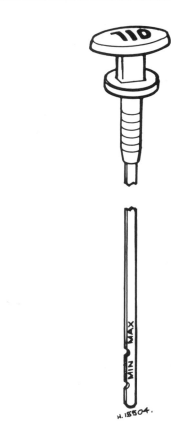

**13.1 Engine oil dipstick (Sec 3)**

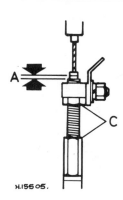

**13.2 Downshift cable at idle (Sec 4)**

*A Cable stop clearance        C Cable adjuster and locknut*

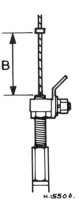

**13.3 Downshift cable at full throttle (Sec 4)**

*B Cable stop clearance*

16 Drain the transmission fluid and refit the drain plug.
17 Unbolt and remove the valve body cover. This is the larger of the two covers (Fig. 13.4). Be prepared for some loss of fluid.
18 Rotate the downshift cam and release the cable nipple. Withdraw the cable.
19 On some transmissions, an adjustable cam mounting bracket is fitted; do not touch the bracket fixing screws otherwise it will have to be reset in the following way.
20 Have the screws just tight enough to permit the cam bracket to slide, then move the bracket towards the cam.
21 Insert a 1.0 mm (0.040 in) thick feeler gauge between the heel of the cam and the downshift valve. Hold the cam in contact with the feeler gauge, and then slide the bracket away from the cam until the gap between the throttle valve and the exhaust port in the transmission is just eliminated. Tighten the bracket screws and remove the feeler blade.
22 Transmissions incorporating a sliding type of cam bracket can be identified by the bevelled top of the fluid filter and its end lip which is angled down to clear the cam. Failure to adjust this type of cam correctly will cause 'clonk' and harsh gear engagement.
23 Fit the new downshift cable and adjust as described earlier.

*Final drive pinion nut (manual transmission)*
24 On later models the final drive pinion nut is secured by a locknut, the lockwasher as fitted to earlier models having been deleted.

## 5  Driveshafts

*Driveshaft nut tightening - revised procedure*
1 Whenever the driveshaft has been separated from the stub axle carrier, it must be refitted in the following way to avoid the split collar jamming on the driveshaft and so preventing the shaft seating fully in its bearings.
2 With the driveshaft inserted into the stub axle carrier, make up a flat steel washer to the dimensions shown in Fig. 13.5 and fit it to the shaft.
3 Oil the shaft threads and screw on the nut tightly to fully seat the shaft in its bearings.
4 Remove the nut and washer and fit the split collar, which must be in good condition.
5 Screw on the nut and tighten to a torque wrench setting of 200 lbf ft (272 Nm). This is very tight; in the absence of a suitably graduated torque wrench, use a piece of pipe to extend the length of a standard ratchet or knuckle bar by about 12 in (305.0 mm). Tighten the nut further if necessary to align the split pin hole.
6 To prevent the hub turning while the driveshaft nut is being tightened, either have an assistant apply the brakes or place a long lever between the wheel studs. If the latter method is used, protect the stud threads from damage.

## 6  Braking system

*Hydraulic system - bleeding*
1 The following additional methods for bleeding the braking system may be used instead of the manual method described in Chapter 9, Section 9.
2 If the master cylinder has been disturbed then the complete system must be bled. If only a component of one circuit has been removed and refitted, then only that particular circuit need be bled.
3 The dual circuits are split so that each circuit includes two of the four cylinders in each of the front disc calipers, plus the rear wheel cylinder on the opposite side of the car.
4 Carry out the bleeding operation in the following sequence on one side of the car.

(a) Rear wheel cylinder
(b) Two caliper inboard nipples
(c) Caliper outboard nipple
(d) Rear wheel cylinder (second application)

Repeat on the opposite side.
5 Unless the pressure bleeding method is being used, do not forget to keep the fluid level in the master cylinder reservoir topped up to prevent air from being drawn into the system, which would make any work done worthless.

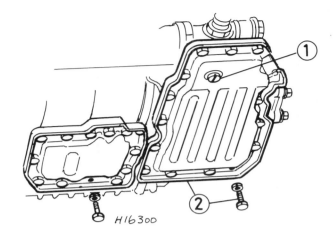

**13.4 Automatic transmission valve body cover (Sec 4)**

*1 Drain plug*            *2 Cover screw*

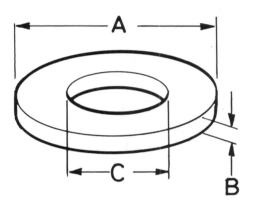

**13.5 Driveshaft temporary washer (Sec 5)**

*A = 65.0 mm (2.6 in)*          *C = 25.0 mm (0.99 in)*
*B = 6.5 mm (0.26 in)*

6 Before commencing operations, check that all system hoses and pipes are in good condition and all unions tight and free from leaks.
7 Take great care not to allow hydraulic fluid to come into contact with the vehicle paintwork as it is an effective paintstripper. Wash off any spilled fluid immediately with cold water.
8 As the system incorporates a vacuum servo, destroy the vacuum by giving several applications of the brake pedal in quick succession.

**Bleeding - using one-way valve kit**

9 There are a number of one-man, one-way brake bleeding kits available from motor accessory shops. It is recommended that one of these kits is used wherever possible as it will greatly simplify the bleeding operation, and will also reduce the risk of air or fluid being drawn back into the system, quite apart from the advantage of being able to do the work without the help of an assistant.
10 To use the kit, connect the tube to the bleed screw and open the screw one half a turn.
11 Depress the brake pedal fully and slowly release it. The one-way valve in the kit will prevent expelled air from returning at the end of each pedal downstroke. Repeat this operation several times to be sure of expelling all air from the system. Some kits include a translucent container which can be positioned so that the air bubbles can actually be seen being expelled from the system.

12 Tighten the bleed screw, remove the tube and repeat the operations on the remaining brakes.
13 On completion, depress the brake pedal. If it still feels spongy repeat the bleeding operation as air must still be trapped in the system.

**Bleeding - using a pressure bleeding kit**
14 These kits too are available from motor accessory shops and are usually operated by air pressure from the spare tyre.
15 By connecting a pressurised container to the master cylinder fluid reservoir, bleeding is then carried out by simply opening each bleed screw in turn and allowing the fluid to run out, rather like turning on a tap, until no air is visible in the expelled fluid.
16 By using this method, the large reservoir of hydraulic fluid provides a safeguard against air being drawn into the master cylinder during bleeding, which often occurs if the fluid level in the reservoir is not maintained.
17 Pressure bleeding is particularly effective when bleeding 'difficult' systems or when bleeding the complete system at time of routine fluid renewal.

**All methods**
18 When bleeding is completed, check and top up the fluid level in the master cylinder reservoir.
19 Check the feel of the brake pedal. If it feels at all spongy, air must still be present in the system and further bleeding is required. Failure to bleed satisfactorily after a reasonable repetition of the bleeding operation may be due to worn master cylinder seals.
20 Discard brake fluid which has been expelled. It is almost certain to be contaminated with moisture, air and dirt making it unsuitable for further use. Clean fluid should always be stored in an airtight container as it absorbs moisture readily (hygroscopic) which lowers its boiling point and could affect braking performance under severe conditions.

## 7  Electrical system

*Steering column combination switch*
1 On later models, the washer/wiper switch can be removed (after withdrawal of the steering wheel) from its mounting plate if the screws are extracted or the rivets drilled out.
2 When refitting the switch, observe the following alignment procedure:

**Right-hand drive up to 1980 and all later models:** *align the arrow on the centre of the switch on the side towards the stalk of the direction indicator switch*
**Left-hand drive up to 1980:** *align the arrow in the direction of the 'pip' on the cover*

*Wiper delay*
3 On models fitted with a wiper delay unit, the wiring diagram is modified as shown in Fig. 13.6.

*Rear fog lamps*
4 Rear fog lamps may be fitted as supplementary accessories in the following way.
5 Remove the rear bumper.
6 Remove the rear interior trim to expose the wiring harness.
7 Mark the rear body panel and drill the necessary holes to accept the lamps and their wiring grommets. Take care not to damage the wiring harness during this operation and make sure that the lamps are positioned as near the rear corners of the body as possible.
8 Refer to Chapter 10, Section 18 to gain access to the rear of the instrument panel, and fit the switch and its illuminating fibre optic.
9 Run the wiring to the facia area and connect in accordance with the wiring diagram (Fig. 13.7). Make sure that the in-line fuse is of 15 A capacity.

*Fuel pump isolation relay*
10 On later models, a relay is mounted on the right-hand wing valance within the engine compartment.

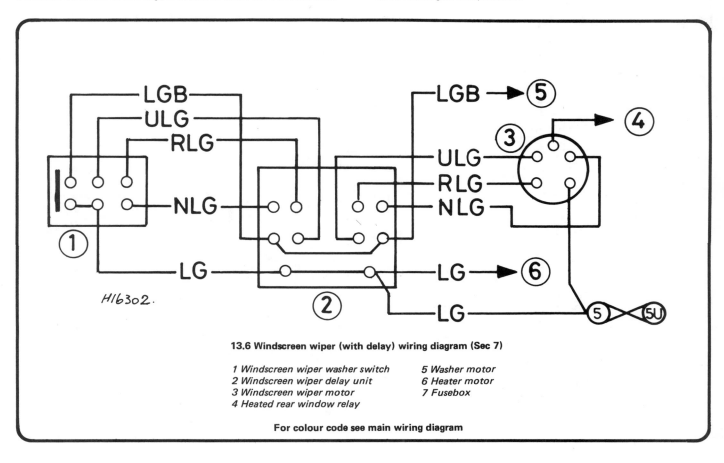

**13.6 Windscreen wiper (with delay) wiring diagram (Sec 7)**

1 Windscreen wiper washer switch
2 Windscreen wiper delay unit
3 Windscreen wiper motor
4 Heated rear window relay
5 Washer motor
6 Heater motor
7 Fusebox

**For colour code see main wiring diagram**

H.12304

**13.7 Wiring Diagram (1980 on) (Sec 7)**

1 Direction indicator lamp (rear LH)
2 Rear lamps (LH)
3 Reversing lamp
4 Stop lamp
5 Direction indicator lamp (front RH)
6 Sidelamp (RH)
7 Sidelamp (LH)
8 Direction indicator lamp (front LH)
9 Indicator repeater lamp (LH)
10 Direction indicator lamp (rear RH)
11 Fuse (in fusebox)
12 Direction indicator switch
13 Warning lamp for direction indicators
14 Indicator repeater lamp (RH)
15 Rear lamps (RH)
16 Number plate lamp (lamps*)
17 Reversing lamp
18 Stop lamp
19 Suction chamber heater* (carburettor)
20 Hazard warning switch
21 Lighting switch
22 Horns
23 Horn switch
24 Headlamp dip switch
25 Headlamp flasher switch
26 Headlamps (dip beams)
27 Headlamps (main beams)
28 Headlamp main beams (4 headlamp system)
29 Fog lamps*
30 Reversing lamp switch
31 Induction heater and thermostat*
32 Stop lamp switch
33 Flasher unit (direction indicators)
34 Combined steering column switch
35 Passenger's seat switch
36 Passenger's seat belt switch
37 Driver's seat belt switch
38 Warning lamp for seat belts
39 Warning lamp for choke control
40 Choke control switch
41 Rear window heater switch/warning lamp
42 Flasher unit (hazard)
43 Windscreen washer/wiper switch
44 Windscreen wiper motor
45 Windscreen washer pump
46 Rear window heater unit
47 Brake hydraulic system pressure differential switch
48 Handbrake switch
49 Warning lamp for pressure differential/handbrake 'ON'

50 Rear window heater relay
51 Clock
52 Thermostatic switch for radiator cooling fan
53 Radiator cooling fan motor
54 Cigarette lighter (lighters*)
55 Automatic transmission quadrant illumination lamps*
56 Cigarette lighter illumination lamp (lamps*)
57 Fibre optics illumination lamp
58 Battery
59 Glovebox lamp*
60 Glovebox switch*
61 Panel lamp switch
62 Warning lamp for sidelamps
63 Fog lamp switch*
64 Interior lamp and switch (front)
65 Door switches (front)
66 Starter motor
67 Battery condition indicator
68 Panel lamps
69 Warning lamp for hazard lights
70 Warning lamp for main beam
71 Heater indicator lamp
72 Panel lamp rheostat
73 Distributor
74 Coil
75 Interior lamp and switch (rear)*
76 Door switches (rear)*
77 Fuel tank unit
78 Fuel gauge
79 Instrument voltage stabilizer
80 Heater fan switch
81 Heater fan motor
82 Luggage compartment lamp
83 Luggage compartment lamp switch
84 Starter motor solenoid
85 Coolant temperature transmitter
86 Coolant temperature gauge
87 Printed circuit for instrument panel
88 Radio*
89 Ignition/starter switch
90 Starter inhibitor switch for automatic transmission
91 Starter solenoid relay
92 Alternator
93 Oil pressure switch
94 Warning lamp for oil pressure
95 Warning lamp for ignition
96 In-line fuse

* Depending upon model specification

**Colour code**

| | | | |
|---|---|---|---|
| B | Black | P | Purple |
| G | Green | R | Red |
| K | Pink | S | Slate |
| LG | Light Green | U | Blue |
| N | Brown | W | White |
| O | Orange | Y | Yellow |

**When a cable has two colour code letters, the first denotes the main
colour and the second denotes the tracer colour**

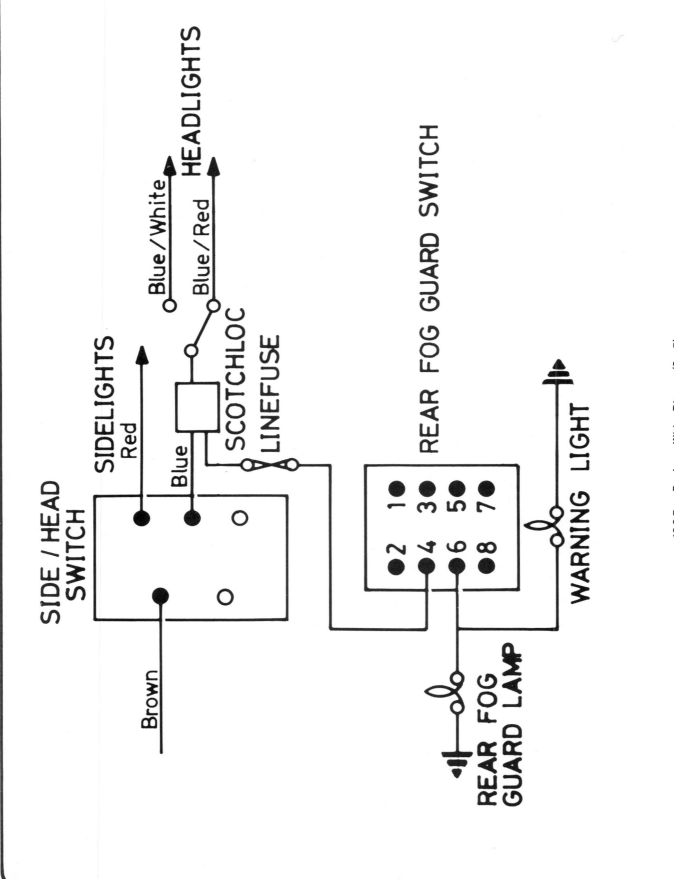

13.8 Rear Fog Lamp Wiring Diagram (Sec 7)

11 If the relay must be removed, pull off the connecting plug and extract the relay fixing screw.

*Choke control warning lamp switch*
12 This device is fitted at the control knob end of the choke operating cable.
13 Access to the switch is obtained by extracting the two screws from the left-hand shroud on the steering column.
14 Pull the shroud away so that the switch leads can be disconnected.
15 Release the switch locknut and slacken the clamp screw. Slide the clip from the switch and remove the switch.
16 Refit by reversing the removal operations.

## 8  Suspension and steering

*Rear suspension - low appearance*
1   It is possible that even with the suspension correctly set (Chapter 11, Section 18) the rear of the vehicle may appear to hang low.
2   Should this condition occur, a spacer (Part No 22A 1201) is available for fitting between the rear displacer strut and the knuckle joint on each side of the vehicle.

*Front hub bearings - renewal*
3   Before renewing front hub bearings remember that hub endfloat of up to 0.006 in (0.15 mm) is permissible before the bearings must be

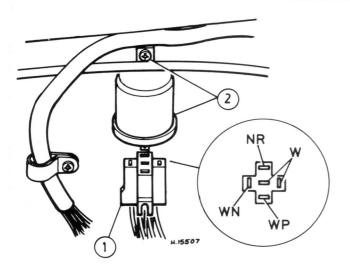

**Fig. 13.9 Fuel pump isolation relay (Sec 7)**

*1   Connecting plug*    *2   Relay and fixing screw*

**See main wiring diagram for colour code**

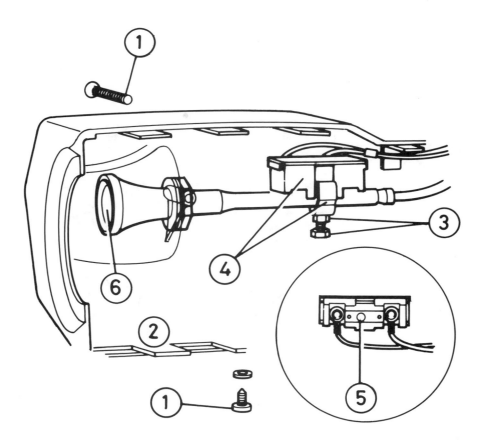

**Fig. 13.10 Choke control warning lamp switch (Sec 7)**

*1   Steering column shroud screws*    *3   Clamp screw and locknut*    *5   Switch plunger*
*2   Shroud*    *4   Clip and switch*    *6   Choke control knob*

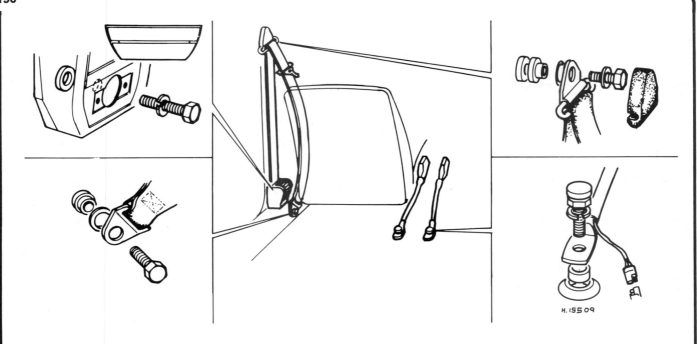

Fig. 13.11 Front seat belt anchorages (Sec 9)

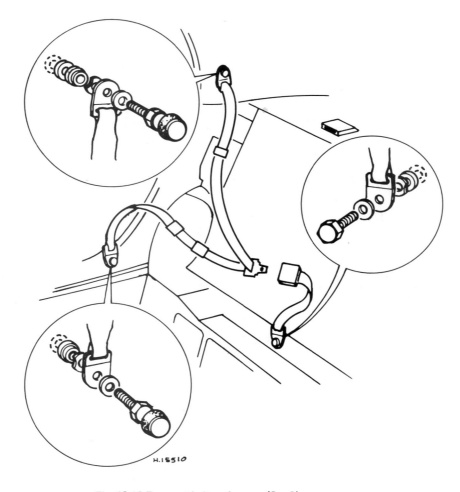

Fig. 13.12 Rear seat belt anchorages (Sec 9)

considered worn. The specified endfloat will give a noticeable 'rock' if the vehicle is raised and the roadwheel gripped at top and bottom.

*Power steering pump - drivebelt adjustment*
4   When adjusting the drivebelt tension, ensure that the fluid pipe union nut is slackened half a turn first in order to prevent the pipe twisting. Retighten after adjustment is complete.

## 9  Bodywork and fittings

*Seat belts*
1   Front inertia reel type seat belts are fitted as standard.
2   Keep the belts clean by wiping them with detergent and warm water - nothing else.
3   Never alter the anchorage points, and if the belt is disconnected, make sure that the sequence of spacers and washers at the anchor points is carefully retained when refitting.
4   Refer to Chapter 10, Section 31 for details of the seat belt warning system.
5   All Princess models from Chassis No 186868 have weld nut anchorages on the rear parcel shelf for fitting child safety seats. To use the nuts, simply pierce the vinyl covering on the shelf.
6   Rear seat belt lower anchorages are located under the rear seat cushion.

*Rear quarter trim panel - removal and refitting*
7   Working inside the luggage area, compress the tabs on the retaining buttons of the rear parcel shelf liner and remove the liner.
8   If a rear interior lamp is fitted, remove it. Tape the leads to prevent them from slipping into the body aperture.
9   Pull the door seal from the rear quarter body flange.

10  Peel the trim at its front and lower edges from the body flange and pillar.
11  Unclip the trim panel upper edge and remove it.
12  Refitting is a reversal of removal.

*Front door trim panel - removal and refitting*
13  Although the procedure is similar to that described in Chapter 12, Section 9, the armrest is of modified design.
14  To remove the armrest, extract the two screws and swivel it to the vertical position to release its bayonet type fixing.

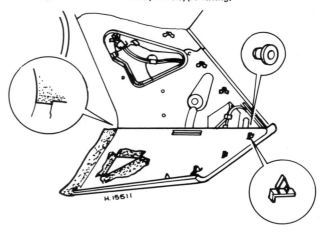

**Fig. 13.13 Rear quarter trim panel removed (Sec 9)**

# Safety first!

Professional motor mechanics are trained in safe working procedures. However enthusiastic you may be about getting on with the job in hand, do take the time to ensure that your safety is not put at risk. A moment's lack of attention can result in an accident, as can failure to observe certain elementary precautions.

There will always be new ways of having accidents, and the following points do not pretend to be a comprehensive list of all dangers; they are intended rather to make you aware of the risks and to encourage a safety-conscious approach to all work you carry out on your vehicle.

## Essential DOs and DON'Ts

**DON'T** rely on a single jack when working underneath the vehicle. Always use reliable additional means of support, such as axle stands, securely placed under a part of the vehicle that you know will not give way.

**DON'T** attempt to loosen or tighten high-torque nuts (e.g. wheel hub nuts) while the vehicle is on a jack; it may be pulled off.

**DON'T** start the engine without first ascertaining that the transmission is in neutral (or 'Park' where applicable) and the parking brake applied.

**DON'T** suddenly remove the filler cap from a hot cooling system – cover it with a cloth and release the pressure gradually first, or you may get scalded by escaping coolant.

**DON'T** attempt to drain oil until you are sure it has cooled sufficiently to avoid scalding you.

**DON'T** grasp any part of the engine, exhaust or catalytic converter without first ascertaining that it is sufficiently cool to avoid burning you.

**DON'T** syphon toxic liquids such as fuel, brake fluid or antifreeze by mouth, or allow them to remain on your skin.

**DON'T** inhale brake lining dust – it is injurious to health.

**DON'T** allow any spilt oil or grease to remain on the floor – wipe it up straight away, before someone slips on it.

**DON'T** use ill-fitting spanners or other tools which may slip and cause injury.

**DON'T** attempt to lift a heavy component which may be beyond your capability – get assistance.

**DON'T** rush to finish a job, or take unverified short cuts.

**DON'T** allow children or animals in or around an unattended vehicle.

**DO** wear eye protection when using power tools such as drill, sander, bench grinder etc, and when working under the vehicle.

**DO** use a barrier cream on your hands prior to undertaking dirty jobs – it will protect your skin from infection as well as making the dirt easier to remove afterwards; but make sure your hands aren't left slippery.

**DO** keep loose clothing (cuffs, tie etc) and long hair well out of the way of moving mechanical parts.

**DO** remove rings, wristwatch etc, before working on the vehicle – especially the electrical system.

**DO** ensure that any lifting tackle used has a safe working load rating adequate for the job.

**DO** keep your work area tidy – it is only too easy to fall over articles left lying around.

**DO** get someone to check periodically that all is well, when working alone on the vehicle.

**DO** carry out work in a logical sequence and check that everything is correctly assembled and tightened afterwards.

**DO** remember that your vehicle's safety affects that of yourself and others. If in doubt on any point, get specialist advice.

**IF,** in spite of following these precautions, you are unfortunate enough to injure yourself, seek medical attention as soon as possible.

## Fire

Remember at all times that petrol (gasoline) is highly flammable. Never smoke, or have any kind of naked flame around, when working on the vehicle. But the risk does not end there – a spark caused by an electrical short-circuit, by two metal surfaces contacting each other, or even by static electricity built up in your body under certain conditions, can ignite petrol vapour, which in a confined space is highly explosive. Always disconnect the battery earth (ground) terminal before working on any part of the fuel system, and never risk spilling fuel on to a hot engine or exhaust.

It is recommended that a fire extinguisher of a type suitable for fuel and electrical fires is kept handy in the garage or workplace at all times. Never try to extinguish a fuel or electrical fire with water.

## Fumes

Certain fumes are highly toxic and can quickly cause unconsciousness and even death if inhaled to any extent. Petrol (gasoline) vapour comes into this category, as do the vapours from certain solvents such as trichloroethylene. Any draining or pouring of such volatile fluids should be done in a well ventilated area.

When using cleaning fluids and solvents, read the instructions carefully. Never use materials from unmarked containers – they may give off poisonous vapours.

Never run the engine of a motor vehicle in an enclosed space such as a garage. Exhaust fumes contain carbon monoxide which is extremely poisonous; if you need to run the engine, always do so in the open air or at least have the rear of the vehicle outside the workplace.

If you are fortunate enough to have the use of an inspection pit, never drain or pour petrol, and never run the engine, while the vehicle is standing over it; the fumes, being heavier than air, will concentrate in the pit with possibly lethal results.

## The battery

Never cause a spark, or allow a naked light, near the vehicle's battery. It will normally be giving off a certain amount of hydrogen gas, which is highly explosive.

Always disconnect the battery earth (ground) terminal before working on the fuel or electrical systems.

If possible, loosen the filler plugs or cover when charging the battery from an external source. Do not charge at an excessive rate or the battery may burst.

Take care when topping up and when carrying the battery. The acid electrolyte, even when diluted, is very corrosive and should not be allowed to contact the eyes or skin.

If you ever need to prepare electrolyte yourself, always add the acid slowly to the water, and never the other way round. Protect against splashes by wearing rubber gloves and goggles.

When jump starting a car using a booster battery, for negative earth (ground) vehicles, connect the jump leads in the following sequence: First connect one jump lead between the positive (+) terminals of the two batteries. Then connect the other jump lead first to the negative (–) terminal of the booster battery, and then to a good earthing (ground) point on the vehicle to be started, at least 18 in (45 cm) from the battery if possible. Ensure that hands and jump leads are clear of any moving parts, and that the two vehicles do not touch. Disconnect the leads in the reverse order.

## Mains electricity

When using an electric power tool, inspection light etc, which works from the mains, always ensure that the appliance is correctly connected to its plug and that, where necessary, it is properly earthed (grounded). Do not use such appliances in damp conditions and, again, beware of creating a spark or applying excessive heat in the vicinity of fuel or fuel vapour.

## Ignition HT voltage

A severe electric shock can result from touching certain parts of the ignition system, such as the HT leads, when the engine is running or being cranked, particularly if components are damp or the insulation is defective. Where an electronic ignition system is fitted, the HT voltage is much higher and could prove fatal.

# Tools and working facilities

## Introduction

A selection of good tools is a fundamental requirement for anyone contemplating the maintenance and repair of a motor vehicle. For the owner who does not possess any, their purchase will prove a considerable expense, offsetting some of the savings made by doing-it-yourself. However, provided that the tools purchased are of good quality, they will last for many years and prove an extremely worthwhile investment.

To help the average owner to decide which tools are needed to carry out the various tasks detailed in this manual, we have compiled three lists of tools under the following headings: *Maintenance and minor repair, Repair and overhaul,* and *Special*. The newcomer to practical mechanics should start off with the *Maintenance and minor repair* tool kit and confine himself to the simpler jobs around the vehicle. Then, as his confidence and experience grow, he can undertake more difficult tasks, buying extra tools as, and when, they are needed. In this way, a *Maintenance and minor repair* tool kit can be built-up into a *Repair and overhaul* tool kit over a considerable period of time without any major cash outlays. The experienced do-it-yourselfer will have a tool kit good enough for most repair and overhaul procedures and will add tools from the *Special* category when he feels the expense is justified by the amount of use to which these tools will be put.

It is obviously not possible to cover the subject of tools fully here. For those who wish to learn more about tools and their use there is a book entitled *How to Choose and Use Car Tools* available from the publishers of this manual.

## Maintenance and minor repair tool kit

The tools given in this list should be considered as a minimum requirement if routine maintenance, servicing and minor repair operations are to be undertaken. We recommend the purchase of combination spanners (ring one end, open-ended the other); although more expensive than open-ended ones, they do give the advantages of both types of spanner.

Combination spanners - 10, 11, 12, 13, 14 & 17 mm
Combination spanners - $\frac{7}{16}$, $\frac{1}{2}$, $\frac{9}{16}$, $\frac{5}{8}$, $\frac{11}{16}$, $\frac{3}{4}$, $\frac{3}{16}$, $\frac{15}{16}$ inch
Adjustable spanner - 9 inch
Spark plug spanner (with rubber insert)
Spark plug gap adjustment tool
Set of feeler gauges
Brake bleed nipple spanner
Screwdriver - 4 in long x $\frac{1}{4}$ in dia (flat blade)
Screwdriver - 4 in long x $\frac{1}{4}$ in dia (cross blade)
Combination pliers - 6 inch
Hacksaw (junior)
Tyre pump
Tyre pressure gauge
Grease gun
Oil can
Fine emery cloth (1 sheet)
Wire brush (small)
Funnel (medium size)

## Repair and overhaul tool kit

These tools are virtually essential for anyone undertaking any major repairs to a motor vehicle, and are additional to those given in the *Maintenance and minor repair* list. Included in this list is a comprehensive set of sockets. Although these are expensive they will be found invaluable as they are so versatile - particularly if various

drives are included in the set. We recommend the $\frac{1}{2}$ in square-drive type, as this can be used with most proprietary torque wrenches. If you cannot afford a socket set, even bought piecemeal, then inexpensive tubular box spanners are a useful alternative.

The tools in this list will occasionally need to be supplemented by tools from the *Special* list.

Sockets (or box spanners) to cover range in previous list
Reversible ratchet drive (for use with sockets)
Extension piece, 10 inch (for use with sockets)
Universal joint (for use with sockets)
Torque wrench (for use with sockets)
'Mole' wrench - 8 inch
Ball pein hammer
Soft-faced hammer, plastic or rubber
Screwdriver - 6 in long x $\frac{5}{16}$ in dia (flat blade)
Screwdriver - 2 in long x $\frac{5}{16}$ in square (flat blade)
Screwdriver - 1$\frac{1}{2}$ in long x $\frac{1}{4}$ in dia (cross blade)
Screwdriver - 3 in long x $\frac{1}{8}$ in dia (electricians)
Pliers - electricians side cutters
Pliers - needle nosed
Pliers - circlip (internal and external)
Cold chisel - $\frac{1}{2}$ inch
Scriber
Scraper
Centre punch
Pin punch
Hacksaw
Valve grinding tool
Steel rule/straight-edge
Allen keys
Selection of files
Wire brush (large)
Axle-stands
Jack (strong scissor or hydraulic type)

## Special tools

The tools in this list are those which are not used regularly, are expensive to buy, or which need to be used in accordance with their manufacturers' instructions. Unless relatively difficult mechanical jobs are undertaken frequently, it will not be economic to buy many of these tools. Where this is the case, you could consider clubbing together with friends (or joining a motorists' club) to make a joint purchase, or borrowing the tools against a deposit from a local garage or tool hire specialist.

The following list contains only those tools and instruments freely available to the public, and not those special tools produced by the vehicle manufacturer specifically for its dealer network. You will find occasional references to these manufacturers' special tools in the text of this manual. Generally, an alternative method of doing the job without the vehicle manufacturers' special tool is given. However, sometimes, there is no alternative to using them. Where this is the case and the relevant tool cannot be bought or borrowed, you will have to entrust the work to a franchised garage.

Valve spring compressor (where applicable)
Piston ring compressor
Balljoint separator
Universal hub/bearing puller
Impact screwdriver
Micrometer and/or vernier gauge
Dial gauge
Stroboscopic timing light

*Dwell angle meter/tachometer*
*Universal electrical multi-meter*
*Cylinder compression gauge*
*Lifting tackle (photo)*
*Trolley jack*
*Light with extension lead*

## Buying tools

For practically all tools, a tool factor is the best source since he will have a very comprehensive range compared with the average garage or accessory shop. Having said that, accessory shops often offer excellent quality tools at discount prices, so it pays to shop around.

Remember, you don't have to buy the most expensive items on the shelf, but it is always advisable to steer clear of the very cheap tools. There are plenty of good tools around at reasonable prices, so ask the proprietor or manager of the shop for advice before making a purchase.

## Care and maintenance of tools

Having purchased a reasonable tool kit, it is necessary to keep the tools in a clean serviceable condition. After use, always wipe off any dirt, grease and metal particles using a clean, dry cloth, before putting the tools away. Never leave them lying around after they have been used. A simple tool rack on the garage or workshop wall, for items such as screwdrivers and pliers is a good idea. Store all normal wrenches and sockets in a metal box. Any measuring instruments, gauges, meters, etc, must be carefully stored where they cannot be damaged or become rusty.

Take a little care when tools are used. Hammer heads inevitably become marked and screwdrivers lose the keen edge on their blades from time to time. A little timely attention with emery cloth or a file will soon restore items like this to a good serviceable finish.

## Working facilities

Not to be forgotten when discussing tools, is the workshop itself. If anything more than routine maintenance is to be carried out, some form of suitable working area becomes essential.

It is appreciated that many an owner mechanic is forced by circumstances to remove an engine or similar item, without the benefit of a garage or workshop. Having done this, any repairs should always be done under the cover of a roof.

Wherever possible, any dismantling should be done on a clean, flat workbench or table at a suitable working height.

Any workbench needs a vice: one with a jaw opening of 4 in (100 mm) is suitable for most jobs. As mentioned previously, some clean dry storage space is also required for tools, as well as for lubricants, cleaning fluids, touch-up paints and so on, which become necessary.

Another item which may be required, and which has a much more general usage, is an electric drill with a chuck capacity of at least $\frac{5}{16}$ in (8 mm). This, together with a good range of twist drills, is virtually essential for fitting accessories such as mirrors and reversing lights.

Last, but not least, always keep a supply of old newspapers and clean, lint-free rags available, and try to keep any working area as clean as possible.

### Spanner jaw gap comparison table

| Jaw gap (in) | Spanner size |
| --- | --- |
| 0.250 | $\frac{1}{4}$ in AF |
| 0.276 | 7 mm |
| 0.313 | $\frac{5}{16}$ in AF |
| 0.315 | 8 mm |
| 0.344 | $\frac{11}{32}$ in AF; $\frac{1}{8}$ in Whitworth |
| 0.354 | 9 mm |
| 0.375 | $\frac{3}{8}$ in AF |
| 0.394 | 10 mm |
| 0.433 | 11 mm |
| 0.438 | $\frac{7}{16}$ in AF |
| 0.445 | $\frac{3}{16}$ in Whitworth; $\frac{1}{4}$ in BSF |
| 0.472 | 12 mm |
| 0.500 | $\frac{1}{2}$ in AF |
| 0.512 | 13 mm |
| 0.525 | $\frac{1}{4}$ in Whitworth; $\frac{5}{16}$ in BSF |
| 0.551 | 14 mm |
| 0.563 | $\frac{9}{16}$ in AF |
| 0.591 | 15 mm |
| 0.600 | $\frac{5}{16}$ in Whitworth; $\frac{3}{8}$ in BSF |
| 0.625 | $\frac{5}{8}$ in AF |
| 0.630 | 16 mm |
| 0.669 | 17 mm |
| 0.686 | $\frac{11}{16}$ in AF |
| 0.709 | 18 mm |
| 0.710 | $\frac{3}{8}$ in Whitworth; $\frac{7}{16}$ in BSF |
| 0.748 | 19 mm |
| 0.750 | $\frac{3}{4}$ in AF |
| 0.813 | $\frac{13}{16}$ in AF |
| 0.820 | $\frac{7}{16}$ in Whitworth; $\frac{1}{2}$ in BSF |
| 0.866 | 22 mm |
| 0.875 | $\frac{7}{8}$ in AF |
| 0.920 | $\frac{1}{2}$ in Whitworth; $\frac{9}{16}$ in BSF |
| 0.938 | $\frac{15}{16}$ in AF |
| 0.945 | 24 mm |
| 1.000 | 1 in AF |
| 1.010 | $\frac{9}{16}$ in Whitworth; $\frac{5}{8}$ in BSF |
| 1.024 | 26 mm |
| 1.063 | $1\frac{1}{16}$ in AF; 27 mm |
| 1.100 | $\frac{5}{8}$ in Whitworth; $\frac{11}{16}$ in BSF |
| 1.125 | $1\frac{1}{8}$ in AF |
| 1.181 | 30 mm |
| 1.200 | $\frac{11}{16}$ in Whitworth; $\frac{3}{4}$ in BSF |
| 1.250 | $1\frac{1}{4}$ in AF |
| 1.260 | 32 mm |
| 1.300 | $\frac{3}{4}$ in Whitworth; $\frac{7}{8}$ in BSF |
| 1.313 | $1\frac{5}{16}$ in AF |
| 1.390 | $\frac{13}{16}$ in Whitworth; $\frac{15}{16}$ in BSF |
| 1.417 | 36 mm |
| 1.438 | $1\frac{7}{16}$ in AF |
| 1.480 | $\frac{7}{8}$ in Whitworth; 1 in BSF |
| 1.500 | $1\frac{1}{2}$ in AF |
| 1.575 | 40 mm; $\frac{15}{16}$ in Whitworth |
| 1.614 | 41 mm |
| 1.625 | $1\frac{5}{8}$ in AF |
| 1.670 | 1 in Whitworth; $1\frac{1}{8}$ in BSF |
| 1.688 | $1\frac{11}{16}$ in AF |
| 1.811 | 46 mm |
| 1.813 | $1\frac{13}{16}$ in AF |
| 1.860 | $1\frac{1}{8}$ in Whitworth; $1\frac{1}{4}$ in BSF |
| 1.875 | $1\frac{7}{8}$ in AF |
| 1.969 | 50 mm |
| 2.000 | 2 in AF |
| 2.050 | $1\frac{1}{4}$ in Whitworth; $1\frac{3}{8}$ in BSF |
| 2.165 | 55 mm |
| 2.362 | 60 mm |

**A Haltrac hoist and gantry in use during a typical engine removal sequence**

# Fault diagnosis

## Introduction

The vehicle owner who does his or her own maintenance according to the recommended schedules should not have to use this section of the manual very often. Modern component reliability is such that, provided those items subject to wear or deterioration are inspected or renewed at the specified intervals, sudden failure is comparatively rare. Faults do not usually just happen as a result of sudden failure, but develop over a period of time. Major mechanical failures in particular are usually preceded by characteristic symptoms over hundreds or even thousands of miles. Those components which do occasionally fail without warning are often small and easily carried in the vehicle.

With any fault finding, the first step is to decide where to begin investigations. Sometimes this is obvious, but on other occasions a little detective work will be necessary. The owner who makes half a dozen haphazard adjustments or replacements may be successful in curing a fault (or its symptoms), but he will be none the wiser if the fault recurs and he may well have spent more time and money than was necessary. A calm and logical approach will be found to be more satisfactory in the long run. Always take into account any warning signs or abnormalities that may have been noticed in the period preceding the fault – power loss, high or low gauge readings, unusual noises or smells, etc – and remember that failure of components such as fuses or spark plugs may only be pointers to some underlying fault.

The pages which follow here are intended to help in cases of failure to start or breakdown on the road. There is also a Fault Diagnosis Section at the end of each Chapter which should be consulted if the preliminary checks prove unfruitful. Whatever the fault, certain basic principles apply. These are as follows:

**Verify the fault.** This is simply a matter of being sure that you know what the symptoms are before starting work. This is particularly important if you are investigating a fault for someone else who may not have described it very accurately.

**Don't overlook the obvious.** For example, if the vehicle won't start, is there petrol in the tank? (Don't take anyone else's word on this particular point, and don't trust the fuel gauge either!) If an electrical fault is indicated, look for loose or broken wires before digging out the test gear.

**Cure the disease, not the symptom.** Substituting a flat battery with a fully charged one will get you off the hard shoulder, but if the underlying cause is not attended to, the new battery will go the same way. Similarly, changing oil-fouled spark plugs for a new set will get you moving again, but remember that the reason for the fouling (if it wasn't simply an incorrect grade of plug) will have to be established and corrected.

**Don't take anything for granted.** Particularly, don't forget that a 'new' component may itself be defective (especially if it's been rattling round in the boot for months), and don't leave components out of a fault diagnosis sequence just because they are new or recently fitted. When you do finally diagnose a difficult fault, you'll probably realise that all the evidence was there from the start.

## Electrical faults

Electrical faults can be more puzzling than straightforward mechanical failures, but they are no less susceptible to logical analysis if the basic principles of operation are understood. Vehicle electrical wiring exists in extremely unfavourable conditions – heat, vibration and chemical attack – and the first things to look for are loose or corroded connections and broken or chafed wires, especially where the wires pass through holes in the bodywork or are subject to vibration.

All metal-bodied vehicles in current production have one pole of the battery 'earthed', ie connected to the vehicle bodywork, and in nearly all modern vehicles it is the negative (–) terminal. The various electrical components – motors, bulb holders etc – are also connected to earth, either by means of a lead or directly by their mountings.

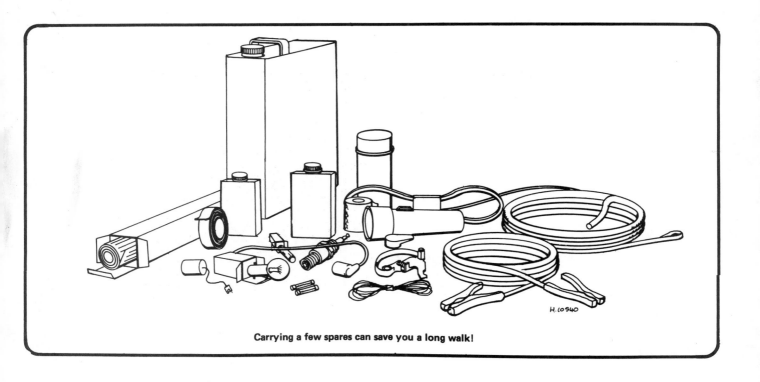

H.10540

**Carrying a few spares can save you a long walk!**

Electric current flows through the component and then back to the battery via the bodywork. If the component mounting is loose or corroded, or if a good path back to the battery is not available, the circuit will be incomplete and malfunction will result. The engine and/or gearbox are also earthed by means of flexible metal straps to the body or subframe; if these straps are loose or missing, starter motor, generator and ignition trouble may result.

Assuming the earth return to be satisfactory, electrical faults will be due either to component malfunction or to defects in the current supply. Individual components are dealt with in Chapter 10. If supply wires are broken or cracked internally this results in an open-circuit, and the easiest way to check for this is to bypass the suspect wire temporarily with a length of wire having a crocodile clip or suitable connector at each end. Alternatively, a 12V test lamp can be used to verify the presence of supply voltage at various points along the wire and the break can be thus isolated.

If a bare portion of a live wire touches the bodywork or other earthed metal part, the electricity will take the low-resistance path thus formed back to the battery: this is known as a short-circuit. Hopefully a short-circuit will blow a fuse, but otherwise it may cause burning of the insulation (and possibly further short-circuits) or even a fire. This is why it is inadvisable to bypass persistently blowing fuses with silver foil or wire.

*Spares and tool kit*

Most vehicles are supplied only with sufficient tools for wheel changing; the *Maintenance and minor repair* tool kit detailed in *Tools and working facilities,* with the addition of a hammer, is probably sufficient for those repairs that most motorists would consider attempting at the roadside. In addition a few items which can be fitted without too much trouble in the event of a breakdown should be carried. Experience and available space will modify the list below, but the following may save having to call on professional assistance:

*Spark plugs, clean and correctly gapped*
*HT lead and plug cap – long enough to reach the plug furthest from the distributor*
*Distributor rotor, condenser and contact breaker points*
*Drivebelt(s) – emergency type may suffice*
*Spare fuses*
*Set of principal light bulbs*
*Tin of radiator sealer and hose bandage*
*Exhaust bandage*
*Roll of insulating tape*
*Length of soft iron wire*
*Length of electrical flex*
*Torch or inspection lamp (can double as test lamp)*
*Battery jump leads*

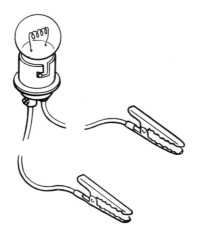

**A simple test lamp is useful for checking electrical faults**

*Tow-rope*
*Ignition waterproofing aerosol*
*Litre of engine oil*
*Sealed can of hydraulic fluid*
*Emergency windscreen*
*'Jubilee' clips*
*Tube of filler paste*

If spare fuel is carried, a can designed for the purpose should be used to minimise risks of leakage and collision damage. A first aid kit and a warning triangle, whilst not at present compulsory in the UK, are obviously sensible items to carry in addition to the above.

When touring abroad it may be advisable to carry additional spares which, even if you cannot fit them yourself, could save having to wait while parts are obtained. The items below may be worth considering:

*Clutch and throttle cables*
*Cylinder head gasket*
*Alternator brushes*
*Fuel pump repair kit*
*Tyre valve core*

One of the motoring organisations will be able to advise on availability of fuel etc in foreign countries.

## Engine will not start

### *Engine fails to turn when starter operated*
Flat battery (recharge, use jump leads, or push start)
Battery terminals loose or corroded
Battery earth to body defective
Engine earth strap loose or broken
Starter motor (or solenoid) wiring loose or broken
Automatic transmission selector in wrong position, or inhibitor switch faulty
Ignition/starter switch faulty
Major mechanical failure (seizure)
Starter or solenoid internal fault (see Chapter 10)

### *Starter motor turns engine slowly*
Partially discharged battery (recharge, use jump leads, or push start)
Battery terminals loose or corroded
Battery earth to body defective
Engine earth strap loose
Starter motor (or solenoid) wiring loose
Starter motor internal fault (see Chapter 10)

### *Starter motor spins without turning engine*
Flat battery
Starter motor pinion sticking on sleeve

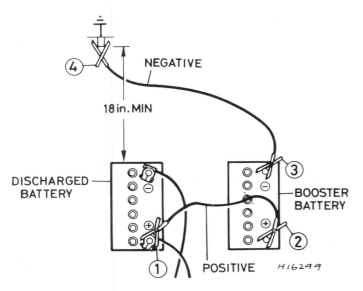

**Correct way to connect jump leads. Do not allow car bodies to touch!**

Flywheel gear teeth damaged or worn
Starter motor mounting bolts loose

## Engine turns normally but fails to start
Damp or dirty HT leads and distributor cap (crank engine and check for spark)
Dirty or incorrectly gapped distributor points
No fuel in tank (check for delivery at carburettor)
Excessive choke (hot engine) or insufficient choke (cold engine)
Fouled or incorrectly gapped spark plugs (remove, clean and regap)
Other ignition system fault (see Chapter 4)
Other fuel system fault (see Chapter 3)
Poor compression (see Chapter 1)
Major mechanical failure (eg camshaft drive)

## Engine fires but will not run
Insufficient choke (cold engine)
Air leaks at carburettor or inlet manifold
Fuel starvation (see Chapter 3)
Ignition fault (see Chapter 4)

### Engine cuts out and will not restart

## Engine cuts out suddenly – ignition fault
Loose or disconnected LT wires
Wet HT leads or distributor cap (after traversing water splash)
Coil or condenser failure (check for spark)
Other ignition fault (see Chapter 4)

## Engine misfires before cutting out – fuel fault
Fuel tank empty
Fuel pump defective (check for delivery)
Fuel tank filler vent blocked (suction will be evident on releasing cap)
Carburettor needle valve sticking
Carburettor jets blocked (fuel contaminated)
Other fuel system fault (see Chapter 3)

## Engine cuts out – other causes
Serious overheating
Major mechanical failure (eg camshaft drive)

### Engine overheats

## Ignition (no-charge) warning light illuminated
Slack or broken drivebelt – retension or renew (Chapter 1)

## Ignition warning light not illuminated
Coolant loss due to internal or external leakage (see Chapter 2)
Thermostat defective
Low oil level
Brakes binding
Radiator clogged externally or internally
Electric cooling fan not operating correctly

Engine waterways clogged
Ignition timing incorrect or automatic advance malfunctioning
Mixture too weak

**Note**: *Do not add cold water to an overheated engine or damage may result*

### Low engine oil pressure

## Gauge reads low or warning light illuminated with engine running
Oil level low or incorrect grade
Defective gauge or sender unit
Wire to sender unit earthed
Engine overheating
Oil filter clogged or bypass valve defective
Oil pressure relief valve defective
Oil pick-up strainer clogged
Oil pump worn or mountings loose
Worn main or big-end bearings

**Note**: *Low oil pressure in a high-mileage engine at tickover is not necessarily a cause for concern. Sudden pressure loss at speed is far more significant. In any event, check the gauge or warning light sender before condemning the engine.*

### Engine noises

## Pre-ignition (pinking) on acceleration
Incorrect grade of fuel
Ignition timing incorrect
Distributor faulty or worn
Worn or maladjusted carburettor
Excessive carbon build-up in engine

## Whistling or wheezing noises
Leaking vacuum hose
Leaking carburettor or manifold gasket
Blowing head gasket

## Tapping or rattling
Incorrect valve clearances
Worn valve gear
Worn timing chain
Broken piston ring (ticking noise)

## Knocking or thumping
Unintentional mechanical contact (eg fan blades)
Worn fanbelt
Peripheral component fault (generator, water pump etc)
Worn big-end bearings (regular heavy knocking, perhaps less under load)
Worn main bearings (rumbling and knocking, perhaps worsening under load)
Piston slap (most noticeable when cold)

# Conversion factors

## Length (distance)

| | | | | | |
|---|---|---|---|---|---|
| Inches (in) | X | 25.4 | = Millimetres (mm) | X | 0.0394 = Inches (in) |
| Feet (ft) | X | 0.305 | = Metres (m) | X | 3.281 = Feet (ft) |
| Miles | X | 1.609 | = Kilometres (km) | X | 0.621 = Miles |

## Volume (capacity)

| | | | | | |
|---|---|---|---|---|---|
| Cubic inches (cu in; in³) | X | 16.387 | = Cubic centimetres (cc; cm³) | X | 0.061 = Cubic inches (cu in; in³) |
| Imperial pints (Imp pt) | X | 0.568 | = Litres (l) | X | 1.76 = Imperial pints (Imp pt) |
| Imperial quarts (Imp qt) | X | 1.137 | = Litres (l) | X | 0.88 = Imperial quarts (Imp qt) |
| Imperial quarts (Imp qt) | X | 1.201 | = US quarts (US qt) | X | 0.833 = Imperial quarts (Imp qt) |
| US quarts (US qt) | X | 0.946 | = Litres (l) | X | 1.057 = US quarts (US qt) |
| Imperial gallons (Imp gal) | X | 4.546 | = Litres (l) | X | 0.22 = Imperial gallons (Imp gal) |
| Imperial gallons (Imp gal) | X | 1.201 | = US gallons (US gal) | X | 0.833 = Imperial gallons (Imp gal) |
| US gallons (US gal) | X | 3.785 | = Litres (l) | X | 0.264 = US gallons (US gal) |

## Mass (weight)

| | | | | | |
|---|---|---|---|---|---|
| Ounces (oz) | X | 28.35 | = Grams (g) | X | 0.035 = Ounces (oz) |
| Pounds (lb) | X | 0.454 | = Kilograms (kg) | X | 2.205 = Pounds (lb) |

## Force

| | | | | | |
|---|---|---|---|---|---|
| Ounces-force (ozf; oz) | X | 0.278 | = Newtons (N) | X | 3.6 = Ounces-force (ozf; oz) |
| Pounds-force (lbf; lb) | X | 4.448 | = Newtons (N) | X | 0.225 = Pounds-force (lbf; lb) |
| Newtons (N) | X | 0.1 | = Kilograms-force (kgf; kg) | X | 9.81 = Newtons (N) |

## Pressure

| | | | | | |
|---|---|---|---|---|---|
| Pounds-force per square inch (psi; lbf/in²; lb/in²) | X | 0.070 | = Kilograms-force per square centimetre (kgf/cm²; kg/cm²) | X | 14.223 = Pounds-force per square inch (psi; lbf/in²; lb/in²) |
| Pounds-force per square inch (psi; lbf/in²; lb/in²) | X | 0.068 | = Atmospheres (atm) | X | 14.696 = Pounds-force per square inch (psi; lbf/in²; lb/in²) |
| Pounds-force per square inch (psi; lbf/in²; lb/in²) | X | 0.069 | = Bars | X | 14.5 = Pounds-force per square inch (psi; lbf/in²; lb/in²) |
| Pounds-force per square inch (psi; lbf/in²; lb/in²) | X | 6.895 | = Kilopascals (kPa) | X | 0.145 = Pounds-force per square inch (psi; lbf/in²; lb/in²) |
| Kilopascals (kPa) | X | 0.01 | = Kilograms-force per square centimetre (kgf/cm²; kg/cm²) | X | 98.1 = Kilopascals (kPa) |

## Torque (moment of force)

| | | | | | |
|---|---|---|---|---|---|
| Pounds-force inches (lbf in; lb in) | X | 1.152 | = Kilograms-force centimetre (kgf cm; kg cm) | X | 0.868 = Pounds-force inches (lbf in; lb in) |
| Pounds-force inches (lbf in; lb in) | X | 0.113 | = Newton metres (Nm) | X | 8.85 = Pounds-force inches (lbf in; lb in) |
| Pounds-force inches (lbf in; lb in) | X | 0.083 | = Pounds-force feet (lbf ft; lb ft) | X | 12 = Pounds-force inches (lbf in; lb in) |
| Pounds-force feet (lbf ft; lb ft) | X | 0.138 | = Kilograms-force metres (kgf m; kg m) | X | 7.233 = Pounds-force feet (lbf ft; lb ft) |
| Pounds-force feet (lbf ft; lb ft) | X | 1.356 | = Newton metres (Nm) | X | 0.738 = Pounds-force feet (lbf ft; lb ft) |
| Newton metres (Nm) | X | 0.102 | = Kilograms-force metres (kgf m; kg m) | X | 9.804 = Newton metres (Nm) |

## Power

| | | | | | |
|---|---|---|---|---|---|
| Horsepower (hp) | X | 745.7 | = Watts (W) | X | 0.0013 = Horsepower (hp) |

## Velocity (speed)

| | | | | | |
|---|---|---|---|---|---|
| Miles per hour (miles/hr; mph) | X | 1.609 | = Kilometres per hour (km/hr; kph) | X | 0.621 = Miles per hour (miles/hr; mph) |

## Fuel consumption*

| | | | | | |
|---|---|---|---|---|---|
| Miles per gallon, Imperial (mpg) | X | 0.354 | = Kilometres per litre (km/l) | X | 2.825 = Miles per gallon, Imperial (mpg) |
| Miles per gallon, US (mpg) | X | 0.425 | = Kilometres per litre (km/l) | X | 2.352 = Miles per gallon, US (mpg) |

## Temperature

Degrees Fahrenheit = ($^\circ$C x 1.8) + 32          Degrees Celsius (Degrees Centigrade; $^\circ$C) = ($^\circ$F - 32) x 0.56

*It is common practice to convert from miles per gallon (mpg) to litres/100 kilometres (l/100km), where mpg (Imperial) x l/100 km = 282 and mpg (US) x l/100 km = 235

# Index